Slater Walker

CHARLES RAW

Slater Walker

An investigation of a
financial phenomenon

 ANDRE DEUTSCH

First published 1977 by
André Deutsch Limited
105 Great Russell Street London WC1

Printed in Great Britain by
Lowe & Brydone Printers Limited,
Thetford, Norfolk

ISBN 0 233 96798 2

Contents

AUTHOR'S NOTE

Without the backing of *The Sunday Times* this book would never have been published. I am therefore deeply indebted to its Editor, Harold Evans, for the support and encouragement he has consistently given me in the face of unprecedented obstacles. I also wish to thank my legal advisers, as well as Piers Burnett of André Deutsch, and all colleagues, past and present, who have devoted time and effort to helping me get this book into print - in particular John Barry, Anthony Bambridge, Bruce Page and my research assistant Anna Buxton.

Foreword

When research for this book was started in about April 1973, Slater was on the point of announcing the most important deal of his career – the proposed merger of his company, Slater Walker, with one of the City's leading banks, Hill Samuel. The deal, *The Times* said, 'probably ranks as the most fascinating City development since the war'. Its purpose was to establish a 'substantial and significant presence in world banking'.

Peter Walker, with whom Slater had started his company nine years before, was Minister for Trade and Industry, the rising star of the Tory party and one of the most influential members of Edward Heath's Cabinet. 'He is discussed frequently, whenever the topic comes up, which is often, as a future Prime Minister,' wrote the *Daily Mail*'s political editor that same month.

The Slater Walker share price stood at 245 pence.

The book was essentially completed in the summer of 1975; many profound changes had taken place during the two years since research began. The deal with Hill Samuel had been abandoned and a second 'great crash' had hit financial markets; Slater had systematically dismantled the structure he had created. The Tories had been ousted from power, Heath replaced as their leader and Walker relegated to the back benches.

There have been more cataclysmic events in the two years or so that it has taken to get the book published. Slater has retired from Slater Walker and been replaced by his friend Sir James Goldsmith, knighted in Wilson's resignation honours list. A report by leading accountants has revealed huge losses in Slater Walker, which had only avoided complete collapse thanks to massive support from the Bank of England. The Singapore government has tried unsuccessfully to extradite Slater to face criminal charges and is still pursuing his colleague Tarling; and the Department of Trade is appealing Slater's acquittal on minor charges under the Companies Act.

On the political front, Walker remains a back bencher, but the pendulum has swung back in favour of the Conservatives, putting him perhaps once more on the threshold of power.

The Slater Walker share price has fallen below 10 pence.

The reasons why it was not possible to publish this book when it was originally completed are long and complicated. It is not even possible to attempt to summarize them here without causing yet further delays or even risking the possibility that publication would never take place. Two points must be stressed at the outset, however: (1) that, although this final text incorporates some material obtained in the two years of argument over publication, the great bulk of information in this book was obtained by myself, often from public sources, without any help from Slater or Walker; (2) that my opinions and conclusions about Slater Walker were reached by the summer of 1975, and not in the light of subsequent events.

Slater and Walker naturally do not agree with my views; but they have seen the text and have had every opportunity over the past four years to dispute what I have said, and their side of the argument has been stated where necessary. Slater's own book, *Return to Go*, which Weidenfeld & Nicolson announced in June they would publish in October 1977, was written while he was in possession of the text of this book.

This book was drafted in a very different business and political climate from that which exists today. No doubt if I were starting it now, or if I were free to revise it totally, I would approach the subject differently. I would probably not, for example, have included so much financial detail, which inevitably makes the book hard reading; but at the time, because of the unquestioning acclaim in which Slater Walker was then widely held, I felt that it was necessary to include as much evidence as possible to support my critical conclusions.

Obviously, too, the impact of the book will be less than if it had appeared, as intended, before the effective demise of Slater Walker. I am sorry it did not, if only because it might have saved some people some money. But I hope it still serves a useful function, explaining, perhaps, why that demise was inevitable because of the values on which Slater Walker was based from the beginning.

I hope, too, that the history of Slater Walker contributes towards the understanding of the changes in business and political attitudes. Slater - or rather Slater Walker - was 'the most remarkable phenomenon of the British financial scene in the 1960s and early 1970s', *The Times* wrote in September 1976. Yet its influence went further than the financial world. One forgets, perhaps, today just how closely Slater Walker was identified with the New Tories then emerging under Heath - of whom Walker was such an important member. They accepted the Slater Walker style of capitalism: indeed it was their answer to Harold Wilson's and Tony Benn's 'technological revolution'. Anthony Sampson wrote* that Slater 'is (like Walker) the very paragon of the new Heath-type Tory – self-made, hard-working, unsentimental, competitive'; the Conservative government in its 1970 to 1972 phase has been labelled the 'Slater Walker government', and Clive Irving wrote in the *New Statesman* in February 1974, just before the fall of the Heath government, that Slater and Walker embodied 'the unprecedented nexus between the political and business ethics which the country has still barely comprehended'.

The new Tories were 'the Mr Efficiencies', as Peregrine Worsthorne described them in the *Sunday Telegraph*, the meritocrats and the technocrats who would streamline the running of the state just as Slater Walker and its kind were supposedly 'cutting the dead wood' out of British industry. The free enterprise system was to be reinvigorated: inefficient companies were no longer to be propped up, bad managements no more bailed out. 'The object of Slater Walker from the beginning,' says Walker, 'was to inject better management into a range of existing companies.' The new young 'aggressive' breed of managers would, on the other hand, be encouraged and properly rewarded. Money became the measure of success and ability. 'We are money makers, not thing makers,' Slater used to declare – a direct challenge to Wilson's 1964 pronouncement that: 'What is wrong with our society is that those who make the money are more regarded than those who earn the money.'

Once in power the New Tories came quickly to be regarded as the friends not just of big business but also of the financial operators. The Heath government which removed the penal short-term speculative gains tax was a far cry from Harold Macmillan's which had introduced it nine years before.

But the 'lame duck' version of free enterprise ran into fierce opposition from established City and industrial hierarchies, and was soon abandoned. Indeed Walker says that he himself, together with Reginald Maudling, were strong opponents of the 'lame-duck' concept. More slowly, as the debate over the causes of the chronic shortage of capital investment in British industry widened, the question began to be asked whether this new breed of managers, rather than putting industrial assets to better use, was in reality removing capital to make quick fortunes on the stock market, so that the market itself had ceased to fulfil its function of channelling money into productive industry. The history of Slater Walker helps to answer that question.

* Sampson, *New Anatomy of Britain*, Hodder & Stoughton, 1971.

1   *The Under-Forties*

The origin of the meeting between Slater and Walker, lay, as is well known, in a series of short articles in the *Evening News* around the end of 1961. The then City Editor, David Malbert, and his staff set out to pick out young businessmen – the series was entitled 'The Under-Forties' – who had already made names for themselves in their own industries and who were expected to go further, but who had not hitherto received much publicity.

The series took the form of brief 150- to 200-word summaries of the careers of the thirty men selected, each accompanied by a photograph. Slater was number seven on Tuesday 14 November 1961. He was then, at thirty-two, commercial director of AEC, then an independent manufacturer of buses, trucks and engines, and was chosen for his rapid rise in the motor industry:

> He took a 'short-cut' to the top, qualifying as an accountant in 1953 and entering industry a year later.
>
> His move to the AEC group was in 1955. He answered an advertisement and became secretary of Park Royal Vehicles.
>
> At 29 he was a director of AEC (Sales) Ltd and at 30 he went on to the board of AEC Ltd and of associated overseas companies.
>
> In the last few years he has been mainly concerned with exports.
>
> He reckons to travel well over 50,000 miles each year, and has just returned from a 'round-the-world' trip.
>
> Unmarried, Mr Slater lives in Ealing and is an enthusiastic golfer in his spare time.

Walker, number nine in the series, appeared four days later:

> It's been a quick road to the top for Mr Peter Walker, 30-year-old grocer's son. [Walker was in fact still only 29.]
>
> Starting as an office boy with the General Accident Insurance Company in Gloucester, he now has a seat in five boardrooms, as well as in the House of Commons.

Shortly after finishing his National Service, and still only 22, he formed his own firm of insurance brokers, Walker Moate Ltd.

Beginning with a £200 borrowed stake, in a one-room office with only a table and four chairs, it has been built into a leading City broking firm, specializing in death duty business.

Later Walker helped set up the Unicorn group of unit trusts: he also became financial director of the Rodwell group of property companies.

Politics has taken a lot of his time. A member of the young Conservatives at 14, he was their national chairman from 1958 to 1960.

He was the youngest Conservative candidate in the 1955 General Election, and won a seat in the Worcester by-election early this year.

The rest of the Under-Forties came from a wide spectrum of City and business interests. Some have since faded from the scene; others have continued their successful careers. Probably the most outstanding were Frederick Catherwood, then managing director of British Aluminium, later director general of the National Economic Development Council, knighted in 1971 and today chairman of the British Overseas Trade Board; Lord Melchett, then a managing director of the merchant bank M. Samuel & Co. and later chairman of the British Steel Corporation until his early death; David Nicolson, then with a firm called Production Engineering and today chairman of Rothmans International. There were also Peter Parker, now head of British Rail, John Clay, then as now a director of Hambros Bank, Jessel Harrison, chairman of a textile firm, Slimma, Peter Evans of the restaurant chain, and Sefton Myers, a close friend of Walker's and colleague in the Rodwell group.

In August 1973 Walker told me that he wrote to the Chancellor of the Exchequer after the *Evening News* series had appeared, and to those who had been featured, to arrange a dinner, as he thought the Chancellor would be interested in the ideas of these young businessmen. In July 1977 he told me that it was, in fact, the Chancellor himself who had suggested the idea.

The dinner did not take place until early February 1963, and by then there had been some big changes. A year before, Selwyn Lloyd had been at the Treasury, but his cautious, non-expansionary Budget that year pleased virtually nobody: this was the Budget that imposed purchase tax on sweets and introduced the short-term speculative gains tax. Most displeased was Prime Minister Harold Macmillan, and in July 1962 Lloyd was abruptly dismissed, along with other ministers, to be replaced by the expansion-minded Reginald Maudling.

Maudling himself could not come to Walker's dinner, but he sent his Chief Secretary Ian Boyd-Carpenter. The evening was a failure, as even Walker admits today. About fourteen of the Under-Forties turned up and, perhaps overawed by the occasion, they could hardly muster an original thought between them. There was a succession of dull, trite speeches harping on well-worn themes such as the need to increase productivity and exports. Nevertheless, the Under-Forties agreed to continue to meet from time to time.

Slater himself was unable to go to this original dinner, because he was away on AEC business. But he wrote Walker a long letter outlining his views for the improvement of the economy which, by contrast with the banal generalities of the dinner, impressed Walker by their specificity. Slater wrote, for example, of his belief in the need to give managers adequate incentive, which struck a chord with one of Walker's own favourite themes. Walker replied suggesting that they should get together, and later in 1963 – neither can remember exactly when – the meeting took place.

The occasion was another dinner at the substantial suburban home at Walton-on-Thames to which Walker and his parents had recently moved. There is no record of what the two said to each other, although Walker remembers Slater discussing whether or not he should leave Leyland. But Slater once told the following story about the dinner: he had, he said, expressed his appreciation of the wine Walker served him with dinner; so Walker told an assistant to make a note of its name and have a case sent round to Slater. 'I was impressed with Peter Walker's business acumen,' Slater joked, 'when I found an invoice with the wine.' Walker says this story is totally untrue.

It is unlikely that the two were quickly on intimate terms. Both were men of strong character, although Slater was probably the more dominant figure – he was, at thirty-three, three years Walker's senior, a couple of inches taller than Walker's six feet, and a fluent speaker. Both were self-confident and highly ambitious.

There were however many things that the two men could learn from each other. Slater had spent five years in the motor industry and had only recently started on active investment in the stock market. Like many men in manufacturing companies he did not know a great deal about the ways of the City; but, while Slater may have shared with many of his industrial colleagues a traditional scepticism of the economic value of institutions like merchant banks and stockbrokers, unlike his colleagues he was not in the least daunted by their defensive barriers of class, wealth and esoteric financial jargon.

Walker on the other hand had little direct experience of the heavier end of industry, although he had been on the board of

Adwest Engineering, a company which he says was of high repute with a range of products from the light end of industry to the heavy end. He did however know about the City and how to raise money there – knowledge he had gained not as a born insider but as one who had assailed and was indeed still clambering over those barriers.

The two men had many other things in common. They came from similar lower-middle-class backgrounds – Walker's slightly humbler than Slater's – in West London suburbs. Both were bachelors. Both preferred work to play. Both were opportunists in business and politics. Above all, both wanted financial independence.

Slater and Walker did not then and there decide to go into business together. Slater had not yet made up his mind to leave the motor industry; Walker had already made some money and it might not have struck him that teaming up with Slater would add much to his fortunes.

Walker was also by then emerging publicly as an up-and-coming political figure. Shortly before their dinner, in August 1962, the *New Statesman* had devoted 2½ columns to a profile of Walker. 'It is not,' ran the piece, 'every 15-year-old school leaver who succeeds in making half-a-million pounds by the age of 30 – and who thereby, even more miraculously, crashes the Tory party's traditional social barrier.'

The article was not unqualified praise: there was, for instance a slight dig at Walker's brashness in the title, 'Junior Imp', a pun on Joseph Chamberlain-style imperialism to which Walker's then enthusiastic support for the Commonwealth against the Common Market was compared. But the suggestion that he had made £500,000 by the age of thirty was one of the earliest printed contributions to a myth that was to grow and flourish over the following decade.

Already, then, in 1962 Walker's image was that of the aggressive, successful businessman who had made his way, and his fortune, in the City, from a lower-middle-class background, against the odds, and with plain, no-nonsense ability. In the following three years the Conservative party, searching for a new identity in the aftermath of Macmillan, Home and the Profumo affair, settled on the young, clean-living self-made men who got things done and who would lead the party out of the era of the Primrose League into the age of meritocracy. Walker seemed to have all the qualifications to become the young hope of this movement. He was, as Anthony Sampson writes in *The New Anatomy of Britain*, the 'most obvious prodigy of the New Toryism'.

By the summer of 1964 Walker was rising fast in the Conservative party, projected into close relationship with its leaders through his appointment as Parliamentary Private Secretary to Selwyn Lloyd

when Sir Alec Douglas-Home restored Lloyd to the Cabinet as
Leader of the House in October 1963. But the myth of his wealth still
far outstripped the reality. Slater on the other hand had demonstrated in the previous eighteen months that he had little less than a
Midas touch. Suddenly they could be of use to each other.

The story must now go back to trace the careers of the two principals before that epochal July 1964 when Slater Walker was formed.
Walker's career must come first, partly because it was more varied,
but also because Walker was then the more prominent of the two. As
the *New Statesman* piece shows, he had gained this prominence as
much on his reputation as a successful businessman as on his political
achievements. Without that reputation he would not have had much
to contribute to the partnership and Slater Walker as such might
never have been conceived.

2   *Insuring independence*

In the early summer of 1972, when Walker's standing was at its peak, another profile of Peter Walker appeared, in the *Guardian* by Terry Coleman. Emphasis was placed, as usual, on Walker's youthful achievements '. . . by 1945 he was, at thirteen, probably the youngest Young Conservative, and he went on to become the youngest chairman of the Young Conservatives, the youngest Parliamentary candidate of his year (in 1955 he was twenty-three), the youngest member of the Shadow Cabinet, and the youngest member of the real Cabinet (in 1970 when he was thirty-eight) . . .'

It is one of the minor ironies of the Slater Walker story that, until about 1962, an idea got around that whizzkid Walker was one year *older* than he really was. For official documents, such as Conservative party press releases and Companies House returns, record, until about that date, that Walker's birthday was 25 March 1931. He was in fact born exactly one year later.

Inconsistencies and inaccuracies over age and other details have continued to dog the numerous press summaries of Walker's early life. Nevertheless the basic outline is clear enough.

In Walker's early boyhood the family lived in a semi-detached house in South Harrow. His father Sydney, who died in 1965, was, according to Walker, a capstan lathe operator and setter, and worked in a factory in Hayes: an easygoing man with a neat moustache, he was happier when he was later able to afford to set up in business as a grocer. Walker's parents were Conservatives but it was his mother Rose who provided the dynamism, having been an active Conservative supporter from an early age and becoming head of the women's division of Conservatives in Harrow. Although she was not dominating, she was a much stronger force behind Walker's ambition than his father. Walker also had an elder brother, but he left home to become a naval cadet and then went to work in Canada.

At eleven Walker won a place at Latymer Upper School in Hammersmith, a grammar school which, under a capable headmaster, was then attracting much of the middle-class talent in West London. Walker was there for five years, leaving in July 1948 at the age of sixteen. Although he always managed to stay in the upper streams he was noted neither for his scholastic nor his sporting abilities. There are conflicting accounts about the number of 'O' level school certificate subjects he passed: one says four, another nine. Walker, however, told me he had passed six, with distinctions in maths and history.

Much of Walker's time was anyway already taken up with politics. The story that Walker likes to tell is that at the 1945 General Election, when he was thirteen, he borrowed some books on the competing parties from the library and after reading them decided his parents were right, and took up the Tory cause.

This picture of a thirteen-year-old making such a coolly rational decision must be viewed against the passions of the post-war election, in which many families of the same financial circumstances as the Walkers and also once traditional Tory supporters turned their backs on the triumphant Churchill. But, decision made, Walker pitched into the campaign with characteristic vigour, forming 'Walker's Anti-Labour League' at school and distributing leaflets. He also helped form and became the first chairman of the Harrow Young Conservatives; being only thirteen in 1945 he was below the minimum age of fifteen, and Walker thinks this may be the reason for the misimpressions about his age – although it hardly explains why they persisted for another fifteen years or so.

Walker was undaunted by the Conservatives' failure and his commitment to their cause increased with his determination to get on. This, it seemed, was the party of opportunity and Disraeli became his hero. He also became an admirer of Leo Amery, the die-hard Tory theorist, whom he met at a Conservative party conference. This meeting has become one of those pivotal points which characterize the Walker legend, for Amery took Walker under his wing and advised him that if he wanted to make his way in politics and the Conservative party, then he should make some money so that first, he could afford to travel, and second, if ever he were to reach a junior position in the government he would not be solely dependent on his Parliamentary salary and could resign on an issue of principle if necessary.

The main legend tells us that as a result of this advice Walker remembered that the only man in the street where they lived who owned a car worked in insurance; it was clearly a business in which money could be made and so, on leaving school, he hurried off to the Labour Exchange to ask for a job in insurance.

There have however been other versions. The *New Statesman*, in its 'Junior Imp' article, did not mention the Amery story, but ascribed Walker's early interest in making money to an introduction to the *Financial Times* by his maths master at school – a story which has an interesting parallel in Slater's early life.

By the time that Walker left school in 1948 his family had moved to Gloucestershire. It was there he got his first job, with the local branch of the General Accident Insurance Company. Going to work for this large institutionalized business, efficiently and unextravagantly run from Perth in Scotland, would not normally be regarded as the fastest short-cut to fortune, but Walker's pay of thirty shillings a week would have been a useful addition to the family income. He later recalled winning a staff competition for new business introduced by selling bicycle insurance to his Young Conservative friends.

Walker cannot have worked for the General Accident for more than about a year and a half, for at the end of April 1950, when he was just eighteen, he went off to do his National Service. His period with that company has, however, added one common anecdote to the legend: Walker was responsible for buying the office tea and coffee and, as the *New Statesman* first reported the story in its 'Junior Imp' article in 1962, 'today Mr Walker, as a pluralist company director, proudly recalls how he switched the order from a private grocer to the Co-op and pocketed for three years the 2d. a week dividend.' Walker denied to me that he had told this story, saying that he was never a member of the Gloucester Co-op, but after checking with the author of the article I cannot accept that the *New Statesman* simply invented it. This sort of example of youthful enterprise no doubt went down well as the Tory philosophy of self-help revived in the Sixties, and Walker told a similar story of himself in 1969 in a personal column he was then writing in the *Birmingham Post*: 'My first successful business transaction was when I managed to buy a first edition of Winston Churchill's *My African Journey* for 6d. on a bookshelf in Foyles and I was able immediately to go into the Rare Book Department there, and sell this volume for a substantially increased sum of money.'

More important however, at General Accident Walker learnt the technicalities of the insurance business. He would have discovered that working for a big insurance company was not the way to make big or quick money. The basic business of General Accident and other such companies is underwriting risks, that is issuing the insurance policies and then paying out on the claims. The selling of the policies is mostly undertaken in exchange for a commission, either by agents, who work for specific companies, or by brokers who are free to choose. Good brokers require technical skill to advise their customers on the best insurance for their needs and, like most selling operations, broking can also be highly rewarding for those who combine willingness to work hard with the flair of the salesman.

Walker joined the Army as a private and became a sergeant when he went into the Education Corps. His parents meanwhile moved back to the capital, or rather to Brentford in Middlesex, where the Walkers acquired a grocery shop on the main London road. When Walker finished his two-year National Service stint in May 1952 he too returned to London. He now turned again, 'Dick Whittington-like', as he has described it, to insurance, and this time he chose a broking firm.

Walker saw an advertisement for an 'American' broker for which he applied, believing, he says, that it would entail travelling to the United States. He secured the job, which was with a medium-sized City firm of insurance brokers called Griffiths Tate, but quickly discovered that no trips to the US were involved, for he was hired to help handle the firm's American business in 'the room' at Lloyd's. Nevertheless, he was as a result at once thrown into the heart of the insurance world, for Lloyd's is the centre of the British, and indeed the world's, insurance market. He would have learnt that no insurance broking business could really succeed unless it gained admission to the select club of Lloyd's.

At about the same time that Walker left the Army and went to Griffiths Tate, he met by chance, on a tube station, an old school colleague called David Moate. Moate and Walker had been in the same intake at Latymer Upper, and Moate was in fact ten weeks older than Walker – although he always believed that Walker was his senior by some nine months. Moate had usually been in lower streams than Walker at school and the two had not been particularly close. But as a result of the chance encounter, they now began to discuss plans together.

David Moate was at that time working for his father's accountancy firm, Moate, Thorpe & Co., where he was training for his exams. The firm was in Coleman Street in the heart of the City, but it was a very small and somewhat ramshackle business: in spite of their ostensibly more middle-class livelihood, the Moates were in fact little better off than the Walkers. David Moate had had his National Service postponed because of his exams; but before deciding to take up accountancy he, like Walker, had worked for a large insurance company.

So the two young men decided to combine their insurance and accountancy talents and set up a partnership: Walker asked his employers at Griffiths Tate if they would mind him going part-time into the same line as themselves, and they agreed to let him do it: the sort of business involved would have been too small to be of much interest to them. So on 1 August 1952, Walker and Moate set up in business as insurance agents, using the address of Moate Thorpe & Co., at 25/29 Coleman Street, but with no special space allotted to them.

So began a partnership that was to last seven and a half years. The Walkers and the Moates lived quite close to each other and the two young men spent much time in each other's houses. At the Moates', Walker met David's two younger brothers, Keith and Roger. All of them had ambitions to get on in the world and improve their circumstances; like Walker, David Moate wanted to make money, and had already started thinking up schemes: in 1950 when he was seventeen he had devised a system similar to that which was to be started some five years later by Luncheon Vouchers, and even got as far as forming a company to try to get the project off the ground. Unlike Walker however, and unlike his youngest brother Roger, who was to follow Walker into Parliament as a Conservative MP, David Moate had no political ambitions.

The business of the Walker Moate partnership was indeed small stuff to begin with; after their first year the two friends were able to split something like £60 of brokerage commission. However, they had made one advance: a helpful insurance company official had pointed out that if they called themselves insurance brokers rather than agents they could charge a higher commission.

Walker still depended on his job at Griffiths Tate for a living, and it was now that he landed his first big deal. Walker gave me his own account of it: he read in the *Financial Times* one day that the German airline Lufthansa were buying four Super Constellations. He rang the German Embassy and inquired who was responsible for insuring the planes. The obliging Embassy gave Walker the name of a man in Cologne and even helped fix up an interview.

Walker then asked his directors at Griffiths Tate if they would send him to Germany to try to get the business. They pointed out that a second-class fare to Cologne was a lot of money to risk on their young employee. Walker said he would pay his fare himself on condition that he could take half the brokerage if he got the order. Griffiths Tate agreed.

Knowing little about aviation insurance, Walker quickly collected a correspondence course on the subject from the Insurance Institute, which he read on the train to Cologne. The man there said he was thinking of placing the insurance for the new planes through the firm's usual channels: Walker asked what rate he would be paying and then offered to do the business at a fraction less. He was given the business, although back in London Griffiths Tate had some trouble persuading the aviation underwriters to take the risk on their books at rates acceptable to all parties.

The coup was however not quite such a single-handed achievement as this account might suggest. For Walker did not speak German and wisely took along a contact, John Lowe, who did, and who undertook much of the negotiation.

Walker's share of the commission was two or three hundred pounds. This was roughly equivalent to his annual salary at Griffiths Tate at the time. If, he thought, he could make that sort of money on one deal, he might just as well work for himself full-time. So after about eighteen months with Griffiths Tate he decided to leave to devote his energies to the partnership with David Moate.

So Walker moved in with David Moate in Coleman Street. They took over a room in the offices of Moate Thorpe which they carpeted out and smartened up, so that it contrasted sharply with the dingy rooms occupied by the accountancy practice down the corridor.

It was now 1954. This was a year of stock market boom, in which share prices, which had started to pick up in 1952, now rose rapidly and substantially for the first time since the war – indeed since the Twenties. The rate of new flotations on the stock market doubled and quick fortunes were made. It was a time of great revival in company promotion.

Walker and Moate were soon caught up in this heady atmosphere and for a brief period they were involved with a group of 'young men about the City' in thinking up potential commercial enterprises outside their chosen financial field. The others in the group were for the most part better connected than Walker or Moate: there was David Rutland, another young broker at Lloyd's, an old Etonian and the grandson of Lord Ashfield, the creator of London Transport. There were Dimitri Kasterine, another young Lloyd's broker, and Christopher Keeling, just starting with the blue-blooded merchant bank of Kleinwort, Benson. (Today, Keeling is a director of a leading firm of Lloyd's insurance brokers.) From outside the City were Michael Rice, who like Walker was then active on Conservative party committees, and who also worked for the International Wool Secretariat (today, he heads a public relations firm), and Nicholas Royds, an advertising man who now runs the family firm.

Members of the group would sometimes meet at a coffee shop close to Lloyd's, the brokers trailing their underwriting 'slips', or round at the offices of Walker Moate. There was no clear leader. David Rutland, a personable young man with many friends, perhaps did most to bring the group together. But the Walker Moate partnership provided what organization the group had, and Walker was clearly the dominant figure in that partnership. The two men were now twenty-two, although Moate, with his slight build, fair hair brushed forward and round boyish face, looked younger. Walker on the other hand was imposing, wearing black jacket and pinstripe trousers – the uniform of Whitehall and City traditionalists.

In those days the first thing an ambitious young entrepreneur did was to register a company; it created an impression of substance even if the business itself was far from solid. In the summer of 1954

Walker Moate formed a little clutch of companies through which the partners and their friends hoped to promote their inspirations.

The most important was called Grailand Industrial and Investment, the name being invented by Moate. All seven of the group joined in its formation in July 1954, and the nominal capital was an ambitious £10,000. But only four, including Walker and Moate, actually subscribed for shares, each putting up £100.

Grailand's articles of association opened with a sweeping list of objectives: it was 'to carry on business and trade of merchants, traders, manufacturers, wholesalers, retailers, factors and agents in all kinds of general merchandise . . . ' It was perhaps a somewhat pretentious description for Grailand's initial industrial enterprise: the manufacture of book-ends in a shed in a garden in London's smart Belgravia. The garden belonged to the house of the mother of one of the group in Wilton Street – just a couple of doors from the house to which Edward Heath moved after he lost the premiership in 1974. The book-ends were decorated with small plastic reproductions of pub signs and members of the group helped stick the parts together, either in the shed or at their own homes – although Walker says he did not take part. It was quickly discovered, however, that the book-ends were not heavy enough to support even a couple of paperbacks and they never got as far as selling any.

That, for the time being anyway, was the extent of Grailand's activities, although there was some talk of offering a conversion service, turning corner shops into self-service stores over the weekend so that trading would not be interrupted. But four other companies were formed in July and August 1954. Michael Rice inspired one of them: he had been to America and had noticed there that every drink came with a plastic cocktail stick in it. Talking it over with his friends back home, they decided that it would be a good idea to try to promote the habit on this side of the Atlantic. So Walker and Moate, together with Rutland, formed a little company called Swizzle Sticks Ltd, with a £3 capital. Further investigation showed that most of the hotels and bars had already organized their supplies of sticks.

It was also with the help of Rice that Walker and Moate acquired the rights to market a type of wool wound on a special spindle for use in knitting machines. Two companies were formed, Walmoric Trading – Wal for Walker, Mo for Moate and Ric for Rice – and Conifer Wools to exploit these rights. But nothing ever came of it and the rights were sold back to the textile company concerned, who later marketed the line themselves. Another idea that Walker and Moate had was to try to cash in on the increasing popularity of do-it-yourself. So they formed a £2 company, Make-it-at-Home Ltd. But nobody can recall today what they hoped to persuade people to make at home.

None of these plans really came to anything. For most of the group they were regarded if not as frivolous, at least as just sidelines – 'laughable', as one of them described them to me; 'just something we would do in the evenings,' said another – and the group drifted apart after a few months. With the exception of Grailand, which we will meet again shortly, the companies were dissolved by the Board of Trade as dormant in 1967 and 1968. Walker had resigned his directorships of them on 2 January 1961 and he told me that he would doubt if he spent more than four hours in total on these companies, and that insurance broking never took second place to them. But my inquiries indicate that this somewhat understates their importance, however brief: for example, when, as required by Company Law, Walker gave his occupation on subscribing for shares in the last three of the five little companies to be formed in the summer of 1954, he listed 'company director' rather than 'insurance broker' as he had done before, although the only companies of which he was a director were the two registered just a few weeks before. The potted biographies which state that Walker was a company director at twenty-two would be read in this light: Walker's first appointments to the boards of companies already in business did not take place until he was nearly twenty-five.

The first company in the Walker Moate insurance broking business was formed in February 1955: called Walker Moate (Overseas), its primary purpose was to collect Walker's share of the commission that he still collected from the Lufthansa deal. At home the partners built up a useful connection with the police, persuading the underwriters that policemen were better risks for both car and householders' insurance, and they became brokers to the Metropolitan Police Motor Club. Otherwise it was: 'Motor insurance. Shopkeepers' insurance. Householders' insurance. Anything I could get my hands on,' as the *Birmingham Sunday Mercury* reported, quoting Walker, in 1965.

The business grew slowly: a partner's share of net commission had only risen to £63 by 1955/6. It was hard work, particularly for Walker, as Moate had to go off to do his National Service in the RAF and could only put in occasional appearances on Saturdays. The *Sunday Mercury* again quoted Walker: 'It was a bit tricky at first. One's standard of living was quite low, of course. It was a matter of living from hand to mouth.'

Walker's political commitments increased considerably at this time. He continued to be active in the Young Conservatives, and in 1955 became chairman of the Home Counties North area. In the General Election in May that year he was chosen to fight the Dartford division of Kent: the Conservatives under their new leader Anthony Eden were returned with an increased Parliamentary majority, but Dartford was a Labour stronghold and although Walker reduced the margin he still lost by 4,125 votes. The following year, 1956, Walker was appointed to the general purposes committee of the National Executive of the National Union of Conservative Associations.

On 3 November 1956 Walker got his first non-executive director-ship: he was asked to join the board of a small private company called Aircraft and General Finance, which was owned by a friend of Moate's and acted as the representative and purchasing agent in the UK for a few small foreign airlines. Walker never took an active part in the business and resigned in June 1964.

The Moate connection brought Walker a more important directorship in December 1956: he was asked to join the board of a small property company in Croydon called New British Garden Estates, in which members of the Moate family had an interest. There was no financial reward in the appointment, which Walker says he accepted for the experience and to help the company recover from a fraud.*

So the insurance partnership was, at the end of 1956, still Walker's main hope of making money. While David Moate was doing his National Service the two partners made an important decision: they hired a life assurance specialist called Edward Clouston. Clouston, who was some twelve years older than Walker and Moate, had recently returned from the Far East to work as a life manager for an insurance firm in the City, and thus came into contact with the partnership. Previously Walker and Moate had done little life insur-ance, but in a growing broking concern it is useful to mix life with general business: while the initial sale of a life policy is not always particularly rewarding, in the following years the automatic renewal commission is almost all profit.

By the end of 1957, therefore, the Walker Moate partnership, formed over five years before, was at last beginning to move ahead, with Moate's return from National Service giving it a further impetus. They had picked up odd bits of insurance like the replica ship, *Mayflower II*, launched in the spring of that year through the efforts of a public relations friend. They also canvassed estate agents: insurance brokers often also act as mortgage brokers, putting insurance companies with large sums available to invest in property, in touch with developers. For this they not only earn commission but get the fire and other insurance business on the buildings.

* The Companies House return of Walker's appointment provides an example of an inaccurate statement of Walker's date of birth. Walker said that the wrong date on these returns could well have been supplied by any of the staff of the Moate accounting firm, or the Moates themselves, who had the wrong impression about his age. This does not explain how they got that impression in the first place, or why the Conserva-tive party biographical releases also stated it incorrectly.

More important, they had started opening branch offices. The first was in their own 'home' area, Hounslow, where they acquired a small office with the help of a local friend. Walker's family put up a few hundred pounds towards the cost of the premises. They went after the insurance business of local firms and formed, in June 1957, a £100 company, Walker Moate and Co., in which each partner held fifty shares, to handle the new office's affairs.

The usual practice of Walker and Moate in opening branch offices was to join forces with a local businessman. Thus in 1958 they formed Walker Moate (Midlands) with a young barrister from York called Charles Longbottom, who was also later to become a Conservative MP, and opened an office in Retford; they each took a third of the shares of this new firm. Then in 1960 they took over the Birmingham brokerage of Charles Simpson, a future Lord Mayor of the City.

The Walker Moate partnership did not confine itself to insurance broking. They backed a little engineering firm, Martin King, in 1959; but more important, the previous year they had moved into another business that in the late Fifties looked as if it might be a big money-spinner: hire purchase. This was the time of free-for-all in the never-never trade, after the easing of statutory controls (covering down-payments and repayment period) on cars in 1956 and their complete removal on other consumer durables and furniture in the autumn of 1958.

Walker and Moate started gradually, introducing in February 1958 a scheme they called Securitas Finance to provide car hire purchase for their good-risk policemen clients. Then in November 1958 they resurrected the dormant Grailand Industrial and Investment company to administer the credit business. A year later they formed Grailand Finance, also to do hire purchase.

From November 1958 to the end of March 1960, Grailand earned only just over £1,000 from its credit business. But to finance the expansion Walker and Moate had had to increase the paid-up capital first to £1,000 and then to £3,000 – Moate taking up to two thirds of the shares and Walker only one third. Nevertheless, they needed still more capital to finance the credit they were giving and so, through Securitas, they took deposits from the public: at 31 March 1960 Securitas had taken some £12,000 of money on deposit.

Walker says he was unenthusiastic about expanding the hire purchase business, but his partner's enthusiasm was fired by two factors. First, he had been asked to advise on the public issue of shares by a small hire purchase company, and it had gone well. Secondly, the partnership had formed an association with an ex-Army sergeant and one-time builder turned car salesman called Bill Turner. Turner had a chain of garages in South London, and Walker Moate had opened an office in Hayes to handle its insurance business, installing a young Conservative, David Clarke – a future Parliamentary candidate for Watford – to run it. Turner also forecast a potentially huge hire purchase business linked to his car sales.

Grailand's hire purchase business thus began to expand more rapidly in 1960, with earnings and deposits more than doubling. In June of that year its capital was reorganized, the 3,000 £1 shares being turned into one shilling 'management' shares, so that Moate had 40,000 and Walker 20,000; and 20,000 new £1 shares were created ready for issue. Just what the purpose of this manoeuvre was is not clear, but patently Grailand at that point featured prominently in the plans of the Walker Moate partnership. But then suddenly at the end of 1960 the partnership broke up.

It is difficult now to pinpoint exactly what the causes of the break were. Walker says it resulted from the fact that he and Moate had for some time been pursuing different interests: he had concentrated on the insurance broking, while Moate had handled the hire purchase and other activities, as well as looking after the accountancy practice.

Nevertheless, the full reasons for the break-up are undoubtedly more complicated. It was Moate and not Walker who took the initiative for the split, and although Walker says that Moate did this because he wanted his independence to pursue policies he, Walker, opposed, in particular the decision to provide a substantial hire purchase contract to a road haulier, it is more likely that personal rather than business motives lay behind Moate's move: for over seven years Walker had been the dominating half of the partnership, and Moate simply felt he needed to break away.

Once the two friends had determined to break it was done quickly and cleanly, although Walker was at first annoyed because he felt he had contributed more than Moate. But virtually everything that Walker and Moate had started, bought or earned until then had been shared; even Walker's interests in the unit trust company, Unicorn, and the property development group, Rodwell, whose affairs will be detailed in the next two chapters, were held by him on behalf of the partnership. Accountants were called in to advise on the value of the investments so that they could be split equally.

It was natural that the insurance broking side should be taken by Walker. I do not know what value was put on it but Moate told me that Grailand and the accountancy business were each valued at £3,000 and 'we called it quits'. Walker bought back Moate's share of their joint interest in Unicorn and its associated company Dillon Walker, which was valued at £5,333 10s., but Moate wisely held onto his share of the Rodwell interest.

The Rodwell stake, as we shall see, was the cause of some bitterness, but the split was amicable enough, although the two have only met two or three times since they parted. David's youngest brother, twenty-two-year-old Roger, who had just returned from working for a big insurance broking firm in South Africa, slipped conveniently into David's place on the boards of the Walker Moate companies, allowing continuity of name and maintaining Walker's links with the Moate family. The middle brother Keith took Walker's place at Grailand.

If Walker was annoyed at the break-up, he was also lucky, for David Moate's subsequent business career was not a great success. In the autumn of 1961 he tried to turn Grailand into a public company and raise £100,000, but the issue failed. Then in 1967 Grailand collapsed after an ill-judged takeover of a banking company called Finance & Mortgages.

After the break, Walker immediately set about reorganizing the structure of his insurance broking concern. He had to find new offices, and moved down the road to No. 63 Coleman Street. Walker Moate & Co. was now turned into the main holding company and its capital increased to 10,000 £1 shares, of which Walker took up 3,000, Clouston 2,500, Roger Moate and David Clarke 1,750 each, and Charles Longbottom 1,000. Walker says that with the exception of Longbottom he gave his colleagues the money to obtain their shares.

Less than half the capital was paid up, however, and by City standards Walker Moate was still a very small insurance broking business indeed. It was certainly not the 'leading City broking firm' that the *Evening News* was to call it in the 'Under-Forties' article later in 1961. In fact no broking firm engaged in general insurance could claim such status without the cachet of Lloyd's membership. For only Lloyd's brokers may place business directly with the Lloyd's underwriting market, which then accounted for about a third of all nonlife insurance.

There were then over two hundred firms of Lloyd's brokers, but for a new firm to gain admission was difficult. Not only would it be subjected to detailed scrutiny by the Committee of Lloyd's but membership would also require the payment of large deposits to Lloyd's as security. At that stage there would have been no question of Walker Moate being able to qualify for Lloyd's on its own merits, although it could place business in the Lloyd's market through a member firm, splitting the commission.

Nor at the start of 1961 was Walker nearly wealthy enough to become an underwriting member of Lloyd's, that is, one of the six thousand or so individuals who are in the end responsible for paying Lloyd's insurance claims. Then, as now, a person must show a net worth of £75,000 before he can underwrite, and a part of that must be in readily realizable form and deposited with Lloyd's – although a *working* member, which Walker was later to become, only had to show £15,000.

But in 1961 Walker got his first toehold in Lloyd's. Some eight years before he had made friends with a young colleague at Griffiths Tate called Bryan Harrison, who had subsequently joined a small Lloyd's firm named Hugh Paul. At the end of 1960 Walker was invited to join the Hugh Paul board, because, I was told, they wanted his advice, particularly on investment matters. Once a director, Hugh Paul suggested that Walker should become what is called a Lloyd's subscriber: subscribers are senior executives of Lloyd's firms who are allowed access to the Lloyd's market on behalf of those firms on payment of a small fee.

So at the start of 1961, as Walker reached the age of twenty-nine, he was still a long way from being a wealthy man. He could live cheaply enough, as he was still living at home: his parents had given up the grocer's shop some years before and were now living in a small stuccoed bungalow in Albemarle Avenue in Twickenham – a street that in spite of its name is rather more modest than the typical 'Acacia Avenue' from which the New Tories are traditionally said to spring.

But Walker's political commitments were becoming more onerous. He had been elected National Chairman of the Young Conservatives in 1958, and had held the post for two years. He was awarded an MBE for political services in 1959, and in the General Election in October that year again fought Dartford. The Conservatives, now under Macmillan, again increased their Parliamentary majority, but Walker again lost, although he cut his Labour opponent's majority right back. But he was beginning to be noticed, and new men were moving up in the Tory party: Heath, who had been Chief Whip since 1955, was first appointed to the Cabinet in October 1959 as Minister of Labour and then in July 1960 was made Lord Privy Seal to act as Lord Home's representative in the Commons on foreign affairs.

Walker's chance came at the end of 1960 with the elevation to the peerage of the sitting Conservative member for Worcester. Walker was chosen to fight the by-election and on 16 March 1961 he won a three-cornered fight with a majority of 3,597.

3   *Towards a capital-owning democracy*

One of the Conservative party's principal themes in the late Fifties and early Sixties was the call for the creation of a 'property-' or 'capital-owning democracy'. It was a natural answer to Labour's policies for the redistribution of wealth: rather than levelling down by eroding the property of the richer sections of the community, why not make it easier for the enterprising, hard-working and thrifty to build up their own capital?

At one level the implementation of this policy lay in obscure measures like the Stock Transfer Act – an Act we shall meet again in Chapter 10 – which streamlined the mechanics of capitalism and encouraged the spread of investment in shares. More fundamentally it entailed positive measures to aid the accretion of capital, such as stock options and employees' shares incentive schemes, tax relief on loan interest, and help for people to buy their own homes.

Naturally one of the loudest advocates of the property-owning democracy was Peter Walker: not only had he shown that he could create capital for himself, but he could also claim, unlike most of his colleagues, to have done something to help others achieve the same goal. This was the formation with Edward du Cann, in the autumn of 1957, of Unicorn Securities, the first unit trust to be started in the UK since the war. Like his own reputed wealth Walker's role in the start of Unicorn was to play an important part in his rapid political advancement. As the *Guardian* commented in November 1972, when Walker was at the height of his power, it was characteristic that 'as A New Type of Tory, he should have been in at the start of one of the epitomes of benevolent capitalism: unit trusts, or the giving to the small investor the chance to own some of the country's largest companies.'

Something of the political zeal that lay behind the idea can be found in a short book du Cann published in 1958 called *Investing Simplified.** Suggesting that there had been a diminution in the

---

* Published by Newman Neame.

sense of personal responsibility as a result of the Welfare State, du Cann wrote:

> We must seek to reverse this trend, to give people the opportunity to accept responsibility and to participate in the management and organization of British industry.
>
> This is the social necessity for encouraging a wider spread of share ownership. To spread wealth: to spread responsibility; to spread power; that is the aim.
>
> Every need creates, in time, its own solution. There is a simple answer to all these problems: the Unit Trust method of investment.

Du Cann was nearly eight years older than Walker. After the war he read law at Oxford and then went to work in the City. He joined the huge investment complex of a well-known City figure, Sir Denys Lowson, who was Lord Mayor in 1950/1, and in 1953 was appointed secretary of the unit trust side, the National Group. This then comprised some forty-five trusts, many of which had been started in the Thirties – among the very first of this type of financial creature – and du Cann made it his job over the next three years or so to rationalize these, reducing their number to about twenty, of which only a dozen or so were actively promoted.

Du Cann was appointed a director of National at the start of 1956, just before he was elected to Parliament as MP for Taunton in a by-election. He was however becoming disenchanted with the way his attempts to reform the National's unit trusts were being received: Sir Denys achieved considerable notoriety in 1974 for the way he handled the sale of the National Group at enormous personal and family profit, but within the unit trust business his management has for many years been a matter of much controversy and criticism. Du Cann had also examined the growth of mutual funds – the equivalent of unit trusts in America – and believed that this type of investment was being seriously under-exploited in the UK.

Matters came to a head when his employers suggested that now he was getting an MP's salary and spending time in Parliament, his pay at National should be halved. In early 1957 du Cann resigned, determined to buy or start a unit trust company of his own.

Du Cann thought, somewhat naïvely, that all he would have to do would be to draw up a memorandum of his plans and City banks would be falling over themselves to put up the cash. He was however realistic in his estimate of the sort of money that might be needed – as much as £100,000, a lot of money to ask for in those days for a completely new venture.

After a few months of fruitless attempts to raise the money, du Cann ran into Walker by chance; the two already knew each other, for du Cann, like Walker, had been active in the Young Conservatives, holding the chairmanship of their City branch from 1953 to 1955. Walker, too, had been impressed by the way mutual funds in the United States had been more active than in this country in spreading the habit of equity investment, and he and du Cann now decided to join forces.

Walker had an idea that he believed would make the project successful, and the formula he put forward had far-reaching and important consequences for the British life insurance industry: he suggested that the unit trust should be used as the basis for a new life insurance policy, in which the benefits payable on death, maturity or surrender would be determined directly by the value of the units, i.e. of the ordinary shares quoted on the Stock Exchange in which the trust would invest.

Walker also believed that this new approach to the basic unit trust idea would make it easier to raise the backing that du Cann needed, and he had a specific person in mind. In the City, Walker had done business with an insurance broking firm called Stewart Smith; it was owned by the merchant bank S. G. Warburg & Co. but still run by its founder, George Stewart. Stewart, Walker knew, also controlled an insurance company, the London & Edinburgh, which he was anxious to develop, particularly on the life side. Walker also sensed that Stewart, who was familiar with American mutual funds through his insurance connections in the United States, would be receptive to the idea of an 'equity-linked' insurance policy.

He was right. Stewart agreed to help, putting up an initial £40,000 in share and loan capital through London & Edinburgh Assurance. It was just enough to get the trust going even if, as du Cann later recollected, he interviewed his first secretary 'in a dingy office in the City furnished by two orange boxes, a telephone and a decrepit typewriter'. Walker's outline for a new life policy was then turned over to London & Edinburgh's actuary, Ralph Lane, who refined it into a practicable document; it was, du Cann said, like handing the rough sketch to the architect.

So was born the first equity-linked life assurance policy. It was christened 'Equitas'. In terms of its ultimate effects on the life insurance business and on the people who buy life policies, this plan to link the benefits of an ordinary 'with-profits' policy to the value of a unit trust was in many ways the most significant, if not the most dramatic, development in which Walker was directly involved.

With-profit policies, that is those in which the policy holders share in the investment profits of insurance funds over and above the guaranteed minimum sum assured, had already proved extremely popular – one reason of course being that although such policies were strictly rather more investment than insurance, the premiums still

qualified for tax relief. However, life companies were then dominated by cautious actuaries, and the profits they had actually been
handing out to the policy holders had for the most part been based
only on the income earned by the investments, taking no account of
the rise in their capital value. Just as many people followed du Cann
and Walker into unit trusts, so many also followed them into equity-
linked insurance. One outcome of this was that the increased competition gradually forced the old life offices to abandon their over-
cautious methods and to produce a much better deal for their policy
holders.

But the introduction of Equitas was not solely responsible for this
change. Already by the late Fifties the big life offices had started to
invest a much higher proportion of their premium income in equity
shares and also directly in property; at the start of an inflationary age
they had already made large capital profits as a result, both realized
and unrealized. Already many life assurance officials had begun to
question the fairness of putting all these profits to reserve, and some
companies had even gone a stage further and had declared special
bonuses on their with-profit policies to reflect at least part of the
realized gains. One company, the London & Manchester, had in fact
already produced an equity-linked policy, although it was of limited
appeal, being related only to retirement annuities.

But Walker must be given credit for his part in giving a firm impetus to this trend, perhaps more credit than London & Edinburgh
itself was prepared to give him in its own later account of the origins
of Equitas: 'History – and the press – have variously ascribed the
invention to Peter Walker and Edward du Cann, but tempting
though it is to conjure up a picture of a man with a golden vision, it is
more accurate to report that the equity-linked assurance contract
idea was no one man's brainchild, rather an evolvement from many
business sessions.'

Du Cann's difficulties were not yet over. It had long been recognized that the unit trust form of investment was open to special types
of abuse, and for this reason their operation was surrounded with the
special restrictions encoded in the Prevention of Fraud (Investments)
Act, 1939, and the Companies Acts of 1947 and 1948. (These were
consolidated the year after Unicorn was started in the Prevention of
Fraud (Investments) Act, 1958.) The legislation gave the Board of
Trade tight control over unit trusts, and no scheme was allowed to
operate unless it had been approved by the Board's officials. In particular the Board had laid down firm limits on the charges that could
be levied by the managers of unit trusts. They would not allow a new
unit trust to take, in fees, more than two per cent of the amount initially put up by the investors; thereafter the Board allowed the managers to take a half per cent of the fund each year in a service charge.

This limitation on charges was the main reason why no new unit trust had been started since the restrictions had been introduced. It was widely felt that these charges were too low; certainly it was agreed that it would not be profitable to launch a new trust if the managers could only take two per cent of the money they attracted.

Du Cann set out to persuade the Board to let him charge more, and he submitted a trust deed for approval with an initial charge of five per cent. At first the board officials flatly refused. Du Cann and Bill Fowler, a colleague at the National Group who had left with du Cann to help found Unicorn, were determined; they knew from their experience at National that some trusts were effectively charging more. Du Cann now came up with a face-saving compromise which was to be the key to the expansion of the trust industry from 1958 onwards.

While the Board of Trade did not allow the managers of unit trusts to take more than two per cent of the money put up by investors for themselves in 'service charge', it did allow the managers to levy an extra $1\frac{1}{4}$ per cent on money subscribed through agents like banks and stockbrokers in order to pay them the standard sale commission. The managers were thereafter allowed to charge their customers another half per cent a year. This meant that the maximum amount payable by the customer over the standard twenty-year life of a trust was $13\frac{1}{4}$ per cent, although of course the managers only collected twelve per cent of that.

Du Cann proposed that they should form their own 'agent' through which sales of units could be channelled and on which they would be permitted to collect the $1\frac{1}{4}$ per cent extra themselves. The Board could not very well refuse. In the first place, it was under pressure from other unit trust managers to permit higher charges. Secondly, although customers would not now be able to avoid paying the extra $1\frac{1}{4}$ per cent by going direct to the managers, those who bought through banks and stockbrokers, then the usual method of distribution, would not pay any more than before.

In fact, having made this concession, the Board went further: it permitted du Cann the full five per cent initial charge he wanted. It would not however allow the total charge over the life of the trust to go above $13\frac{1}{4}$ per cent, and as a quid pro quo du Cann had to accept a lower annual service charge of only $\frac{3}{8}$ per cent.

Once the Board of Trade had given in and allowed du Cann his five per cent it was not strictly necessary to form a separate distributor. But nevertheless du Cann created an 'agent' – a company called Dillon Walker. (Du Cann chose to use one of his Christian names in the title rather than his surname like Walker.) For Dillon Walker was not designed just as a device to secure higher charges: it was part of du Cann's plan radically to alter the method of selling unit trusts. He did not want to use only brokers and banks; he wanted to sell direct to the public and he believed that it was best to keep the selling arm of the organization separate from the one managing the trust. The expense of the exercise was, as he said in *Investing Simplified*, 'formidable'; but it had its advantages, one of which was that the distributing company could pursue new kinds of marketing methods.

The new unit trust was unveiled on 25 October 1957. Besides George Stewart, who was chairman, du Cann, managing director, and Walker, there were three other directors: Fearnley Allen, a broking colleague of Stewart's, Admiral of the Fleet Lord Tovey, wartime commander of the Home Fleet and hero of the sinking of the *Bismarck*, and Sir William Charles Crocker, a solicitor who had become famous for his detective work for Lloyd's on fraudulent claims, particularly for his part in the exposure of the notorious fire-raiser Leopold Harris in the Thirties. The trustees were Lloyds Bank.

At once the new company's direct approach to selling was revealed, when Unicorn launched itself on the public by offering 500,000 units at 9s. 6d. each through advertisements in the press.

The technique of the so-called 'block offer' has since become familiar, but in 1957 it was highly unusual. Advertising of units had taken place before – but the advertisements had merely called attention to the merits of the particular trust. The bold approach of Unicorn, similar in style to a new issue prospectus with its 'offer for sale' of '500,000 shares' at a fixed price, soon caused controversy in the unit trust business.

The opposition to block offers was led by the Municipal & General group of unit trusts, whose purist chairman Ian Fairbairn even refused to join the Association of Unit Trust Managers. The main argument against the offers was however best summarized by the Association itself in evidence to the Jenkins Committee on company law reform in 1960:

> It is argued by some people that a block offer is wrong for a number of reasons – the most cogent of which is that this form of offer creates the false impression that the proposed purchaser must invest at once at a price which is predicted in advance, whereas, the whole idea of a Unit Trust is that units shall always be on offer at a price which fluctuates according to the value of the underlying securities.

The proponents of block offers argued that this was over-idealistic – the pragmatists won the day and block offers stayed. We do not like them, unit trust managers would argue, but they are the only way we can get people to buy the units and it is in the customers' interests for the trust to keep expanding. It is not a strong argument, and du

Cann's own defence in *Investing Simplified* is preferable: 'They are helpful to the investor because he knows exactly what to pay.'

The block offer was not the only innovation to run into opposition. Stockbrokers, feeling their livelihood threatened, complained of the new, vigorous promotion of unit trusts. More serious objections, perhaps similarly motivated, were advanced by the established life offices in attacks on London & Edinburgh's Equitas life policy.

The first assault came quickly: on 12 November 1957, in a lecture on 'Life Assurance and Inflation' given to the Insurance Institute, J. A. Shaljean, then life manager and actuary of Yorkshire Insurance, discussed the new type of policy in some detail, but without naming Equitas or London & Edinburgh. Shaljean expressed a number of doubts about the new species, and was worried that people who took out these policies might not understand them. This he feared, might result in the life insurance industry losing its 'reputation for stability and reliability'.

The most serious allegation he made clearly referred to the London & Edinburgh: 'It is all very well for the office to say that the nominal sum assured is a guaranteed minimum. But if the whole of its funds are invested in equity shares – as the nature of the contract demands – and if these decline in value, it would just not be possible for the office to fulfil this guarantee. The money would not be there.'

The lecture was published by an insurance trade paper, *The Post Magazine & Insurance Monitor*, in January 1958. London & Edinburgh were furious, not surprisingly, as, adding insult to injury, the attack on the policy appeared opposite a half-page advertisement for Equitas. Libel proceedings were immediately started against Shaljean and the magazine.

The action was settled when *The Post* printed an extensive 'contradiction' some months later. It pointed out that Shaljean's comments had been based on a false premise, for the Equitas contract did not 'demand' that the whole of London & Edinburgh's funds, or indeed any part of them, *had* to be invested in Unicorn shares, or, for that matter, any other equity shares. Shaljean's hypothesis had been strictly logical; what he had not made clear was that London & Edinburgh were only intending to use the value of Unicorn shares, or units, as a yardstick to determine the benefits payable. Although the company could, and did, buy the units for its life fund, it reserved the right to invest its money elsewhere too.

The echoes of that controversy can still be heard. The inherent risks of a life fund whose liabilities are determined by an index rather than directly by the value of its actual investments are still a matter of debate. Because they were easy to sell, equity-linked policies spread rapidly, but their development in some ways outran the ability of the life insurance industry to understand what was happening. The beneficial effect was to make the old life offices more generous to their policy holders and some even introduced equity-linked policies of their own. But many new firms were attracted into the business, and equity-linked policies often became just a thinly disguised method of securing tax relief on what was no more than direct stock market investment. They also provided a convenient method of bypassing the controls on unit trust charges.

The trend went further: the inventive had soon conjured up the property bond, then the income and growth bonds, the 'managed' bond, even the energy bond. By 1971 there was such concern over the higgledy-piggledy growth of these new policies that a committee under solicitor Sir Hilary Scott was appointed to examine them. But its report was disappointing and did little to help avert the crisis that overtook life insurance in the 1974 crash.

By then London & Edinburgh's original Equitas policy looked the most conservative of contracts; indeed it had proved a sound investment, for a fifteen-year Equitas policy started at the outset in October 1957 would have matured with a value of £2,105 on a total outlay, after tax relief, of about £830. But London & Edinburgh had to pay the price of being a pioneer: the initial opposition made Equitas hard to sell – even Walker Moate did not sell many policies – and it never achieved the widespread success of some of its followers. The link with Unicorn was ended after London & Edinburgh was sold in 1970 to International Telephone & Telegraph, the giant, and controversial, American conglomerate.

The problems of Equitas did not directly affect Unicorn, for the marketing of the policy was left to London & Edinburgh. London & Edinburgh in turn let du Cann and his old colleague Bill Fowler get on with the promotion of the new unit trust. Not that they could look ahead with a great deal of confidence either. Du Cann later recalled: 'I remember several eminent journalists telling me at our first press conference at the Great Eastern Hotel in Liverpool Street, that I was a fool and would be broke within six months. There were a few nasty moments in those first six months, when the stock market, which had been falling when Unicorn was launched, continued down.' Du Cann, with the advice of stockbrokers Fenn & Crosthwaite, decided not to put all the money they had attracted into the advertised list of ordinary shares, but to put a large chunk temporarily into government securities. It may not have been quite what unit trusts were supposed to be about – spreading the risk of equity investment – but it was wise. When Unicorn had its second block offer on 25 April 1958, the price of the units had risen to 10s. 4d., comfortably outperforming the market.

The market had anyway reached its bottom in early 1958 and there followed two years of almost uninterruptedly rising share prices. Unicorn had sold a million units before the trust was a year old, and had 3,600 unit holders and 2,500 subscribers to a regular saving scheme.

By the spring of 1959 the number of Unicorn units sold had risen to over 4.5 million, the fund was worth over £3 million and the price at 13s. 11d. was 46.5 per cent higher than the issue price. At the end of that year du Cann and Fowler decided to start a second trust, which they called Falcon. It was launched in January 1960 and was an astounding success: after the units had been on offer for just a week some 60,000 people had applied, putting up a total of £6,875,000 – a record at that time.

This was the capital-owning democracy in action all right. Anything remotely connected with the general aims of 'wider share ownership', of giving the general public a chance to share in the nation's wealth, was applauded and written about at length in the newspapers. Others were already climbing on the bandwagon in various ways.

One of the first was David Moate, then still Walker's partner. Inspired by an article in the *Financial Times*, he seized on the idea of investment clubs. The article had extolled the merits of investment clubs in the United States and told how they had expanded there since the formation of the American National Association of Investment Clubs some half a dozen years before. In the UK a few groups of people had already for some years been getting together to pool their monthly savings in stock market investments, but there was no machinery for their recognition or for helping them to organize themselves. So in August 1958 Moate formed the National Association of Investment Clubs to promote their growth in the UK.

Du Cann outlined the Association's objectives in *Investing Simplified*: 'The Association gives advice and help to clubs on such technical matters as formation, legal and taxation problems. It arranges fidelity guarantees to provide against defalcations. The Association will also provide a set of draft rules for new clubs.' Walker had no formal role in the Association, of which Moate made himself president, but he came to some of its functions, and Walker and Moate and half a dozen others, mostly friends of Moate's from the RAF, also formed their own investment club which they grandly, if not completely accurately, called the First Investment Club, and by the end of 1958 there were some forty clubs affiliated to Moate's association.*

Unicorn's most important effect however, was the impetus that its success, together with the new charges structure allowed by the Board of Trade, gave to the development of unit trusts. Soon more

---

* Moate left the Association after an internal row in 1964, from which it never fully recovered.

new trusts were appearing, started both by the old management groups and by newcomers. But they did not all find it as easy as Unicorn.

One new company launched in 1959 was called Community, or 'Cupids', short for its full title – cumbersome but chosen in keeping with the spirit of the times – of Community Units (Participating in Industrial Development). It, too, quickly attracted large sums of money – about £5 million – but the minimum investment had been set at only £10 against Unicorn's £50 and this sum was spread between some 65,000 investors. The management was soon in administrative and financial trouble, there was a public boardroom row and investors queued up to get their money out. At the close of 1960, Unicorn absorbed Community – much to the relief of the rest of the unit trust industry, threatened with its first collapse. The lesson: unit trusts were for the not-too-small man.

The enormous but unexpected success of Unicorn brought some financial reward for its promoters but it was not great wealth. Du Cann decided that Walker should have an equal interest with himself for having secured the vital introduction to Stewart, although Walker was only a non-executive director and his duties therefore limited to attending board meetings at which he would give investment advice. Du Cann and Walker were each given an option on 1,500 one pound shares in Unicorn Securities, the management company, Unicorn's initial £10,000 paid-up capital being wholly taken up by London & Edinburgh. Du Cann and Walker, however, each took up 240 shares in Dillon Walker, the distributor company, while the remainder of its £1,000 capital went to London & Edinburgh.

Both Unicorn and Dillon Walker were making money by the end of 1959, the former showing a trading profit of just over £9,000 and the latter one of £7,000. It was in 1960, the year of the great launch of Falcon, that the two companies first made big money: Unicorn's pre-tax trading profit exceeded £80,000 while Dillon Walker made nearly £60,000.

So over two years after backing du Cann, London & Edinburgh found itself collecting its first dividend from its new subsidiaries: from Unicorn it got £9,750 gross, while Dillon Walker paid out £5,000 before tax, of which Walker's and du Cann's share would have been £1,200 each. As Dillon Walker's capital was only £1,000 this represented a rate of 500 per cent, and Admiral Lord Tovey, not fully comprehending the intricacies of capital, had to be persuaded that such a high rate was not immoral.

It was at the end of 1960 that the Walker Moate partnership, to which Walker's interests in Unicorn and Dillon Walker belonged, broke up and Walker bought out his partner. The valuation, which would have been done before the Unicorn and Dillon Walker accounts for 1960 had been finalized and which were made on a break-up basis, put, as we have seen, a figure of only £1,137 10s. on the option on the 1,500 Unicorn shares, but one of £4,196 on the 240 Dillon Walker shares.

Du Cann and Walker took up their Unicorn options in May 1961; but that year turned out less successfully. The stock market no longer rose steadily; it rose and then fell sharply. At the start of the year, an insurance guarantee against loss was offered to Falcon unit holders over ten years; although it was popular with existing investors, it was criticized as a sales gimmick. Nevertheless, overall new sales that year were disappointing and in addition there was the expense of sorting out Community's problems. In the event both Unicorn and Dillon Walker turned in small losses for 1961.

Profits recovered in 1962 to £76,000 pre-tax for Unicorn and £51,000 for Dillon Walker. The stock market fell steeply in the early part of the year but then began to move steadily upward again after expansionist Reginald Maudling replaced the deposed Selwyn Lloyd in the Macmillan 'massacre' of 13 July. In the same government reshuffle du Cann was appointed Economic Secretary at the Treasury.

Du Cann was naturally obliged to resign from the Unicorn and Dillon Walker boards on taking up a post in the government. But it was not, under the rules drawn up for ministers, strictly necessary for him to sell his Unicorn and Dillon Walker shares. Nevertheless, as his post might involve decisions which would affect the fortunes of the investment world, du Cann felt it would be wiser to sell his shares to avoid any possible conflict of interests; London & Edinburgh bought them back in the autumn of 1962.

Some months later the *Sunday Express* reported du Cann's sale: 'It is understood that the price he received for his shares was around £20,000, although he was advised that he could have obtained substantially more if he had waited.' Du Cann told me, speaking from memory, that he thought the amount had been more like £17,000. It covered both the Unicorn and Dillon Walker shares.

Walker did not want to sell his Unicorn shares at the same time, but London & Edinburgh said that if they were to buy out one, then they wanted to buy out the other as well, and furthermore they would give a better price for buying out the whole minority holding. Walker, unlike du Cann, had transferred the bulk of his Dillon Walker holding back to London & Edinburgh in early 1962 and may therefore already have raised some capital. London & Edinburgh bought back his Unicorn shares about four months after du Cann's in early 1963: there is no reason to think that overall Walker's shares fetched a price very different from that realized by du Cann.

Du Cann returned to Unicorn after the Conservative defeat in 1964 to become joint managing director with his old colleague

Fowler. In the autumn of 1967 London & Edinburgh sold the group to Martins Bank for about £450,000. Walker then resigned from the board, but du Cann was elevated to the chairmanship. The following year, Barclays Bank took over Martins. Du Cann's views on the running of Unicorn gradually drifted apart from those of his new masters, and he finally resigned in 1971.

Both du Cann and Walker got considerable kudos from their post-war 'pioneering' of unit trusts. As du Cann says, however, the amount they made personally out of Unicorn was small in relation to the risks. In the Sixties, unit trust management companies were valued like most other companies, either on net asset value or on a formula related to profits. But by the Seventies, when the power that control of large sums of money brings in the stock market had come to be better appreciated, a new method was evolved based on the size of the trust funds. Management companies then changed hands at a rate of around five per cent of the funds they controlled. If Unicorn had been valued on this basis at the end of 1962, when its funds already totalled some £25 million, it would have been worth about £1,250,000. Du Cann's and Walker's share of this would have been nearly £150,000 each.

4   *The man of property*

National Service in the Fifties involved attendance at Territorial Army camps for three and a half years after the basic two-year stint had been completed. Walker did his part-time service with the Royal Army Service Corps as a private, and after one of his camps he was offered a lift back to London by a young lieutenant called Sefton Myers. The occasion stuck in Walker's mind because Myers' Riley broke down on the journey.

Some three or four years later, after the launch of Unicorn and his election as chairman of the Young Conservatives, Walker had started to get a certain amount of publicity as a young man who knew his way about the City and Westminster. It was this growing reputation which led Sefton Myers to renew the acquaintanceship: he called up Walker at the offices of Walker Moate, and, after reminding him of their meeting, said that he would like to ask Walker's advice about how he and his father, Bernard Myers, should set about securing a Stock Exchange quotation for an assemblage of little property companies they had put together. Walker thought he might be able to help and agreed to a meeting with Sefton and Bernard over lunch.

So began Walker's third main pre-Slater business association and his interest in property development. On the face of it, the friendship that developed between him and Sefton Myers was unlikely; Sefton was an extrovert who later developed a passion for the theatre and made many friends in show business. In commercial business Sefton was something of a dilettante, fascinated by new ideas and tempted to back grand but unrealistic schemes. His father Bernard was all of this – and more.

In some ways Walker's association with the Myerses was the most important of his three early business careers. It brought him into the most spectacular financial phenomenon since the war – the great property boom of the late Fifties – and it was the first venture to put him in a position to realize a substantial capital sum. But it also had its embarrassments.

In 1959 the Myerses had only fully completed three property developments, all of them small blocks of flats, in Purley, Eastcote and Addlestone; their total value was a little over £150,000. But this was the height of the post-war office building boom and the Myerses had some ten or eleven office blocks under construction or planned.

Four of these were scheduled for completion in 1960 and 1961. The most important was a block at Kew Bridge, Brentford, with a likely value of over £450,000; there were two others in Eastcote and Isleworth together worth £550,000 and a small building in Kennington estimated at £175,000. In addition the Myerses were developing a residential estate at Northolt valued at over £360,000, and they had further ambitious plans for the following years involving developments worth another £4.5 million or so.

Property development in those days was quite a simple business. Oliver Marriott in his book *The Property Boom** has estimated that some 110 people made roughly one million pounds or more between 1945 and 1965, including Bernard and Sefton Myers. The key to success was to know where to go to borrow money. The insurance companies were then easy sources of cheap long-term loans, but the Myerses did not have particularly good City contacts. This was one area where they thought Walker could help them. But their main objective was to cash in by floating the group on the stock market. The first tangible result of their approach to Walker was that the Myerses were able to raise in March 1960, through Walker Moate, £300,000 from the giant Legal & General Insurance company for the Kew Bridge development. To advise on the proposed flotation, Walker introduced the Myerses to stockbrokers Read, Hurst-Brown and they in turn introduced them to a partner in the leading City solicitors Slaughter & May called Thomas Walmsley.

As is usual in property development, the Myerses had formed a string of separate companies to undertake each development, but there was no financial or legal structure binding the operation into a cohesive saleable package. With the help of their new advisers they formed, around the end of 1959, a new holding company which they named the Rodwell Group, of which the original directors were Bernard and Sefton Myers, who held the £200 capital, their conveyancing solicitor, Robert Egerton, and Peter Walker, who says that Rodwell was a well-run property company which was a pioneer in the building of office accommodation outside the centre of London. Then in September 1960 the Myerses 'injected' their various developments into this company in exchange for 640,000 new five shilling shares. Shortly after a further 359,600 shares were issued for cash: Sefton and his stepmother Sylvia, Bernard's second wife, each took

* Hamish Hamilton, 1967.

up 170,200, giving the Myers family control of 980,800 of the firm's one million shares. Of the remainder 14,400 were allotted to Walker on behalf of the Walker Moate partnership. At 5s. each these would have cost £3,600, but it appears that what had happened was that some time previously the Myerses, in gratitude for Walker's help, had given him for a nominal consideration a few shares in one of the original development companies and the 14,400 in the new parent represented that stake. The final 4,800 went to a company executive, Leonard Woolf, in the same way.

By early 1961, with some of the larger developments in the West London suburbs completed or nearly finished, the new property concern seemed ready for launching on the public. Read, Hurst-Brown drew up a preliminary prospectus for approval by the London Stock Exchange's Quotations Committee, and a short notice – not accurate in all details – appeared in *The Times* of 13 April 1961:

> About 30 per cent of the ordinary capital of the Rodwell Group, a private property company which has specialized in developing offices in the suburbs, will be offered for sale later this month.
>
> Rodwell, which was formed in 1953, has an ordinary capital of £2 m. in 5s. shares. Gross assets are in excess of £6 m. The chairman is Mr Bernard Myers, a partner in Norfolk and Prior, estate agents. The other directors are his son, Mr Sefton Myers, chartered surveyor and estate agent, Mr P. E. Walker, director of Unicorn Securities, and Mr R. Egerton, partner in a firm of London solicitors.
>
> Brokers to the issue will be Read, Hurst-Brown. Full details will be announced in due course.

But the full details never were announced – nor has the full story ever been told before – for at the last minute, disaster struck: it was discovered that the chairman of this proposed new public company had been a bankrupt. The issue, the Stock Exchange decided, had better be called off.

Untangling the affairs of Bernard Myers and the story of the abortive Rodwell flotation was hard. David Moate first suggested to me that the Rodwell issue had to be abandoned as a result of the discovery of Myers' bankruptcy. Read, Hurst-Brown said it was for personal reasons; they did not deny it was because of the bankruptcy but would not comment further. Other reasons advanced were that the government had been expected to take steps to curb property developers' profits, or to tax gains made on the flotation of companies.

Walker himself confirmed that Myers' financial past was the reason: when I asked him why the issue had been put off, he told me that it was because the Stock Exchange had discovered that Myers had been 'involved in the liquidation of a company' back in the Thirties. He had been told, he said, just a week before the proposed issue. Later he also told me that he expressed his anger and sorrow to the Myerses for not telling him about the bankruptcy and they explained that they felt that there was no reason why Bernard Myers should be adversely affected because of events that had taken place many years before and which in no way affected the company. He said he then discussed the matter with his advisers and they all agreed it was right to continue offering their advice to the company as it was, in their view, a sound one.

Bernard Myers told me that the issue was stopped at the last minute because they found a more convenient, cheaper way of going public – as indeed they did, but that was a year later. He denied that he had ever been bankrupted.

In fact Bernard Myers had been twice bankrupted, first in 1933 and then again in 1951.

In the spring of 1961 Myers was fifty-eight years old and on the verge, for the first time in his life, of making big money. He had lived well at one time or another, but now he was about to make over a million pounds for himself and another three million or so for his wife and son. Yet ten years before, after a petition for his bankruptcy had been filed in December 1950, he had informed the Official Receiver that his only asset was a wristwatch worth £3.

Myers' career is best summarized in the cross-questioning he underwent at his public examination in the High Court in Carey Street on 4 May 1951. The Official Receiver started by going over briefly the details of Myers' first bankruptcy; his third question was more a statement of fact:

Q. This is not the first time you have been in this court?
A. No.
Q. Was a Receiving Order made against you here on 5 April 1933?
A. Yes.
Q. At that time had you been acting for some years as a director of John Morley Ltd, tailors, of the Strand?
A. Yes.
Q. And were you adjudged bankrupt in May 1933?
A. Yes.
Q. Did you attribute your failure to the failure of the business of John Morley Limited, and to your liability for nearly £8,000 for guarantees which you had given on behalf of that company?
A. Yes.

Q. Is it a fact that your present failure is due to a very similar cause, giving guarantees for limited companies?

A. Not entirely; it is one of them.

The Official Receiver then reverted to the past bankruptcy:

Q. Did you submit an Amended Statement of Affairs showing liabilities to rank for dividend at £12,404?

A. Yes.

Q. And no assets?

A. Yes.

Q. Nothing, I think, was realized and no payment made to creditors. On the 6th March 1936, were you granted your discharge subject to a suspension of two years?

A. Yes.

Q. May I remind you that the facts which were found against you then were the assets fact, contracting liabilities without reasonable expectation of being able to pay and unjustifiable extravagance.

A. Yes.

The Official Receiver had made his point: Myers had paid nothing back to his creditors in the Thirties. Furthermore, when Myers had applied for his discharge after three years, it had been suspended for another two years by the Court. Suspension depends on which of twelve 'facts' listed in the 1914 Bankruptcy Act have been proved against the bankrupt. The Official Receiver had referred to the three facts proved against Myers in the Thirties, the 'assets fact' being that his assets were 'not of value equal to ten shillings in the pound on the amount of his unsecured liabilities'. One of the principal handicaps of an undischarged bankrupt is that he must not be a director of, or in any way be concerned in, the management of any company without the Court's permission.

The Official Receiver's next questions, and Myers' answers, conveniently summarize the next few years of his career – and his total experience of the property business until the middle of the Fifties:

Q. After that bankruptcy were you employed until 1935 as a shop manager by a new company John Morley (Strand) Limited at the same place?

A. Yes.

Q. Then from 1935 to 1937 were you employed by London & Provincial Properties Limited of Victoria Street as a property manager?

A. Yes.

Q. In 1937 did you become employed by Emm Developments Limited, property dealers?

A. Yes.

Q. A company in which your wife held nearly all the shares?

A. Yes.

Q. Was there an allied company called Property Administrators Limited?

A. Yes.

Q. Were receivers appointed by mortgagees of these companies' properties in 1938 and 1939?

A. On the outbreak of war.

Q. And did the companies subsequently become dormant?

A. Yes.

Q. And now have they been dissolved?

A. Yes, but there were no liabilities.

Q. Just before the war, did you become employed by Norfolk & Prior, estate agents, at Hay Hill?

A. Yes.

Q. As property manager?

A. Yes, as negotiator.

Norfolk & Prior was a respected firm in which Myers had bought himself a partnership with the help of his father. He became senior partner in 1938; the following year the partnership was dissolved. Myers was questioned closely on its winding up both by the Official Receiver and by the presiding Registrar of bankruptcies. Their purpose was to try to establish whether its creditors had been paid in full. Myers was unable to say – which did not impress the Registrar. Myers had, in fact, sold the Norfolk & Prior name to another estate agent, who told me that he had paid a nominal sum for it and that there had been no business to go with it. Myers had had no connection with it since 1939.

The Official Receiver then turned to the events that led up to Myers' new financial plight. Questioning on these affairs was long and detailed and the story must be condensed.

During the Forties, Myers, with two partners, built up a conglomeration of little companies making a wide variety of products. In the war Myers had invented a gas-proof curtain, and had also started, in Oxford, a woodwork company and a firm making coathangers. Later he formed a business called International Wire to handle a load of surplus aluminium wire he had bought, and he acquired a small manufacturer of metal windows and a firm making metal chairs. All these were put under a holding company, Rodwell Investments, the name stemming from a little export company, originally registered back in 1920, that had become part of the group. To raise money, however, Myers had assumed personal liability to the Perseverance Banking & Trust, an organization which was to live up to its name in pursuit of its money.

Disaster struck at the end of 1949: the pound was devalued and quickly Myers' products, which were mostly made from imported aluminium wire but sold abroad, could no longer hold their own against competitive products made from steel. On top of this, one of Myers' partners had become ill and Myers had taken over his shares and obligations, while the other, an accountant with many other interests, ran into problems of his own. (He was also bankrupted in 1951 and was later convicted of fraud on the clients of his accounting firm.)

By April 1950 Myers found himself having to persuade a supplier to let him pay a bill by instalments. He soon defaulted and the supplier obtained judgement. The whole structure then crumbled, his main trading companies were put into liquidation and by the end of the year Myers was being called upon to meet his personal guarantees.

Towards the end of Myers' examination the Registrar returned to his failure to pay anything to his creditors from the first bankruptcy. It had emerged that in 1948 Myers had bought a house in exclusive Bishops Avenue in Hampstead for £13,000. It had immediately been placed in trust for his second wife Sylvia and their children. At that point, therefore, Myers had clearly had plenty of money and the Registrar plainly thought that instead of 'denuding' his estate of the house, he might have considered making a payment to his earlier creditors.

Myers applied to the Court for discharge from his second bankruptcy in early 1952. The Official Receiver reported that his property debts were estimated at nearly £37,000, and his assets at a little over £2,000: the watch had been sold for £3 10s. and money had been raised on furniture and insurance policies. The Official Receiver summarized the case and concluded that four 'facts' had been established against Myers:

1 His assets were not worth 10s. in the £ on his unsecured liabilities.
2 He had 'contracted a debt provable in bankruptcy without at the time of contracting it any reasonable or probable ground of expectation of being able to pay it'. This was the debt incurred to the supplier in the spring of 1950.
3 He had 'contributed to his bankruptcy by unjustifiable extravagance in living'.
4 He had been bankrupted once before.

Myers disputed the second and third facts alleged against him, but nevertheless the Court this time suspended his discharge for four years, starting from 22 February 1952. Nor did the remonstrations of the Registrar appear to have made much impression on Myers: a dividend of just one shilling in the pound was paid to creditors in

August 1957, when Myers was on the way to becoming a property millionaire.

The fortunes of the Myers family were naturally adversely affected by the collapse of Bernard's companies and his bankruptcy. 'Arden' was sold, the Myers moved to a flat in Kensington and Bernard took up yet another trade, as assistant in a chemist's shop. The shop was in Kensington Church Street and it was owned by his wife Sylvia's company, S. Myers (Chemists). Bernard himself, as an undischarged bankrupt, could not become a director or play any part in the management of the company, but he helped his wife out behind the counter.

The chemist's shop provided the Myers with a livelihood for some three or four years, although it too developed financial problems. But salvation was at hand: Bernard's son Sefton, a young man of twenty-three at the end of 1953, had made a timely choice of career – property development, the business that was to make the Myerses and many others rich.

Oliver Marriott pinpoints the cause of this new gold rush in the opening paragraph of *The Property Boom*:

> The starting gun for the most intense phase of the property boom was fired on the afternoon of November 2nd, 1954. Mr Nigel Birch, Minister of Works in the first post-war Conservative administration, announced to the House of Commons that building licences were to be dropped entirely: 'Licences are now issued freely in nearly all areas and neither the cost nor the inconvenience caused to architects and contractors can any longer be justified . . .' There were cheers from the Conservative benches.

Those in the property business had already foreseen the way the wind was blowing when Harold Macmillan, then Minister of Housing and Local Government, had the year before dropped Labour's 100 per cent charge on development value, declaring: 'The people whom the Government must help are those who do things: the developers, the people who create wealth whether they are humble or exalted . . . ' Furthermore, the 'people who create wealth' knew that there was a pent-up demand for office space.

It is unlikely that Sefton Myers foresaw the full implications of these changes. But he knew something about property, for he had worked first for an estate agents and then for some months for a property group called Hammerson. There he had made some money and become friends with a colleague, James Lambert. At the end of 1953 the two decided to leave Hammerson and set up on their own, with Sefton's father as a sort of sleeping third partner, unable to take a front seat because he was still an undischarged bankrupt.

In February 1954, Sefton Myers and James Lambert created two new companies, one which they called simply Sefton Myers and Lambert Ltd; the other named Rodwell Properties, harking back to Bernard's old holding company, Rodwell Investments, which was also temporarily resurrected. They were not in those early days intent on property development so much as on investing in and dealing in properties, and acting as advisers to those who wished to do likewise. They set up offices first in Manchester Square W1, and then moved to No. 9 Hertford Street by Shepherd's Market in Mayfair. Their first ventures into property were in suburban South and West London.

Lambert today still runs a property and financial advisory firm in Croydon. I asked him what role Bernard Myers played in those early days of Rodwell. Lambert told me that Bernard could not effectively take part in the business because he was an undischarged bankrupt, which Lambert himself only discovered once he had started working with the Myerses. Bernard, Lambert said, was a 'consultant', or a 'father figure in the background'. He could not, said Lambert, 'show his hand'. Nevertheless Lambert found his presence in the background increasingly difficult, and he finally pulled out in the autumn of 1955, after little more than a year and a half. He decided to go, he told me, because he did not like being 'one corner of a triangle', the other two corners being Sefton and Bernard.

Lambert's early departure was temporarily embarrassing: Bernard could not immediately take his place, because his discharge from bankruptcy was not due until 22 February 1956, still a few months away. So his wife stepped forward once again and took up Lambert's shares and directorship in the companies that formed the basis of the Myerses' new hopes of prosperity.

Within five days of his discharge from bankruptcy, Bernard Myers was appointed a director of Rodwell Properties, joining his son and replacing his wife. With his added panache the business began to expand.

Reconstructing its early history is hard, because the Myerses kept forming new companies and there was no single master firm to lead the way through the maze. Rodwell Properties, the forerunner of the Rodwell Group which the Myerses tried to float in 1961, was sold in 1958. Rodwell Investments, the only link with Bernard Myers' previous industrial fiasco, was dropped, while Sefton Myers and Lambert became Rodwell Securities, a property and share dealing company.

The Myerses' first major success would appear to have been a building on part of a site known as the Lampton Island on the Great West Road at Hounslow. Their next big projects were to be erected on land they acquired at Field End Road in Eastcote, on which they proposed to build two office blocks and some flats, and on another site nearby at Northolt.

At that time, the Myerses' sources of credit were limited. They had been able to borrow a bit from the banks, but it was not easy in view of Bernard Myers' record, and they were usually committed up to the hilt. To help finance the Eastcote development, they even borrowed from a charitable organization called the Jewish Colonization Association, on whose board many distinguished members of the Jewish community sat. The Myerses also borrowed, fortuitously as it turned out, from another property company called Lombard London & Provincial, from whom they had bought some of the West London land in 1957.

Although first formed in 1920, Lombard London & Provincial's life as an independent property concern really started in 1953. Until then it had been the property-holding arm of a store group, Lennards, but that year it sold the shops and started to reinvest the proceeds in a wide spread of residential, industrial and commercial premises. By 1962, it had also built a couple of office blocks, but it remained primarily a property investment rather than development company. It was conservatively managed by a financier called John Solomon Cohen and his twenty-eight-year-old son Richard, and was about the same size as Rodwell, with properties in the same areas of Middlesex.

The Cohens and the Myerses knew each other, of course, as a result of the deal over the land in West London. There had been little risk in lending the Myerses the money to buy it, because Lombard had kept a charge on the land. The Myerses kept promising they would be able to pay off the debt once they went public. But the failure of the attempt to float their company forced them to consider an alternative method of achieving a Stock Exchange quotation – and the Cohens an alternative means of settling the debt. It could, of course, be settled by Lombard taking back the land. But if the two companies merged instead, it would become an internal book-keeping affair, and Lombard could bring to the marriage an invaluable dowry: its stock was already quoted on the London Exchange. The Myerses could achieve all the advantages of going public without encountering the obstacles which had prevented their independent flotation.

The merger was announced on 22 February 1962. The properties of each company were valued by Jones Lang & Wootton, a leading firm of chartered surveyors, and the terms of the merger were to be based on net assets of each company: in the event Rodwell's value came out at £2.2 million against Lombard's £1.75 million. But it was agreed that Lombard should add another twenty per cent to their figure in order to recognize the potential long-term value of their investments. It was not much for the Myerses to give away, for Rodwell's value still remained slightly above that of Lombard, so that the

Myerses ended up with a majority – 50.4 per cent – of the shares in, and therefore control of, the new group.

To facilitate the retention of the Stock Exchange quotation, the merger was effected by the issue of new Lombard stock to the Rodwell shareholders. As Lombard was the smaller company, it was what is called a 'reverse' takeover. On the basis of the relative values of the two companies, the Rodwell shareholders were given 16,413 new 1s. shares in Lombard in exchange for every one of their old 5s. shares in the Rodwell group.

The terms of the alliance were announced on 14 March 1962, and the following day the *Daily Mail* proclaimed the new millionaires in an article headlined: 'Myers – the new name in millions'.

'A tailor's son who was never paid for his first property deal turned himself, his wife, and son into millionaires last night,' the article began, and it went on to estimate that Bernard Myers was now worth £1,793,000, his wife Sylvia £953,000 and Sefton no less than £2,746,000. Bernard Myers, the *Mail* said, had begun his property career as an estate agent. 'He said of his first deal: "I was supposed to earn £500, but, in fact I was never paid."' The *Mail* asked him if he felt elated at being a millionaire. 'No,' Myers is reported to have replied, 'if you've got two good cigars you smoke them only one at a time.'

The Lombard share price, which had started the year at about 4s. 9d., had been rising very fast in the weeks preceding the deal. The *Mail*'s figures for the Myerses' wealth were based on a price of about 6s. 9d. The highest it in fact reached was 7s., at which the Myers family was worth nearly £200,000 more.

Nevertheless the *Mail* had much exaggerated the value of Walker's interest in the new group, thus helping to propagate the myth of his early wealth: 'Thirty-year-old Mr Peter Walker (Tory MP for Worcester), who is a director and financial adviser to the Rodwell Group, has his holding valued at £80,000 under the deal.'

In fact, at 7s. a Lombard share, the deal was worth just £29,871 16s. to Walker. What the *Mail* presumably did not know was that Walker's holding in Rodwell had already been considerably reduced. In the first place, as already noted, half the 14,400 originally registered in Walker's name belonged to David Moate, who had held on to them when the partnership broke up. Walker had written to Moate a week before the merger was announced offering to buy them back, because, he says, Moate had written to him expressing his anxieties that the flotation had not taken place and he gathered Moate wished to use the cash from the Rodwell shares for building up his own business. Walker says he told Moate he had no knowledge when the matter would be resolved or what the eventual price would be, and Walker also told me that he did not know at the time of the plans to merge with Lombard which would have made the shares worth more. In any event, Moate did not accept the price offered by Walker and retained the shares. Secondly, Walker had sold 2,000 shares to Bryan Harrison, his friend and colleague at insurance brokers Hugh Paul, in early 1961 because, they both say, Harrison had asked him if he could make an investment in Rodwell. Harrison paid Walker something like £3,000 for the shares, less than a third of the value they reached on the merger. Walker's remaining Rodwell holding of 5,200 shares was converted into 85,348 in Lombard.

As part of the terms of the merger the Myerses, with a majority of the shares, took the powerful jobs in the enlarged concern: Bernard became chairman and Sefton managing director. John Cohen took the title of president, while his son Richard became deputy managing director. Walker was appointed to the new six-man board, the last director being Lombard's solicitor, Roderick Purves.

The speculation that preceded the merger announcement had driven the Lombard price up to 7s. a share. This considerably over-priced the merged company and the market quickly realized this when the full details were revealed in a letter to shareholders sent out on 14 March 1962. By the end of that week the price was down to 6s. and by the end of May to 5s. 3d.

On 30 May 1962 John Cohen presided over the annual meeting of the company as deputy chairman and president elect: he gave a cautiously optimistic view of the future, and the price recovered to 5s. 9d. The seal was put on the merger by the shareholders' vote to change the company's name to Rodwell London & Provincial.

The share price of the new Rodwell London & Provincial dropped to 4s. 6d. by the end of June and for the rest of 1962 it fluctuated in the 4s. 6d. to 5s. 6d. range. That year proved to be the peak for property shares, and in the next three years they fell back sharply: Rodwell's shares fell with the rest, reaching a first 'low' of 2s. 7d. in 1965, and another of 2s. 1d. in 1967.

The steady decline in the share price coincided with the fortunes of Rodwell London under Bernard Myers' chairmanship. The later history of Rodwell will be told in another chapter, but readers will perhaps not be surprised to hear that once again Myers ran into financial straits. By the end of 1965 the board of Rodwell had no alternative but to oust Bernard Myers. Walker says it was he who went into his office and told him he must go, but the power lay with John Cohen, who told me that he had come to the conclusion that Myers should not remain in charge of a public company.

But how had he got there? How much did Cohen, Lombard and its advisers and the Stock Exchange know about Bernard Myers' past when they agreed to the merger in early 1962? I asked John Cohen at least twice in the summer of 1973 if he had been told about Myers' bankruptcies before the merger. He told me that 'they never made any disclosure'.

When I first spoke to Walker about the abortive flotation of Rodwell, at the interview in which he indicated that the 1933 bankruptcy had been the reason for calling off the proposed flotation in 1961, he told me that he had never heard that Bernard Myers had been bankrupted again. I was, it seems, telling him about it for the very first time.

Walker's explanation of why he had not anyway told the Cohens in 1962 about the first bankruptcy was that neither he nor the solicitors Slaughter & May were involved in the merger negotiations which were conducted by the Myerses and the Cohens directly. But Thomas Walmsley of Slaughter & May had, he said, as a friend of the Myerses told them that they should inform the Cohens about it and he had been given to understand by the Myerses that they had done this.

From my own conversations with both Walmsley and Roderick Purves, who advised Lombard and was the sixth man on the merged group's board, it was clear that John Cohen was in a position to know at least that Myers was persona non grata with the Stock Exchange; for Lombard's advisers, on asking why the smaller Lombard had to take over the larger Rodwell, were told that it was because the Stock Exchange would not 'wear' Myers.

John Cohen died suddenly in early 1974 and I was not able to ask him about this. It is not, however, inconsistent with what he had previously told me, for he had said that while he had been given no firm information about Myers' bankruptcies, he had heard 'whispers' about him from friends.

It must be asked, then, why John Cohen agreed to the merger if he knew there was some sort of cloud over Myers. He and Myers could not anyway have been more different, the one cautious and reserved, the other an extravagant speculator. Cohen, however, had reached sixty and unlike Myers, who in 1961 was also approaching that age, was already a wealthy man, with other interests besides Lombard. He told me that he had wanted to pull out from active business himself and he thought that running Lombard with the Myerses might be good experience for his son. Furthermore, whatever John Cohen thought of Bernard Myers, there is no doubt that Sefton, a model of responsibility beside his father, had a flair for the business; and although Rodwell's developments were rather too speculative for Cohen's taste, its properties had value.

Walker and Walmsley in fact later told me that the Stock Exchange did not rule out completely the possibility of an independent flotation of Rodwell because of the 1933 bankruptcy; they said that in the light of it they felt the issue should wait until more of the group's developments had been completed.

I had previously asked the man who was head of the Stock Exchange's quotations department in 1961 about the case, but he said he could not remember the details. The Exchange's attitude at the time to former bankrupts taking part in the affairs of quoted companies is, however, demonstrated in one of its publicity films called *The Launching* (made, coincidentally, shortly after the Rodwell affair). The high point of the film is when the Exchange's officials dramatically discover at the last minute that the father of two brothers trying to raise money from the public for their yacht-building concern has been bankrupt back in 1929. The Stock Exchange, however, graciously decides that this damaging fact need not be revealed in the prospectus because the father is no longer closely involved in the business, and, more important perhaps, because he has paid off his debts in full.

To judge from the film the Stock Exchange would hardly have been happy to see an independent flotation of Rodwell with Bernard Myers as chairman even if they knew only about the first bankruptcy. But knowledge of this bankruptcy alone was not apparently enough to make the Exchange stop the merger with Lombard, which they had to approve because new, quoted shares were issued – presumably because they knew that the Cohens would still be on the board and could in the last resort act as a restraining influence, as indeed they did. It is less likely that the Exchange would have allowed the merger had they known about both bankruptcies. It is remarkable that their investigations apparently uncovered the first but not the second.*

Cohen, Walmsley and Purves all later found out about the second bankruptcy, but it seems that Walker was not told. Some time after I had told him about it and after talking to Walmsley, Walker said that when Walmsley himself found out he decided it was too late to take any further action and so Walmsley decided not to inform him.

The Myers episode was a messy one. The marriage between Lombard and Rodwell proved extremely unhappy, and Lombard shareholders had been badly misled when they were told that their new chairman Bernard Myers 'has been engaged in property development for virtually the whole of his business life'. Also, anyone who bought shares in the immediate pre-merger enthusiasm must have lost money. But the deal provided the Myerses and Walker with tangible wealth.

Commenting on the merger, the *Financial Times*' influential 'Lex' column had said on 15 March 1962: 'A public quotation for Rodwell had been talked of in the autumn, but with the change of investment

---

* I found out about the second bankruptcy *first* from the public index of bankrupts at the Law Courts. The names are filed in separate sections, each covering a different period of years. There are two cards for Bernard Myers, with no indication that they are both for the same man.

climate deferred until more of the company's projects became income producing. Rodwell now has a painless quotation and gets it in advance of the Budget – though in fairness its directors have no intention of reducing their holdings.'

The importance of doing such a deal before the Budget was that this was the year the Conservatives were widely expected to crack down on speculators – as indeed they partially did by introducing the short-term speculative gains tax which treated profits realized within six months of purchase as income. Nevertheless the *Financial Times* was not strictly accurate over the reason for 'deferring' the Rodwell issue, and its attempt to be fair to the directors was also misplaced.

The Rodwell register records that Walker had transferred 70,100 out of his 85,348 shares by the autumn of 1962, the first transfer out of his name being the very first transfer of shares of the new Rodwell, London & Provincial company. Walker told me the average price he received was about 5s. 2d., and so he would have realized about £15,000. He used the proceeds to buy a house in Walton-on-Thames, and Walker says the only reason he sold the shares was because his father had suddenly been struck down by a form of polio and was unlikely to live long, and he wanted him to have a pleasant home and garden for the remainder of his life.

Walker said he was never asked by the *Financial Times* or anyone else if he intended to reduce his holding, but he told me he wrote to the Myerses explaining why he wanted to sell, and that they were very understanding. This is not surprising, as now that Rodwell had got its 'painless' quotation Bernard Myers himself was only too anxious to raise some ready cash, and so he 'placed' large blocks of his newly marketable shares with friends, relations and associates. Now he was wealthy at last he wanted fully to indulge his passion for racehorses. He had bought the 400-acre Walton Manor estate in Buckinghamshire and he lavishly modernized it as a stud farm at a cost of some £500,000. Walton Manor was to contribute to Myers' later problems.

5 *Who wants to be a millionaire?*

In his profile of Peter Walker in the *Guardian* of May 1972 Terry Coleman states that Walker was probably the youngest self-made millionaire of his day. Coleman then reported this exchange: 'Had he really got this million by the time he was 30? "I forget," he says.' A good throwaway line, Coleman commented.

Walker says he made this remark because he had no wish to go into detail with Coleman as to when he was a millionaire and that it was intended to ensure that they passed on to another topic. But the point is too important to let pass as easily as that. For the 'millionaire-at-thirty' myth became an essential part of the Walker image and, as such, was of considerable help to his political career as the archetypal self-made New Tory.

Walker himself denies that either his reputation as a youthful millionaire or his business career itself was of any help to his political advancement; this cannot be accepted. He also denies any responsibility for the myth; he says he always avoided the topic of his wealth in press interviews, and when I confronted him with such quotations as 'I'm a rich man' – from the *Sunday Times* in October 1970 – he said any remarks he might have made about being rich were only in the context of references to his fortune in politics in having financial independence. The myth, he claimed, was entirely the responsibility of journalists looking at each other's press cuttings and commenting that his wealth was greater than it was. But again, after checking with a number of the reporters concerned, I cannot accept that journalists should take all the blame. While Walker may not have actively encouraged the myth, he did not take positive action to ensure that it was laid.

Nor was it a matter of a year or two either way, or a few thousand pounds. The fact is that at thirty Walker was not remotely in the millionaire league. His thirty-first birthday was on 25 March 1963 and makes a convenient, as well as significant, point at which to assess his real financial status.

The Rodwell/London, Lombard merger in the spring of 1962, touch-and-go as it was, had provided him with £15,000 or so of realizable capital, while the sale of his Unicorn shares back to London & Edinburgh around the end of that year, unwilling though it may have been, had given him some £20,000 more.

This is quite a substantial amount of money for a thirty-year-old to have amassed, but it is still a long way short of the magic million. The meeting with Slater, which also took place about this time following the Under-Forties dinner on 6 February 1963, was not to yield tangible results for another year or so. But there is still Walker's insurance broking firm to take into account.

On this front, too, Walker had an important breakthrough at this time, for he achieved the coveted status of Lloyd's broker for his insurance business. As recounted in Chapter 2, it is not easy for a firm of brokers to gain admission to Lloyd's by direct application. But there is a simpler way: merge with a firm that already is a member. In 1962 Walker found a candidate: a small but old-established business called Rose Thomson Young.

The origins of Rose Thomson Young dated back to 1818; it was run in an unassuming manner by Jimmy Young, then fifty-seven, whose grandfather had come into the business back in the 1850s. There may well have been some restlessness among some of Young's younger assistants at the firm's lack of vigorous growth; at any rate one of them, who had met Walker, suggested to Young that he should meet him too.

Young did not follow up the suggestion. Then, two or three months later, his employee urged him again more strongly to talk to Walker. Young inquired why, and was told that Walker had been told that Young wanted to sell the firm. Young might not have been the most self-assertive of figures, but he knew that he did not want to sell the family business. Luckily for Walker, however, Young thought he had better telephone him to tell him he had been misinformed.

Now Young, who had no son in the firm to take it over when he himself retired, was quite happy to listen to proposals for its future expansion, and when he telephoned Walker he agreed to meet him for lunch. In the subsequent conversation plans for a merger on equal terms arose, but in the final event Young, who had started out not wanting to sell his firm, found himself agreeing to cede control.

The formal agreement was signed on 31 December 1962, although the merger effectively took place a few weeks before. It had been decided that exactly the same value should be put on each share of the two constituent companies, Walker Moate and Rose Thomson Young. The amalgamation was affected by forming a new holding company, Walker Young, in which the shareholders of the two merging firms would get the same number of new shares as they had held in their respective firms. As Walker Moate had an issued capital of £10,000 in one pound shares, and Rose Thomson Young one of £15,000, Walker Young had to issue 25,000 new one pound shares.

Walker himself was no longer the largest shareholder in Walker Moate: he had transferred 650 of his 3,000 shares to his friend and colleague at Rodwell, Sefton Myers, who had joined the Walker Moate board in December 1961. Myers had also acquired some shares from the other directors and owned a total of 3,025. There was one other new shareholder, a Birmingham stockbroker with the firm of Smith Keen Barnett called Alan Beaumont Dark, who had joined the board of the local Walker Moate subsidiary.

The shares of Rose Thomson Young were divided among about a dozen owners of whom the largest was naturally Young. As a result of the equal terms of the merger the Rose Thomson Young men had a majority of the shares in the new Walker Young. But it was part of the agreement that the Walker Moate team should buy out part of the shareholding of the Rose Thomson Young men, so that Walker and his colleagues ended up with three quarters of the shares of Walker Young. They also took control of the five-man board of the holding company: Walker became chairman and Sefton Myers and Clouston were appointed directors. Apart from Young, the only other representative from Rose Thomson Young was thirty-three-year-old Max Herbert Despard, whom we shall meet again in the early years of Slater Walker.

So Walker secured his entrée to Lloyd's, a crucial advance, as he could now place insurance directly in this market and earn a full commission. From 1963 onwards the bulk of the insurance broking was done through Rose Thomson Young which, as the Lloyd's member firm within the group, continued to function as an active subsidiary and of which Walker also became chairman, Young taking the title of president. Walker Moate itself became otiose at least as far as insurance was concerned and its broking activities were run down. But, as we shall see, it re-emerged later as an active share dealing subsidiary.

Young, however, did not do badly from the deal. He had retained a separate insurance business for himself to look after; named Rose Thomson Young (Agencies), this was not a broking firm but a manager of a Lloyd's syndicate of underwriters.* Young had also ensured future growth for his family firm, even if its progress was henceforth directed by others, and he also retained a substantial share interest and the presidency of Rose Thomson Young.

---

* An insurance broker introduces its clients to the underwriter, which can either be a company like the Commercial Union, or a syndicate at Lloyd's. A syndicate is a group of wealthy individuals, each worth at least £75,000, whose affairs are handled for a fee by professional managers. The managers can form themselves into a limited company.

At the time of the merger with Rose Thomson Young, Walker held 2,350 shares in Walker Moate: what were they worth?

Any valuation of Walker Moate at this time must be rough, as few exact figures are available: private companies like Walker Moate did not have to file balance sheets at Companies House until after the 1967 Companies Act. Walker himself told me, speaking from memory in the summer of 1973, that at the time of the merger the brokerage income of Walker Moate had been between £15,000 and £25,000 a year, and then later he told me that the merger with Rose Thomson had been made on the basis that both firms expected to contribute brokerage income of at least £45,000 each in 1963.

One method of valuing a broking firm is to multiply its brokerage by a factor of between two and three. Using a factor of $2\frac{1}{4}$ – suggested by Walker himself – on the prospective brokerage of £45,000 values Walker Moate at the end of 1962 at just over £100,000. Thus Walker's $23\frac{1}{2}$ per cent stake in his firm was worth about £24,000.

Because the merger was on equal terms Walker received 2,350 out of Walker Young's 25,000 £1 shares in exchange for his Walker Moate stock, but the capital of Walker Young was immediately increased to £100,000 by a free issue of three shares for each of the 25,000, raising Walker's stake in the new firm to 9,400 shares. He immediately increased this to 17,625 by acquiring shares from some of the old Rose Thomson Young owners, but as he would have had to pay for these they would not have added to his net worth.

The merger with Rose Thomson Young of itself added to the value of Walker's insurance interest because he now had a stake in a Lloyd's firm, and these normally command a higher price. But the amalgamated group remained small by City standards, with a joint brokerage in its first year, according to Walker, of £100,000, or a little more than forecast, and a profit of only £6,600 – although, as Walker indicated, in the early years the profit could have to some extent been depressed because the benefit of expanding by taking on new personnel would only have been obtained after several years of their accumulated brokerage.

Walker Young was finally taken over by Slater Walker itself in early 1970 and was valued then at £1,345,000; Walker, then nearly thirty-eight, received £188,494 3s. 9d. for his stake in that deal. We shall be looking at this transaction in a later chapter, but in order to give some idea of the growth of the business, here is a table of Walker Young's brokerage income and broking profits prepared from figures on record:

	Pre-tax profits	Brokerage
1963	£6,629	Not available
1964	£7,466	Not available

	Pre-tax profits	Brokerage
15 months to		
31 March 1966	£5,239	Not available
Year to 31 March		
1967	£20,767	£255,000
1968	£26,049	£265,000
1969	£67,723	£321,000
1970	£167,318	£442,000

The Walker Moate partnership itself had been formed ten years before the merger with Walker Young. As Walker said, when faced with the statement in a radio interview in August 1974 that he made a lot of money pretty quickly: 'It wasn't a quick, speedy affair, alas.'

So by his thirty-first birthday, Walker had not made anything like a million pounds out of insurance broking, unit trusts or property development. In fact these reputed sources of his great wealth had totalled roughly £60,000. He had one or two other small interests, and he may have made some money in shares on the stock market, but these have never been said to have contributed much to his wealth, and indeed there is no evidence that they did. As we shall see he actually lost money on one of his other interests.

By 1963 Walker's total income was relatively high, but not enormous. In the first place, there was his Parliamentary salary of £1,750. Then there was his earnings from his various directorships: in 1963 the five directors of Walker Young shared remuneration of £9,250, the five non-executive directors of Unicorn and Dillon Walker £5,884, and the six directors of Rodwell £18,890. His other directors' fees would have been purely nominal or non-existent.

Walker had already achieved one of the objectives of Leo Amery's advice to make himself some money: he travelled widely. He often went to America, combining business with an opportunity to observe the American political system. In 1962, when Macmillan and Heath launched Britain's first attempt to join the Common Market, Walker committed himself to the Commonwealth cause and went on a month's tour through Australia, New Zealand, India and Canada. On the business front, he started to set up overseas links for Walker Young, forming in 1963 a little firm in Canada called Walker Whitehead – sold some two years later.

At home, the first tangible evidence of Walker's improved financial circumstances was the purchase of the house in Walton-on-Thames for his parents to replace the bungalow in Twickenham. The Walkers' modern, red-brick house, 'Broadston', was in a private road just round the corner from a house that Walker's friend Sefton

Myers had built for himself a couple of years before. Walker also had a small flat in the City, he says, and went to Broadston at weekends – and to his Worcester constituency, where he had another flat in Droitwich.

So by his thirty-first birthday in 1963, Walker was comfortably off, but not in the millionaire bracket nor even to be classed among the rich. Yet already the myth of great wealth was well established.

The earliest mention of Walker's money I have traced was in an article on Unicorn in the *Sunday Times* in April 1961, stating that Walker, one of the 'brightest young men' in the City and the House of Commons, was 'reputedly well on the way to his first personal £500,000'. This was written just after the split with David Moate in which Walker had taken the insurance broking side of the partnership in exchange for its other interests valued at just a few thousand pounds, at about the time that Rodwell was being denied a flotation of its own by the Stock Exchange, and at the start of a year in which both Unicorn and Dillon Walker lost money. Walker was thus far from being well on the way to half a million. He told me that at no time did any *Sunday Times* journalist consult him as to the use of a figure estimating his wealth, but the author of the article told me it was written after a long interview in which Walker's wealth was discussed.

The *New Statesman*, too, favoured the half-million in its 'Junior Imp' profile in August 1962, also written after a personal interview. It gave a résumé of his interests:

> Behind him today stands not one city interest, but three. Insurance (his first love), unit trusts (his second – with Edward du Cann, now Economic Secretary to the Treasury, he pioneered their post-war boom) and property development (in which he now has his major personal holding – of £100,000) all combine to provide the kind of passport that the Tory party understands. And among the Tories these credentials have looked all the more impressive as they have never been flashed about in an ostentatious way: there are no vulgar number-plates on his Austin Princess, not even a town house, just his parents' bungalow home in Twickenham.

The article highlights the importance of the Rodwell shares, but, as we have seen, these were already being sold and raised not £100,000 but about £15,000, the proceeds enabling the Walkers to move from Twickenham to Walton-on-Thames. But the *New Statesman* article was significant because it clearly described the importance of Walker's reputed wealth to his political career. It called Walker 'intelligent and progressive', quoting his anti-hanging position and the concern he expressed over the Common Market's effect on the economic growth of Commonwealth countries in Africa and Asia. But if Walker's view on such matters carried weight, it was clearly because his reputed success in making half a million pounds by the age of thirty had enabled him to crash 'the Tory party's traditional social barrier. Within the Conservative party in Parliament Peter Walker has never suffered from the grammar-school working-class label: he has risen above it simply by reason of his business success.'

But not all reports were so exaggerated. In November 1963, the *Birmingham Sunday Mercury* referred to Walker's hand in controlling Unicorn's £30 million of funds and then quoted Walker: 'What I am worth isn't anything like that of course. But I have enough to do what I want to do. I live comparatively simply, mind you, but I have the expense of two homes, in London and Worcester. There are secretarial services, research and travelling: they all take up quite a bit.' Nevertheless the *Mercury* still described Walker as 'very rich'.

By the start of the Seventies, when Walker was the rising star of the Conservative Cabinet, the repetition of the millionaire-at-thirty myth was an almost automatic reaction of journalists and commentators. For example, in October 1970 the *Observer* wrote: 'Everyone knows that Peter Walker made a million (or thereabouts) by the age of 30.'

By then Walker had made quite a lot more money by selling his insurance firm to Slater Walker, and by selling Slater Walker shares. As we shall see, these sources alone were still not enough to put him squarely in the millionaire bracket, although Walker has told me there were times when doubtless he could have called himself a millionaire, taking into account land values of farms he later bought. But he had, after some seventeen years in business, undoubtedly reached Amery's second goal: financial independence enabling him to devote his life to politics. But by 1970 the myth of his early wealth had become part not just of the Walker image but of the Tory party itself. As the *Daily Mirror* said in November 1970: 'Unlike any other leading Conservative politician of his generation, he is part of the Tory Dream. For what Walker embodies is the belief that self-help can gain a man life's glittering prizes and that riches once achieved are not simply a means of pleasure but also a means of serving society.'

But back to 1963. In January that year de Gaulle blocked the UK's attempt to join the EEC and with his 'Non' also removed any obstacle that Walker's anti-Common Market campaign might have created to his appointment to a government post. In October that year, Sir Alec Douglas-Home replaced Macmillan as Prime Minister, and he immediately restored the deposed Selwyn Lloyd to the Cabinet as Leader of the House. Walker was appointed Lloyd's Parliamentary Private Secretary, succeeding his colleague Charles Longbottom, who had been PPS to Iain Macleod, the previous Leader. As the *Sunday Mercury* observed, Walker was 'on the threshold of political power'.

Walker was also on the threshold of his fourth and most famous business partnership – with James Derrick Slater.

6   *Slater—industrialist*

The career of James Derrick Slater up to 1963 had been more straightforward than Walker's but no less remarkable. For Slater had, at the age of thirty-four, established himself in firm line of succession to the leadership of Leyland, Britain's leading motor manufacturer, when he became deputy and right-hand man to Donald Stokes, then emerging as the new 'strong man' of the car industry.

Like Walker, Slater had already made a bit of money for himself when they met, by playing the stock market. But he had not fully developed the overriding ambition to make himself financially independent, which was to determine him to leave Leyland. Nor in Slater's case was there any political motive behind the ambition. Nevertheless, in this common aim lay the foundations of Slater Walker.

Born on 13 March 1929, Slater is three years older than Walker. He was brought up little more than a couple of miles away in Wembley, but the Slaters were more comfortably off than the Walkers. Slater's father, Hubert, owned a small building and decorating business in Kensington – the same kind of business, as Anthony Sampson points out in his *New Anatomy of Britain*, as Heath's father – and their semi-detached house in Windermere Avenue placed them more firmly in the middle class.

Slater went to Preston Manor County, the local grammar school, where, like Walker, neither his sporting nor academic record was particularly distinguished: he used to come about tenth in his class, he once said. He developed, however, a passion for and considerable skill at chess, and his ability to play 'blindfold' is evidence of the keen memory that was later to impress those who worked for him. He is also reputed to have been fond of playing practical jokes. *Nova* magazine quoted a former master in a profile in 1973: 'In the staff room, whenever some schoolboy villainy was mentioned, there was a tendency to think of Slater and Tomlin in the same breath.' Tomlin was Slater's best friend.

Slater also left school at sixteen and was immediately articled to a firm of chartered accountants called Croydon & King, based in Grosvenor Street, Victoria, a small firm with only sixteen people. Slater spent five years with Croydon & King, with a break for National Service in the Royal Artillery, but he did his final year of accountancy training with the leading and exacting firm of Cooper Brothers.

Although it was at his father's instigation that Slater became an accountant, as with Walker, his mother Jessica appears to have been a more important figure. There is evidence, too, that the striking self-confidence that became crucial to his business success did not emerge until after his National Service. The *Nova* account says that at Croydon & King Slater feared he might fail his examinations, and that in the Army he chose to remain a lance-bombardier for fear of being turned down if he applied for a commission. Sampson, too, citing Slater himself, says that it was 'his experience in the ranks, with men who saw no prospects in their lives' that gave him the 'urge to push ahead'.

When Slater qualified as a chartered accountant in 1953 at the age of twenty-four, he immediately left the profession to seek a job in industry, as many accountants do. He answered an advertisement – which stipulated that 'persons without a keen sense of economy need not apply' – for a position with the Dohm Group, and was appointed company secretary and chief accountant of Renu Plating, a Dohm subsidiary, in February 1964 at a salary of £650 a year.

Renu, a metal finishing company based in London, was one of a dozen or so small industrial concerns, scattered around the country and engaged in various metal, mineral and plastic processes, owned by Svend Dohm, a Danish financier who had settled in the UK. Slater gave an account of his career there in an interview with the magazine *Accountancy Age* in 1970:

> For various reasons the board [of Renu] fell out with him [Dohm], and I was suddenly made general manager after only three months. The firm had been losing money, but within six months it started to make profits again. Then Dohm made me manager of two of his other subsidiaries, and gradually I went through his group as a sort of trouble-shooter.

In the course of his trouble-shooting tour of the Dohm organization, Slater met the man who was to become his first business partner: a chemical engineer some two years older than himself called Kenneth Meyer. Meyer had gone to work for another of Dohm's companies at about the same time as Slater, and the two became close friends.

Slater probably learnt a certain amount about finance from Dohm, for Dohm was interested in so-called asset situations and made use of the Exchange Telegraph card service, on which the details of public companies are summarized. The Dohm group was small however, and privately owned by the family; Dohm's son was being groomed to take over and there was little scope for an ambitious young man.

After nearly two years with Dohm, both Slater and Meyer decided to leave. There were two main factors behind Slater's decision: his father had died and he wanted to put the family building business on a profitable basis. But also Slater and Meyer had determined to try to exploit their managerial talents on their own account. In the autumn of 1955, Slater and Meyer set up in business as industrial and management consultants, through a company they called Commercial & Industrial Development. They hoped to hire themselves out to do one-off reorganization jobs.

But the partners quickly found they had been too ambitious; neither had any money, and they just did not have enough capital to get the business off the ground. Within three months they realized that they could not make a living out of it and both sought other employment.

Meyer went off to work for an engineering firm which he and Slater had been trying to interest in their consultancy services. Slater meanwhile replied to an advertisement for the position of company secretary at Park Royal Vehicles in West London, then, as now, a leading builder of bus bodies.

Slater nearly did not get the job. Though Bill Shirley, general manager of Park Royal, favoured him over two other short-listed applicants, Bill Black – later Lord Black – then managing director of Park Royal, wanted to make an internal appointment. But when Black met Slater he quickly changed his mind. The backing which Black, also a self-made man and then already sixty, subsequently gave Slater was an important factor in his rapid rise through the group; today they remain close friends.

Slater was appointed on 1 January 1956. He was then twenty-six and his career in the motor industry was to cover eight years of radical change. It started humbly enough, though. The duties of a company secretary are not particularly glamorous. He tends to be the man who does the chores: ensuring that the company complies with the minutiae of the law, dealing with the auditors, collecting figures for the accounts, drawing up the minutes of board meetings, and, in the case of a public company, looking after the shareholders. It is unlikely, after his experience with Dohm, that Slater ever contemplated a career as a professional company secretary. Within a few months of joining Park Royal he confronted Shirley and explained he wanted a larger role in the management of the company. Shirley agreed: Slater retained the title of company secretary, but the routine work was delegated to a deputy and Slater was promoted to Shirley's management team. This consisted, in addition to Shirley and now Slater, of the production manager, the body designer and the commercial director.

Park Royal was owned by Associated Commercial Vehicles (ACV) and employed about a thousand men putting bodies onto chassis supplied by ACV's main subsidiary the Associated Equipment Company (AEC). The truck and bus market in the UK was at the time dominated by ACV and its arch-rival Leyland. But in the mid-Fifties the fortunes of Leyland were on the up, thanks largely to their dynamic young sales director Donald Stokes, while those of ACV were falling: it had been formed by a loose amalgamation of independent companies and there had never been any real attempt at rationalization. Each unit, including Park Royal, was left to go its own way, the only co-ordination being through a sales company run by Black.

Leyland had even succeeded in breaching Park Royal's traditional monopoly of the London bus market. This was no tragedy, as the business was not particularly profitable. But in 1956 London Transport wanted to place a big new order to replace their ageing fleet, and decided that the best way to keep the cost down was to tell suppliers that there was to be just one simplified design, that this alone would be used for twenty years, and that the full order would be awarded exclusively to one manufacturer.

Such an order was highly attractive to Park Royal. It would take up half the firm's production capacity and the prospect of steady work for twenty years was inviting. The management team were set to do their figuring: Slater's job was to produce an estimate of cuts that could be made in overhead costs with continuous production of a single model.

Park Royal got the order: a firm contract for 1,500 'Routemaster' buses over three years with deliveries starting in 1958, plus an understanding that this would be followed by 350 a year for the remainder of the period and that no other manufacturer would be used. Although it was to backfire on Park Royal some ten years later, when London Transport abandoned the Routemaster in favour of one-man operated buses, initially this was good business. But once the factory was busy churning out Routemasters, life at Park Royal became somewhat uneventful. Slater might just as well have included himself in his tally of redundant head office staff. Shirley, recognizing that Slater would be restless in any job but his own, told Black that if he wanted to keep him he had better find him another position in the group.

About a year after Slater had joined Park Royal, major changes had taken place in the structure of the ACV group. Pressure had been brought on Lord Brabazon, its chairman, to reorganize with the aim of introducing some sense of unity, and in early 1957 Black was made managing director of the whole group - the only executive director on the main ACV board. As part of the reorganization all the part-time directors on the boards of the subsidiary company resigned and full-time executives were appointed in their places. The job that Black found for Slater was as commercial director of the principal motor and chassis manufacturer, and backbone of the group, AEC.

Before Slater took up his new appointment in early 1959, however, Black assigned him a special task. Black's plans for the revival of ACV included the complete closure of Crossley Motors, a Birmingham firm which had been one of the original constituents of the group. Black himself handled the redundancies and the sale of the factory, but he asked Slater to help with the disposal of the machinery and equipment. The production men were reluctant to see it go, saying that it could be used elsewhere in the group. Slater, however, demonstrating perhaps for the first time his talent for realizing assets, obtained such good prices for the plant that there could be no argument.

It was during the closure of Crossley that Slater first came into close contact with his new boss, John Bowley, the managing director of AEC. Bowley was afraid that Slater's appointment as a director at just thirty might cause resentment among his new colleagues, who were mostly, like Bowley himself, lifelong motor industry men, but Black insisted.

Slater, however, settled in at AEC in Southall without upsetting anyone. His job, according to Bowley, was 'to see we made money'. One of his particular responsibilities was to keep a watch on the prices charged for trucks and paid for components. AEC's prices were not fixed and the salesmen had some freedom to negotiate with customers; Slater had to ensure that they did not offer unprofitably low prices. Graham Turner, in *The Leyland Papers*,* his book describing the mergers that led to the formation of the British Leyland Motor Corporation, says that Slater 'believed that the policy of trying to undercut Leyland was foolish (particularly at a time when home market sales were just beginning to pick up) and therefore increased new vehicle prices by 10 per cent, of which he gave $2\frac{1}{2}$ per cent to ACV's distributors and dealers'.

Slater's most important contribution in the three years he was at AEC was the development of the company's overseas markets. Although Slater has been credited with some responsibility for the decision to reorganize AEC's operations, in fact Black had already made up his mind. Slater, however, together with John Bowley, implemented Black's policies most effectively.

Slater's first task abroad was to change AEC's sales arrangements in

* Eyre and Spottiswoode, 1971.

South Africa. Shirley, Slater's former boss at Park Royal, had introduced ACV to a South African called Jack Plane, whom Shirley knew
from the days before he joined Park Royal. Shirley had recommended that AEC switch its sales agency in South Africa from the firm
they were using, Dowson & Dobson, to Plane's company. Black had
accepted this, and Slater was dispatched to South Africa to wind up
the Dowson & Dobson arrangement and settle the deal with Plane.

Slater's trip to South Africa was to have important consequences
both for himself and for AEC. He got on very well with Jack Plane and
his brother Cyril. ACV bought a stake in the Planes' company, whose
shares were quoted on the Johannesburg Stock Exchange, and the
relationship became particularly close. Plane sold such a large
number of AEC trucks that they had soon usurped the position of their
main competitors Leyland, whose organization in South Africa
found itself in bad trouble as a result. This was the first marked reversal of the years of ACV's decline.

The Plane arrangement became the model for new AEC sales companies in other countries and Bowley and Slater travelled many miles
setting them up. Wherever possible they would go into partnership
with a successful local firm, and such deals were made in France,
Belgium, Holland and Spain. The new sales companies did not all
achieve the same startling results of South Africa – the Dutch one in
particular was a failure – but the new network was largely responsible
for the vigorous expansion in AEC's exports.

At home, too, ACV was expanding. The group was given the
chance to buy the Basingstoke motor manufacturing factory of the
Thorneycroft engineering group; Black sent Bowley and Slater to
investigate and advise on the price he should pay. Bowley looked at
its manufacturing potential; Slater looked at the balance sheets. They
decided that each would give Lord Black his valuation separately, in
sealed envelopes. In the event, Slater's price, based on what he
thought he could get by selling off the plant, was a few hundred
thousand pounds lower than Bowley's, who had calculated what he
thought he could earn from employing the extra capital. But Black
disregarded both their figures; he said a loss-making firm was worth
nothing to its owners and bought the Thorneycroft factory at a much
lower price than even Slater had put on it. It was an argument that
Slater was not to forget.

The new life that Black had put into ACV was supported by a good
demand for commercial vehicles, and profits quickly recovered.
After a bad 1958 the group earned just under £1 million before tax in
the year to 30 September 1959; in two years this had almost doubled
to over £1.9 million. Encouraged by this rate of progress some of the
ACV men, including Slater, who for years had had to live with the fear
that they might be swallowed up by their stronger rival Leyland,

began to hope that ACV might one day become the dominant partner if a merger became inevitable.

The hopes were not to be fulfilled. Partly because ACV wanted to avoid falling into the lap of its main competitor, its directors had agreed in the early summer of 1961 to open negotiations with the country's biggest car makers, the British Motor Corporation, on possible areas of collaboration. Slater himself took part in the discussions of what the two might do together in export markets. The talks went on through 1961, and at one point Rolls-Royce was also brought in. But the proposal that emerged was a straight takeover of ACV by BMC, to which ACV's ageing chairman and managing director, Lord Brabazon, and Black agreed.

Graham Turner, in *The Leyland Papers*, has given the reasons for the last-minute failure of this proposal. The BMC board suddenly decided that its own financial position was not at that moment strong enough to be subjected to the detailed scrutiny involved in a formal takeover. The negotiations were therefore postponed.

News of the talks had reached Donald Stokes and his boss at Leyland, Sir Henry Spurrier. Not wishing to let ACV escape them, they now made a direct approach. Black was not happy, but could not refuse to talk. Leyland offered a reasonable price – four of its own shares of about £4 each for five of ACV's which stood at about £3. Black, according to Turner, insisted on improving the ratio to one Leyland for each ACV share. The intervention of the American Chrysler, who wanted to buy a stake in Leyland, helped Spurrier and Stokes to make up their minds to accept Black's terms and the deal was done. Leyland paid a stiff price, but the acquisition of ACV was crucial to the effective dominance of Leyland over BMC when the two eventually merged in 1968 to form the British Leyland.

The ACV men had many misgivings about the merger, but the two managements were no strangers. The two companies had had a jointly owned business, British United Traction, since 1948, when they had merged their trolley-bus manufacturing capacities. Slater had been made a director of this company, and at its board meetings he first met and impressed Stokes. Slater was also one of the few executives outside the main board of directors who knew of the ACV-Leyland talks before the conclusion was announced.

After the merger in the summer of 1962, Slater was brought up from AEC to Berkeley Square, where both Leyland and ACV had their headquarters. As he told *Accountancy Age*, he was appointed 'commercial manager of the Leyland Group, which at that time embraced Standard Triumph, Leyland, Albion, Scammell, and, of course, AEC'. He worked closely with Black and Stokes, who found themselves running the rationalization programme as Sir Henry Spurrier, chairman of the new motor giant, had been taken ill.

But the Leyland men did not agree with all Slater's ideas. Shortly before the merger, Slater had persuaded his directors that ACV should buy a trading company in South Africa; it was a proposal based on financial, not industrial considerations – in fact a proposal to diversify. The Leyland board rejected the plan, as it ran counter to their established policy of confining their activities to the manufacture of vehicles.

By early 1963 Slater's rise through the motor industry had been extraordinary. At only thirty-four, after six years in the industry, he had reached a senior position in one of the country's most important firms. To some extent he had been lucky – he had by chance chosen a company that was badly short of good management, and he had benefited from events beyond his control which had led to Black's emergence at the top, followed by his successful efforts to revive the group carried out against a background of firm demand for vehicles. But Slater had been an important part of that revival. His direct contribution had been principally to the growth of overseas sales, for which he had been chosen by the *Evening News* for its Under-Forties series. But in the group's attempt to become more profit-conscious, Slater's purely financial approach, devoid of sentimental attachment to the process of making lorries or buses, was important.

Slater was also well off financially by 1963. He had already been earning a substantial salary at AEC and when he moved to head office he was being paid over £5,000 a year, a big salary in those days for a man of thirty-four. But by then Slater's eyes had been opened to a much quicker and easier way of making money.

Slater's story, like Walker's, has its pivotal points. One of these concerns Slater's discovery of his talent for stock market investment. The *Nova* profile encapsulated this part of the legend: '1961: Catches virus on business trip to Spain; convalescing in Bournemouth with nothing to do, starts taking interest in stock market. Evolves system of looking for shares with below average rating, but above average growth prospects.'

The *Sunday Express* gave a fuller version in May 1965 in an article which placed Slater's illness in 1960 and which quoted Slater:

Suddenly it occurred to me that I was not financially independent. I decided to set about changing that, so I started reading the financial papers. I couldn't understand why some shares existed with both high earnings yields and good profit records. So I totted up my capital – it came to around £2,000 – and started buying shares. The first two I bought were Bernard Wardle and Klinger Manufacturing. Luckily I caught them just at the right time. Klinger were around 7s. at that time, and Wardle, adjusting for scrip issues, less than 1s. Inside six months I had nearly doubled my capital. Then I went along to my bank and borrowed as much money as the manager would advance me. Fortunately I had an accommodating manager and soon I had borrowed four times as much money as I could put up myself.

There is evidence, however, that Slater's interest in shares had been developing gradually, perhaps even from his time with Dohm. Slater told me that he could not remember when he first became interested in stock markets; he had, he said, bought one or two shares from time to time over the years, but only became really interested after his illness. Shirley, his old boss at Park Royal, remembers that lunchtime conversation would often turn to shares, especially when Slater and a similarly inclined colleague were both there, and he thought that Slater was first 'bitten with the bug' there. Bowley, Slater's chief at AEC, also told me he thought that Slater was already fascinated by the stock market when he joined AEC in 1959.

Legend, too, has sometimes distorted the system that Slater devised; rather than looking for companies with 'good profits records' Slater, it was said – for example by the *Financial Times* in 1968 – 'stumbled on a system the basis of which was that the market was very loath to upgrade the investment rating of companies emerging from losses'. The first version is the more accurate, according to Slater, who also says that a lot of detailed work was involved; but either fits one of his favourite descriptions of the companies as 'due for a status change'. As we shall see, his system was in reality considerably more sophisticated.

Nor does the £2,000 figure perhaps convey the full picture of Slater's financial position at the start of 1961, for he had 2,000 ACV shares worth nearly £6,000, and in March that year he subscribed for a further 2,100 in an issue at 30s. each. He also sold the family building business for £3,500, but this belonged to his mother, who also had some ACV shares.

Slater's illness was clearly some sort of turning point, however. After his convalescence, former colleagues like Bowley remember that he had a new enthusiasm for the stock market. Bowley also told me how Slater appears to have secured his first investment 'client', and the circumstances suggest that Slater's career as stock market analyst and investment adviser owes something to the whims of a seventy-seven-year-old industrialist – Slater's chairman at ACV, Lord Brabazon.

Slater had to attend a board meeting of one of ACV's subsidiaries in Berkshire, over which Lord Brabazon presided. Afterwards, they all went to lunch at a local hotel, and there Slater started praising the merits of the shares of Bernard Wardle. The assembled commercial vehicle manufacturers were able to appreciate some, at least, of

Wardle's attractions, for it supplied their related industry, the car manufacturers, with artificial cloth for seat coverings. As they filed out from lunch, Lord Brabazon turned to Slater and said: 'Buy me some of those Wardle. If they go down by as much as a halfpenny – you are out!'

The purchase was duly made: in about April 1961 Lord Brabazon and Slater each acquired a block of 5,000 shares in Bernard Wardle when the price was about 3s. 9d.* Slater bought a further 15,000 shares at 3s. 8¼d. and 3s. 9d. and the total cost of his investment was thus about £3,734, excluding costs like stockbrokers' commission. The shares were registered in Slater's own name, which suggests that he had not borrowed to buy them, for banks lending against securities usually require them to be put into their nominee company names.

It was just as well that Brabazon's threat was not serious, for by the end of 1961 the price of Wardle had dropped to 2s. 9d., its profits having fallen some sixteen per cent as a result of the recession in the motor industry.

But while there was no possibility of Slater doubling his money in Wardle in six months, he was able to make a small dealing profit. For the share price had initially risen to a little over 4s. in the early summer of 1961, and Slater had promptly resold 15,000 of his shares, retaining only the 5,000 rights. He thus realized a gross profit of about £360.

But hardly had he finished selling the 15,000 than he started buying again, as the Bernard Wardle share price fell. Between July 1961 and the start of 1962 he bought back a total of 22,500 at prices from 3s. to 3s. 6d. and a total cost of £3,701 10s. 11d. His holding was now 27,500 shares.

From a high point in May 1961 the stock market as measured by the *Financial Times* Industrial Ordinary Index fell by thirty-one per cent to a 'low' in July 1962. From this point Slater's fortunes seemed to have considerably improved. Also by then colleagues including Stokes – but not Black – at Leyland had begun to follow Brabazon's example and take Slater's investment advice, which he was freely giving to all and sundry.

The Plane brothers, in particular, are to be found frequently in the records of Slater's early favourite shares. Cyril Plane first acquired 6,000 Wardle shares at 3s. 3d. each in the autumn of 1961 at the same time as Slater was buying for the second time, while Jack Plane had had a very small holding from early 1960. Then in the

---

* More accurately they acquired rights to shares which were later converted into full shares. In March 1961 Bernard Wardle had made a rights issue to raise new capital. In such an issue the new shares are offered to existing shareholders at a favourable price. The shareholders do not, however, have to buy the new shares but can sell the 'rights' on the market.

summer and autumn of 1962 the brothers moved heavily into the shares, buying another 93,000 at 3s. 7¼d. to 4s. 5¼d. to give them a total investment of nearly 100,000 shares at a cost of over £20,000.

Meanwhile Slater himself was doing the opposite: selling Wardle shares. In the summer of 1962 he disposed of 17,500 of his 27,500 shares for around £3,300 and a gross profit of about £380. Slater told me that he could not remember exactly why he sold some of his Wardle shares at this point. He said that there might have been pressure from his bank to reduce his borrowings, that he might have wanted funds for other domestic reasons or some shares might have been sold to help pay interest charges. Whatever the reason, he said he clearly believed that Wardle remained an excellent investment because he retained a substantial number of shares.

We will become familiar with Slater's explanations for selling shares, and on this occasion, as on others, it is not possible to accept that his account represents the full story. Certainly, Slater may have believed that Wardle was still a good investment at the time he sold; but in Slater's sale can be seen the first sign of his personal, unpublicized investment system - to be fully unfolded in succeeding chapters.

Twelve thousand of the Wardle shares sold by Slater were actually bought by the Planes. They may well have been aware that some of their shares came from Slater himself, for the buyer had to sign a transfer form - the document sent by the Stock Exchange to the company so that it can register the change of ownership - and in those days this would normally have already been signed by the seller. In any case the Planes had no cause for complaint, for Wardle turned out to be a very successful investment for them.

Slater's suggestion that he had to sell his Wardle shares to raise cash must also be seen in the light of the fact that at the same time as he sold he reinvested about £1,000 in Clear Hooters, another supplier of the motor industry - horns and other electrical parts - which was to become a firm favourite. Slater acquired 14,650 shares in the summer of 1962, when the price was about 1s. 6d.

Towards the end of that year, Slater also bought 5,000 shares in Spark, an industrial holding company with clothing, engineering and timber interests. His stake rose to 5,500 as a result of a rights issue the company was making and the price, adjusted for the issue, was about 13s. 6d. a share.

In the autumn of 1962 Slater had also bought back another 5,000 Wardle shares at just over 5s. each for a cost of £1,273 8s. 9d. - double the £750-or-so profit he had already realized on his Wardle dealings. But by the end of the year the Wardle price had risen to around 5s. 6d., so his 15,000 shares were worth about £1,125 more than the £3,000 he had paid for them.

His Clear Hooters and Spark had probably cost a little over £5,000 but were not at the end of 1962 showing much appreciation. These are the only investments of Slater's that I have been able to trace at that point. Slater suggested in his *Sunday Express* interview in 1965 that he had invested in Klinger Manufacturing at about the same time as Wardle, but there is no sign of his name in the Klinger register at Companies House and Slater told me that he could not understand the article's reference to Klinger: 'I know that I identified the shares because they fulfilled my investment criteria and I also recommended them to some friends. It is possible that I held some shares although my records do not confirm this.'

At the end of 1962 the *Financial Times* Industrial Ordinary Index was nudging the 300 mark, having risen steadily from the July low point of 252.8. It was to continue to rise to a peak of 377.8 on 1 October 1964, with only one serious falter at the start of that year. It was to be a marvellous time for stock market speculators, and Slater was to profit from it to the full.

Among those who prosper in a stock market boom are newspaper share tipsters. The star of the financial pages in 1963/4 was an anonymous columnist in the *Sunday Telegraph* called Capitalist. Capitalist was in fact none other than Jim Slater, prominent Leyland executive, part-time investment adviser and now freelance journalist.

Slater—Capitalist

It is said that the hardest million to make is the first. It is also said that much the most interesting part of the story of any first million is 'how its owner got his grubstake', as one City contemporary not unfamiliar with Slater's story put it. To persuade others to put up capital to get a new, untried venture off the ground, you have to put up a bit of your own – the grubstake. Without the money that Slater made in the stock market before he left Leyland, it is unlikely that Slater Walker would ever have taken shape.

The speed with which he made his grubstake has been accelerated in the Slater legend. 'Invests savings; turns it into £50,000 within year,' said *Nova* in 1973. It took rather longer, as Slater told *Accountancy Age* in 1970: 'I saved about £2,000, and I didn't start investing seriously till I was 32. Between the age of 32 and 35 (when I left Leyland) I had turned my £2,000 into £50,000.' He also explained how he had increased his initial capital by borrowing: 'I borrowed £8,000, so I had £10,000 to invest; and then the £10,000 became £20,000, I repaid the £8,000 which left me with £12,000.'

What Slater did not tell *Accountancy Age* is that he made some £20,000 and possibly more of his capital dealing in shares he was recommending in the *Sunday Telegraph*. Slater today claims that he made no secret of the fact that there were many similarities between his own portfolio and the shares he wrote about for the paper and states that he had agreed with the City Editor of the *Sunday Telegraph* that he was free to invest in the shares he wrote about. But not once in all the many occasions on which the legend of the £2,000 turned into £50,000 has been repeated has it been publicly stated that he was dealing in the shares he was writing about.

In the winter of 1962/3 Slater wrote out of the blue to Nigel Lawson, the Conservative MP who was then City Editor of the *Sunday Telegraph*, suggesting that he should write a monthly investment column. Slater told me he did so because: 'I thought it was a novel, personal challenge and I was rather proud of the investment system

which I had developed as a hobby while working mainly in industry.'
He wanted to emphasize, he said, that he wrote 'as a successful investor and not as a professional journalist'. Lawson was initially against
the idea, according to Jonathan Aitken, former journalist who later
went to work for Slater Walker and also became a Conservative MP,
in his book *The Young Meteors*:* Aitken suggests – wrongly – that
Slater had already made his £50,000 and then quotes Lawson: 'To
have an outsider from industry tipping shares in a serious newspaper
is completely against the traditions of financial journalism, but Jim
Slater was so good that one simply could not turn him down.'

Lawson's caution was natural. The tipping of shares in newspapers
has long been a matter of contention. In 1973, the City Editor of the
News of the World was sacked after the *Sunday Times* had exposed
that he had dealt in shares he was tipping and engaged in other questionable practices. But it was not the first time it had happened, and
even before 1964 the City Editor of another Sunday paper had been
hauled before the Stock Exchange Council for making money out of
his column in a scandal that never became fully public. The possible
abuse is clear: the recommendation of a share by a national or leading provincial newspaper often results in an increase in the price as
readers rush in to buy and stockjobbers mark up the prices. A
journalist can therefore easily make money on the side by buying
shares before recommending them and selling them afterwards, so
that the merits of the share as a long-term investment need not be of
any consequence to him. Lawson knew too that an outside contributor would be more difficult to supervise than a staff man.

In the early stages of my inquiry, in August 1973, I asked Slater if
any understandings were reached or rules laid down covering his own
investment activities while writing for the *Sunday Telegraph*. Slater
replied: 'There were no rules laid down as I made it clear to Nigel
Lawson that if I were going to be prevented from dealing in shares it
could not possibly be worth my while to write the column.' Much
later, however, in early 1975, Slater told me that there had, after all,
been an understanding with Lawson: Slater undertook to Lawson
that he would not exploit the column for his personal financial gain.
Lawson confirmed to me that Slater was perfectly free to continue as
an active investor, including in the shares he wrote about.

Black, Slater's boss, also agreed to let Slater become a part-time
journalist, although he laid down that it must not interfere with his
work at Leyland, and that his identity must not be revealed.

Slater's first column, under the pseudonym Capitalist, appeared in
the *Sunday Telegraph* of 3 March 1963. Slater began his article with
a repetition of the claim to a successful record which had persuaded

* Secker & Warburg, 1967.

Lawson to let him write the column. 'I have,' wrote Slater, alias Capitalist, 'over a period, developed a set of standards for equity investment which have resulted in a very substantial capital appreciation being achieved during the last few years, at a time when share prices in general have been, at least for the past three years, on balance declining.' He says that he had shown Lawson details of his early share dealings and that these had obviously impressed him. As we saw at the end of the last chapter, I have only been able to find three investments in Slater's name at the start of 1963 – Bernard Wardle, Clear Hooters and Spark Holdings. Only on the former, his first traceable investment which he had made less than two years before, was he showing a relatively large gain of about 37½ per cent on an investment of some £3,000, after realizing dealing profits of £750. Slater remembers buying some Wardle shares at 4s. each in late 1961 and that their price had risen to 9s. at the time he began his column in the *Sunday Telegraph*. This does not accord with my own analysis of his holding. Slater may well have had other investments in nominee names, for it would be normal for the bank from which he had borrowed to require some shares to be held under its own nominee company; but it is unlikely that these would have been more successful than Wardle, since this was Slater's favourite share.

Slater went on to say that the shares which satisfied these standards were basically those which 'couple an above average earning yield with above average growth prospects'. They would usually be among smaller and less-known companies – there would be no 'blue chips' in his portfolio. There was, he said, perhaps an extra element of risk in his system. The real object of the exercise was capital gain.

Deciding which companies have 'above average growth prospects' is naturally a matter of subjective judgement. But Slater also laid down nine quite strict criteria for his shares. He would, he wrote, allow only minor infringements of these criteria:

1 The dividend yield must be at least 4 p.c.
2 Equity earnings must have increased in at least four out of the five years.
3 Equity earnings must have at least doubled over the last four years.
4 The latest Chairman's statement must be optimistic.
5 The company must be in a reasonable liquid position.
6 The company must not be vulnerable to exceptional factors.
7 The shares must have a reasonable asset value.
8 The company should not be family controlled.
9 The shares should have votes.

There are two main determinants of any share price. On the one hand there is the performance of the company itself, its profits and dividends, its sales, the competitiveness of its products, the competence of its management and the efficiency of its workforce. These are the so-called 'fundamentals', and most of Slater's criteria related to them.

The other determinant is the state of supply and demand for the share, sometimes called the 'technical position'. There are many reasons why people buy and sell a particular share, often so difficult to pinpoint that they are lumped together by commentators as 'sentiment'. There are purely external factors, like changes in taxation or death duties, or the availability of credit. The technical situation, however, is influenced by the fundamentals, or rather by what investors believe them to be, which may bear little relation to reality. For what investors expect to happen is as important as what actually happens.

Stockjobbers, the men who make the market in shares, operate principally by assessing the supply and demand, not by trying to analyse fundamentals. They know a newspaper recommendation can influence investors' expectations and decisions, and so they usually 'mark up' a share following a tip. They do this particularly when small companies are recommended, because it only takes a handful of new buyers to upset the 'normal ' supply and demand position. Some newspapers have more effect than others of course: the *Sunday Telegraph*, with a readership then of about $2\frac{1}{2}$ million, spanning just about anyone with an interest in investment, could be expected to have more influence than most. But Slater frequently warned Capitalist followers not to chase up prices on the Monday following publication and advised them to place a limit on their own purchase price of a modest premium over the Capitalist price. On at least one occasion, in September 1964, he asked the *Sunday Telegraph* that this warning be inserted, as it had often been omitted.

Slater for the most part wrote his column as if only the fundamentals mattered, and he was often right about the companies he chose for Capitalist, although by no means always. Either way however, the movements in the shares were exaggerated by the recommendations themselves, and further enhanced by the money that Slater could himself direct into the shares. But while the public Capitalist purported to deal for the most part on fundamentals, Slater personally often benefited from the technical position he was helping to create.

Before proceeding with an analysis of Slater's own investment activities in contrast to those of Capitalist, it is necessary to explain some of the intricacies of tracing share dealings.

A company must by law make its register of shareholders available to the public. It can be inspected either at the company's own office or at the office of its registration agents if it employs, for example, a bank to do this work. The information provided by the company register is considerably fuller than that available from the annual returns of shareholders which a firm must also make to Companies House.

Nevertheless there is a limit to the conclusions that can be drawn from the entries on a company register. In the first place, as stated in an earlier chapter, the entries represent transfers in and out of an account. These transfers are not necessarily purchases or sales, for they may represent the switching of a holding into or out of a nominee name.

It is however possible to get some idea of whether a transfer does represent a genuine purchase and sale. Each transfer is numbered, and for every transfer into an account there must somewhere be a matching number showing a transfer out of another account. It is therefore possible, but a most laborious job, to match transferor and transferee; if there is no nominee company involved in the transaction and if it is one between two private individuals, then the chances are that it must be a proper purchase and sale. It may of course also be a genuine purchase and sale, even if one party is a nominee company, but this cannot be assumed from the registry alone.

Then there is a further problem. Each transfer on the register is dated, but the date does not represent that on which the shares were bought and sold; it is merely the date on which the company registered the transaction. The change of ownership itself takes place when a stockjobber and a stockbroker conclude the deal on the floor of the Stock Exchange. The lapse of time before the deal is registered may vary considerably for many reasons, but will normally depend on the efficiency of the stockbrokers and company registration officials concerned. If there is a muddle it can be a year or more; if it is done efficiently it could be as little as two weeks. The average delay is probably somewhere between a month and six weeks. But this means that it is not normally possible for a member of the public to discover the exact date on which shares were bought and sold.

These problems are all immensely simplified with access to the transfer forms from which the company register is compiled. There is a form for each transfer, giving the name of buyer and seller, or indicating if there is no change of beneficial ownership. They also usually carry a date, often on a stockbroker's or official Stock Exchange stamp, which will be much closer to the actual date of the deal. Most important, the forms carry the consideration paid for the shares, and from this - especially if the share price was rising or falling sharply in the market - it is possible to deduce almost exactly when the purchase was made.

Buyers and sellers are matched in the complex Stock Exchange settlement procedure. The transfer forms do not carry the price received by the seller and therefore it is not possible to be as precise about sales as purchases. Normally, however, the sale would have taken place in the same two-week Stock Exchange account as the purchase was made.*

Capitalist wrote his column in the first person, and it is possible that some readers believed that the anonymous author was actually buying and selling shares exactly as the column described. It is even more likely that they would have been most surprised to learn that Slater personally sometimes did the opposite of what he was advising them to do.

Slater chose three shares to start the portfolio on 3 March 1963: B. Elliott, a machine tool manufacturer, and two companies in which he had already invested, Spark Holdings and Clear Hooters. Capitalist 'bought' 225 Elliott shares at 17s. 6d., 270 Spark at 14s. 3d. and 1,900 Clear Hooters at 2s. 0¾d. each for an all-in 'cost'- for Capitalist allowed for dealing expenses of brokers' commission and stamp duty – of £605 8s.

Slater had, as we have seen, acquired 14,650 shares in Clear Hooters in the summer of 1962 when the price was around 1s. 6d. They had risen a little by the start of 1963 when Slater got another 1,000 shares a few weeks before tipping them at 2s. 0¾d. The price rose 6d. after the tip and another 6d. in April. On 26 March the transfer of 750 shares out of Slater's name was registered by Clear Hooters, and by 8 May the transfer of his entire holding, in sixteen blocks, had been recorded.

A member of Clear Hooters' registration department told me he remembers the Capitalist tip well: the company had previously only had about 900 shareholders and the publicity resulted in an increase to around 2,000. This in itself demonstrates the influence that Slater's column had right from the start. Clear Hooters was a very small company by stock market standards: with two million shares in issue, its value at 2s. a share was only £200,000.

By October, the Clear Hooters share price had doubled and, as we shall see, it was a 'star performer' in the Capitalist portfolio. But Spark Holdings was not a success.

Spark's price also jumped about 6d. to 14s. 9d. on the Monday after the tip, and had reached about 16s. 9d. by early May. The transfer of the 5,500 shares that Slater had acquired around the end of 1962, when the price had been about 13s. 6d., was registered on 15 May 1963. The shares remained in the Capitalist portfolio until November 1964, and at one point showed a profit of over twenty per

---

* In a number of cases, where the registered holder is a nominee company, the forms also carry the name of the real owner.

cent; but they were 'sold' for a loss of 3.5 per cent, the price having failed to maintain its higher level largely because the company's profits had been static.

There is no trace of Slater himself in Elliott, but his mother and Donald Stokes both became registered holders of 1,000 shares shortly after they were tipped. Mrs Slater's shares were transferred around the end of 1963 at the same time as Capitalist 'sold' at 24s. 6d. but Stokes' holding was built up to 5,000 shares during 1963 and transferred in the summer of 1964. Stokes also acquired 2,000 Spark shares, registered on 5 April 1963, which were not transferred until early 1965.

I have not seen the transfer forms for Slater's initial disposals of his own holdings in Clear Hooters and Spark, and I tried to establish with him whether the shares had been sold shortly before, rather than shortly after, he tipped them. In early 1977 Slater said that the first 750 Clear Hooters 'may well have been sold before the Capitalist recommendation and the balance about a month later'. He said this would not have been out of line with his agreement with Lawson, which he understood only precluded him from dealing within a few days, or the same two-week Stock Exchange 'account', of his recommendation. He said this was quite different from doing the opposite of what he was advising the *Sunday Telegraph* readers. This must, however, be rejected, for the transfers of the bulk of Slater's Clear Hooters were registered between 2 and 11 April and so, because of the inevitable delay between transaction and registration, the only conclusion is that Slater sold his shares within a matter of days of his recommendation. Several blocks of his shares, including the first 750, were in fact sold to first-time buyers of Clear Hooters who were thus almost certainly *Sunday Telegraph* readers. Slater also produced the same argument for Spark, and it is possible, although unlikely, that he did delay before selling these. Slater also said that he had a valuation of his investments which showed that he held 2,000 Spark on 3 January 1964, and so he would appear to have reinvested in the shares.

Slater also reinvested in Clear Hooters, as we shall see; he could have made a greater profit on his initial investment if he had not sold, but the sale allowed him to take advantage of his next tips, for he lost no time in reinvesting the proceeds. He bought 7,000 shares in UK Optical, makers of lenses for glasses, just before he tipped them in his second Capitalist article on 31 March 1963. Slater 'bought' for his public portfolio 420 shares at 9s. 3d. Personally, he paid 8s. 1½d. for 5,000 and 8s. 9½d. for 2,000.

These must have been bought about a week before the article appeared; although the transfer forms are dated 10 April, some of them bear a Stock Exchange stamp of 22 March, and after they had been tipped, UK Optical shares did not fall below 9s. 6d. As the price rose, Slater bought another 6,000 at 11s., to bring his total investment to 13,000 shares costing £6,215 12s. 6d.

UK Optical announced excellent results within a few weeks of Slater's recommendation, and the share price rose thirty per cent during the next seven months. Slater tipped them again on 20 October 1963, 'buying' 284 more shares for the Capitalist portfolio at 12s. 1½d. with the comment: 'I would expect the market to give these shares a better rating'; and within a few days the shares had risen to 14s. Slater's own action hardly reflected this confidence. Within a matter of weeks of his additional purchases in the summer of 1963, he had resold 6,000 of his holdings at about 11s. 3d. Slater said that he may well have changed his view of the shares as a result of the substantial boost in earnings that had been announced, and that the later chairman's statement could also have been of some significance. But if Slater's private, personal view of the shares had changed, it was less than frank of him to re-recommend the shares in October, especially as he also disposed of the rest of his holding at this time. The evidence suggests that he sold shortly after the booster, for the transfer forms were dated 15 and 18 November, and nearly all the fourteen purchasers of his shares paid prices unobtainable in the market before 20 October. So by November 1963 Slater had realized a total of probably more than £8,000, to make a useful profit of the order of £1,800 to £1,900. Donning his Capitalist hat, Slater did not 'sell' until 31 March 1964, when UK Optical had slipped back to 13s.

Slater did not discuss the details of his Capitalist strategy with his friends, but they did benefit at times apparently from following his dealing – although as we shall see this was not always so. UK Optical provides a good example of how the Capitalist column, and those who were getting the benefit of Slater's investment advice more directly, supported each other. It, too, was a smallish company with two million shares valued, before Slater came on the scene, at less than £900,000. After the initial rise which followed the *Sunday Telegraph* tip, their performance was helped not only by the announcement of good results in May but also by the money that Slater himself could direct into the shares. For at least 100,000 UK Optical shares passed through the hands of Slater and his friends, or nearly five per cent of the equity – enough to influence the market in the shares. The timing of the purchases and sales was staggered, some being luckier than others.

For example, Stokes got 2,000 shares before they were tipped at 8s. 4½d. each; then he too bought more afterwards – 3,000 at 11s. 1½d. Slater's mother, who had, as Slater pointed out, relatively slender resources, acquired 3,000 after the tip at 10s. 1½d. and another 2,000 later in the summer at 11s. 3d. – which suggests that

Slater's view of the company had not at that point changed. Jack Plane, investing through 29 Gracechurch Street Nominees, poured over £33,000 into 60,000 shares throughout the summer (150 came from Slater himself) and his brother acquired nearly 20,000. Mrs Slater and Stokes sold before Capitalist but after Slater himself and so got slightly lower prices; still, they made a few hundred pounds profit each. The Planes started selling before Capitalist but some of their shares were not disposed of until later.

As Capitalist disposed of his Spark, he advised his followers that: 'One of the most important investment rules is to cut your losses and let your profits run on. In this way, you ensure small losses and help ensure large profits.' Cut your losses and let your profits run was to become a great Slater public maxim. His private rule was rather different in Clear Hooters; likewise in Bernard Wardle, his first love, which he selected for Capitalist in his third column of 21 April 1963, 'buying' 430 shares at 9s 0d. each.

At the end of 1962, as we have seen, Slater held 15,000 Wardle shares. He bought another 4,000 just before he tipped them. The price was already rising fast, and he paid almost as much as Capitalist, getting 2,000 at 8s. 9d., 1,000 at 8s. 10½d. and 1,000 at 9s. each, for a total of £1,768 15s.

As usual, the share price was marked up the following Monday to 10s., although Wardle was a rather larger company than Clear Hooters, with a market capitalization of about £1.8 million. It rose again the next day to 10s. 3d. and was then quoted at 9s. 6d. to 11s. for two weeks. The price then started to rise again, reaching 11s. 9d. at the end of May 1963, where it remained for the first week of June before falling back again slightly. In that period Slater sold all his 19,000 shares: at an average price of 10s. 3d. he would have realized £9,737.

Again, Slater would have made more if he had held the shares longer, for the price reached 16s. by the autumn of 1963. But Slater had not done badly; the 19,000 shares had cost £4,758, an average of just over 5s. each. He had therefore more than doubled his money with a gain of about £5,000; but it had not been done in six months, as some of the shares had been bought back in the late summer of 1961. The 4,000 shares that Slater bought just before tipping and sold just after – the sort of dealing that most clearly demonstrates the abuse of a tipster's power – would have produced a profit of nearly £300.

Slater insisted in early 1977 that the 'hard core' of his Wardle holding was 'run' for a profit. He said that the apparent position from the share register might be confused by the fact that he borrowed money to buy Wardle shares and it was possible therefore that some of them were held in banks' nominee names. He said he did not recollect consciously using nominee names during this period and that most shares appear to have been purchased in his own name. As we shall see, this explanation somewhat undermines part of Slater's earlier defence of his Capitalist dealings; and it must also be rejected, for I have found no example of an investment in Slater's name on which the profits were allowed to run. There is therefore no reason to think that shares in nominee names were handled in a different manner. In any event, Slater may have been surprised that the Wardle price continued to rise so fast, for on 20 October 1963, Capitalist wrote that although the company announced that profits were up, he thought that the shares were 'adequately priced' at 15s. 9d., until the terms of an expected rights issue to raise capital for expansion were known.

He did not however suggest that the shares should be sold. His motor industry colleagues, were doing just that. Stokes had acquired 3,000 shares in early 1963 at 6s 5$\frac{1}{2}$d. and a further 7,000 just before the tip at 8s. 5$\frac{1}{4}$d. and 8s. 11$\frac{1}{4}$d. All were resold in the autumn when the price was 15s. 9d. to 16s. for a gain of some £4,000. The Planes also did well: Cyril, for example, started selling in the late summer, and by the end of November had sold all his 35,000 shares for a profit of about £17,000. Slater's explanation of the inconsistency of advice was that different considerations apply to individual portfolios – an explanation whose inadequacy will become apparent in later chapters. Slater also said that it would be impossible for everyone to sell at once. This is, of course, precisely why it was so useful to have a newspaper column through which he could tell the public to buy while he sold for himself and his associates.

This pattern was to continue for most of the two years that Slater wrote the Capitalist column. Slater tipped twenty-one shares altogether: he also dropped thirteen of them later, keeping the portfolio to ten or less. Of the thirteen 'sold', seven lost money for Capitalist. Slater's name is to be found in ten of the Capitalist shares, and one in a joint account. Motor industry colleagues, other associates and, later, investment clients are to be found in nearly all the companies. Slater himself, after selling out his initial holdings, is usually to be found dealing before advising his readers.

Slater invested in four of the seven that were losers: we have already seen that he made money out of one, Spark. Here are brief details of the other three:

Winn Industries – group with engineering and building interests, tipped 26 May 1963 at 17s. Capitalist says shares are depressed because of unpopularity of industrial holding companies but Winn has good profit record. Slater became registered holder of 5,000 on 22 July 1963, but shares must have been bought before 13 May, last day on which they could be bought with entitlement to free one-for-three issue in which Slater gets further 1,666. Mrs Slater and Stokes acquired 1,919 and 2,000 each. Winn price reaches 17s. 6d. a week after tip, then falls. Transfer of 6,166 of Slater's shares registered on 1 October and of remaining 500 on 14 November 1963.

Capitalist announces he has 'sold' on October 1963 at 15s. 9d., explains that main reason price has gone ahead is that recent take-over paid for by stock issue 'has put more Winn shares on the market'. Slater himself may have realized small profit on his investment. Mrs Slater's and Stokes' shares transferred between November 1963 and March 1964.

Symonds - precision engineers, tipped 1 September 1963 at 9s. 9d. Slater in joint account with Anthony Roberts, later chief accountant of Slater Walker, has 2,750 bought in June at 8s. 10½d. and 8s. 11d. Capitalist 'sells' 2 February 1964 at 7s. 6d. after company says profits likely to be down.

Slater and Roberts also sell at about 7s. 6d. Other losers: J. Plane who had about 40,000 bought through second half 1963; Stokes who sold 20,000 - bought both before and after tip for £9,593 15s. - for £6,000 in May 1964.

Hunt & Moscrop (Middleton) - paper textile machinery manufacturers, tipped 6 October 1963 at 3s. 9d. Company has just announced good results for year to 30 June 1963. About same time, Slater buys 20,000 at 3s. 5½d. to 3s. 10½d. Total paid £3,706 17s. 6d., average price 3s. 8½d. 5 November 1963, H & M chairman says profits might be lower in current year: 1 December Capitalist writes: 'The statement by the chairman of Hunt & Moscrop (Middleton) Limited was a surprise and a disappointment,' sells at 3s. 6d. Slater had already sold and may have come out ahead: buyers of his shares paid up to 4s. 9d. Stokes also in and out.

To replace Hunt & Moscrop, Capitalist chose, on 1 December 1963, Sidney Flavel, a manufacturer of gas appliances. Flavel did not meet Slater's criteria, for it had had only two years of rising earnings. Its share price had already risen substantially and Capitalist 'bought' at 29s. 11½d. Two weeks after the tip the price had reached 35s. 6d. Slater himself had acquired 4,000 shares in the spring of 1963 when the price was around 13s.; the transfer of these shares was registered on 20 February 1964. Slater told me he might have sold a few Flavel shares six or seven weeks after he had tipped them.

By 5 January 1964 the Capitalist portfolio had risen by fifty-six per cent since its inception the previous March. In the same period the *Financial Times* - Actuaries All Share Index* had risen by about twelve per cent.

---

* This index is much more widely based than the more popular *Financial Times* Ordinary Index, which is compiled only from thirty 'blue chip' companies.

But 1963 had been a year for stock market 'high fliers'. Robert Heller, then Business Editor of the *Observer*, singled out ten in an article headlined 'What a year for profit!' on 22 December. One thousand pounds invested in these ten alone would have produced a capital gain of £3,229. There were two Capitalist shares among them: Bernard Wardle and the recently added Flavel. But Klinger Manufacturing, that other reputed favourite of Slater's, was also in the ten.

The 'high fliers' were anticipating the boom that had been gradually building up since Maudling's first expansionary Budget in April 1963. It was not just a good year for stock market profits, but also for industrial ones. Wardle, as Heller pointed out, was 'bounding along on a boom' in cars. So too was Clear Hooters.

It was at the height of the car boom that Slater decided to leave that industry, for he took the decision in the autumn of 1963. His life was now changing dramatically; he had met Walker and had bought a large red brick house with leaded windows, called High Beeches, on a private estate near Esher, close by the Walkers' house at Walton-on-Thames.

Financially, he was now very well off. His pay at Leyland had been increased to about £10,000 a year. On top of that he was *charging* stockbrokers for investment advice, and at the end of 1963 his income from this was running at the rate of £9,000 a year.*

Around the end of 1963 Slater started looking around for a vehicle for his investment activities. The hectic events of the following months will be examined in the following chapters. Slater, however, continued to write his anonymous *Sunday Telegraph* column until 7 February 1965. I shall complete the analysis of Capitalist but it must be remembered that from early 1964 stock market investment was no longer Slater's hobby but his full-time job.

This fact and Slater's identity as Capitalist leaked out in the small circulation (now defunct) *City Press* on 8 May 1964. Three days later Slater wrote to Kenneth Fleet, who had taken over from Lawson as City Editor of the *Sunday Telegraph* the previous October, saying: 'I have been giving a lot of thought to my position during the last few days, and now this announcement has been made it does, to some extent, bring matters to a head. I feel there is now an obvious conflict of interest between the *Sunday Telegraph* Capitalist article and my clients, and under the circumstances, I think it would be better for me to resign from my position with you.' He said he was sorry if this let the *Sunday Telegraph* down and offered to reimburse the paper

---

* I have not usually allowed for costs in my estimates of dealing profits. Although Slater would have had to pay commission and stamp duty, his fees from brokers could have been set off against them. The people he was advising would have had to pay these costs and their profit would have accordingly been less.

for the cost of a publicity campaign it had started. Slater wrote, however, that he wanted to continue writing about 'share systems' and said he had drafted an article on 'blue chip' shares, where, he said, there could be no question of influencing the market – for the *Sunday Telegraph* was worried at the small size of some of the companies chosen by Slater. Slater says that Fleet persuaded him to continue to write the column for the time being. Fleet, however, was not informed that Slater had often acted in the opposite manner to the advice he was giving, but even so Fleet's concern over the declared conflicts of interest did grow over the coming months, although Slater says he was never told about this. The conflict had, of course, existed from the start, but from early 1964 more of Slater's widening circle of associates are to be seen in the shares he was recommending. Two share dealing companies of which Walker was a director appear, for instance, in Allied Ironfounders, Slater's first tip of 1964, made on 5 January.

Allied Ironfounders, makers of baths, pipes and other cast iron appliances, was much larger than most Capitalist companies, being valued in the stock market at about £27 million. Capitalist 'paid' 103s. 6d. for its shares. Walker Moate and Rodwell Securities, the share dealing subsidiary of the Rodwell property group whose formation we followed in Chapter 4, each owned 1,000 shares at the time. The transfer forms were dated 7 January 1964, but Walker Moate and Rodwell each acquired 250 shares at 96s. 9d. and 750 at 96s. 10½d., prices unobtainable in the market after about 14 December 1963.

If Slater had inspired the original purchases, the Master's touch is missing from the subsequent transactions in these two companies. The Allied Ironfounders' share price was rising fast because it, too, had announced much higher half-year profits in early December. In spite of its size – and this demonstrates the importance stockjobbers attached to Capitalist's selections – the price was marked up a further 4s. 9d. to 107s. 6d. on 6 January 1964, the day after Slater had tipped it. But within ten days the price was back to 102s. 6d. and Walker Moate, which sold by early March, thus probably made a gross profit of only about £250 on its in-and-out investment.

Rodwell hung on. In March 1964 Allied Ironfounders split its 'heavy' shares into four, and the price rose again. Rodwell now bought 1,200 more of the new shares at 28s. 0¾d. each, equivalent to 112s. 3d. in the old form. Rodwell's original stake, increased to 4,000 shares in the split, was then sold in June 1964 as Allied Ironfounders duly announced record profits. Rodwell realized a gain of some £700 on these shares, but the over-enthusiastic market had been disappointed with the results, the share price had slipped back, and Rodwell was showing a loss on its remaining 1,200 shares. The price recovered again later in the year, however, and Rodwell succeeded in getting out of it its last shares in the autumn for a profit of around £90.

Capitalist also 'sold' his Allied Ironfounders in the autumn of 1964, on 4 October, to realize a profit equivalent to 6s. a share. Another seller about that time was an investment club called Tiger; named after an old Leyland trade mark, its membership comprised senior Leyland executives, and both Brabazon and Black were on the board of Tiger Nominees, through which the club's investments were held. It had been formed in the summer of 1963 with the help of David Moate's National Association of Investment Clubs, but its investments were naturally handled by Slater. Tiger had acquired Allied Ironfounders' shares at about the same time as Walker Moate and Rodwell in December 1963, paying the equivalent of just under 23s. 8d. a share: it sold about the same time as Capitalist, to realize a profit of some £950 on its £2,318 investment.

But not everyone connected with the motor industry was so lucky. Lady Winifred Spurrier, the wife of Sir Henry Spurrier, ailing former chairman of Leyland who died in June 1964, did not get her Allied Ironfounders until after the *Sunday Telegraph* tip and they were not sold until the spring of 1965, when the price had fallen right back to the equivalent of 89s. 6d. She must have lost about £150.

Slater himself does not appear in Allied Ironfounders. But his next two Capitalist selections were highly profitable for him – and for his public portfolio:

Musical & Plastic Industries – distributors of plastic guitars signed by the Beatles. 'Backing the Mersey beat', Capitalist 'buys' at 8s. 3d. on 2 February 1964. 11 March Slater became registered holder of 40,000, half of them acquired in one-for-one free issue, for which last qualifying date was 7 February; Mrs Slater gets 22,000, Stokes 25,000. June 1964, Capitalist writes that controlling shareholders of MPI have sold out, but expects shares 'to continue their upward path'. Price then 6s. 7½d., against adjusted buying price of 4s. 1½d. Reach 7s. by August; 17 August transfer of all Slater's and Mrs Slater's shares registered. Slater's possible profit £4,500 to £5,000.

Cannon Holdings – gas appliance manufacturer, tipped 1 March 1964 at 98s. 6d. Capitalist says 'Very often the best time to buy is immediately after excellent results are announced during a period of market indigestion and profit taking.' Slater has 1,750 shares. June 1964 GEC takes over Cannon at 127s. 6d. cash. Capitalist profit subject to capital gains tax. So also probably Slater's of around £2,500.

At the end of 1963 and in early 1964, Slater also turned again to his motor industry favourites, Clear Hooters and Bernard Wardle.

In November 1963, Clear Hooters had announced profits that were almost twice the previous year's and the dividend was doubled.

Slater gave the shares a boost in his 1 December column: 'They could still practically double in price without looking unduly expensive.' They were then 6s. 3d.

The following day, the shares were marked up 1s. 3d. to 7s. 6d., and two days later they rose again to 8s. This was a useful rise for Slater, for shortly before he had bought 20,000 shares; of these 15,000 were registered in December 1963 and 5,000 in February 1964. The transfer forms for 1963 could not be traced but those for 1964 make it clear that all 20,000 must have been bought before 1 December, for Slater paid 6s. each for the last 5,000 – a price unobtainable in the market after his column.

Clear Hooters then decided to raise more money by a rights issue, but the terms were attractive, as shareholders were asked to subscribe only one shilling for each new share, one of which was offered for every two held. Capitalist announced he would 'take up' his rights. Slater also took up his, getting another 10,000 for £500. The average cost of his 30,000 shares must therefore have been 4s. or less.

Capitalist 'sold' some of his Clear Hooters at 7s. 1½d. on 3 May 1964, saying the holding had become a disproportionate part of the portfolio; he retained the bulk of the holding, however, because he thought that 'this fast growing company must continue to benefit from the buoyant motor industry'. On 2 August, Capitalist 'sold' most of the rest of the holdings at 7s. 'in an endeavour to accelerate my rate of capital appreciation'. Slater kept a few shares in the portfolio, because he was 'looking for exceptionally good results'.

By August 1964, Slater himself had sold all his 30,000 Clear Hooters: at the price range of 6s. 6d. to 7s. 6d., the proceeds must have been about £10,800 and his gain of the order of £4,300. In the summer of 1964, Walker Moate also engaged in an in-and-out operation, buying 4,000 at 6s. 11¾d. and selling six weeks later at 7s. 5d.to 7s. 6¼d. Walker Moate used the stockbrokers Smith Keen Barnett,of which Walker's colleague Alan Beaumont Dark was a partner: Smith Keen were also Clear Hooters' official brokers.

Wardle's 1963 profits had also risen well, being up sixty per cent on the previous year. The share price had climbed to over 21s. by 1 March 1964, when Capitalist wrote: 'Prospects for this company for 1964 must again be excellent as they are substantial suppliers of plastic and leather cloth to the car, furniture and shoe industries, all of which are doing exceptionally well.'

Shortly before, Slater had bought 5,000 shares for himself at 18s. 0¾d. each. The company had also announced a capital reconstruction in which not only did it propose to issue shareholders with one free share for each one held, but also it offered another share by way of rights at just one shilling each. After these issues Slater owned 15,000 shares at a cost of £4,765 12s. 6d. or 6s. 4½d. each.

Stokes also went back into Wardle, acquiring 12,000 shares mostly at 18s. 6d. but a few at £1: after the issues Stokes held 36,000 shares, an investment of nearly £11,867. The Tiger investment club acquired a rather smaller holding of 7,350, after the issues, for £2,371. As Capitalist said, the shares were indeed attracting 'further investment support'.

The Wardle price reached a peak of about 8s. 6d. towards the end of March – equivalent to over 24s. for comparison with pre-March prices – but then dropped back to 8s. It fluctuated around this level for the rest of the year, and it was at this price that Slater sold his 15,000 shares in the autumn to realize £6,000 and a profit of about £1,200.

On 22 March 1964, the *Sunday Telegraph* published an unsigned letter which was critical of Capitalist's methods. The writer raised two main points: first, that the performance of the portfolio was to some extent self-generated, because the recommendations themselves pushed the share prices up; similarly, the 'selling' of a share by Capitalist knocked the price down in the market, making it impossible for readers to realize as high a figure. Secondly, Capitalist did not pay enough attention to the 'technical market situation', that is the supply and demand for the shares as opposed to the fundamentals. The writer then went on to challenge Capitalist to a competition in which each would select six shares to be held for six months.

Slater's reply was printed in the same issue. He agreed that the performance of the portfolio might be helped by the fact that it was printed in the press, but said that he warned readers not to chase prices up. He also agreed that he did not give a great deal of attention to the technical situation, but did not discuss this point; to do so accurately he would, of course, have had to reveal his own activities. Slater accepted the challenge and chose six Capitalist shares: Wardle, Musical & Plastic, Allied Ironfounders, Sidney Flavel, Spark and Newrith Group, a company he had tipped in the summer of 1963.

On 27 September 1964, Capitalist duly announced that he had beaten his challenger, only one of whose shares – a rubber company called Greengate & Irwell, which we will meet again – had performed well. Slater's six had appreciated by an average of 14.5 per cent, the best being Musical & Plastic and Sidney Flavel. Wardle had actually fallen by 4.4 per cent. Capitalist wrote that by selecting for his challenge portfolio six shares from the monthly portfolio, some of which had already risen in price very substantially, he considered he had 'proved that it is the intrinsic merit of the shares that is really the determining factor', as opposed to the technical position.

Nevertheless, Capitalist continued to back Wardle. The *Sunday*

Telegraph now threw the challenge open to all its readers, asking them to choose six shares to outperform another six selected by Capitalist for the coming half-year. Slater this time included some bigger companies like GEC and Lombard Banking, into which he was also putting his clients, as we shall see; he only chose two from the Capitalist portfolio: Wardle and Harmo Industries, makers of replacement exhaust systems. It was, of course, about this time that Slater sold his last 15,000 Wardle, on which, whatever his published view of their intrinsic merit, he was showing a gain of some twenty-five per cent. He held, however, some 3,500 Harmo which he had selected for Capitalist in August 1964 at 13s. 5½d.

Slater returned to the question of the technical position: 'I do not worry if a share has already trebled in value in a relatively short period, and I am always far more concerned with its fundamental merits at the time I buy it.' Mentioning two examples, he pointed out that 'profit takers from earlier price levels were matched by new buyers and the share price moved ahead relatively sharply'. He did not, of course, say that he was one of those profit takers and that his readers were the new buyers. His explanation to me for this omission was that it would not have been appropriate to describe in the Capitalist articles each month the details of his own portfolio and neither would any reasonable person expect him to do so. 'The whole essence of my approach to building up an investment portfolio,' Capitalist continued, 'is to select relatively few shares which have very strong upside potential and a minimal downside one. Generally speaking, I then cut losses and let profits run on.' Capitalist speaking, please note, not Slater.

But Capitalist was even then ignoring an important factor affecting fundamentals: the balance of payment crisis that the new Labour government was running into. On 1 October the *Financial Times* Industrial Ordinary Index reached its peak of 377.8, after rising fifty per cent since July 1962. In the last three months of the year it went into sharp reverse, dropping over eleven per cent as the government grappled with the run on sterling.

The high fliers, as always, led the way down. As Robert Heller remarked in his review of the year in the *Observer*, '1964 has been a great year for *losing* money – all you had to do was to invest in a few well-chosen 1963 stars.' It was not just that they stood to be more affected by the measures that would be needed to defend the pound, but also that their share prices had simply been overinflated. For example in the third week of November, Clear Hooters duly announced the excellent results that Capitalist had expected, profit up sixty-one per cent, a dividend even higher than forecast. But the shares dropped 1s. to 6s. 6d. on the news.

On 10 January 1965 Slater announced that he would cease managing the Capitalist portfolio the following month 'owing to pressure of other commitments'. That month there was no new selection for the portfolio, but instead Capitalist discussed 'some recent changes' in his 'investment thinking'. In a bull market, Capitalist wrote:

> I largely ignored technical factors and concentrated on funda-mental analysis. This means for example that I was not con-cerned in any way if a share had already doubled in price in the previous six months provided that its fundamental statistics (and in particular its earnings yield and future growth rate) were well above average. In a bear market I now intend to give consider-ably more attention to the technical position of my share selec-tions as investors always prefer taking profits rather than cutting losses.

Capitalist went on to say that he had added 'two more criteria in the light of recent events': he now also required a reasonable technical position and, in all except outstanding growth stocks, a strong asset position.

As Slater had announced that he was no longer to write the column, this talk of future plans could only purport to refer to his own personal policy. The reality, as we have seen, was that even in the early days of the bull market Slater sold out his personal holdings once he was showing a good profit, ignoring the fundamental merits he was often - rightly - extolling. As the bear market set in he held only one Capitalist share that I have been able to trace - Harmo.

In spite of the deterioration at the end, there was enough fat behind Capitalist's selections to ensure that when Slater wrote his last column on 7 February 1965 he was able to announce that his port-folio had shown an overall rise of 68.9 per cent in the two years he had been running it, against an increase of only 3.6 per cent in the *Financial Times* Actuaries Index. Most of Capitalist's gains had been in 1963 and the first half of 1964: most of the Index's appreciation had been wiped out in the last three months of 1964. Still, it was a very good record for the *Sunday Telegraph*, although they had been worried by the performance at the end; and, as Slater himself admit-ted in the column, no reader could have benefited to the same extent as the Capitalist portfolio. Furthermore Slater, whose identity was re-vealed in the final column, continued to be bullish about the nine shares left in the portfolio. Readers who followed his advice would have seen much of their profit rapidly whittled away, for this is what happened to four of the shares:

Clear Hooters were down to 5s. 10½d. Still, as Slater reported, they had been the 'star turn of my portfolio', making a substantial contri-bution to the overall performance. The shares, Slater advised, 'should be held'.

About this time, Walker made a strange incursion into Clear Hooters, buying 1,000 at 6s. 11¼d. each and reselling them a couple of weeks later. As the price was falling he may have lost money. By June 1965 the price was down to 4s. 3d. and by the end of the year it had fallen forty-nine per cent to 3s. as the firm's profits dived seventy-five per cent.

Musical & Plastic – then at 6s. 6d. – Slater said 'could move to higher ground after the results'. This they did in March 1965, but later in the year disaster struck: profit for the first half of the year slumped and the dividend was cut. By the end of 1965 the shares were down to 2s. 6d., a fall of over sixty-one per cent. Worse was to follow when the 1965 accounts were heavily qualified by the auditors. It was to take Musical & Plastic seven years to get over its troubles.

Wardle were down to 7s. 5½d. but the company, Slater reported, had been a 'star performer' in 1962 and 1963, and he still considered that the earnings and dividend yield were 'attractive for a growth company'. By the end of the year, the price had fallen nearly forty-three per cent to 4s. 3d. There were no 'fundamental' disasters at Wardle: profits in 1964 had again risen substantially and then in 1965 they fell, but only by nine per cent. Slater said that it was this shift from a high compound growth rate to declining growth that led to the fall in price. But this is not the whole story, for the 'technical situation' had also changed as Slater moved on to other things.

Harmo had fallen to 12s. 10½d. by 7 February 1965. Slater expected 'further improvement' and said the shares should 'be held until the results are announced in April'. In the event 1964's profits turned out to have fallen by about ten per cent. By the middle of May, the shares had fallen to about 9s.: the transfer of Slater's 3,500 holding was registered on 10 and 31 May. By the end of the year, Harmo's price had recovered to 10s. 6d. as the firm's profits turned up again. Still, this was a fall of over eighteen per cent since Slater's last column.

On 4 April 1965, Slater wrote an article, now under his own name, reviewing the performance of his second challenge portfolio. His six shares had fallen by an average of 10.9 per cent against a drop of 8.9 per cent in the *Financial Times* Actuaries Index. Slater said he was disappointed, and attributed the result mainly to his failure to take account of the 'technical position' which he thought was more important in a bear market than a bull one. The following month the *Sunday Telegraph* announced the result of the competition: there had been 4,000 entries – more evidence of the following of Slater's column – and the winner's selections had appreciated by an average of 21.81 per cent, while those of 150 other entries had succeeded in rising rather than falling in value. The *Sunday Telegraph* did not say how many readers had beaten their champion.

By the end of 1965, only two of the nine shares left in the Capitalist portfolio had risen in value, Flavel being the best performer with a rise of twenty-three per cent. The average fall was 18.62 per cent, compared with a rise of 2.5 per cent in the *Financial Times* Actuaries Index over the same period. Nevertheless the portfolio was still nearly forty-three per cent above its starting level, against a rise of just over six per cent for the market.

Whether or not the performance would have been better if Slater had continued to manage the portfolio through the bear market is a matter of speculation, although we shall be seeing some of the effects of these falls on Slater's investment clients in later chapters and it is ironic that a number of these clients had been among his most avid followers as Capitalist: for the revelation of Slater's name and new profession in his final column brought him many requests from readers to look after their investments.

In the autumn of 1974, after I had analysed his dealings, I reminded Slater that he had told me in August 1973 that he 'did not speculate short-term' in the Capitalist shares and pointed out that I did not think his investments in Capitalist shares could be called long-term. Slater said that I must remember he was a dealer and that any share he held for as long as three, four or six months was a long-term investment to him. Indeed, he said that any share not bought and sold within a two-week Stock Exchange account could be said to be long-term investment. I said I did not think his definition of long-term was the one in normal use, and he agreed that I could have misunderstood him.

Later, on seeing the text, Slater said that the words 'not short-term' did not necessarily mean 'long-term' in the accepted sense of the word; 'not short-term' to him meant 'not account dealing'. Still later, he added that it also meant 'not a few days'. What Slater had actually written, of course, was that he 'did not speculate short-term' and all this is obvious quibbling. Slater's original answer of August 1973 clearly created a misleading impression of his dealings in Capitalist shares; and it also, of course, later emerged that his claim that 'there were no rules laid down' was not the full picture – although it was Slater himself who gave fuller details. He wrote to me in January 1975: 'Nigel Lawson and I did not enter into a formal written agreement. In general terms, I undertook to Nigel Lawson not to exploit the Capitalist column for personal financial gain, and Nigel Lawson reserved the right to reject any Capitalist recommendations at any time, which I remember he did on one occasion.' (Lawson rejected Klinger because he did not think it met Capitalist's criteria.)

Lawson told me that, while it had clearly been impossible to lay down precise rules for Slater's personal dealings, he had attached considerable importance to Slater's undertaking. Lawson, however, confirmed, as Slater had written to me, that: 'He knew from the outset that I was already a holder of shares in certain companies that Capitalist was likely to recommend and that some similarities be- tween my own personal portfolio and that of Capitalist were to some extent bound to continue.'

Slater went on: 'Indeed, the whole basis of the Capitalist series was that it was putting forward the system and method of a successful and active personal investor. The shares in the Capitalist column were the ones which fulfilled rigorous investment criteria and they were extremely hard to identify. For this reason, I would obviously not have agreed to be precluded from investing in them.' Slater also told me: 'Clearly, I could not invest in any of the shares at exactly the same time as Capitalist, as the article was only once a month. How- ever, I agreed orally with Nigel Lawson that I would not, for example, invest a few days before the articles or sell a few days afterwards.'

Slater, as we have seen, on a number of occasions either bought shortly before tipping, or sold out shortly afterwards. Lawson told me he would have regarded it as wholly contrary to the agreement if Slater had bought a share just before tipping it and then sold out afterwards. This Slater did on at least one occasion – the 4,000 Wardle he bought and resold in the spring of 1963 just after he had started the column. Slater naturally claimed that all his dealings – with the possible exception of the 4,000 Wardle – were in accordance with the agreement with Lawson. That in itself would not, of course, have made them acceptable; but anyway Lawson also told me he would have regarded it as contrary to Slater's undertaking if Slater had sold out his personal holding in a company – a holding he might have held for some months – shortly after recommending that share in his column. This Slater did on a number of occasions, although Lawson and Fleet were unaware that Slater had personally done the opposite of what he was advising the *Sunday Telegraph* readers.

Before early 1977 Slater's only comment on his dealings in Bernard Wardle, the details of which I had put to him on three occasions in writing, was that he could not recollect having sold and that he did not have personal records going back that far. (Later it emerged that Slater had found a schedule of investments of early 1964.) I had also put the details of Slater's dealings in UK Optical to him and he replied, in early 1975:

> I think the example you have given of UK Optical literally proves my point. Capitalist was only dealing once a month and clearly was not going to be as active a dealer as I was personally. There was no capital gains tax at the time. There were no discussions

with Nigel Lawson about the length of time that I would personally hold any of my investments but it was understood that Capitalist was going to be quite an active portfolio and that I was similarly free to pursue an active policy. Indeed, as you can see in the case you have mentioned of UK Optical, Capitalist sold the shares that he bought at the end of October at the end of March the following year. Capitalist therefore only held the share for a five month period and this was the sort of period that would generally apply to my own investments.

It was in reality not at all clear whether Capitalist was going to be more or less active than Slater himself; and the facts of UK Optical were as follows: Capitalist 'bought' on 31 March 1963 shortly after Slater himself had bought 7,000 shares. Slater then bought another 6,000 but resold the same number within a matter of two or three months. Capitalist 'bought' some more on 20 October 1963 and Slater sold out his remaining 7,000 shares; Capitalist 'sold' on 1 March 1964, having held the share for eleven months.

Slater had also overlooked the fact that there was a capital gains tax at the time, the Conservatives having introduced their short-term – or speculative, as they called it – tax on gains realized within six months in 1962. The tax, at top personal rates, naturally reduced the attractions of the quick in-and-out type operation. Not all Slater's dealings were outside the six-month limit, but no doubt he was in a position to reduce his tax bill by offsetting the interest he paid on his borrowings – and any losses he may have realized.

Slater had also written in early 1975 that 'my personal dealings during the time I was Capitalist were done in my own name and clearly I felt I had nothing to hide'; and he has recently added that the position would have been clear to stockbrokers and others, that it would also have quickly become general knowledge that he was abusing his position, that the shares would have risen just before the articles in this event but he says they did not do so, and that his actions, and in particular his letter to Fleet, were those of a man with nothing to hide. I had always thought it likely that Slater had had other investments in addition to those that I had traced in his name, and in early 1977 Slater himself asked me to point out that some shares would have been in banks' nominee names to explain the fact that he had patently not run the profits on the Wardle shares held in his name. Slater clearly did not take any steps to prevent his name getting onto the records, but his column was anonymous, and only the few who knew he was writing it would have recognized his name if they had undertaken the laborious task of searching the registers, in which, anyway, a transaction does not show up until several weeks after the event; and, as I have said, there is no reason to think that the pattern of dealing in shares that I have not been able to trace was different from that which had been described.

Just how much Slater's colleagues in the motor industry knew is hard to assess. Stokes, who was most active in Capitalist shares, told me that he was grateful for any advice Slater or anyone else gave him, but responsibility for his private investments was his own affair. He also said that he only became a client of Slater's after Slater left Leyland, and that: 'I had no knowledge whatsoever of any recommendation that he made to the paper before it was published; in fact I do not think we even knew that he was writing in his spare time for the newspapers until it became general knowledge.' But another colleague, who did not invest, told me he had asked Slater outright if he was writing the column 'for the benefit of his own investments' - 'like the man from the *News of the World*', he explained to me. Slater, he said, replied 'No.'

In October 1974 Slater told me that he had made about £20,000 out of Capitalist shares; my own estimate, based only on dealings in his name, puts it nearer £25,000. His starting stake can be said to have been roughly £14,000, the value of the three Capitalist shares - Wardle, Clear Hooters and Spark - he owned when he started the column, all of which were sold after early tips and therefore provided the means for Slater to reinvest in the later ones, and so on. Thus Slater himself could have increased the value of his own portfolio by perhaps as much as 180 per cent, against Capitalist's sixty-nine per cent. Slater argued that my calculation ignored the effect of gearing on his capital, but that is irrelevant to this comparison: a *Sunday Telegraph* reader might also have borrowed to follow Capitalist - although to make anything approaching sixty-nine per cent he would have had to have sold out the whole portfolio after the last column, which is exactly what Slater told him not to do.

In the spate of self-exposure by City editors that followed the *News of the World* affair in 1973, Sir Gordon Newton, former editor of the *Financial Times*, wrote that the 'general conduct' of financial journalists had 'improved beyond measure in the last 25 years and, notably, within the last ten'. He may have exaggerated, and I myself had a serious and difficult problem with a member of the *Guardian* staff who was suspected of dealing when I was City Editor of that paper in 1972.* Slater alleged that I was looking at the whole question of 'Capitalist' in the light of today's standards; but whether or not conduct has improved, the expected standards are much the same. Lawson required an undertaking that Slater should not exploit the column for personal financial gain: today a more common rule of

---

* It was never established that he had abused his position: Slater claimed he knew all about it and could corroborate it, but he refused to tell me how he knew.

thumb is, as Newton put it, that a journalist 'must behave as an honest man, as one who would not have a qualm if his affairs were investigated by anyone at any time and be made public'; and Patrick Hutber, current financial editor of the *Sunday Telegraph* and a friend and supporter of Slater, suggests that if his staff have any doubt about their own dealings they should ask themselves: 'Would I mind the full facts of this transaction being published to the world?'

I leave readers to judge whether Slater could meet these criteria, bearing in mind that I discovered the facts without any help from him. Slater, of course, was not a full-time professional journalist, as he kept emphasizing to me – although I see no reason why the same ethical standards should not apply to outside contributors. In any event in many ways the most fascinating aspect of the Capitalist story is not that it shows how Slater exploited his position as a part-time journalist, but what it reveals about Slater's personal investment strategy.

In its profile of Slater written shortly after the end of Slater's Capitalist column in May 1965, the *Sunday Express* said:

> Slater claims that there has been very little original in his method of operating. In fact, on the share dealing side, he claims only to have carried out a plan which anyone with intelligence and courage could have applied.
>
> 'The secret', he says, lies in only two factors – 'method and gearing'. By gearing he means obtaining as much credit as possible from banks and brokers to give full scope to your method.
>
> 'What, then,' I asked him, 'was his method?'
>
> 'Basically,' he told me, 'it consists of picking out shares with good records and high earnings yields. Then – and this is important – the will power to cut your losses and run your profits. The natural inclination of many people is to do precisely the opposite.'

But Slater did not let his profits run. He took them early. What Capitalist shows about Slater is that however right he may have been about the 'fundamentals' he himself took more account of the 'technical position'. He was a dealer, not an investor; a market manipulator – but not a speculator, for a speculator takes a risk and Slater did not do that because he could influence the market. Slater was, in fact, following the maxim of many a shrewd financier. You make more money by getting out while the going is good: never mind if you leave some of the profits to others, for you leave them the risks too. When you have a buyer, take your profit, as a realized profit is a lot better than an unrealized one. So much the better if you can generate your own buyers.

8   *A company – and a plan*

Slater's decision to leave Leyland was taken in the autumn of 1963, about six months after he had started the Capitalist column. Slater had already met Walker; at their dinner together they had discussed Slater's dilemma over his future career. Slater, however, did not resign from Leyland to go into business with Walker: that idea only came up later, in the early summer of 1964 when a suitable opportunity presented itself. When Slater resolved to give up his industrial career, his plans for an alternative were somewhat hazy.

Nevertheless the reasons why Slater gave up a successful and secure career are clear enough. In the first place, in his seven years with ACV and Leyland Slater had been promoted very rapidly and, at thirty-four, had reached a level from which little real advancement was possible in the near future. Although Stokes was not formally elevated from sales to managing director of Leyland until 31 October 1963, he had effectively been holding down the senior job, for Sir Henry Spurrier had been ill for some time before he resigned the chairmanship in June 1963 and Black had been deputizing for him. Stokes' responsibilities were further extended when Stanley Markland, a long-serving Leyland engineer who had risen to be deputy chairman, retired early when Black was chosen to succeed Spurrier. So the title of deputy sales director, which Slater had been given earlier in 1963, did not fully reflect the extent of his duties.

The lines of succession were thus already clear by the autumn of 1963. Stokes, at forty-nine, would obviously follow the seventy-year-old Black as executive chairman, and although Slater seemed to be directly in line behind Stokes, if Black's precedent was anything to go by, he could look forward to the prospect of playing second fiddle for some twenty years.

But there were more mundane reasons why Slater left Leyland: the business of selling cars was getting in the way of his stock market operations. As he explained later in a speech:

I found that when Donald Stokes said to me: 'I'd like you to go to

Finland; we are having trouble with our distributor there. Would you get on a plane and go tomorrow?' I'd think to myself: 'Now, I've got an open position in these eight shares, and the results of two of them are coming out in a few days' time.' It was becoming very difficult for me to leave the country, which meant that I could not do justice to my job.

Slater was, as we have seen, beginning to make a lot of money out of his share dealing, and the urge to make more was probably as important a factor as any in his decision to leave Leyland. He was being paid £10,000 a year and was offered a full executive directorship, but this could not compete with the capital he was building up in the stock market or the fees his activities generated. 'They could not have paid me enough to stay,' he told the *Financial Times* in 1968.

There were personal reasons, too. Slater wanted to be his own boss, to work the hours he chose and to take his holidays when he liked. He has always been concerned about his health and had already contracted one nasty illness in the service of the motor industry; and the travelling that inconvenienced his investment activities held no particular fascination for Slater. He preferred life at home.

Slater was, of course, a 'money-maker', not a 'thing-maker'. He was no more interested in cars or buses for their own sake than he was in the products of the companies that Slater Walker later acquired. When he joined the motor industry the companies in it knew there had to be further rationalization; this engendered a new profit consciousness, as the most successful companies would obviously come out on top in the inevitable mergers and takeovers. Slater played a useful role in ensuring that ACV did not become completely subservient to Leyland, and then in building the base that ensured that Leyland would dominate the merger with British Motor Corporation five years later; for when he left, Leyland was more successfully exploiting the industry boom, its profits were rising and it could hardly meet the demand for its products.

Black and Stokes tried hard to make Slater stay and Black chided him for going off to be a 'City slicker'. But the parting was very friendly and Slater maintained close links with Leyland; he was asked by Stokes to advise on the merger with BMC and, on its completion in early 1969, he was invited to join the main British Leyland board as a non-executive director.

In the event, the Stokes regime failed to fulfil its promise and British Leyland, like Slater Walker itself, had to seek the backing of public funds to survive the 1975 crisis; Slater left the board in the restructuring of the group that summer, when Stokes fell from power. What would have happened had Slater duly taken his place as second in command of the British-owned motor giant is a matter for interesting, if academic, speculation.

The most important link that Slater maintained with Leyland was the money he managed for his colleagues at Leyland. Until the autumn of 1963 he had done this informally: he would, according to friends at the time, dispense advice freely to anyone who would listen, from the doorman upwards. Even wives of colleagues were lectured by Slater on the merits of his favourite shares. Slater had not up to that point been charging his colleagues, but with the formation of the Tiger Investment Club the arrangement had already become more businesslike, and on his decision to leave Leyland Slater determined to make his ex-colleagues into 'business associates', as he himself once described them.

Slater initially proposed to levy a fee based on the performance of the funds in his charge. These already totalled £1.5 million at the end of 1963, according to the *Sunday Express* May 1965 profile, but this might not have been quite enough to ensure an adequate income; but, as the *Sunday Express* reported: 'At this point, Leyland appointed me to run their pension fund for them and I thought that, with this backing, I could branch out on my own. So, almost exactly a year ago, I walked, a rather frightened man, out of Leyland.'

The pension fund was then around £4 million, and managing it alone could well have been almost a full-time job. Slater maintains that he even thought of quietly retiring to an office in Staines, near his home, to conduct his own stock market operations and advise his new business associates.

It is difficult to imagine Slater, who, according to contemporaries, was extremely confident and ambitious, either doubting his ability to succeed on his own, or having such humdrum plans. In any event, several weeks before his resignation from Leyland came into effect on 30 April 1964, Slater was already engaged on a grander project: to secure effective control of a company with a Stock Exchange quotation.

It must have been around the end of 1963 that Freddie Cheshire, chairman of a little rubber company, Productofoam Holdings, received an unusual telephone call. Slater introduced himself as the man who wrote 'Capitalist' and said he was interested in Cheshire's company as it was one of the smallest quoted on the London Stock Exchange. He asked if they could meet. Now Cheshire, himself something of a dealer, was not one to turn any proposition away lightly, and as he happened to be free, he suggested lunch that day. It was easily arranged, for Cheshire's office was in Mount Street, just around the corner from Slater in Berkeley Square; they met at a club in Curzon Street.

Over lunch, Slater outlined his plans for Productofoam; Cheshire was impressed but pointed out that Slater must meet his friend Jan Rabl, managing director and largest shareholder of Productofoam. Slater had in fact already been in touch with him on the telephone without explaining his full intentions, but now a meeting was arranged.

The company that Slater had set his sights on was a far cry from Leyland. Productofoam had its origins in a firm called Latex Surgical Products, which had been started in 1941. When Rabl, who had come to England from Czechoslovakia, took over shortly afterwards, he found its principal stock consisted of contraceptives. He pulled out of that market and switched production to household rubber gloves. The firm became one of Boots' main suppliers and also sold to a chemists chain, Barclay & Son, of which Cheshire was a director. (This company was years later itself to come into the Slater orbit – as the vehicle for asset stripper John Bentley.)

Rabl also acquired a manufacturer of foam rubber, Productofoam Rubber (London), and a public quotation was secured at the end of the Fifties, with Cheshire's help, by merging both businesses into an old 'shell' rubber plantation company, which was then renamed Productofoam Holdings. Rabl also expanded by going into laminating, a process by which rubber latex or plastic foam is stuck to cloth for weatherproofing and other purposes, in conjunction with a leather and textile firm called John Loveys, on whose board Cheshire also sat.

When Slater first arrived on the scene, Productofoam's main factory was in Sheep Lane, Hackney, where both the gloves and the rubber foam were made. But its most profitable asset was its fifty per cent interest in the jointly-owned plastic foam laminating business, Sebec Laminations, which had a factory just off the Commercial Road in East London and another on the Moss Industrial Estate, Lowton-St-Mary, Lancashire. Productofoam also owned a small business in Slough, which traded under the Sebec name, engaged in cutting up and distributing foam.

It was not Productofoam's products that interested Slater, but its stock market quotation and its size. In its last financial year before Slater started negotiations, to 30 April 1963, Productofoam had made pre-tax profits of only £12,000 – although Sebec had made rather more substantial profits which were not consolidated in Productofoam's accounts. At the end of 1963 the company was valued on the Stock Exchange at about £234,000, its 986,664 shares being quoted at 4s. 9d. each.

Slater's basic idea was 'to build up Productofoam Holdings Limited to a very much higher level of profitability and thereby all existing and future shareholders should enjoy substantial capital profits'.

To achieve this end Slater recommended three basic steps:

(1) To buy out Loveys' half of Sebec so that this company's expected profits of £60,000 could be fully consolidated. Productofoam's own profits, before any contribution from Sebec's laminating business, were forecast to be a meagre £5,000.

(2) To form a share dealing company which he would manage and whose profits would be injected into Productofoam. This was, of course, somewhat foreign to Productofoam's traditional operations, but Slater pointed out that as the 'capital for this project is relatively negligible, it would not interfere with the present Stock Exchange quotation of Productofoam Holdings which is in any event described as a Holding Company. The share dealing company could be described as a small Finance Company for this purpose'.

(3) Slater would form a company to handle his investment advisory business, which he reckoned was pulling in £9,000 a year in fees which he was charging stockbrokers for financial advice and another £6,000 in profit sharing arrangements with clients, and this company would then be sold to Productofoam for £45,000.

The effect of these proposals would, he estimated, in the short run boost profits to £93,000 of which £9,000 would be provided by his investment advisory business and £19,000 by the dealing company, after allowing for interest on their working capital loans. Such profits he thought would lead to an increase in the share price to 10s. Further ahead, he forecast profits of £185,000, of which investment advice would contribute £30,000 and share dealing £50,000. This would justify a share price of 20s., but by then Productofoam should already have undergone a 'status change' – not to mention transformation – and Slater reckoned the price could be 30s.

Clearly, it was more than Productofoam's status that was going to change. Though the plans made some obeisance towards improving the basic rubber business, it was clear that it was not going to claim a great deal of Slater's energy or attention. The deal had two principal attractions for Slater as he stood on the threshold of his new career. Firstly, by allowing his advisory business to be absorbed into a public company, he no longer had to worry about the surtax bills which his success had begun to bring in. At the same time he would be in a position to influence directly the fundamentals which dictated the market price of the Productofoam shares. The company's results would depend on his skills; skills which he clearly intended should be exercised in the financial rather than the industrial field. And as one of the principal shareholders Slater would be one of the main beneficiaries of a rising share price. Rabl would also benefit to some extent at least, for he was to retain most of his holding; Slater's initial stake was to come from John Loveys, who were happy to part with some of the new Productofoam shares they received in exchange for their fifty per cent of Sebec. Rabl, however, had been ill, and was not averse to gently pulling out of the partnership; he was therefore ready to concede an option on some of his shares.

To run the rubber business itself, Slater proposed that his old colleague Kenneth Meyer should be brought in to help Rabl. Slater and Meyer had remained in touch in the seven years since their first attempt to set up in business; Meyer had made a rather more modest industrial career of his own, and a rather more modest sum of capital.

The first stage of the deal – the purchase of the outstanding half of Sebec from Loveys – was announced on 6 February 1964, but no mention was made of Slater, Meyer or the rest of the plan. The share price was then 5s. 6d.; it proceeded to rise even faster than Slater had foreseen, reaching nearly 12s. by 10 April 1964. That day a circular was dispatched to Productofoam shareholders giving more details of the Sebec acquisition. Loveys' half interest had been bought for the issue of 500,000 new Productofoam shares. Loveys however had wanted to sell most of these, and so it had been arranged that a small merchant bank called P. P. Rodocanachi should 'place privately' 400,000 at 5s. 1½d. each.

Still no mention was made of Slater's and Meyer's role, although they had signed an agreement with Cheshire and Rabl on 26 February. Under this Slater was to acquire 200,000 of the Rodocanachi shares and Meyer 100,000. In addition Slater had an option to buy two blocks of 10,000 shares under Cheshire's control at 6s. and 7s. a share, and Meyer an option to buy 50,000 of Rabl's total holdings of 300,000 shares at 10s. each. Slater and Meyer were to be appointed to the Productofoam board, Slater to look after dealing and Meyer industrial development. Slater was to get a basic salary of £1,000 plus ten per cent of dealing profits over £10,000, with a maximum of £2,500. Meyer was also to get £2,500. Both were provided with company cars costing about £2,000.

The agreement stipulated that Productofoam would in due course announce a rights issue to raise another £100,000 or so of capital.

It also stated that Slater would be forming a company 'for his present investment advisory service business and after holding this for six months to avoid Capital Gains Tax, consideration will be given to selling it to Productofoam Holding', and the following day, 27 February 1964, Slater and Meyer became directors of a new registered company, Dayside Finance, later rechristened Investment Analysis, through which Slater's fees were subsequently channelled.

Slater apparently did not feel that his ambitious plans for Productofoam were going to absorb all his energies, for the agreement with Cheshire and Rabl also included a statement that Slater planned to form a personal share dealing company with a capital of £100,000, half of which he would put up and half of which would be borrowed from brokers. Slater estimated that the profits of this venture would average £50,000 a year. It is not clear why this plan was outlined in the agreement - in any case it was not, apparently, put into effect. But it does make it clear that even at this point Slater's ambitions extended beyond Productofoam and that they were centred upon the Stock Exchange. Slater had hoisted his banner as a financier; 'making things' was in future to be a secondary objective. Two months before he left Leyland - on 30 April 1964, shortly after his thirty-fifth birthday - Slater had determined that his career was henceforth going to be concerned with making money.

In his new role as financier, Slater got much help from Cheshire, who also provided Slater with his first office, a room in Mount Street, which was divided with a partition. Cheshire, who was then fifty-three, had had, by his own admission, something of a controversial career as a financier. Like Bernard Myers, Walker's colleague at Rodwell, he had had a difficult start, having been bankrupted in the Thirties when he was twenty-five. The circumstances were, however, very different from Myers'. The son of a wealthy businessman, Cheshire was well off as a young man; on holiday one year in the South of France a smooth-talking Frenchman persuaded him to invest the proceeds of a successful night at the tables in pepper.

Now pepper is at the best of times a tricky commodity in which to dabble. In the Thirties it was especially dangerous in view of the notorious attempt of one Garabed Bishirgian and others to corner the market. The attempt failed in early 1935 and the inflated pepper price collapsed: among the victims, Cheshire found himself with debts of some £45,000, much of it owed to his father. He walked into the nearest solicitor's for advice, and the lawyer, having ascertained that Cheshire had enough in his pocket to meet his bill, suggested a brisk walk round to Carey Street.

Unlike Myers, Cheshire resolved to pay off all his debts; it took him until 1948, when he reimbursed all his creditors, father included, in full and with interest.

Throughout the Fifties, Cheshire was involved in deals of various kinds, but he always remained on the fringes of the big league, probably because he was the sort of financier to whom the epithet 'ruthless' cannot be applied. In 1964 he had a tally of some forty directorships, including a series of investment trusts, the three most important of which were Marvan, Preferential and Rights & Issues and which he managed from Mount Street with the help of two colleagues: his friend Bertie Hardman and a young accountant about Slater's age called John Robertshaw, who also had ambitions to set up on his own.

In April, the plan for injecting share dealing profits into Productofoam was put into motion, but in a modified form. A new dealing company, Moss Securities, was registered, but its £10,000 capital was put up jointly by Productofoam and Rights & Issues, so that it was a subsidiary of neither. Slater, along with Cheshire, Hardman and Robertshaw were its initial directors; and on 1 May 1964 Slater also became a director of Rights & Issues itself – it was in fact his first appointment to the board of a company quoted on the London Stock Exchange.

Cheshire, with his wide range of acquaintances and contacts in the financial and business world, was just the man to show Slater around. Two introductions were particularly important: John Gommes, the head of Rodocanachi, the bank which 'placed' the Productofoam shares, and Eric Knight, the founder of a successful hire purchase finance house, Lombard Banking. It was these two who provided much of the backing for Slater's grubstake.

Slater's 200,000 Productofoam shares, at 5s. 1½d. each, cost him £51,250: they were already valued at £120,000 in the market when he had to pay for them on 10 April 1964. Slater told me he used £25,000 of the capital he had made in share dealing and borrowed the other half from Lombard. Slater also quickly took up his option on the further 20,000 shares, and for these he would have had to find another £6,500. Slater's total of 220,000 shares and the bulk of Meyer's 100,000 – of which 40,000 were actually taken up by his mother – were all put into the name of Lombard Street Nominees, a Martins Bank Company.

With Meyer's option on Rabl's shares, the two partners controlled about twenty-five per cent of Productofoam's capital. Cheshire and Rabl had also undertaken not to sell any of their remaining 400,000 or so shares without first offering them to Slater and Meyer. Slater soon effectively controlled a larger percentage, for his friends and new business associates were now rapidly buying Productofoam shares in the market. Among those who got shares in the early summer of 1964 were Walker Young (7,000), Stokes (3,000), John Ford, who was then working for Leyland but who later joined Slater (4,000), and Despard at Rose Thomson Young (1,650).

On 1 July 1964, Slater and Meyer were finally appointed to the board of Productofoam, along with another accountant friend of Slater's, Ronald Brand, whom he had met when they were articled at Croydon & King. But by then, as we shall see, Productofoam, originally intended as the main vehicle for Slater's new career, had taken second place to another, more appealing proposition that Cheshire had put his way.

The attractions of Productofoam itself were diminished by a series of misfortunes, and if Slater had had to rely on it alone, his hopes might literally have gone up in smoke. Just a week before Slater and

Meyer were appointed to the Productofoam board, at eight in the evening of Sunday, 21 June 1964, a fire broke out at the foam depot of Productofoam's Sebec subsidiary in Slough. It was caused, Meyer told me, by children who threw a match into a pile of foam stacked outside. As no one was at the factory at the time, the fire took hold and it was four hours before the brigade was able to bring it under control, by which time the premises had been completely destroyed. A week later, most of the workforce were sacked with just a day's pay in lieu of notice, causing considerable local ill-feeling. But as Ronald Brand, who was the manager, told the local newspaper, the *Slough Observer*, since they were hourly paid, the firm was under no obligation to pay them anything. Damage was estimated at £40,000.

The Slough business was one of the group's smaller subsidiaries, according to a letter to shareholders dated 10 July informing them of the fire and also of Slater's and Meyer's appointments; one result, however, would be to delay the accounts.

Just a month later, however, in the early hours of Monday morning 20 July 1964, Productofoam's main factory in Hackney caught fire. It was another bad blaze, watched by a crowd of people on their way to work: substantial damage was caused to the ground and first floors of the factory. The fire was brought under control before the part where the rubber gloves were made was much affected, but the section making foam for car seats was burnt out.

By contrast, the new opportunity that Cheshire brought Slater not only had money-raising potential more in keeping with Slater's ambition, but was not encumbered with any embarrassing industrial operations to go wrong. It was a pure 'shell', called H. Lotery & Co.

9   *A chance too good to miss*

In April 1970 Slater told *Accountancy Age* that he bought control of
H. Lotery & Co. 'after quite a lot of deliberation'. In fact, his takeover of Lotery was much more opportunistic than his move into
Productofoam. That, as we have seen, was a planned operation
initiated by Slater. Lotery was a different matter. It was offered to
Slater by Cheshire after he had joined him in Mount Street in May
1964. Slater was already committed to Productofoam, but he saw at
once that this was too good a chance to miss. To judge from what he
told Lotery's public shareholders and the way he changed his mind,
he had no time to work out detailed concrete plans for Lotery when
he grabbed it. This had to be done afterwards, and the very ease and
success of the acquisition itself led Slater to raise his sights.

In the spring of 1964 Lotery was controlled by a small building
firm called Hawkins Developments, of which Cheshire was a director, and it was classed as a property investment company. Formed in
1870 by an East End tailor, Hyman Lotery, it had, however, been
best known as a manufacturer of uniforms. Its fortunes rose during
and after World War One, when it was a large supplier to customers
like the Army, the post office, London Transport and the nursing
services. It became a public company in the Thirties, and also built
what was then one of the most modern clothing factories in the
country in Gravel Lane on the eastern boundary of the City.

The Lotery business declined after World War Two. The clothing
manufacturing was moved to Wales, then the company's shops and
smaller properties were sold off, as finally was the clothing business
too. All that remained was Beaufort House, as the Gravel Lane
factory was called. The freehold was sold to the Prudential Assurance, but Lotery retained a long lease and the building was converted into a 176,000 square foot office block; in 1964 it had a number
of tenants the largest of which was the Peninsular & Oriental Ship-
ping Line.

Until the start of the Sixties the rump of Lotery remained in the

control of the Lotery family, among whose members there was dis-
agreement over the future of the firm. Harold Lotery, chairman and
grandson of the founder, was happy to sell, but Arthur, his younger
brother, had wanted to keep the family business going. But from
about 1961 onwards, the company was effectively up for sale, and
over the next couple of years, as Arthur Lotery remembers, there
seemed to be a new set of faces at each board meeting, with even that
of Maxwell Joseph, one of Cheshire's many acquaintances, who was
then just beginning to build up his huge hotel business, making a
brief appearance. The outstanding shares became quite a well recognized speculation on the market.

Cheshire had dabbled in them, and in August 1963 he persuaded
Hawkins to buy the forty-eight per cent block that had once
represented the family's major interest and constituted control.
Hawkins decided to run Lotery as a conventional property investment company, and one of the first things they did was to have the
eighty-three-year Beaufort House lease revalued; on 19 September
1963 they were advised that it was worth £1,347,000, or £791,000
more than its book value.

This value was neither startling nor unexpected, and over the
following months the Hawkins men became disillusioned with their
investment. Wanting to buy more properties and to raise money,
they started negotiating a mortgage from the Prudential on the
security of the Beaufort House lease. But the market was unsettled; it
was known that the Conservatives could not postpone the General
Election beyond the autumn of 1964 and, with the polls suggesting
that it would be a close-run thing, there were fears of the effect the
return of a Labour government might have on property values.

In the early summer of 1964 this disillusion came to a head. As
Cheshire had put them into Lotery in the first place, Hawkins now
asked him to get them out. Cheshire felt he should offer to resign in
the face of the criticism – his resignation took effect on 7 June 1964 –
and returned to the Mount Street office, where he told Slater what
happened. It did not take Slater long to decide that he would offer to
buy Hawkins' Lotery shares at 10s. each. So Cheshire put this proposal to Hawkins who, after some hesitation, agreed, and a provi-
sional agreement was signed on 30 June 1964. The price valued
Lotery at £1.5 million – slightly more than the value of its assets on
the new valuation of Beaufort House – but the attraction to Slater lay
in what he thought he could do in the stock market with the capital
he would control if the negotiations for a mortgage could be
concluded.

Some evidence of the speed with which the deal was made is given
by the fact that the Lotery annual report for 1963, which contained
details of the revaluation of Beaufort House and which was dated 3

July 1964, made no mention of the fact that Hawkins had agreed to sell out. But on 16 July, Hawkins issued a brief statement that 'in pursuance of an agreement dated June 30th 1964 which has now become unconditional Hawkins had agreed to sell to Mr J. D. Slater its entire holding of 1,442,415 ordinary shares of 5s. in H. Lotery & Co.' The *Financial Times* reported the announcement in a brief, down-page statement the next day; otherwise, the rebirth of the corporate infant that was subsequently to be christened Slater Walker went unnoticed.

Nevertheless, Slater knew the value of public relations and had hired a consultant he knew, Alexander Thomson, a former City Editor of the *Evening Standard*. So, although the appointment of James Slater, Peter Walker and Kenneth Meyer to the Lotery board on Friday 24 July 1964 went unnoticed, Slater's first task, as the new chairman, of presiding over the annual meeting the following Monday received some coverage.

The *Evening Standard* reported:

> Shareholders who turned up for today's annual meeting of H. Lotery, the small property firm whose main asset is an office building in the City, were given plenty to digest. First, they were told that every one of their former directors had moved out of the boardroom to make room for three newcomers. Then they learned that the company's name was to be changed to Slater Walker & Co.
>
> Behind the moves are Messrs Slater and Walker, of course. Mr Slater is the man who almost accidentally discovered he had quite a knack when it came to handing out investment advice while working for the Leyland lorry giant. Mr Peter Walker is a young Tory MP who has already made a mark for himself in City circles. Together they bought the 48 per cent of Lotery's capital which was owned by Hawkins Developments. Now they intend to increase the emphasis on the investment side of the company's business.

To raise the money to do this, Slater said a mortgage would be raised on Beaufort House. It was not their present intention to sell the lease, he added.

Slater had clearly seen, and seized, the opportunity which Lotery offered; but it was not an opening which he could afford to exploit on his own. It was at this point that he turned to his fellow Under-Forty, Peter Walker, and an alliance was formally concluded. It is one of the strange features of the Slater Walker legend that vagueness surrounds not only the occasion when Slater and Walker first met – most accounts wrongly state that it was at the first Under-Forties dinner and suggest that it took place much earlier than it did

- but also what brought the two together again in the summer of 1964. Slater says that they had been in touch since their first dinner together, which probably took place about a year before negotiations to buy Lotery began. He also told me: 'I should think I saw Peter Walker six or seven times for lunch or dinner during the summer of 1964 and before Slater Walker was formed.'

It has been said that the suggestion that brought the two together was that they should combine Slater's investment advisory business with Walker's insurance broking firm to form a financial services group. This proposal would have had considerable logic to commend it; but logic, other than as a useful aid to the 'selling' of a proposition, was not what primarily interested Slater; and certainly that kind of long-term planning was not uppermost in his mind in the summer of 1964. His most pressing need was money – £720,000 to be precise – to pay for the Lotery shares he had agreed to buy from Hawkins. To raise it Slater had to mobilize all the connections he could muster.

As for Walker, he was still looking for new business opportunities. He remained a non-executive director of Rodwell and Unicorn, but these only took a small amount of his time; his considerable energy was principally devoted to building up his insurance broking business, where he could work in the morning before going to the House of Commons. Walker was, however, anxious to get more direct experience of industry – it was Slater's ideas on industrial efficiency that attracted him, he says – and in 1963 he had been appointed to the board of the Adwest Group, an engineering firm of which Thomas Walmsley, the Slaughter & May solicitor, was a director. Then in early 1964, just before he teamed up with Slater, Walker joined a syndicate formed to take control of and develop a shell company called E. C. (Holdings).

The syndicate was headed by a Canadian financier named Douglas Bayle, whom Walker knew because Walker Moate had handled the insurance of Bayle's West London group of garages. Bayle had in fact acquired Bill Turner's Grange Group, which had once been such an important part of the Walker Moate partnership's plans,* but by 1964 he had resold all his garages. Through E.C., however, he planned to go back into the motor business, hoping to buy a big coach company. This, Walker says, is why he came in, for he was developing an interest in transport at the time.

E.C. (Holdings) had once owned the Earls Court exhibition hall – hence its name – but had sold it and retained some £630,000 of free and easily realizable assets together with its stock market quotation. Bayle's syndicate bought a block of 1,200,000 E.C. shares, sixty-seven per cent of the capital, at 7s. 8d. each, of which Walker's

* See Chapter 2.

quota was 50,000 at a cost of over £19,000. The appointment of Bayle, Walker and a third member to the E.C. board was reported in the *Financial Times* on 15 May 1964.

It is not clear whether Walker and Slater had already discussed specific plans at this point; in any event Bayle's plans, although in some respects similar, were less ambitious than Slater's. He formed a share dealing subsidiary for E.C. called Avasvilla Properties, to whose board Walker was appointed on 10 July, and made an abortive bid for a little company making pillows and cushions. Bayle anyway had other preoccupations at this time, for he was closely involved with John Bloom, the flamboyant tycoon whose affairs dominated the financial news in the summer of 1964 and whose washing machine company, Rolls Razor, collapsed spectacularly on 17 July. Bayle had been arranging finance for Rolls Razor's associated investment company English & Overseas, and on the collapse of the washing machine business he engaged in lengthy and ultimately successful negotiations to save the other firm.*

On the political front Walker's appointment as PPS to Selwyn Lloyd, Leader of the House, in the autumn of 1963 had projected him into a position of close contact with the leaders of his party as the Conservatives searched for a new image during Sir Alec Douglas-Home's interregnum. He continued to beat the drum of the property-owning democracy/meritocracy, which was to become one of the main themes of the New Tory Philosophy: with Ian Gilmour, PPS to the Minister of Science, he wrote, in the summer of 1964, a pamphlet called 'Ownership, Opportunity, Obligation', in which they made proposals for social reform and advocated measures to ease and extend share and house purchase. For himself and his mother and father, he bought a sixteenth-century half-timbered house, the Old Parsonage, fully modernized and standing in two acres of garden, in Warndon, Worcestershire, to replace the Droitwich flat.

By the summer of 1964, therefore, Peter Walker could bring to a partnership with Slater not only valuable contacts in the City, and a considerable experience of the intricacies of raising money, but also a reputation as a thrusting young politician whose name would add lustre to the board of Slater's latest brainchild. For Walker's part, he was no doubt not averse to having his name coupled with Slater's in

---

* The collapse of Rolls Razor was of considerable concern to another of Walker's interests – the Unicorn group. At du Cann's initial instigation the trusts were heavily invested in Bloom's companies. Du Cann, of course, had been in the government for two years at the time of the liquidation; he had been moved from the Treasury and was now Minister of State under Heath, the 'Secretary of State for Industry, Trade and Regional Development and President of the Board of Trade'. Heath ordered an official inquiry into Rolls Razor on 23 July. Walker was the registered holder of 1,000 Rolls Razor shares at the time it went under.

the title of the new venture: an image of a go-ahead entrepreneur assorted well with the political gospel that he preached.

Slater, Walker and Meyer between them were still not nearly wealthy enough to put up personally the £720,000 needed to pay for Hawkins' Lotery shares, and the bulk of the money had to be raised either by borrowing or by persuading others to take the shares. This is where Walker's contacts came in useful to supplement those that Slater had built up for himself through the Leyland connection and Cheshire's introductions.

It has not been possible to work out an exact breakdown of where Hawkins' 1,442,415 Lotery shares, sold for 10s. each, went, for most of them were transferred into nominee names. Slater has confirmed however, that he took 700,000, for which he paid £25,000 of his own money – the remainder of the £50,000 he had made dealing on the stock market – and borrowed the £325,000 balance. 'That's called gearing in a very substantial way!' he remarked to *Accountancy Age*: he says he borrowed 'from several diverse sources some of which were Rodocanachi, Lazards and Lombard Banking'. Walker had introduced him to Lazards, while the Rodocanachi loan was eased by a guarantee arranged by Cheshire.

One hundred thousand shares from the Hawkins' block were put into Walker's name, of which 20,000 were transferred in the coming weeks to friends and relations, including his father and mother. The remaining 80,000 were switched into Acons Nominees, a Westminster Bank company, but Walker told me that 'as far as I can trace in the records available to me from the beginning I personally held in my own name and for my own interests 50,000 shares', and it is not clear who were the beneficial owners of the rest.

The share register shows that Walker Moate, the share dealing subsidiary of Walker Young, took up 52,415 which it also redistributed to associates like Despard, Roger Moate, Sefton Myers and the Rodwell Group. Walker Young itself acquired 40,000 shares which it held and which became a most remunerative investment.

Of the remaining 550,000 shares, about 175,000 went to Meyer, while the rest would appear to have been 'placed', some only temporarily, with or by Rodocanachi, Lombard and Lazards.

The sale of the Hawkins' block naturally did not go through the stock market in the ordinary way. But Slater quickly started buying Lotery shares for his clients and from the beginning of July through to the autumn of 1964 shares were distributed among clients, friends and associates. As this money chased the shares and as market rumours elaborated the brief announcements, the price of Lotery began to soar. From 10s. 7½d. on 30 June, the date of the initial agreement, it jumped to 14s. 6d. by the Hawkins' announcement on 16 July. On Monday 27 July, the day of the annual meeting, it was marked up to 16s. 6d., and by that Wednesday it had reached 17s. 6d.

That day Slater received some more publicity in the *Evening Standard*:

> At 35 Mr Slater has rapidly built up a reputation as a shrewd detector of choice investment possibilities and he now handles investments totalling at least £6,000,000. Last year, he claims, the value of his clients' portfolios jumped up 45%. Slater himself takes 10% of any capital appreciation for his management and advice. But if he fails to outstrip the FT Index by a 'substantial margin' his charge is nil. He refuses to handle accounts worth less than £5,000. He honestly admits that it is short-term capital gains – outside the six months tax period – that he is after. 'I'm just not interested in long-term investments,' he says.

The article brought Slater more new clients, including a Dr William Stott from Brighton, who gave Slater the minimum £5,000 to manage and whose investments we shall follow in some detail. Slater also later had to alter his fee structure, for he discovered that the Board of Trade did not approve of 'performance' charges linked to appreciation. Such fees are thought to encourage speculation and are effectively prohibited under the detailed regulations covering dealing in securities issued under the Prevention of Fraud (Investments) Act: anyone who enters into an agreement with another the purpose of which is 'to secure a profit to any of the parties from the yield of securities or by reference to fluctuations in the value of securities' must secure a dealer's licence from the Department, and anyone who wanted to charge a performance fee would not normally succeed. Investment Analysis did not get such a licence until July 1965, although its activities up to that point would appear to have fallen within the definition of dealing. Slater says that at this time he knew little about City practices and the regulations governing dealing in securities, and he also told me that he did not remember ever, in fact, charging on performance, but said he had contemplated doing so before he heard about the attitude of the Board of Trade. But, as related in the last chapter, he had estimated in early 1964 that his income from profit-sharing arrangements was running at £6,000 a year. I have not been able to establish exactly when Slater switched to a flat rate charge.

At the rate Slater's investment advisory business was growing he could no longer manage it alone. Slater had originally planned to make John Robertshaw, Cheshire's colleague, another partner in Slater Walker, but the two drifted apart as it became clear that their respective attitudes were very different. Robertshaw was not adventurous enough for Slater and was content to move more slowly. For his part Robertshaw was becoming alarmed at some of Slater's stock market tactics. But it was Slater who took the initiative in proposing the break, paying Robertshaw £5,000 for an option he had on a share of the business.

Slater advertised for an assistant and selected Simon Pendock, whose optimistic attitude to share prices fitted in better with his methods. Jonathan Aitken later wrote of Pendock that he 'talks about share-buying as though it was an activity mid-way between a religious experience and the seduction of a beautiful woman'.* Pendock, a thirty-two-year-old accountant, had given up his job with a finance group, the Minister Trust; he had some money of his own and ran a private investment company. He brought with him from Minister a market technician, Eric Farrell.

Nevertheless, the initial structuring of Slater Walker was essentially carried out by Slater single-handedly. Walker was not completely 'non-executive' and he and Slater consulted frequently on the telephone – it became their habit to talk regularly in the early morning – but the late summer and autumn of 1964 was a busy political time with the run-up to the General Election of 20 October. Meyer had been delegated to look after Productofoam and the only other director, appointed on 20 August 1964 and strictly non-executive, was Walker's solicitor friend Thomas Walmsley.

Slater's new executives had to be 'incentivized' and Slater lost no time in reorganizing the company's capital to give them the opportunity of acquiring shares. On 28 August 1964 he sent his new shareholders a two-page letter which proposed the granting of stock options, at not less than ten per cent over the market price and exercisable after between three and ten years' service up to a maximum of five per cent of the capital. Slater also announced that the arrangements to mortgage Beaufort House for £850,000 had been completed, that £500,000 had been paid over already and that the remainder would be available in three months. 'With the moneys thus made available your Directors consider that they at present have sufficient resources to enable them to carry out their investment programme in accordance with their policy statement made on 27th July last,' said Slater, without amplifying what the policy was.

Within two months, however, Slater's plans had acquired yet another dimension, and far from content with his £850,000, he had set out to raise another £1.5 million: this time it was to be raised not on Slater's claim to be a stock market wizard but on the strength of his reputation as an expert industrial manager. He was in fact planning to ask City institutions and other investors to put up cash so that he could buy large enough stakes in companies to enable him to

* *Evening Standard*, 1 July 1968.

demand that their managements listen to his advice on how they could be more profitably developed 'either by the elimination of unprofitable aspects or by applying resources more efficiently or towards more easily exploitable opportunities'.

The outline of the new plan and of the emerging structure of Slater Walker was first revealed in a statement issued by Slater to the press at the end of October 1964. First, as the *Daily Telegraph* and the *Financial Times* reported, he had incorporated his investment advisory business as 'Investment Analysis'; this was in fact the new name for Dayside Finance, the company he had formed the previous February, and which he had originally planned to sell to Productofoam under this agreement with Rabl and Cheshire. All Slater's fees from his clients had been channelled through the company since April: it was now 'injected' free into Slater Walker and Walker and Pendock joined Slater and Meyer on the board.

Slater also revealed how the mortgage money had already been spent: about half, according to the *Daily Telegraph*, had been invested in 'special situations' and the balance in 'general quoted equities'.

The most important of the special situations was Productofoam, in which Slater Walker itself had now bought 467,000 shares. These were acquired from Cheshire's investment trusts, John Loveys and from Rabl, who had decided to pull out and hand his company completely over to Slater and Meyer, his last job being to sell off some of the plant salvaged from the Hackney fire. Slater, of course, still personally owned 220,000 Productofoam shares and Meyer and his mother now had 130,000, Meyer having exercised his 10s. option over 30,000 of Rabl's shares.

Slater Walker's next most important 'special situation' was George Wilson Gas Meters, a Coventry firm which, in addition to meters, made gas heaters and burners and was another company to benefit from the revival in the popularity of gas. Among Slater Walker's general equities the *Telegraph* listed GEC – Slater was an early admirer of the techniques of its managing director Arnold Weinstock – and a little electronics company named Astaron-Bird, of which we will be hearing more.

Slater Walker had made these investments through three dealing companies which Slater had quickly activated. Two were old subsidiaries of Lotery, one called Clamond Securities and the other renamed Status Change Investments after Slater's famous maxim. The third, registered as Arrowfold Investments, was later somewhat inappropriately rechristened SW Industrial Holdings. It was, however, a dealing company and not to be confused with Slater Walker Industrial Group. The Slater Walker Industrial Group, or SWIG, was to be the instrument through which Slater Walker implemented its new policy of using large shareholdings to influence the management of industrial companies to adopt Slater's gospel of efficiency. It was also the receptacle into which investors were to be invited to pour large amounts of cash.

Slater says that the logic of creating a separate company for the industrial interests was that they wanted, at that stage, to keep Slater Walker itself a purely financial operation. It was however also much simpler and quicker to issue backers with shares in a new private company than to go through the process of arranging an issue of further Slater Walker shares.

There seemed no shortage of people willing to put up money to back SWIG, even though the investment climate had sharply deteriorated in the balance of payments crisis that followed the Conservative defeat in the General Election. Slater was greatly helped, when going round the City, by the fluent and confident exposition of his plans, by the reputation that he had made for himself at Leyland and the good words that Lord Black was prepared to put in for him. The Leyland connection, for instance, secured him an introduction to another first-line City merchant bank, Schroders; and after Robertshaw had introduced him to Angus Ogilvy, Black spoke to Ogilvy's boss, the financier Harley Drayton. Lord Cowdray's Whitehall Trust also invested in SWIG.

It was Walker, however, who gave Slater one of his most important introductions. His political colleague Ian Gilmour was the son of Sir John Gilmour, then a senior partner in a big stockbroking firm, Joseph Sebag; and Slater quickly hit it off with David Eastham, Sebag's partner responsible for promoting new companies. Eastham introduced Slater to the man who gave Slater his biggest backing: Basil Samuel of the property group Great Portland Estates. Great Portland subscribed £200,000 of the £1.5 million Slater and Walker raised for SWIG.

SWIG was a remarkable achievement, for the list of backers willing to put up substantial sums included the names of impeccable banks like Schroders, Lazards and Drayton's 117 Old Broad Street Group. Most of them subscribed cash, but the investment trusts associated with Cheshire, with whom, of course, Slater was still closely in touch, got their stakes in exchange for quoted securities. A few close associates were also allowed to invest: Black and Stokes each put up £5,000 and Walker Young £10,000. Two other investors in SWIG deserve a special mention – and another short digression from the narrative: a one-time knacker from Hull called George Wiles and a second-line City merchant bank, Dawnay Day.

George Wiles had made a fortune when Dawnay Day had floated his Wiles Group on the stock market in March 1964. The one-time animal byproducts and fertilizer business had already diversified, and in August 1964 it acquired two important North of England motor distributors, Oswald Tillotson, run by a young man called James Hanson, and Commercial Vehicles, which had been built up by Jack Brignall. Slater knew them both from his motor industry days, and Hanson was, a year later, to succeed Wiles as chairman of the Wiles Group, which he turned into an operation that was part associate, part rival of Slater Walker itself. But a more immediate result of the association was that Slater acquired some more wealthy investment clients: Jack Brignall and George Wiles' brother Leonard signed up for advice, while George himself became even more closely involved with Slater, for together they formed a private finance company and an investment trust; it was through the latter that George Wiles subscribed £300,000 towards SWIG.

Through Wiles, Dawnay Day came to hear of Slater's plans; but their opportunity to subscribe for shares in SWIG arose as a result of the affairs of E.C. Holdings, for Walker's colleague there, Douglas Bayle, was coincidentally also a client of the bank. It had been suggested that E.C. itself should take up a slice of SWIG, but the Stock Exchange authorities would not allow it, as they felt that SWIG was an unknown quantity and they do not usually allow 'shell' public companies like E.C. to invest too large a part of their resources in such projects. Instead Dawnay Day took up the SWIG shares earmarked for E.C., while Walker resigned from E.C. at the end of 1964 'owing to his increasing commitments' – just before it finally did buy into the coach business – and sold his shares at about 1s. profit each.

Over the year end of 1964 the investments that Slater had made with the £850,000 Beaufort House mortgage loan were switched out of Slater Walker itself into SWIG in exchange for one million shares, or forty per cent, of the new company. The fact that the august institutions which Slater had persuaded to invest in SWIG were prepared to accept this arrangement is a tribute to Slater's salesmanship. For Slater Walker's stake in SWIG depended on the market values of these investments at the end of 1964, most of which were very much higher than when Slater Walker had first bought them. Productofoam shares, for example, were roughly $2\frac{1}{2}$ times higher than they had been barely nine months before. It was remarkable, anyway, that leading City merchant banks should have accepted that this versatile but minute rubber company should become SWIG's largest investment, representing more than one fifth of its total assets. Productofoam was to come close to bringing the whole structure crashing down, and we must therefore see what had been happening to SWIG's rickety foundation, and to Slater's personal share stake in it.

The first hard news that the Productofoam shareholders received from their new management was in a letter which Slater, as chairman, sent them on 24 November 1964. This announced that they had bought, for £70,000 cash, Foam Textile Laminators, another company engaged in the process of adding a layer of foam to materials to make weatherproof or furnishing fabrics. Slater continued with some details of the reorganization:

> As a result of the reassessment of the activities of two of the wholly owned subsidiaries of your Company namely Producto-foam Rubber Company (London) Limited and Sebec Limited in July 1964 it was decided to discontinue most of the manufacturing side of both these Companies. The moulds and goodwill of Productofoam Rubber Company (London) Limited are therefore being sold. The foam conversion business of Sebec Limited has been sold for a nominal consideration and arrangements are being made for the disposal of that Company's leasehold factories at Slough.

These two companies, which had not been doing well, were those whose premises had been partly destroyed by fire, and Slater went on to say that for this reason, and because of the reorganization, the accounting period had been extended beyond 30 April to cover a seventeen-month period up to 30 September 1964. During this period, and for the same reasons, he said, there had been little change in the rate of profitability; but he forecast a 'very substantial' improvement for the coming year.

Slater, characteristically, did not personally wait to see his predictions fulfilled. He had told shareholders in his letter that Slater Walker now owned 551,500 shares in Productofoam, an increase of 84,500 on the end-October figure. What neither Productofoam nor Slater Walker shareholders were told was that Slater and Meyer had themselves sold nearly all these shares to Slater Walker from their personal holdings. For in the closing months of 1964 the whole of the Lombard Street Nominee holding of 316,000 shares, representing Slater's and Meyer's initial stake in Productofoam acquired at 5s. 1½d. a share the previous April, was disposed of: the bulk were sold to investment clients and other associates, while the records suggest that 84,000 went to Slater Walker itself.

I asked Slater at what price he and Meyer had sold their Productofoam shares. He told me that of his 220,000 shares, 182,000 had been sold at 13s. 5¼d., 28,000 at 13s. 4d. and 10,000 at 13s. 7d. Meyer, he said, had sold at 14s. each. (In addition to his shares held through Lombard Street Nominees, Meyer had acquired another 38,000 in his own name.) Slater continued:

> We are unable to say definitely whether or not these shares were sold to investment clients as you suggest, although this is a possibility. We are able to confirm that 80,000 shares were acquired

by Slater Walker. As the purchase price was 14s. they were not part of my holding, but we assumed that they were Kenneth Meyer's although we are unable to positively substantiate this as a fact.

But Meyer – and his mother – had only 96,000 Productofoam shares in Lombard Street Nominees, and as 40,000 of these were now transferred back into Mrs Meyer's name, at least 24,000 (or 28,000) of the 80,000 (or 84,000) acquired by Slater Walker must, it would seem, have come from Slater's personal holdings. In any case he was getting out in the most unorthodox way and at a remarkable profit. His stake in Productofoam had cost £57,750; now, little more than six months later, he had resold for £147,739 11s. 8d. – a profit of nearly £90,000.

Among those to get shares from Lombard Street Nominees were Slater's mother (6,000), Stokes (7,000 to add to 3,000 he already had), Lady Stokes (1,250), Black (3,000), Lady Spurrier (3,600) and John Brignall and his wife (10,000). Slater had been investing client money heavily in Productofoam in the last half of 1964; among associates who bought were Walker Moate (14,500 shares) and Avasvilla Properties (2,000). Two more interesting shareholders were Eric Knight, head of Lombard Banking, of which Slater was a substantial creditor, and Iain Macleod, who had become an executive director of Lombard on his refusal to serve in Home's government; they each acquired 1,000 shares. Slater also spent £358 of Dr Stott's £5,000 on 500 Productofoam shares. Under this buying pressure the share price had reached the 14s. level in November. It had thus already far outstripped Slater's projections earlier in the year when he had forecast that the price might reach 10s. on profits of £93,000.

Slater later told me that he sold his Productofoam shares at this point in order to degear, and that he was concentrating his main personal investment in Slater Walker Securities – which was about to sell its own stake in Productofoam to SWIG – and that his interest in its welfare thus continued through his indirect holding. He said he would have known that his shares were placed with clients and would have asked for some to be allocated to his mother. He said it was 'inconceivable' that he would have committed any of her 'slender resources' to Productofoam shares unless he thought them a very good investment.

I asked Slater why he did not tell his clients and other shareholders in Productofoam that he was selling his stake, for obviously they might have taken a different view of the investment if they had known. He replied that he was not in touch with every client, but those with whom he was in touch on a personal basis would have been

told and so would his mother. His recollection was that shareholders
of Productofoam were 'advised at the appropriate time'.

It was not possible to check the details of the financial arrangements between Slater and his mother; but Stokes, a client with whom
Slater was in touch, had previously told me that he knew of no
occasion when he had been sold shares from Slater's personal
holding; and the appropriate time to tell Productofoam shareholders
would have been in the circulars issued during this period. In fact
they were not told then, or at any other time.

Slater's explanation for the sale of his shares to his clients in this
manner was that he knew little about City practices at this time. He
pointed out, however, that clients wanted to participate in the companies in which Slater Walker itself was interested, some of which, as
we shall see, were profitable investments for them. But Productofoam was not: the shares were only once again briefly to see such high
levels. Slater, an optimist, at least as far as the investments of others
were concerned, no doubt genuinely believed he would be able to
keep Productofoam's profits and share price rising; but the fact is
that he was once again taking advantage of the buyers he controlled
to create a favourable situation for his own profitable exit. This was
more serious than a newspaper tipster exploiting his job: Slater was
now in the fiduciary relationship of a fee-taking adviser and also of a
director of public companies.

The Productofoam results for the seventeen months to 30 September 1964, released in December, showed that the company had only
made £38,898 even with the inclusion of eight months' trading
profits from Sebec Laminations, control of which had been acquired
in early 1964 in the deal which gave Slater his first stake in Productofoam; and even though the burnt-out factories had been insured,
additional capital losses had to be charged to reserves on that
account.

In his first annual statement to shareholders of a public company,
Slater told the Productofoam shareholders that 'we have cut out all
activities which made insufficient contribution to the Company's
profitability, and we have developed those activities which have a
good profit potential'. Apart from the two businesses that had burnt
down, the Sebec Commercial Road factory had been closed and the
business moved to the newly-acquired Foam Textile Laminators.
Slater said it was not easy to make an accurate profit forecast for the
coming year, 'particularly bearing in mind the general industrial
outlook'. Still, he ventured the opinion that Productofoam would
make at least £100,000 profit in the coming year, made up of 'not less
than £65,000 on laminating and £35,000 on rubber glove manufacturing', which had been considerably developed with a new machine
to make lined gloves. The profits estimate, Slater added, was 'essen-

tially a base-line as we intend in the years to come to expand substantially our business both by internal development in our existing and allied lines and by further acquisition. We are engaged in growth industries and with a strong management team we look forward to the future with considerable confidence'.

Slater made no mention of what was to be Productofoam's principal growth industry, share dealing. In fact Moss Securities had only made £83 since its formation at the end of September 1964; but the following year its role was to be crucial, as we shall see.

Slater wanted more money for Productofoam too, and with his annual report he sent shareholders a letter explaining that he proposed to raise some £150,000 by a rights issue. He offered shareholders one new share for every five that they owned for 10s., an attractive enough price as the shares were then standing at about 12s. 6d. in the market. Slater repeated the £100,000 profit forecast, although this time he qualified it slightly by saying:

> In making this forecast however you will appreciate that your Directors while aware of the present general uncertain business climate are quite unable to quantify its possible effects, if any, on the potential profitability of your Company and have therefore relied in making their forecast on the current trends as demonstrated by the figures available to them.

Slater told shareholders that Slater Walker intended to take up its rights – although by the time the new shares were issued the investment had been switched to swig, which had to fork out £58,150 for an extra 116,300 Productofoam shares. The brokers Joseph Sebag underwrote the rest of the issue; that is to say, for a fee, they agreed to find buyers at 10s. for any new rights shares that could not be sold to existing shareholders or on the market at that price. But there was not much chance of the issue flopping with so many shares under Slater's control: and also a new big buyer emerged, the Community Unit Trust, one of the Unicorn group of which Walker was a director. It acquired 20,569 shares by buying rights shares and went on to build up a holding of 47,000. (When I asked Walker about this, he replied: 'I certainly would not have advised Community Unit Trust to purchase any shares closely linked with my own activities.')

Slater's financial agility, at least, throughout the closing months of 1964 demands admiration. But he still had two major problems to solve: firm hands had to be found for the Lotery/Slater Walker shares that had only been temporarily placed the previous summer; and Slater's own enormous borrowings had to be further reduced.

They were in fact dealt with simultaneously. Great Portland Estates, as well as backing swig, decided first to buy 40,000 and then yet a further 200,000 shares in Slater Walker itself. This not only solved the problem of the 'floating' shares, but allowed Slater to realize further capital, for, as he told shareholders in a letter dated 3 February 1965: 'To make up the number of shares required by Great Portland Estates Limited I was obliged, in order that the deal could go through, to sell to them 150,000 of my personal holding shares in your Company but none of your other Directors were involved.'* Basil Samuel and a colleague then joined the Slater Walker board.

Slater told me he sold the 150,000 to Great Portland at 13s. 3d. each – a total of £99,375. The Slater Walker share price had fallen sharply with the stock market, and this was only a little below the level ruling throughout most of December 1964 and early January 1965.

The drop in the shares created problems for Slater. 'They fell back to 13s. 6d. and were still going down,' he told the *Sunday Express* in 1969. 'I was frightened. Imagine my position – faced with interest charges of £30,000 a year and no income to pay them with. Even though the shares were worth more than 10s. I would have been in-solvent if they had fallen much below that.' But the price had never-theless 'shot up by 46 per cent this year, on hope', as Heller com-mented in the *Observer*, and it began to move up again in early 1965. At this time Slater sold another 100,000 at, he told me, 15s. each, to Securities Agency Nominees, a company in Drayton's 117 Old Broad Street Securities Group. From this sale Slater realized another £75,000 and a profit of £25,000. Finally Dawnay Day insis-ted on having shares in Slater Walker as well as swig, for they felt that the company likely to do best was the one in which Slater had the greatest personal interest. Slater duly sold them 75,000 from his own holding in March 1965 at 15s. 6d. each to raise another £58,125, of which £20,625 was gain.

So including the sale of his Productofoam shares, within six months Slater had raised a total of £354,000 – enough to pay off at least the capital element of his borrowings – and the total gain of £134,000 meant that the 375,000 Slater Walker shares he was left with had effectively only cost him £53,500, although their market value, at 15s. each, was over £280,000.

The Productofoam issue was not the last money that Slater was to raise around the turn of the year 1964/5: on 15 January 1965 it was announced that P & O, the main tenant, had bought the lease on Beaufort House for £1,850,000 – more than £500,000 over its book value.

Slater has in retrospect been credited with shrewd foresight in realizing, when he offered 10s. a share for Lotery, that the Beaufort

---

* Slater's last sentence creates a small mystery, for 25,000 of the 80,000 shares trans-ferred out of Walker's name into Acons Nominees were also sold to Great Portland; but Walker says he only owned 50,000 from the start.

House lease was undervalued: indeed his 'asset spotting' talent has been traced back to this deal. Lotery was an asset situation, but Slater told me that at the time he bought control he did not realize that the lease would be so valuable.

With this deal accomplished Slater was ready to announce his grand strategy to the world at large, and on 3 February 1965 he dispatched a 2,500-word letter to the shareholders of Slater Walker and the press. He first outlined the developments of the six months since he had taken control, the most important of which was the sale of Beaufort House following the 'unsolicited' offer from P & O. The net proceeds, after repayment of the mortgage, were £900,000, of which £155,500 would be used to repay the company's other borrowings. The balance would 'be applied progressively over the course of the next 12 months in the several branches of your Company's business' as follows:

(a) Property. Slater said that the few remaining properties from the old Lotery portfolio, which had a book value of just over £100,000, would be kept.

(b) Investment. Slater Walker planned to use £250,000 of the Beaufort House surplus to form an investment trust. Unlike SWIG, this would not aim to take control of companies. Slater pointed out that the return from this development could not be assessed until the details of taxation changes proposed by the Labour government were known. (In the event the trust was never formed because of the effect of new taxes introduced in the 1965 Budget.)

(c) Trading. Two hundred thousand pounds of the group's resources would be devoted to trading in securities through the share dealing companies, Clamond, Status Change Investments and SW Industrial Holdings. Slater expected to make £20,000 a year in short-term gains.

(d) Investment Management. Slater told shareholders that he had transferred his advisory business, Investment Analysis – 'an entirely new business commenced in April 1964' – to Slater Walker for the nominal sum of £100. It was expected to make a profit of £75,000, the largest contribution to Slater Walker's total forecast profits of £165,000 for 1965.

(e) Management Services. A separate company was to be formed to collect fees from subsidiary and associated companies for services provided by the executives of the main company. Its purpose was purely administrative and it was not intended to add to the profitability of the group.

(f) Industrial Group. Slater described the formation and purpose of SWIG and named its two principal investments, namely Productofoam and George Wilson Gas Meters, Slater's other main 'special situation'; Slater and Meyer had joined the Wilson board in November 1964 and SWIG's stake was now up to 151,500 shares. SWIG's other investments were not named, nor were two private companies in which it had invested about £50,000. These were Young Chemical Engineers, a firm which Slater and Meyer had helped start just a few weeks before, and which was to specialize in water purification; and Kintslaid Engineering, which had also just been formed, with the backing of Walker's friend Sefton Myers, to develop a knitting machine for the textile industry.

(g) General. Slater reckoned that there would still be some £300,000 left from the surplus on Beaufort House, and this would be 'used for the development of any branch of your Company's business whose requirements exceed those for which your Directors have budgeted'.

This orderly plan represents a considerable intellectual feat. For Slater was, essentially, rationalizing into apparent coherence the result of a series of unplanned, opportunistic ventures. It is worth noting that very little remained of the equally orderly plan Slater had outlined over a year before in the agreement by which he acquired his original Productofoam holding. In retrospect it is clear that the structure Slater now described was dictated not by a carefully formed vision of the way a financial company ought to be designed, but simply by the best immediate use that Slater thought he could make of the opportunities that came his way.

Slater Walker was thus not a great discovery, as it has been portrayed in the legend. But as a result of its opportunistic origins it was a new sort of corporate animal. It combined within itself functions which had previously been shared by professions as diverse as the investment adviser and the management consultant. This combination of functions would have tried the most punctilious of men. At first glance, Slater's plan suggests that the enterprises he lists under his seven headings were each to be independent and autonomous. But it is clear that, in Slater's own mind, they were interwoven and mutually supporting.

With benefit of hindsight it is easy to see just how open to abuse Slater's elegant structure was. The larger part of his company's profit was to be derived from investment advice to clients whose combined resources represented a significant sum of money in stock market terms, especially in relation to the size of many of the companies selected for investment. Simultaneously, another corporate limb was to find companies deemed to be in need of management help and to press that help upon them by acquiring effectively controlling shareholdings – yet, on its chairman's own admission, he was not interested in 'long-term' investment. Add to this combination a plethora of share dealing companies and a stated interest in 'special situations', and it is not hard to see the danger that existed.

10 *Other people's money*

It was Clement Stone, a Chicago insurance tycoon, who formulated the idea of PMA – Positive Mental Attitude – a concept to which he attributes his own success. If, he argues, we all made use of PMA we could all be as rich as he, and a notion of the extent of Mr Stone's wealth can be gleaned from the fact that he contributed some $2 million to Richard Nixon's ill-fated campaign in 1972. Stone also suggests that the effect of PMA can be much enhanced by the use of OPM – Other People's Money. OPM is a very much older prescription for success than PMA, and its virtues have been proven many times over. There is, of course, nothing wrong in the idea of persuading people to allow you to make use of their money to your mutual benefit. But, as Mr Stone points out, there is a basic 'unwritten premise' involved in the arrangement: that premise, according to Mr Stone, is that you will apply the highest standards in your business relationship.

There are of course innumerable ways in which OPM can be used; what Stone had primarily in mind was borrowing from a bank to start or enlarge your business. That is, however, a rather unsubtle use for OPM. For the borrower remains at risk; if the worst comes to the worst he may lose OPM but he will almost certainly lose his own as well – and banks have a tiresome habit of asking for security on their loans. A less risky procedure is to persuade OP that you can perform such feats with their M that they should pay you a fee for the service rather than you paying them interest on a loan. This has the additional advantage that if things go awry all you stand to lose is your fee. This was the business that Slater set up in when he undertook to manage investments for clients in return for a fee. It is clear that he was entering into a particularly sensitive association with OPM, and that the observance of Mr Stone's premise was more than ever desirable. The essential point implied in that premise is that Slater's clients were trusting him to handle their money with the same skill, care and concern as if it were his own.

By the autumn of 1964 Slater had collected quite a number of investment clients and was getting more all the time. There were in the first place his old Leyland colleagues whom he was now charging for advice, and the Leyland pension fund, to which was added later a new fund of about £500,000 set up at Standard-Triumph in Coventry. The Leyland connection had also brought Slater clients like the Brignalls and the Wileses. His association with Cheshire led to more business: first and most important Cheshire had introduced Slater to Eric Knight at Lombard Banking, who asked him to manage £100,000 of his company's money, and then to John Gommes of City bankers Rodocanachi, who also gave Slater some business. Then Rabl gave him some £50,000 to look after and two of his and Cheshire's friends, Charles Stein and Claude Farlow-Jones, asked Slater to manage their investments; and later Pendock recruited his dentist.

Other clients were also introduced in the same way by friends or people whose money Slater was already managing. Others like Dr Stott had read about him in the *Evening Standard*, and had written in, and a new influx came when the identity of Capitalist was revealed in the *Sunday Telegraph* in February 1965. It was then also revealed that his advisory business was now a wholly-owned subsidiary of Slater Walker and that he advised the Leyland and Standard-Triumph funds.

The *Sunday Telegraph* readers must have applied to Slater because they had found it rewarding to follow his column; for, questionable though Slater's own dealings in Capitalist shares were, at least it can be said that they had in general not cost his followers money during the rising markets of 1963 and 1964. But in the difficult Stock Exchange conditions of 1965 and 1966 this changed, and investigation shows that a number of Slater's clients lost money and were most unhappy with the treatment they received. Nor was this simply a matter of the advice they received being bad, or of Slater losing his touch in a changing market. It was not even a case, as with 'Capitalist's selections', of Slater advising one thing and doing the opposite with his own money. For Slater and his colleagues now, in effect, controlled large amounts of OPM, money which they were entrusted with and asked to invest for the benefit of the owners. In practice they could use it to buy and sell shares at their discretion. Given the structure and the nature of the company Slater had created it would have tried a saint to conduct its clients' business in a disinterested fashion. For this ability to dispose of large amounts of OPM on the stock market made possible a second degree of subtlety. It was possible to use OPM not only to earn fees but to influence the market itself; indeed if quantities of OPM were invested in small companies and the market in their stock was narrow, it was very difficult to avoid it. Given that Slater Walker was in the share

dealing business on its own account, it is clear that Mr Stone's un-
written premise was going to be severely strained.

When Slater announced the structure of Slater Walker in early
1965 he had painted a picture of a group divided into distinct
sections – investment counselling, share dealing, industrial. In reality
they were interdependent: clients' money was used to help secure
control of companies whose managements Slater Walker hoped to influence through its industrial arm; the dealing companies traded in
and out of the same companies' shares. The power of OPM was
deployed in the service of Slater Walker's own share dealing
businesses, and in support of its industrial ambitions.

In return, the performance of the clients' portfolios often
benefited from the activities of Slater Walker's industrial arm, when
either Slater Walker itself or its corporate clients made bids for the
companies in which the clients' money had been invested. But in
1965 and 1966 the failure rate was high and some clients lost large
amounts on a number of investments. Much of the dissatisfaction
focused on one particular share: a little electronics company called
Astaron-Bird. For this reason, and for the light the story throws on
Slater Walker's attitude to OPM, we shall examine this case in detail.

The Astaron-Bird group had taken shape in June 1963, when a
little Poole-based engineering company, Sydney S. Bird, took over
Astaron Electronics. Bird had been losing heavily, but a substantial
reorganization followed the merger with Astaron, whose managing
director, Harold Whitfield, took over the running of the whole
group. Losses, however, had not been completely eliminated by the
end of the year, and on 14 May 1964 the company announced a
much reduced deficit of just £9,067 for 1963; it did not propose to
pay its shareholders a dividend.

Astaron-Bird's fortunes were related mainly to those of the consumer durable market: it made car radios and electric organs and
was also a supplier to the television manufacturers, principally of
tuners. Not only, therefore, were its fortunes expected to improve in
1964 as a result of the reorganization, but also the expanding
economy was bound to help trading. On top of that, the introduction
of BBC2 would, it was thought, lead to an increase in demand for
televisions.

As a result the price of Astaron-Bird shares started to rise in the
spring of 1964: it jumped from 5s. 6d. at the beginning of April to
7s. 6d. at the start of June. Then, on 3 June, its chairman, Sir Ian
Stewart-Richardson, released his annual statement: he said, as the
Financial Times briefly reported, that both production and the order
book were showing 'very considerable' increases and that the results
for 1964 should show a 'further marked improvement' with the company operating once more on a profitable basis.

The share price rose again to 8s. 3d., but even at this price Astaron-Bird was a very small company by stock market standards with a total value of a little over £520,000. There were 1,263,000 shares in issue spread among about 1,500 shareholders, none of whom held anything approaching a controlling interest.

It was about this time – just as he was also negotiating to buy Lotery – that Slater first became interested in Astaron-Bird. He heard of the company from John Robertshaw, who knew one of the directors, and in the early summer of 1964 Robertshaw, Cheshire and Slater invested in the shares, both personally and on behalf of the Mount Street Investment Trusts.

But Slater soon took the company in hand, and Robertshaw became alarmed when he realized what he had unwittingly started. In July and August so much money was poured into the shares that the price, which had reached 10s. by the end of June 1964, doubled again in two months. For the following year Slater Walker dealt in and out of the shares while the price remained more or less on a plateau. The price then collapsed, and clients saw the value of their investments rapidly diminish. Slater Walker relieved some clients of their shares on the way down and lost money heavily itself; but, as we shall see, Slater and Walker sold personal holdings in Astaron-Bird at a profit and their clients bought their shares.

There is little doubt that at the outset Slater believed that Astaron-Bird had great potential and today Slater says that he believed it was an outstanding investment up to a price of above 20s. because it appeared an excellent recovery situation and he had a good idea that profits would be in the region of £250,000, against which valuable tax losses could be set.

Having found this outstanding investment Slater did not buy first for his clients: he bought first for himself, acquiring 15,000 Astaron-Bird shares at the end of June 1964. Using a Birmingham firm of stockbrokers called Ryland Smith and a London firm, Walker Crips, he bought 3,000 shares at 8s. 4½d. each excluding costs. These shares were not registered in Slater's name at the outset, but were put into Barclays Nominees (Birmingham). Then Slater bought 1,000 shares in his own name at 9s. 9d. using a broking firm called Moy Davies, and he used the same brokers to buy another 11,000 at 9s. 7½d., 10s. 3d. and 10s. 4½d., but these were registered in the name of Midland Bank (Threadneedle Street) Nominees. The cost of the 15,000 shares was £7,396 17s. 6d.

It was only possible to trace the 14,000 shares which were registered in nominee names because they were subsequently switched into Slater's own name, with a declaration that they had always belonged to him. Walker Crips and Ryland Smith bought another 5,543 shares at the same time and same price as Slater's which were also registered in the name of Barclays Nominees (Birmingham), and Walker Crips bought many thousands of shares which went into various Midland Bank nominee companies, but Slater maintains that the 15,000 was his total personal holding and said that the other purchases were quite possibly connected with the Mount Street Investment Trusts whose offices he shared; and he explained that he had bought first for himself rather than his clients because:

> In June 1964 the investment advisory side was in a state of transition from being a hobby of mine to a properly organized and professionally run business. At this point in time the investment side was in its infancy and the clients were mainly friends and ex-colleagues. Staff had not been hired and I only had two small rooms in Mount Street, one of which was a waiting room.

The reality is that the transition from hobby to profession had already taken place: as we have seen, Slater himself had estimated, in early 1964, that his part-time advisory 'business' was, after six months of operation, earning him £6,000 a year in profit-sharing arrangements with 'clients' and £9,000 in fees for advice he was giving stockbrokers. Investment Analysis itself had begun trading on 7 April 1964, and Slater had started Productofoam's share dealing offshoot, Moss Securities – for which he bought 400 Astaron-Bird shares at the same time as his own at 9s. 6d. each. Still, the first money from Slater's clients, friends and other associates hit Astaron-Bird almost simultaneously with the last of Slater's own purchases: Leonard Wiles, for example, acquired 9,500 towards the end of June at 10s. 7½d. each and Slater's housekeeper at High Beeches, Lilian White, got 500 shares at the same price.

Overnight from Tuesday 30 June to 1 July 1964 the Astaron-Bird share price was marked up 2s. to 12s. Next week, at this price, the second wave of money was sent rolling in: a group of about a dozen investors acquired more than 20,000 shares, adding over £12,000 to the demand. They were not all strictly clients – they included, for example, Jessel Harrison, chairman of a company called Slimma, who had been one of the *Evening News'* Under-Forties, and Harley Drayton's Securities Agency. But for the most part they invested through a small London broking firm, Sutherland Pershouse Millar, with which Slater had a special but not exclusive relationship.

Long before, when Slater was still at Leyland, Harry Graham Sutherland, the firm's senior partner, had seen an advertisement in the *Financial Times* asking for brokers interested in a guaranteed £1 million of business. Sutherland answered and found himself one among about a dozen being interviewed by Slater; Sutherland met

Slater's colleagues at Leyland, he says, and came away with the business. Later a friend of Slater's, Derek Rawlins, joined the firm to help with the Slater business, and also the firm started paying Slater fees for investment research, which of course was useful for its other clients, they said.

On Monday, 13 July 1964, the Astaron-Bird price jumped again to 13s. 1½d. and for about two weeks the shares were traded around the 13s. mark. It was during this period that the third wave of Slater Walker money was sent rolling into the market, with Walker and his associated share dealing companies riding on the crest. On 22 July, using Sutherlands, Walker and these companies bought 10,000 Astaron-Bird shares in the market at 13s. each with the exception of one block for which slightly less was paid: the cost was £6,499. Two thousand of these shares, or £1,300 worth, were put into Walker's own name; 3,000 went to Walker Moate for £1,950; 2,500 to Rodwell for £1,625 and the same number, but for £1,624, to Avasvilla Properties, the share dealing subsidiary which Walker and Bayle had started for their 'shell' operation E. C. Holdings.

The same day Lady Spurrier acquired 3,000 shares also at 13s., while Securities Agency bought 9,000 to add another £5,850 to its investments in the tiny electronics company.

In the narrow market inevitable in the shares of a company the size of Astaron-Bird, the price quickly began to move again; some £50,000 had now gone into the market through Sutherlands on top of over £75,000 through Walker Crips and Moy Davies. There was however plenty more money to keep the price moving up and in the last week of July 1964 Sutherlands acquired 15,000 shares for another client at 13s. 3d. and 13s. 6d. This helped push the price up to 15s. by the last day of the month.

While this was going on, Slater and Walker were also busily negotiating for the finance with which to buy H. Lotery. It was only Friday 24 July, with their appointment to the board, that they took formal charge of their new company. They had had to borrow heavily to buy Lotery, and the mortgage arrangements on Beaufort House were not completed until the end of August; but Lotery did have some spare resources, of which Slater was able to make immediate use through its share dealing subsidiary, Clamond Securities, and he decided that there were still profitable opportunities in Astaron-Bird even at these higher levels.

As the stock market got going again on Wednesday 5 August 1964, after the Bank Holiday weekend, Clamond moved heavily into the market for Astaron-Bird shares. It managed to buy 3,000 at 14s. 6d., then had to pay 15s. 3d. for 2,000 and finally 15s. 7½d. for 6,000. After this bout of buying the quotation was lifted to 16s. Few clients acquired shares at this level but Lady Spurrier got another 500 shares at 15s. 9d. to bring her total investment to 3,500 shares costing £2,331 5s.

Clamond came into the market for another 7,000 or so shares at 16s. on 10 and 11 August, and by Friday 14th the quotation was up to about 16s. 6d. That day Clamond bought another 3,000 at 16s. 9d. and small parcels were also bought for clients. There was also still considerable activity in the nominee companies' holdings at around this level, with Midland Bank (Threadneedle Street) buying a large number at about 16s. 4½d. through Gull & Co., another broker favoured by Slater. Many of these shares were bought for the client Charles Stein, who acquired in all about 30,000 Astaron-Bird shares. Midland (Threadneedle Street), of course, also held 11,000 of Slater's personal holding but the 3,000 held for him by Barclays (Birmingham) were now transferred into his own name.

Slater associates continued buying early the following week: Kenneth Meyer's mother got 1,500 at 17s. and Securities Agency another 2,000 at that price and a further 3,000 at 17s. 6d. each, bringing its total stake to 15,000 shares costing £10,775. Clamond acquired another 3,000 at 17s. and 500 at 17s. 10½d.

Under this pressure the Astaron-Bird share price reached 18s. 1½d. on Wednesday 19 August 1964. It had been a great run: on 1 April the price had been 5s. 6d.; on 1 May 6s. 6d.; on 1 June 7s. 6d. Since Astaron-Bird's chairman had issued his optimistic but nevertheless unspecific forecast in early June, the shares had doubled. Yet the company's last recorded results had shown a loss and it had paid no dividend to shareholders for four years: it therefore had neither earnings nor dividend yield by which the value of its shares could be related to other securities in the market. It could not begin to meet Capitalist's nine criteria. Share prices can and quite often do lose all touch with reality when stocks are 'taken in hand' in this way, but at some point the market usually decides enough is enough. Slater and other buyers were speculating on how far back into the black the company had gone, and now the market decided things had gone far enough.

On 27 and 28 August, Walker sold his 2,000 shares in Astaron-Bird. The startling aspect of the transaction was that Walker's shares, which he had bought for 13s., were sold to investment clients of his own company, Slater Walker, at 17s. 1½d. Five hundred of his holding went to Slater's old AEC colleague Brian Shepherd in a joint account with his wife, and the other 1,500 were sold to a client called John Kutchera; he had first met Walker in the Army and was later introduced to Slater by Walker's insurance colleague David Clarke. Walker sold through Sutherlands, who also handled the clients' purchases: Walker told me that he did not know his shares had been sold to clients. He could not recall why he had sold the shares, but said he had no knowledge of the future of Astaron-Bird at the time.

It was not a particularly rewarding deal. After costs Walker would probably have got less than 17s. a share, or a total of under £1,700, of which his profit would have been less than £400. He would also have been liable to short-term speculative gains tax at his own personal rate of taxation as the shares were bought and sold within six months.

On 2 September 1964, Astaron-Bird announced that it had made a profit of £101,000 in the first six months of the year. The directors also said that business was continuing on a high level, but warned again that a large proportion of the group's production went to the 'highly volatile' radio and television industry; to counteract this vulnerability, the group was expanding into other fields.

Excellent though these results were, there was a disappointment for the market; the directors said that because the business was expanding so rapidly, they felt they should not at once restart paying dividends but they should use the profits instead to strengthen the company's cash position. The share price, which had risen to 18s. before the results, dipped slightly, but then made a valiant attempt to continue its upward spiral. It was helped by more Slater Walker money, including £925 from Jack Plane, who acquired 1,000 shares at 18s. 6d. on Friday 4 September. Slater points out today that even at this level the prospective price earnings yield, on the pessimistic assumption that the company would have to meet a full tax charge, was nearly double the market average. On top of this, he says, he believed there was a good chance of a bid from Marconi.

On Monday 7 September, the Astaron-Bird share price started on a final fling, opening at 19s. and then jumping to 19s. 6d. the following day and to 19s. 9d. on Wednesday 9 September, at which price Clamond grabbed an odd parcel of 400 shares, suggesting that someone at Slater Walker still had confidence in the shares. But Moss Securities' 400 shares, bought back in June, were sold that day to a client at 19s. 3d. for gross profit of £195 on the £190 investment. That day, too, Jan Rabl, who had sold Productofoam to Slater Walker, was allotted 2,000 shares at 19s. 9d.

That Wednesday, the offical Stock Exchange list recorded the highest marks ever made for Astaron-Bird shares: 20s. and 20s. 1½d. Such prices were not to be missed and next day Avasvilla Properties, the E.C. Holdings dealing company, decided to take its profit and parted with 1,500 of its shares. Although the middle market price had fallen to 19s., the man who bought Avasvilla's shares – and so provided it with its £500 or so profit – paid £1 each for them: it was Slater's Brighton client, the unfortunate Dr Stott. Sutherlands again acted for both sides. As with Productofoam, Stott seemed fated to pay the top price: Slater bought him another 350 Astaron-Bird shares that day for 19s. 9d. each, committing a total of £1,845 12s. 6d. (plus £40 or so costs) of the doctor's £5,000 to this little electronics company. The price of its shares promptly fell 1s. to 18s. the following day, Friday 11 September, and Sutherlands found a purchaser for Avasvilla's last 1,000 shares at 18s. 3d.

For nearly a month, until the first week of October 1964, the middle market quotation for Astaron-Bird shares remained at 18s. Towards the end of this period, more Slater client money found its way into the shares; on 25 September the Tiger Investment Club bought 3,000 at 18s. and 18s. 4½d. and three days later another 4,000 at 18s. 9d.

The market price was raised to 18s. 9d. on 7 October, and on the 9th Tiger paid 19s. for a further 3,000. The Leyland executives' club now had a total investment of 10,000 shares which had cost it £9,350. In the first week of October, Charles Stein's wife, using Gull & Co. rather than Sutherlands, bought 2,500 at 19s. 4d. Slater Walker's dealing company, Clamond Securities, also bought a final 5,000 shares on 13 October at 18s. 3d. and 18s. 4d. to bring its holding to about 32,000 shares.

After this, the price relapsed to 18s. and 18s. 1½d., which was not surprising, as the *Financial Times* Industrial Ordinary Index had passed its peak on 1 October 1964 and proceeded to drop sharply after Labour won the election of 15 October. Nevertheless, against the trend, the Astaron-Bird price edged up again in November: the directors had changed their minds and decided to pay an interim dividend of ten per cent or 4.8 pence a share. On Monday 23 November 1964, the shares went 'ex-dividend' – meaning new buyers would not get the recently announced payment – and the shares were marked down from 18s. 3d. to 16s. 9d.; they fluctuated widely that week, but dropped again to 16s. on Monday 30 November. At this point Stokes was put into Astaron-Bird for the first time: Sutherlands bought 2,000 shares at 16s. each for him. The following day Pendock's dentist got 2,000 at 16s. 4½d.

Jack Brignall's wife acquired 4,000 shares even more cheaply on 14 December 1964, at 15s. 10½d., but this was still enough to provide a useful profit to the seller of 3,000 of them: it was Walker Moate, which had bought its shares back in July at 13s. each and so realized a gain of about £430. Cyril Plane also now got some shares rather more cheaply than his brother had done: 1,500 at 16s. 6d.

On 21 December 1964 Pendock of Investment Analysis bought 4,500 shares for himself at 16s. 6d., so the shares were still clearly regarded as a good investment at that level. By the end of the year, Slater Walker had control of some fifteen to twenty per cent of the Astaron-Bird capital; clients and associates alone owned some 100,000 while Clamond had over 30,000. Slater Walker was thus well on the way to accumulating a stake 'of sufficient significance to afford, if necessary, a measure of effective control', as Slater described the purpose of the newly-formed Slater Walker Industrial Group, into which it had been decided to transfer the Astaron-Bird investment.

On 31 December 1964 Astaron-Bird shares stood at 17s. in the market, a bit lower than four months before – a fall much in line with the stock market – but still substantially above the level of six months before. The higher the price, the better for Slater Walker, for as indicated in the last chapter, the size of Slater Walker's own stake in swig depended on the market level of the investments it exchanged for swig shares.

swig acquired a total of 100,000 Astaron-Bird shares: 30,400 of Clamond's holding of some 32,000 shares were put through at 17s. 1½d. each, giving Slater Walker a paper profit of over £6,500. Many of the rest were acquired from the Mount Street Investment Trusts, for Cheshire and Robertshaw had sometime before decided to get out of Astaron-Bird; further shares were bought in the market mainly through Sebags. swig's total investment was nearly £87,000 or an average of 17s. 4d. a share.

The share price then rose again slightly in January 1965 to 18s. 1½d. and there is further evidence that the men at Investment Analysis were still extremely optimistic for Astaron-Bird, because at this level Slater's mother acquired 1,000 shares, and Pendock, together with Farrell, acquired another 3,000 shares at 17s. 9d. to 18s. 3d. This demonstrated according to Slater, 'in the most tangible possible way', their belief in Astaron-Bird's investment prospects.

Contact had also been established with the Astaron-Bird management. They were not keen on Slater's interference, Whitfield told me. They had, after all, restored the company to profitability before he came on the scene. But they cooperated to begin with, and one result was that Astaron-Bird bought, in February 1965, a little private company of which Pendock was a director and shareholder; called Gemco, it had developed an altimeter for hovercraft, whose pilots needed to know precisely how far they were above the surface. The following month – but not at Slater Walker's instigation – Astaron-Bird bought a larger company, Coastal Radio; based in Edinburgh, it made marine communication equipment and would, it was hoped, fit in nicely with Astaron-Bird's own navigational radar set unit, as well as reducing the group's reliance on consumer durables.

Throughout the first four months of 1965 dealings in Astaron-Bird were rather less hectic than before and the price was relatively stable at around 17s. 6d. to 18s. There were, however, some movements among Slater Walker clients and associates: Rodwell, for example, the only one of the dealing companies associated with Walker still to hold shares, sold its 2,500 investment at this level for a profit of some £560, and other early investors also disposed of some of their holdings gainfully. Strangely, Tiger, which had bought near the top the previous September, resold its 10,000 during this period at 17s. 3d. to realize a loss of £725.

On 6 April 1965 came the Labour government's first Budget: the extension of capital gains tax and other socialist fiscal measures tended to draw attention away from the economic aim, which was to take £250 million of home demand out of the economy. It was all-in-all, however, 'not a budget for the investor', as the *Financial Times* Lex column highlighted. Nevertheless initially the stock market rose sharply and it was not until a week later that realism set in and the *Financial Times* Industrial Ordinary Index dropped back fourteen points in two days.

Slater sold his 15,000 Astaron-Bird shares on 22 April 1965, having shortly before switched the 11,000 held in Midland Bank (Threadneedle Street) Nominees into his own name. Slater sold through Sutherlands, who also acted for the buyers, of whom there were four. They paid 17s. 11¼d. each for their shares. The largest block, 7,000 shares, went to 29 Gracechurch Street Nominees acting for Jack Plane and brought his holding up to 8,000 shares costing £7,203 2s. 6d. Five thousand shares were sold to Donald Stokes for £4,484 7s. 6d. to bring his total investment to 7,000 for which he had paid £6,084 7s. 6d. Then 2,000 were passed to a new client called Jack Willis: he had applied to Slater Walker after the final Capitalist column, and Slater had sold out his existing 'blue chip' portfolio, and £1,793 15s. of the proceeds (plus £41 costs) were put into the little electronics company. The last 1,000 shares went to a Lloyds Bank Nominees account and it has not been possible to identify the recipient.

The buyers paid a total of £13,453 2s. 6d. excluding costs. Slater had paid £7,396 17s. 6d. for the shares. His net profit, however, as he told me, was less than £6,000 – probably £5,700 to £5,800. Slater would not have had to pay any of the new long-term capital gains tax, for Astaron-Bird stood at 18s. 3¾d. on the starting date.

I asked Lord Stokes if he thought it right for an investment adviser to sell shares to his clients: he said he was sure it had never happened to anyone at Leyland and was surprised when I said it had. Willis was also not aware that his Astaron-Bird shares had been sold to him by Slater personally, although he came to suspect it in the light of the performance of this and other investments he was put into.

In October 1974 I asked Slater and Walker if they thought it was an acceptable practice for an investment adviser to sell shares to his clients without disclosing it. They both said they could not remember the details of the case and said that they would not have been aware that their shares had gone to clients. Slater said shares were often transferred from one client to another, a practice which I also questioned. Slater then said that I must remember that he had just left the motor industry and that he did not know about the technicalities of the regulations governing securities dealings. He had relied on people like Pendock and Farrell, whom he had hired to run the investment advisory side.

I argued that Walker, as a director of a unit trust company, should have been aware that it was not acceptable practice for a principal to sell shares to his clients at a profit without disclosing it, and that clients who lost money on shares acquired in this way might have been even more aggrieved if they had known where they came from. Walker, I understood, agreed but argued that the amounts involved were relatively small.

More than two years after the meeting and a year after seeing the text, however, Walker said he did not agree with my version of the interview, which he claimed gave a false impression. He said that I had asked him directly if he considered it would be wrong for an investment adviser to sell his own shares to his clients without the clients knowing that this had been done, and continued: 'I stated categorically that yes, I did think it would be wrong.' He said he was very surprised when I suggested he had done this and that he had 'pointed out immediately' that he had never done this.*

In an exchange of correspondence after the October 1974 meeting Slater said that he reserved the right to revise off-the-cuff reactions to my questions, and so I put the details of his Astaron-Bird share sales to him in writing. I also said that as Slater Walker dominated the dealings in Astaron-Bird at the time – Sutherlands alone accounted for about half of all transactions in the shares – Slater might have realized that his shares had a good chance of ending up with clients, and that, as he was already worth a substantial figure, he would not presumably have had to sell his Astaron-Bird shares reluctantly in order to raise money.

In a detailed reply Slater repeated that at the time he knew 'very little personally about the mechanics of a licensed dealership or indeed professional investment management', as all his previous experience had been industrial. For this reason he had employed Pendock and Farrell, although Slater later added that there were many problems concerned with actually obtaining approval for the

---

*I do not accept Walker's account of the meeting. My notes and those of a colleague who was present confirm that I asked Mr Walker outright if he thought it wrong, but his initial reaction was to excuse the transaction on the grounds of size, and it was only when it was pointed out to him that this was a matter of principle that he agreed it was wrong. There is no record of his pointing out immediately that he had never done it.

licensed dealership and arranging for it to be properly administered, especially when the number of clients increased rapidly. Slater said that his own main personal effort in the early days was on the industrial side and on acquisitions, and that he had delegated the day-to-day running of the investment advisory side to Pendock.

While it is true that in the spring of 1965 Slater had industrial problems on his hands, particularly at Productofoam, as we shall see, but also at George Wilson Gas, that he was setting up SWIG and was also about to mount his first takeover bid, Slater's whole argument is remarkable. He had effectively left Leyland well over a year before to set up as an investment counsellor, and many clients came to him because of his personal reputation, created largely by his *Sunday Telegraph* column, as an investment expert. Furthermore, although Slater claims there was a clear division between the investment and industrial sides of Slater Walker, all evidence points to the fact that at this time and throughout its career, overall investment policy on 'special situations' like Astaron-Bird was decided by Slater himself.

As far as his personal dealings were concerned, Slater said that if he decided to buy or sell any shares he would ask Farrell, or whoever was in the dealing room in his absence, to arrange it. He said he would not have known the shares would inevitably end up with clients as 'I was not to know that they were not sold on the market in the normal way.'

Slater told me that, as he was trying to build up his business, he would not have wanted knowingly to prejudice the performance of his clients' portfolios. His sale, he argued, did not indicate that his view of Astaron-Bird had changed, and the principal evidence for this that he advanced was a memorandum Pendock had written after he and Slater had visited the company two months later on 18 June 1965. It concluded: 'Our overall impression was that the shares of this company provided a quite outstanding investment and that the profit potential over the next three years, given reasonable economic conditions, was tremendous.' The reason he sold, Slater said, was to degear:

> I had borrowed an enormous amount in relation to my net worth when I purchased both my shares in Productofoam and my shares in Slater Walker, and I therefore had massive interest charges to meet. In addition to this, I obviously had to reduce my gearing as much as possible to get it to an acceptable level with which I could live without undue worry. Although I cannot remember the exact and detailed circumstances at the time, this is almost certainly the reason that I sold my shares in Astaron-Bird as well as a significant number of shares in Slater Walker.

Slater had borrowed about £350,000 to buy his stakes in Slater

Walker and Productofoam, and in the months preceding April 1965 he had resold 325,000 Slater Walker shares for £232,500 of which £70,000 was profit. He had also resold all his 220,000 Productofoam shares for about £148,000 of which nearly £90,000 was profit – and, as we have seen, many of these were sold to clients *with* Slater's knowledge. The total proceeds of these sales were therefore over £380,000, and Slater's remaining 375,000 Slater Walker shares were worth £310,000 in early April 1965. Although, therefore, Slater had become a very wealthy man extremely rapidly, it is fair to say that after interest and other costs, his liquid position in April 1965 might still have been quite tight, explaining his desire to arrange his personal finances on a 'more prudent basis' with a programme of sales, as he later amplified his explanation. But there were other reasons for being prudent at this time; Slater himself had written in his first chairman's statement of Slater Walker issued at the end of March 1965 that 'the stock market as a whole could well find a lower level during the next few months,' and there was little in the early April Budget which followed to warrant a change in such a view.

As to the sale of Walker's Astaron-Bird shares the previous August, I had originally understood from my meeting with Slater and Walker on 16 October 1974 that the decision to sell would have been taken by somebody at Investment Analysis on his behalf; but more than two years later I was told the sale would have been at his initiative. He said that he sold his shares 'to a stockbroker' and that it was essential that I made clear that at no stage did he have any knowledge of the investments of the Slater Walker investment advisory service. 'Only twice in my life have I ever physically entered their offices,' he wrote. 'On no occasion did I know what shares they were buying or selling and I was never consulted by them nor did I ever seek any information as to their activities.'

Walker did not sell 'to' just any stockbroker: he sold *through* Sutherlands, the brokers being used to handle much of the Slater Walker dealing at this period. While there is no reason to dispute that Walker would not have known that Investment Analysis and Sutherlands between them would have passed his shares on to clients like his long-standing friend John Kutchera, Walker's claim that he had absolutely no knowledge of Investment Analysis' activities is extraordinary. This was then the main subsidiary of the firm of which he was co-founder and semi-executive deputy chairman, and Walker was himself coopted onto the Investment Analysis board on 28 October 1964 and remained a director until 9 August 1965; and while Walker may have visited the Mount Street offices only twice, the whole group moved to its new headquarters in Hertford Street in early 1965. But Walker remains adamant that on no occasion was he ever present at either an investment management meeting or a board meeting of Investment Analysis, that he introduced no investment clients to them and that he did not even know that Kutchera had been a client.

Walker's claim is also incompatible with what both he and Slater previously told me when I was trying to discover who would have taken the investment decisions, including those relating to Astaron-Bird, of the dealings companies associated with Walker – Avasvilla Properties, Rodwell Securities and Walker Moate. Slater told me that Investment Analysis had managed a small discretionary fund for the insurance broking group for a period of time, but had not looked after the funds of the other two. He said, however, that: 'As I was personally friendly and in frequent touch with Peter Walker, I would quite often mention individual transactions of minor significance to him before completing them. On several occasions I would probably deal on a discretionary basis especially if the amounts of money were relatively minor.'

Walker himself wrote, in January 1975, that the dealings of these companies 'were in the main carried out on decisions taken by myself, or whoever was my Personal Assistant at the time. All of them were made on our general assessment of the prospects of the companies concerned and there was obviously by conversation an inter-change of views between myself and Mr Slater and other Directors of Slater Walker, and for example, from memory Shaw Carpets was a suggestion of mine.' (Shaw Carpets was a successful investment for clients of Investment Analysis.) Two years later Walker said the sales by the dealing companies would have been 'almost certainly done by a member of my staff through a stock-broker with no knowledge of the investment activities of Slater Walker in this sphere. Almost certainly the decision would have been taken because the person concerned considered that a profit had been made and should be taken.' That is profit made at the expense of Slater Walker client Dr Stott in the case of Avasvilla. But 'almost certainly I would have played no part in the decision,' Walker concluded, for 'minor decisions such as this would have been left to the person I put in charge of the portfolio.'

As already indicated, Slater's main argument for there being nothing wrong with his own sale was that:

> At the time I decided to sell my shares in Astaron-Bird they were rated as a 'buy' by the investment department and the transactions were matched in the stock market. To illustrate this point, on 22 April 1965, not only were the 17,000 shares purchased by clients as you suggest but also a further 3,000 were purchased directly in the market. Indeed, Investment Analysis continued to rate Astaron-Bird shares as a 'buy' and purchased

them in the market for clients as an investment in May, June and July.

Slater also said that following the visit to Astaron-Bird on 18 June 1965 both Slater Walker and Pendock personally bought more shares.

I had not in fact mentioned anything to Slater about 17,000 shares being purchased for clients on 22 April, but it is worth looking at some of the other transactions at this time. In the first place Pendock and Farrell also chose this moment to sell the 7,500 shares they had acquired around the end of 1964. The shares were all sold through Sutherlands, who also acted for the purchasers of 5,000 of them: the clients paid 17s. 10½d. or 17s. 11¼d. The remaining block fetched around 17s. 9d. and the total profit was some £300. On 21 April, too, Sutherland himself sold 3,000 shares from an account with Miss Mollie Joy Sutherland, but they did not make a profit for they sold at the same price they had originally paid – 17s. 10½d. The buyer was the Standard-Triumph Pension Fund, which acquired a further 8,000 shares for 17s. 10½d. for an investment of £9,831: the fund's purchases were not made through Sutherlands but through the other firm popular with Slater, Gull & Co. Derek Rawlins of Sutherlands also sold 2,000 shares about this time and Miss Lilian White, Slater's housekeeper at High Beeches, disposed of her 500 shares on the same day as Slater for about 18s. each and a profit of some £180.

I asked Slater about these further sales and he replied, at the end of March 1975: 'I would guess that Simon Pendock, Eric Farrell, the Sutherlands and Mr Rawlins simply sold their Astaron-Bird shares because they had realized a good profit, needed the cash or they followed my example seeing that I was selling my shares.' He said he had himself recommended Astaron-Bird to Miss White and, he said, he 'probably mentioned to her, at the time, that I was selling mine and she probably expressed the wish for me to sell her shares when I sold mine.' He later pointed out that he had left his mother's holding undisturbed as well as those of other close friends.

Some of Slater's own shares were, of course, sold to his former boss Donald Stokes, and the same day that Slater sold his shares, Investment Analysis bought 2,000 more shares at 17s. 11¼d. each for Cyril Plane, another important colleague turned client, to bring his total investment in Astaron-Bird to 3,500 shares costing over £3,000. But at the end of our exchanges Slater left important questions unanswered. Why did he not point out to Miss White that he still regarded Astaron-Bird as an outstanding investment and advise her not to sell? Why did Pendock and Farrell, the experts at the rules and practices of investment, allow their and Slater's shares to be sold to clients? Why should they have sold to realize a good profit if they believed that by holding the shares they could have made a still better one? There were, as we shall see, good economic reasons for choosing this moment to take a dealing profit and, while it may be true that Investment Analysis continued to believe in the long-term prospects of Astaron-Bird, the simultaneous sales by its three executive directors inevitably suggest that they believed that in the immediate future the shares were more likely to fall than to rise.*

Slater's statement that the sales of his own shares 'were matched in the stock market' raises the question of the relationship of Slater Walker with its brokers, and in particular Sutherland Pershouse. Stockbrokers who get simultaneous orders to buy and sell the same shares can use what is called a put-through. This means they do not have to deal through the market in the ordinary way, but can match the orders directly; they must, however, get a jobber's approval of the price (for which he is paid a small commission instead of the normal 'turn') and the deal must be 'marked' on the official Stock Exchange list, unless the Exchange specifically gives permission for the mark to be withheld.† There are no marks on the official list at 17s. 11¼d. on 22 April 1965, but attempts to find out precisely how Sutherland Pershouse handled its Slater Walker business were not fully successful.

Sutherland himself held the view that small put-throughs at the market price did not have to be marked, and in practice a lot of Stock Exchange transactions are effectively put-throughs without being technically such, for a broker who has two customers, one wanting to sell and the other to buy, can always just go to the jobber, sell the shares and then immediately buy them back. He can then cross the orders in the office without feeding them into the ordinary Stock Exchange system.

As far as Sutherlands were concerned, an order to sell on behalf of one Slater Walker client and an order to buy on behalf of another could be regarded as separate transactions even if the instructions came from the same place. This was because the contract notes were sent direct to the clients by Sutherlands and were not channelled through Slater Walker.

Sutherland did, however, tell me at first that when shares were put through from one client to another, he assumed both sides knew what was happening; but he also said that Slater would only accept fully discretionary business. Rawlins on the other hand told me he did not think he had put shares through from one client to another. Sutherland said he was only acting as Slater Walker's agent and on

---

*In addition to their sales, a further 500 shares were sold at this time which appear to have belonged either to Clamond or another Investment Analysis executive.

†Stock Exchange rules on put-throughs have been considerably tightened since 1965.

their instructions: he would not have wanted to know why they asked for shares to be put through. He would only have objected if asked to do anything against the Stock Exchange rules or anything he thought might be wrong. He did not seem to think he should have questioned the transfer of shares from Slater to his clients, although he recognized that the clients might have kicked up a fuss if they had found out later.

Rawlins, however, had said he would look up the records but later wrote to me to say they had been destroyed. He said, however, of the 22 April 1965 transactions that:

> Assuming your facts are correct, instructions would appear to originate from Slater Walker's dealing department. As we acted for both the buyer and seller in certain instances I think it almost certain that the transactions were regarded as put-throughs. I do not know the reason for them not having been marked but it was most likely an administrative oversight on our part.

Rawlins added:

> If you are criticizing the fact that the transactions mentioned were dealt with as put-throughs, I can only say that, where a broker is buying and selling shares at the same time for different clients, it is obviously economic and administratively convenient to deal with the orders in the way that we would have done at the time.

Further inquiries of Slater produced the answer:

> I understand that my Astaron-Bird shares would simply have been put through the market by Sutherland Pershouse. The dealing department would know that shares were being bought for clients and also that shares were being sold. The transactions would, therefore, have been matched by them. Assuming therefore that the investment department wanted to purchase 20,000 shares or more that day they would have taken and matched the 17,000 that were being sold and bought a further 3,000 in the market. The matching would in effect be a put-through even if it was not officially marked. In practice, brokers did not always mark their bargains.

Within a month of the sales by Slater and his two colleagues at Investment Analysis the Astaron-Bird share price started to fall. The slide began in the week starting 17 May 1965. It was a bad week for the stock market anyway: the *Financial Times* Industrial Ordinary Index fell three points on Monday and was down another 3.5 by the end of Thursday 20 May. That day Chancellor Callaghan warned that the credit squeeze 'had hardly started'. The Index fell another 6.1 points the following day.

Slater argued that Astaron-Bird shares started to fall because of 'the onset of the credit squeeze on 20 May. This carried particularly serious implications for a consumer orientated company like Astaron-Bird.' Slater then said that he and Pendock 'could not knowingly have foreseen this event when they sold their shares.' While it is certainly true that the credit squeeze was a threat to Astaron-Bird's prospects, the rest of Slater's explanation, given after more than two years of exchanges on the subject, must be rejected when put into context. The banks had been given their first directive to be selective in their lending long before – at the end of 1964 when Bank rate had been lifted to seven per cent to defend the pound. By April 1965, however, with only a brief warning by Callaghan in his Budget speech that he would take further measures to reinforce this control if it were to prove necessary, the City began to overlook the fact that there was supposed to be a squeeze, and there was speculation each Thursday that Bank rate would be reduced from its crisis level. This reached its height on Thursday 22 April – the day Slater sold his Astaron-Bird – and there were no doubt many disappointed punters in gilt-edged securities when Bank rate was *not* reduced. The clear intention was to show the City that the credit squeeze was serious: the *Financial Times* the following day devoted its main leader to the 'future of the credit squeeze', saying that a reduction in Bank rate would anyway not mark its end and that the Chancellor had 'made it clear that he sees tight credit as one of the major means of keeping the home economy under control and diverting resources to exports.' A week later, on 29 April, the banks were asked for £95 million of special deposits, and a week after that they were issued with a further directive.

But the tightening of the squeeze was not the only reason for the fall in Astaron-Bird. The company chose 19 May 1965 to release its results for 1964. On the face of it they were excellent: profits of £156,785, no tax to pay because of the past losses, and a final dividend of fifteen per cent. The share price, which had fallen from 17s. 6d. to 16s. 9d. with the market, at first did not react. Then on 20 May it fell to 15s. 7½d. The shares, the *Financial Times* commented, 'came on offer on further consideration of the results'. Consideration had not only been given to the likely effects of the squeeze on a company so dependent on the consumer durable market, but also to the fact that, since Astaron-Bird had made £101,000 in the first half of 1964, the rate of profitability must have fallen again sharply in the second half of the year. Further consideration of these points pushed the shares down to 15s. on Friday 21 May 1965.

In view of the company's success in 1964, the annual review of chairman, dated 8 June 1965, was reserved. The results, he commented briefly, could 'be considered very satisfactory'. He continued immediately with a prominent and clear warning: 'I must remind shareholders that a large part of the Group's production still goes directly or indirectly to the "consumer durable market".' This market, he pointed out yet again, was a highly volatile one seldom producing an even pattern of sales over any prolonged period. He explained too, that the introduction of BBC2 had not resulted in the hoped-for upsurge in demand for TV sets at the end of 1964 and as a result 'stocks had accumulated in the pipeline resulting in a serious curtailment of our tuner production.' The stock position had since improved again, however, and the chairman said that 'an upturn in demand could be expected under normal trading conditions'.

The share price had fallen to about 14s. at the beginning of June 1965 – not helped by the announcement of stiffer down-payment terms on hire purchase and rental agreements which accompanied the eventual reduction in Bank rate on 3 June. Investment Analysis had not in fact continued to buy Astaron-Bird shares in May, as Slater had originally stated; he explained later that between the end of April and the end of June there was a sharp shake-out in the market – particularly in the consumer durable sector, which fell about twelve per cent – and there was no point in resuming buying the shares until the stock market looked more stable.

The shake-out had actually started in mid-April, and Slater Walker began buying Astaron-Bird again some weeks before the market hit its 1965 low – and *before* the Slater/Pendock visit to the company. The first purchases were made by Pendock personally, who acquired 2,000 at 14s. 3d. on 8 June. Slater Walker, through its oddly-named dealing company SW Industrial Holdings – not SWIG – came in on 14 June for 1,000 at 14s. 10½d. (the shares were bought from a client whose substantial holding was being redistributed) and acquired a further 3,980 on the 16th at 14s. 11¼d. Pendock also bought 1,000 more that day at the same price. The Astaron-Bird price was now rising against the general market trend and SW Industrial paid 15s. 4d. for another 1,000 on 17 June 1965.

Following the joint visit of Slater and Pendock to Astaron-Bird on 18 June 1965 – which itself is hardly indicative of a clear distinction between the investment and industrial departments of Slater Walker – Slater Walker bought several thousand more Astaron-Bird shares: they paid 15s. 3d. for some but the share price had started to slip again, and many were bought at 14s. 7½d., the level reached by 2 July 1965. The Astaron-Bird annual meeting of shareholders was held on 7 July, and on the 9th the share price fell to 13s. 9d. On 13 July, following a visit to the company by a reporter, the *Sunday Times* produced a favourable note on the company, but on 20 July the price dropped to 12s. 6d.

So far, the Astaron-Bird price had fallen faster than share prices overall, but in August and September it recovered, again more rapidly than the stock market, to reach 16s. by the end of September. But during this time there were some more unorthodox dealings in the shares.

In July 1965 Investment Analysis was granted a principal's licence to deal in securities. This was an important development, for the licences, issued under the provisions of the Prevention of Fraud (Investments) Act of 1958, allow individuals or firms to offer securities to the public, to act formally as advisers in takeover bids, to 'place' shares and so on. It also meant that Slater Walker could now transfer shares from one client to another without using a stockbroker – in fact could arrange its own put-throughs – and charge a commission for so doing. It would not however allow Slater to sell his own shares directly to clients without disclosing it, for one of the regulations requires a licensed dealer to reveal if he is acting as principal – evidence of the authorities' concern over this sort of transaction.

The first put-throughs by Investment Analysis were in August 1965. One thousand of Jack Plane's Astaron-Bird shares were sold to a client called John James, while the 7,000 that Slater had himself passed on so profitably to Plane were now shifted to another client, John Hurst. Both James and Hurst had applied to Slater after seeing his name in the *Sunday Telegraph* They paid 12s. 10½d. a share; Plane therefore still lost a hefty £2,000 or so on his investment.

Jack Plane's brother Cyril was also relieved of his Astaron-Bird shares: Investment Analysis passed 1,000 of his 3,000 on to James again at 12s. 10½d.; the other 2,500 went to a Kenneth Smith at 12s. 8½d. Cyril Plane thus lost about £800.

Investment Analysis later took 2,000 of Leonard Wiles' shares as the Astaron-Bird share price retreated from its autumn revival and sold them to Mr and Mrs Macdonald, clients who had been introduced to Slater's advisory business back in early 1964. The Macdonalds paid 15s. 3d., plus 2d. a share commission, enabling Wiles to make a profit of perhaps £450 on this batch, for he had been one of the lucky clients to be brought in near the start at 10s. 7½d. Still he was left with 7,500 shares.

The decision to take the Planes out of what two months before had been considered to be a 'quite outstanding investment' at a loss was bizarre indeed. When I mentioned to Slater that the 7,000 shares which had once belonged to him had been passed on yet again, he said he knew nothing about this and could give me very little further help about it.

Before replying to me Slater had consulted Pendock, although Pendock himself refused to discuss the details of Astaron-Bird, or indeed of anything to do with Slater Walker, with me. Pendock did tell me, however, that Slater would not have known about individual shares being transferred from one client to another. On the general issue of the propriety of taking clients in and out of the same shares at widely varying prices Pendock said: 'Clients join and leave at different times, clients have differing tax positions, differing financial requirements and differing mental attitudes.' This suggestion that clients were being closely consulted in the early days is unreal. Slater Walker had absolute discretion and clients only knew what was being done when the contract notes arrived from the broker or when they received their quarterly reports.

Slater himself argued, on the question of switching shares from one client to another, that this was not automatically prejudicial to the interests of one of the parties:

> If one particular client wants some funds withdrawn for a specific purpose, he may wish to sell some shares. In the event, we may reluctantly agree that the client in question should sell shares which we would normally rate as a 'buy' and in this event they might well be too heavy for a particular portfolio or, as happened in later years, a client may wish to sell a share to realize a capital gains tax loss.

Slater continued:

> In the early years there may well have been some transfers of this nature. In recent years, we have tended to consult our clients very much more and if indeed we were to transfer any shares on that basis the client would know the exact position and detailed circumstances beforehand.

This statement was, of course, made before Slater resigned from Slater Walker: just whether standards did improve in later years will be a matter on which some light is thrown in later chapters. In any case, the concern of the counsellors of Hertford Street with the weight of a particular share in a portfolio suffered a strange lapse when they committed over £1,800 of Dr Stott's £5,000 to Astaron-Bird.

By the end of October 1965 the Astaron-Bird price was down to 13s. and in November the market knew that something was wrong: the interim profits statement was overdue. The share price was down to 10s. when the figures were finally released on Friday 26 November.

They turned out to be not quite as disastrous as feared, but they were bad enough. Profits for the first six months of 1965 had been only £18,400 against the £101,000 in 1964. Sales to the consumer durable market had fallen by forty per cent, and although sales of electronic equipment had more than doubled, overall turnover was down fifteen per cent. The dividend was halved to five per cent.

The good news lay in the short statement with the figures. The reason for the delay was because of the reconstruction found necessary to Coastal Radio. It had still been found impracticable to integrate this new subsidiary's figures, but, the company said, 'it is not considered that they will materially effect the result of the Group as a whole for the period in question'. The company also said its order book had improved again and that if the improving trend were maintained, they would consider paying another dividend before the following April.

It has not been possible to pinpoint the precise moment of Slater Walker's final disenchantment with Astaron-Bird. Clamond Securities sold a thousand or so of the shares it had bought the previous year, but which it had not passed on to SWIG, at around 16s. in September 1965 to realize a loss of about 3s. a share, but about the same time 5,000 shares were bought for Moss Securities at 15s. 6¾d. and 15s. 10½d. There were a number of purchases for clients at the end of September and early October 1965 at this level, the latest probably being the transfer of shares from Wiles to the Macdonalds at 15s. 3d. which was made on 19 October. Then sw Industrial Holdings sold one thousand of the shares it had bought the previous June at the 13s. level reached shortly before Astaron-Bird made its interim profit announcement. The disillusionment appears to have been prompted not just by these figures but also by the discovery that Harold Whitfield, the group's managing director, had sold some 20,000 shares in the preceding weeks. Many of these were picked up by Sutherlands and found their way into the Slater Walker camp: 2,500 for example were bought by the Tiger Investment Club in its second bite at Astaron-Bird at 15s. 10½d. Slater and Pendock were furious, not without justification.

In the early days, Slater explained to me, it was not fully realized by all concerned how difficult it would be to sell out some of the smaller company investments when there were sudden reversals in their fortunes. Now the mistake was fully realized, the problem was that with SWIG's, sw Industrial's and the clients' holdings, Slater Walker was locked in. The market could only absorb a dribble of shares and the question was who to get out first. Among the earliest sellers was Slater's mother, whose 1,000 shares fetched around 11s., but she still lost some £300 of her £906 investment. The Sutherlands, who had gone back for another 5,000 shares in the November trough, may even have come out slightly ahead. Basil Samuel of Great Portland, however, who had bought 2,100 shares a year earlier at 17s. 3d., sold at about 9s. to lose about £850. Tiger also sold its recently acquired 2,500 at around 9s. to lose another £850, and Moss

Securities sold 1,000 of its 5,000 at about 9s. 6d.; and a few thousand of the shares bought by Pendock and sw Industrial in the summer of 1965 were disposed of at about 10s.

In the third week of March 1966, with the price down to 7s. 6d. in spite of Astaron-Bird's decision to pay the second dividend, Investment Analysis took some of the clients out. John James, for example, who had paid £1,287 10s. for 2,000 of the Planes' shares the previous summer, was sold out at this level to lose £550. One thousand of Willis' 2,000 stake, acquired from Slater the previous April, were sold at 7s 4½d. to realize a loss of £548 14s., but he was left holding his other 1,000. Willis' shares were bought back by Slater Walker itself and about twenty clients were relieved of their shares in this way at 7s. 4½d., to establish tax losses, and Slater Walker took in all about 25,000 shares back on its own books.

By May 1966 the price had fallen to 6s. 6d. sw Industrial Holdings had resumed selling the shares it had acquired the previous summer, and Pendock now resold the balance of his personal holding at this price. Moss Securities also sold the rest of its investment, losing heavily, and Slater Walker resold the shares it had bought back off its clients at a shilling loss apiece in May and June.

In June, Astaron-Bird announced that 1965's profits had fallen to £36,484 from the previous year's £156,785. It could have been worse for this meant at least that the second half of the year had been better than the first. But the company, it was revealed, had had to absorb a loss of £21,000 at Coastal Radio, and on top of this £89,000 of goodwill had been written off mainly on account of the new subsidiaries: Gemco, too, had been a poor investment, for after its acquisition a government order for the hovercraft altimeters was cancelled.

The share price was down to 6s. by July 1966, and SWIG, which now started to get rid of its investment, managed to secure this price for its first sales. But the quotation quickly dropped to 4s. 4½d. in August, and SWIG waited till the end of the year, when the price had recovered slightly, before selling the rest of its holding. Nevertheless SWIG's total loss was of the order of £60,000, or nearly seventy per cent of its original investment.

Astaron-Bird never recovered. Whitfield, the former managing director, felt bitter about Slater Walker's operation and was reluctant to talk about it. But he told me that 'they stampeded us', and that the company had had to resist strong pressure, particularly on its dividend policy. He said it could not get over the collapse in its share price.

This never again rose above 8s., and at the end of 1969 it was down to 3s. 9d. At that point those of Slater Walker's original clients who were still holding the shares – and there were quite a number of them

– were lucky to see a small revival when a successful bid, worth a little under 5s. 6d. a share, was made for Astaron-Bird by the alarm manufacturers, Brocks.

Among the first clients to become disenchanted with Slater because of Astaron-Bird were Rabl and Stein, who lost several thousand pounds on that one share. What alarmed them was the discovery that they had been put into the shares in 1964 after their friend Cheshire had decided to sell out and his investment trust holdings had been bought up by Slater. Rabl even wrote to Sutherlands inquiring how his original investment had been made.

But Dr Stott was one of the first to voice his disquiet about Astaron-Bird. His 1,850 shares – of which 1,500 had been acquired at 20s. each from Avasvilla, the dealing company in which Walker had an interest – had fallen right from the moment he got them. By June 1965 they were already down twenty-five per cent, and, although his overall portfolio had only performed slightly worse than the market, he was so alarmed that he decided to remove his money from Investment Analysis' care. But he still did not know what to do about the investment, and when the shares had fallen to 12s. Stott called in on Pendock to ask what to do about them. This was in the summer of 1965 at about the time that Pendock and Slater Walker were reinvesting in Astaron-Bird and Pendock told Stott to hold on. He gave the same advice when Stott inquired again when the price was down to 8s. Stott finally took the matter into his own hands and sold in June 1966 at 5s. 10d. to realize a loss of £1,302 3s. 9d. Including dealing expenses his original investment of £1,887 had been reduced by a staggering £1,351 to just £536, a loss of nearly seventy-two per cent – and this was out of a portfolio of only £5,000.

It was later that Willis and Macdonald also became disenchanted with Investment Analysis. Again, it was not so much the overall performance of their portfolios that concerned them but the speed with which Astaron-Bird and a selection of other shares were falling. Macdonald was left with the impression that they were no longer interested in handling accounts of his size and so ended the arrangement. Willis at first asked Pendock to start switching him back into 'blue chips' but then decided to take his money away. Willis sold a further 500 of his holding in 1967 at 5s. 6½d. for a further loss of £320, but in 1974 still held some Brocks shares exchanged in the offer. Mr and Mrs Macdonald held onto theirs until Astaron-Bird had been taken over and then sold their Brocks shares for £478 2s. 6d. for a loss of £1,046 17s. 6d.

There were, of course, other clients who, in spite of losing money in Astaron-Bird, were quite happy with Slater Walker's management of their money. Kutchera and Shepherd, for example, who got Walker's shares, made money in other securities, as did Stokes and

Hurst, and therefore had no complaints.

Slater, however, has recently reiterated that he and Walker did not know that their shares in Astaron-Bird had been sold to clients, and that:

> Astaron-Bird was unrepresentative of investments made by Slater Walker, but with the benefit of hindsight was the biggest single error of investment judgement they made;

> Slater Walker wrongly considered Astaron-Bird to be an outstanding investment and that at most times it appeared to them to be very attractively priced in relation to the market as a whole;

> Slater's mother remained an investor during the critical period and Slater Walker, in which the bulk of Slater's money was invested, was a big buyer of shares;

> the portfolios of the clients who left had performed reasonably well in relation to the market;

> Slater Walker built up a very successful business in both unit trusts and clients' portfolios; in particular they became Managers of the Year in unit trusts on several occasions and clients' portfolios grew mainly by recommendation;

> the kind of money involved in both Slater's and Walker's purchases of Astaron-Bird shares was insignificant to them;

> Slater Walker helped many clients out of their investment in Astaron-Bird even though they lost money in doing this and that the main purpose was to establish capital gains tax losses for those clients; that they never bought any shares for clients for improper motives; and finally that the reason he sold his shares was simply to degear, which he was also doing with his Slater Walker shares, implying no loss of confidence in that company either.

Walker too has recently re-stated his own account of this matter in the following words:

> 1. None of the shares purchased by me or by the two companies with which I was connected were purchased in nominee names, an action which would certainly have taken place by anyone wishing to rig markets and to place shares with clients without the clients being informed.

> 2. The amounts of money involved were not only small but of the three investments with which I was supposedly connected the smallest of them was in my own name and the largest of them was in a company in which I had only a minor shareholding and would therefore not have benefited from the result.

3. My shares were sold openly in the market substantially below what turned out to be the peak in that market and long before the various Directors connected with the Investment Department of Slater Walker purchased shares for themselves.

4. Of my own shares (and unbeknown to me) the largest number went to a person who was, and is, a very good personal friend of mine, an unlikely thing to happen if I was getting rid of a share I considered had reached its peak. Mr Kutchera himself will validate that it is quite inconceivable that I would have done such a thing in order to obtain a minute profit of probably something like £200.

5. The reality of this whole transaction as far as I am concerned is that probably in conversation Jim Slater informed me that he considered, as he did genuinely consider, that Astaron-Bird was a good investment. I picked up a small number of shares for myself and for two companies with which I was connected, and then made my own decision as to when to sell them. I dealt openly through a stockbroker with no knowledge whatsoever as to what buying and selling was taking place at Investment Analysis. On being asked for the first time whether I was opposed to the practice of Investment Managers selling their own shares to their clients without disclosing the fact, I categorically answered that, yes, I was against this and this remains my view and certainly has been my practice.

But these are not in my opinion adequate excuses for the manner in which Slater Walker handled the affairs of its clients in the Astaron-Bird episode, and nor can it be explained away as just a matter of bad investment judgement. In particular the fact that Slater and Walker both personally bought shares and then sold them at a profit and their clients bought those shares and lost money on them indicates that in using other people's money for its own ends, Slater Walker failed to pay sufficient attention to the premise with which we opened this story.

Willis, Stott and Macdonald did not know where their Astaron-Bird shares had come from. Clearly their views on whether Investment Analysis was acting in their best interests would have been strongly influenced by the knowledge that they were being sold shares by its principals, or companies associated with them, or indeed other clients. It might be imagined by those unfamiliar with Stock Exchange procedure that buyers of shares would be able to tell from the documentation from whom they were acquiring their shares; and indeed, this was the case before the autumn of 1963 when the Stock Transfer Act came into operation.

The provisions of this Act meant that the buyer would no longer see the transfer form with the seller's name already entered on it, as he had done when he had had to sign it before the Act came into force. As Macdonald, who had been investing on the Stock Exchange before 1963, remarked to me: 'It used to be rather interesting to see from whom one was buying.'

The Stock Transfer Act had been passed in the summer of 1963; it was sponsored by a private member but had the backing of the Conservative government in the person of du Cann, then Economic Secretary at the Treasury. Its purpose was to streamline the transfer procedure following recommendations made at the end of 1960 by a committee of representatives from the Stock Exchange and City institutions.

Walker found an opportunity in the short debate on the bill to bring up his favourite theme of the property-owning democracy:

> There is, unfortunately, in existence the situation that the City of London has shrouded itself in a mystique with lots of jargon and words which the normal person does not come across in everyday life. As a result, there is a basic fear of the unknown when the ordinary family man living in the provinces con-templates the possibility of purchasing some shares.

Simplifying the transfer procedure alone would not have much impact, Walker thought, unless followed by:

> a process of educating the public as to what actually physically happens when a share changes hands. This is a task for the London and provincial stock exchanges. It is absurd that at this time when there is a need to encourage investment in the private sector of industry – and I think both sides of the House will agree that there is this need – this investment should be confined basically to persons who happen to have contact with a stock-broker or with a bank manager who is not prejudiced against equity investments . . .

The sort of practices that we have seen in the market in Astaron-Bird shares is another main cause of the 'basic fear of the unknown' of the so-called small investor who believes he will be at the mercy of the professionals if he ventures into stocks and shares. Nor does it do much to enhance the Stock Exchange's reputation as a channel of long-term capital into industry; and as far as Slater and Walker were concerned, it is just as well that their clients were not educated as to what physically happened when Investment Analysis took their Astaron-Bird shares and sold them to their clients.

11   *Laminating – and other activities*

In January 1972 Graham Turner wrote a major two-part profile of Slater Walker in the *Sunday Telegraph*, the newspaper that had done so much to advance Slater's career as an investment adviser. Turner reported a decision by Slater to launch an insurance company in 1970: insurance was, Turner quoted Slater, 'basically just investing other people's money, at which we're very good'.

Whatever other criticisms have been levelled against Slater Walker, from its earliest days the company's skill at investing other people's money has rarely been publicly questioned. The general impression, fostered by quotations like the one above, has been of uninterrupted success. The reality is different: in the bear market of 1965 and 1966 Slater Walker's handling of other people's money can in no way be called 'very good'.

Investment 'counselling' had been the main plank in Slater's grand plan announced at the start of 1965, and in that year Investment Analysis levied fees of £90,000, on which it made a profit of £64,000, the most important single contribution to the group's total earnings of £191,000. But the following year growth came to an abrupt halt and Investment Analysis was allowed to slip into temporary obscurity – Slater did not even mention this subsidiary in his 1966 chairman's statement and later accounts by Slater Walker men have tended to play down the role of investment management at this time.

Slater argued that the reason for this was that the investment side had been 'dramatically overtaken by the other sides of the business'. Slater Walker's other activities at this time are fully described in this and other chapters, but what Slater says begs the question – which is why should the investment side have declined in relative importance? The answer is that this reflected the dissatisfaction of investment clients touched on in the previous chapter. It has not been possible to establish just how many customers decided to remove their money: Slater first told me that records no longer existed and then later said some records had been found but refused to produce them on the grounds that they were confidential. He accepted that there had been a decline in the number of clients but said it was estimated that new clients joining brought in more than enough to offset withdrawals. But my own researches suggest that withdrawals were sufficient both in number and size to cause a serious setback, not just a minor one as Slater was prepared to concede.

When Slater had unveiled his grand design he had said that investment counselling was 'still in its infancy in the United Kingdom'. There were, of course, lots of people in the business of giving investment advice: merchant banks and stockbrokers for a start. Then there were the unit trusts that were being set up following the lead of du Cann and Walker at Unicorn. Initially, however, Slater filled a gap by undertaking to look after amounts of as little as £5,000 - the sort of capital that was not really big enough to interest other professional advisers but whose owners wanted more individual attention than they would have got from a unit trust. But Slater soon abandoned that, too; indeed, he argued that the decline in the number of clients at this time was to a large extent due to a deliberate effort to phase out the very small portfolios. There was thus really nothing particularly novel about his investment counselling; what distinguished it were its built-in conflicts of interest, conflicts that investment advisers must recognize in order to safeguard their clients' interests. We have seen what happened in Astaron-Bird: it was not the only example.

Conditions in the stock market in 1965/6 were, of course, much more difficult than any Slater had encountered before; as the Labour government struggled to hold the parity of the pound, the stock market fluctuated before finally plunging at the end of 1966 when the *Financial Times* Industrial Ordinary Index reached a low of 284.2 on 8 November, against its 1 October 1964 high of 377.8. There is, as already recorded, evidence that Slater himself foresaw the difficulties when he wrote, in the Slater Walker annual statement at the end of March 1965, that the 'stock market as a whole could well find a lower level during the next few months'. In spite of this statement, Slater maintains that he continued to invest for Slater Walker in 1965. This is not, however, supported by the evidence: after the transfer of its portfolio to SWIG at the end of 1964 Slater Walker was left with one investment - a £125,000 stake in Lombard Banking which was to be resold to Maxwell Joseph. At the end of 1965 Slater Walker was liquid, with £175,000 in local authority deposits and only £23,000 of equity shares - much of which must have been the Astaron-Bird shares bought in the summer of that year when, according to Slater, Slater Walker resumed buying after the market shake-out. Slater also argued that SWIG had continued to invest in 1965, building up its portfolio from £1.2 to £1.8 million worth of shares. Slater Walker only had forty per cent of SWIG obtained for £1 million worth of investments, and just how many other shareholders subscribed in stock rather than cash is not recorded; so there is no way of checking Slater's £1.2 million figure, or, accepting that SWIG was an active investor during 1965, when during the year it bought. In the spring of 1965, Slater himself sold shares in order, he says, to reduce his substantial bank borrowing, although, he says, he himself remained fully invested. The point is that at the same time new clients had their existing portfolios cleared out and replaced with Slater Walker favourites shortly before the prices of a number of them fell sharply.

Before we look in more detail at the fortunes of some of the early investment clients, we must look at the structure of the organization that Slater was creating. The Astaron-Bird episode shows that any suggestion that Slater Walker was a neat compartmentalized group, with an industrial department and an investment department each quietly pursuing its own policy, is not credible: often, as in that case, all available money – clients', SWIG's, the dealing companies' – was piled into the same situation. But nevertheless, at the start of 1965, with Pendock and Farrell looking after the day-to-day affairs of Investment Analysis, Slater had no one to help him tackle the other objectives of his plan, apart from his original partner Ken Meyer. Slater had therefore quickly to build up a team, whose initial function was to find suitable companies – private and public – for Slater Walker to move in on. Slater's first recruits, however, had financial rather than industrial experience. First to arrive in April 1965 was Walker's co-director at Walker Young, Herbert Despard, then thirty-five. An old Etonian and already quite wealthy, Despard came from a different background to most of Slater's early colleagues. Next to join, on 1 July 1965, was Malcolm Horsman, then thirty-two. He had become restless working for a City factoring or bill discounting firm, and had replied to an advertisement placed by Slater. Richard Tarling was the first man with industrial experience to reach Slater Walker but he did not come until later in 1965. He was then just thirty-one and had resigned his job as youngest-ever commercial director of AEC, having succeeded Slater, whom he had known since the age of twenty-four.

To house his expanding team, Slater moved out of Mount Street and took over, in early 1965, the Hertford Street offices of Rodwell, which the Myerses had vacated in favour of a new head office they had built. All activities of the group were now centred on Hertford Street, although in 1966 the investment department moved out again to new offices in the City – a move which, together with the hiring of more staff, affected its 1966 profits, according to Slater. Hertford Street, like Mount Street, was just a few minutes walk from Slater's old employers at Leyland, who had been so important to his business career – and his personal life, for in the autumn of 1965 he married his former Leyland secretary.

Throughout 1965 the main board of Slater Walker – renamed Slater Walker Securities – was mostly non-executive apart from Slater, its full-time working chairman and mastermind. The deputy chairman, Walker was rather more active than Walmsley, or than Samuel and his colleague Wallace, who were there because of Great Portland's massive investment. (The only other backer to get representation was Schroders, who appointed Gordon Popham to the board of SWIG.) Finally there was Meyer – but he had his hands full with Productofoam, and it soon became apparent that he would need the help of Slater and the men at Hertford Street if Producto-foam was not to threaten the early downfall of the whole structure.

In spite of the huge extension in the scope of Slater's plans since he had first bought into Productofoam in early 1964, the performance of the little rubber company remained vital a year later. Slater Walker owned forty per cent of SWIG and SWIG owned forty per cent of Productofoam. That investment represented nearly £450,000 of SWIG's resources of £2.5 million. Many more Productofoam shares were owned by investment clients. Productofoam was thus the base on which the stability and growth of Slater's corporate structure largely depended.

At the time of the Productofoam rights issue in December 1964, Slater had forecast that the Company would make 'at least £100,000' profit in its financial year to 30 September 1965. 'We should,' he had said, 'make a profit of not less than £65,000 on laminating and £35,000 on rubber glove manufacture.'

But as 1965 progressed, it became clear that Productofoam was not going to make anything like £100,000 from either of these industrial activities. We will be looking at Productofoam's career in more detail in the next chapter; but briefly what happened was, firstly, that installation of new plant at Latex Surgical, the glove subsidiary in Hackney, resulted in a temporary loss of capacity. The real problems however were in laminating. This is a tricky process, involving the heating of materials to just the right temperature before applying the rubber latex or plastic foam. The materials for the most part remain in the ownership of the customers, the clothing and furniture manufacturers for example, but the firm doing the laminating is naturally responsible for the stock while it is being pro-cessed. Losses can quickly mount up if the materials are damaged or discoloured by overheating. 'Laminating material for other people,' Slater told me when admitting that Productofoam had not been an overwhelming success, 'is not to be recommended for prospective entrepreneurs of the future.'

But Slater was stuck with it, and the stock market does not easily forgive prospective entrepreneurs who fail to live up to optimistic forecasts. But Productofoam did not fail to meet Slater's predictions – thanks to its little share dealing subsidiary, Moss Securities. In the event Productofoam turned in pre-tax profits for the year to 30 September 1965 of £107,669. Slater, as we shall see in the next chapter, had other things to tell his Productofoam shareholders and did not dwell on past performance in his annual statement dated 6 January 1966. He remarked briefly that profits were 'in line with our forecast'. The directors' report, however, contained the following breakdown:

Rubber Gloves	£24,542
Laminating and other activities	£83,127
	£107,669

It was therefore at least revealed that gloves had failed to meet Slater's forecast of not less than £35,000. But search as you might, nowhere in the Productofoam report and accounts, or in Slater's annual statement, which even included a little diagram of the structure of the group, was there any revelation that the bulk of the £83,127 had been made by share dealing on the Stock Exchange. There was not even an item for 'quoted securities' in the accounts, for they had all been sold by the end of September.

We have seen that when Moss's shares were first issued in April 1964 its £10,000 capital was subscribed jointly by Rights Securities, a subsidiary of Rights & Issues Investment Trust (one of Cheshire's Mount Street trusts), and by Productofoam. I asked Slater in the summer of 1973, what was the role of Rights & Issues Investment Trust and Moss Securities. He replied: 'I joined Rights & Issues Investment Trust as a director and I ran a dealing company for them which I think was called Moss Securities. We made quite good dealing profits and at a later stage I resigned on an amicable basis.' As far as Rights & Issues was concerned, Slater's answer was accurate enough, but as a description of his relationship with Moss Securities, it must rank as, at best, disingenuous.

In its first six months of operation to 30 September 1964, Moss made a trading profit of £1,227. On 1 January 1965, Rights & Issues transferred its shares to Millstoke, the little merchandising company recently bought by Productofoam. Moss therefore became a wholly owned subsidiary of Productofoam. Shortly afterwards, the Moss shares registered in the name of Productofoam were also transferred to Millstoke, Moss thus becoming a subsidiary of a subsidiary, the last in a chain of three.

Slater allowed his directorship of Rights & Issue to lapse in early 1965, but he remained a director and became chairman of Moss, a position he held until 6 December 1966. The resignations of the other original directors of Moss – Cheshire, Robertshaw and Hardman – are not filed at Companies House, but by July 1965 they had been replaced by Pendock and one of his assistants, and in the year to 30 September 1965 Moss made some excellent profits: £61,928.

It is not clear whether all of this was consolidated in Producto-foam's profits of £107,669, for Moss was only wholly owned for nine months out of the year. But it is clear that of the £83,127 attributable to 'laminating and other activities' the 'other activities' were a euphemism for Moss, and it was Moss that saved Productofoam's and Slater's reputation.

Even including the entire Moss profit, it is hard to follow the calculation by which the £83,127 was reached. For on 31 May 1965, Foam Textile Laminators, acquired for £70,000 cash in the autumn of 1964, and which had taken over the business of Sebec's East End factory, ceased trading with accumulated losses of £25,000. To balance this loss, and to make up the £21,199 needed to account for the total after bringing in Moss's £61,928, there was only £29,125 from the Sebec subsidiary in Lancashire. A new acquisition, W. S. Heaton, added only a few thousand pounds.

At all events, Moss must have provided roughly half, and probably more, of Productofoam's profits that year without so much as a hint in the accounts. It also provided the bulk of the cash needed to pay Productofoam's dividend, for Moss paid a gross dividend to its immediate parent, Millstoke, of £48,500 and Millstoke, which appears to have succeeded in losing money on its own operations, paid one of £40,000 to Productofoam – a rate of 40,000 per cent on its £100 capital. Productofoam's twenty-five per cent payment to its shareholders cost, gross, about £48,500.

By the autumn of 1965 SWIG had increased its stake in Producto-foam to forty-eight per cent, so its share of the dividend was about £23,000, over a quarter of SWIG's total dividend income in 1965. This was in its turn helpful to SWIG when it came to paying its £100,000 dividend for 1965, out of pre-tax profits of £137,500 – including a few thousand pounds from share dealing, for the industrial group, too, had spawned a subsidiary, Dukersbrook, to operate in the stock market.

Slater Walker's share of that dividend was £40,000, and so SWIG failed to make the £50,000 predicted for it in Slater's grand design of February 1965. The backbone of Slater Walker's profits in that critical first full year came from the investment clients' fees, while share dealing profits from the main subsidiaries engaged in this activity – Clamond, SW Industrial Holdings and Status Change – reached £40,000, double the anticipated rate, and helped to push the total profits to some £36,000 above the forecast.

The usefulness of the investment clients was not confined to the fee they paid. Moss's profit was a vital link in the chain, helping to ensure that the structure did not topple; and it was convenient that in order to realize dealing gains in time to be included in Productofoam's profits, Moss was able to sell shares to Slater Walker's investment clients.

From the summer of 1964 a new generation of companies took over from the early Capitalist shares as Slater's favourites. They included some larger companies, like Lombard Banking, General Electric, Grand Metropolitan Hotels, Joe Hyman's textile group, Viyella International, one or two goldmining shares and Leyland. But for the most part the emphasis was still on little companies, like Astaron-Bird; a number of them had been floated for the first time in the 1964 market boom, and their shares naturally responded to concentrated buying.

One example was a little Liverpool-based paint company called Beaver, whose shares were quoted only on the local Stock Exchange. Control of Beaver changed hands in early 1965 and a new board of directors was appointed including Tim Reeve, a partner in a London stockbroking firm called Rowe Reeve (today renamed Rowe Rudd), which was creating something of a reputation for itself as a new issue specialist. The new management started to develop Beaver by taking over other business; and Slater Walker, via Moss, became closely involved in the process over the next two years.

In the spring and early summer of 1965 Moss acquired, in its own name, a mixture of ordinary and preference shares and loan stock in Beaver at a total cost of just over £23,646. But so small was Beaver that this amounted to about ten per cent of its capital. The Beaver share price had started the year at about 8s. and Moss secured its first ordinary shares at 9s. each. By the end of September, the price had soared to 15s. 6d.

On 27 September Moss sold out this investment for £28,727 and a profit of £5,080: the shares were distributed by Investment Analysis to twenty-four of its clients at 13s. 6d. each, along with a block of new shares which had been issued to Moss by Beaver in a deal which will be explained in the next chapter. As Slater points out, this price was below the then ruling market quotation of 14s. 3d. to 15s. 3d., and clearly the men at Slater Walker believed that Beaver shares would continue to rise, for Pendock and Despard each personally took 1,000 of Moss's holding. Beaver shares did go on up, but Pendock and Despard had resold within a matter of weeks, passing their shares on to the Tiger Investment Club at 15s. 3d. Tiger in turn resold to yet other clients at 17s. 6d.

We shall be looking later at some of Beaver's further dealings with Moss and Slater Walker but, briefly, Beaver continued to expand until 1966, when it had to raise more capital by a rights issue. Then in 1967 both share price and profits collapsed. Shortly before the issue the share price had reached a peak of over 24s.: on the way up Moss had acquired some more Beaver shares of which a small parcel of 4,000 were placed with Investment Analysis clients at no less than 23s. 4½d. Another Slater Walker dealing company, Status Change Investments, also made a quick dealing profit of £300 just before the peak, at the expense of a client who had to pay 21s. for the shares. Some (Slater says most) of the clients who had been sold shares in the original 1965 placing and who resold before the spring of 1966 made good profits; others (Slater says only a few) were not taken out until after the collapse and realized only small - if any - profits. One or two who had been sold shares at 13s. 6d. eventually realized losses, although by then they were no longer clients.

This pattern was typical of Slater Walker's investment counselling. While the shares rose everyone could make money, but inevitably those who were allocated their shares at the higher levels were exposed to greater risk. Slater argued that this was not a fair description of the activities and method of operation of Investment Analysis, which he described as 'basically very conventional with investments in hundreds of different shares involving several millions of pounds'. While it is true, as already noted, that client money was not exclusively invested in shares of little companies like Beaver, my own researches could find no support for the suggestion that the funds were spread over 'hundreds' of companies. The relationship between Slater Walker and Beaver may have been especially close, but nevertheless what characterized the operation at this time was the investment of a substantial slice of clients' portfolios in companies in which Slater Walker and swig were interested, and the consistent transfer of shares between clients and Slater Walker companies; and while clients undoubtedly benefited from some of these investments, in no way can this be called conventional - on the contrary, it overrode all established conventions of money management. Slater's most recent explanation of the transfer of shares between clients and Slater Walker companies was that 'most clients joined Slater Walker to participate in special situations with the company.'

Take another example - Tayside Floor Coverings, a Scottish company in which Slater took an interest in early 1965. It was, again, a small firm, with two million shares then standing at about 7s. each. At around this level Moss bought a total of 67,160 shares - again in its own name.

Throughout the summer clients were put into Tayside shares, but the price rose more gradually than usual and by July it was only a little above 7s. The Moss holding was then sold: 60,500 shares were bought directly by swig at 7s. 4¾d. and, of the remainder, 6,000 were sold at the same price to the Standard-Triumph Pension Fund and 320 at 7s. In all Moss realized a profit of about £1,450.

Again, we shall hear more of Tayside later. It proved a profitable investment for most clients whose shares were this time sold at the top of the market – about 8s. 6d. in early 1966 – when another big buyer appeared to compete with SWIG. (At least one client's shares were acquired by SWIG itself at this level, but others were sold in the market.) But not all clients were taken out at that point. The Standard-Triumph Pension Fund, for example, was not so lucky: it had bought a total of 28,000 Tayside shares, many of them acquired from Slater Walker dealing companies' holdings built up through Barclays Nominees, and these were all bought back by SWIG in the summer of 1966 when the price had fallen back to 6s. 6d. The Fund thus lost about £1,000.

Another share which, like Astaron-Bird, cost Slater Walker clients dear, was a publishing company, Caxton Holdings. This concern was being reorganized in 1964 and 1965 by a man called Hedley Le Bas, after making heavy losses. Slater Walker was again introduced to the company by brokers Rowe Reeve, and once Slater Walker had taken it on the share price went roaring away, from about 7s. in October 1964 to 23s. 6d. in May 1965.

The old share registers of Caxton could not be traced but the general – and familiar – picture can be pieced together from Companies House returns. It was another little company with only 1.3 million shares outstanding at the end of 1964. In the early summer of 1965, about the time the price reached its peak, Moss Securities sold some 11,000 shares, while Barclays Nominees (Angel Court), which was used at this time by Slater Walker dealing companies, disposed of about 50,000. But while these sales were being made, Slater Walker was buying on behalf of its clients: the Standard-Triumph Pension Fund, Willis, Stott and others. The rationale behind the investment was that profits would jump, as indeed they did – from £140,649 to £301,562 for the financial year to 26 June 1965. But the share price had already started to fall back even before the figures were announced as Caxton ran into 'unexpected difficulties', including adverse press publicity over door-to-door selling of encyclopedias. Slater Walker was by then too involved to extricate itself quickly. Horsman was dispatched to try to solve its problems and even more client money – the main Leyland pension fund this time – was put into the shares. In spite of this, profits dropped back to the £140,000 mark and the shares to 8s., at which price the company was bought by Robert Maxwell's Pergamon Press in early 1967.

In view of such investments it is not surprising that some of Slater's clients became anxious and a number made the trek to Hertford Street to complain about the performance of their shares. The

Brighton doctor, William Stott, was particularly alarmed at the way his Astaron-Bird had fallen from the day they had been bought (by June 1965 he had a paper loss of £500 on them), but Investment Analysis had also, amazingly, resold some of his Productofoam shares at a loss, retaining only those acquired in the December 1964 rights issue. Unsatisfied by Pendock's explanations, Stott took his money away from Slater Walker's care in June 1965. This was then the state of his portfolio and of the realized gains and losses:

Company	Number of shares	Date bought	Price	All-in-cost	Price on termination	Value
Astaron-Bird	1,850	10.9.64	20s. & 19s. 9d.	£1,887.	15s.	£1,387.10.
Harmo	1,000	28.9.64	14s. 3d.	£ 730.	9s.	£ 450.
Productofoam	100	15.1.65	10s.	£ 50.	10s. 3d.	£ 51. 5s.
Kenwood	2,000	1.4.65	11s. 1½d.	£1,138.	13s. 4d.	£1,333. 6s. 6d.
Caxton	500	30.3.65	21s. 10½d.	£ 553.	23s. 3d.	£ 581. 5s.
G. & M. Power	500	25.5.65	19s. 9d.	£ 505.	19s. 9d.	£ 493. 15s.
				£4,863.		£4,297. 1s. 6d.

Stott's money had also been invested in three other shares that had been resold before he removed it from Investment Analysis' care:

Company	Number of shares	Date bought	Price	Cost	Date sold	Price	Proceeds	Gain/ loss
GEC	550	10.9.64	39s.	£1,099	20.4.65	40s.	£1,093	−£6
Lombard Banking	1,000	15.9.64	17s. 7½d.	£ 901	7.1.65	19s. 3d.	£ 950	+£49
Productofoam	500	20.11.64	14s.	£ 358	5.4.65	10s.	£ 250	−£108
								−£65

Although the overall performance of his portfolio during the time it was under Slater Walker's management had been about the same as the market as a whole, there were further nasty surprises in store for Stott. We have seen that he finally lost no less than £1,351 of his Astaron-Bird investment. To that he had to add a loss of £343 on Caxton, which he sold in June at 8s. 6d., and £280 on Harmo, sold at 9s. 3d. in October 1965. To set against these he only had a gain of £200 realized on Kenwood – one of the few of Slater's new favourites that did well for most clients – and a few pounds recouped on his remaining 100 Productofoam sold in early 1966. So on the shares chosen for him by Slater Walker Stott's final overall loss, including costs, out of the original £5,000 he had entrusted to their care, was about £1,800 or about 36 per cent, though the bulk of this fall took place after he had resumed responsibility for managing his own funds.

The Macdonalds had joined Investment Analysis shortly before Stott, and their portfolio got off to a more auspicious start; they were put into Leyland at 117s. 6d. and GEC at 88s., and into Shaw Carpets, a firm floated by Rothschilds in the summer of 1964, to whose merits

Walker says he drew Slater's attention. Slater also bought 4,000 Lotery shares each for the Macdonalds on 3 July 1964 at 10s. 5¼d. each, so that they benefited from the rise that followed the announcement of his acquisition of control a few days later.

The Macdonalds' Lotery/Slater Walker shares were sold in March 1965 at 16s. 1½d. each and they thus made a good profit of £2,069, nearly fifty per cent. Some of the proceeds were invested in a company called Cork Manufacturing which, as we shall see in the next chapter, Slater was investigating as a possible takeover target, and which as a result also proved a profitable investment. Their Leyland shares were also sold in 1965 for a profit of £458 and they realized a gain of £220 on GEC. But the Macdonalds became disturbed by four of Investment Analysis' choices to replace these early successes.

In June 1965 Investment Analysis bought them 500 shares in James Halstead, a manufacturer of floor tiles and waterproof clothing, at over £1 each – a total cost of £517. The shares, already on their way down from a May peak, continued to fall sharply. Then in October 1965 Investment Analysis put them into both Astaron-Bird and Caxton, both of which were then at the top of temporary revivals in their prices: as we have seen the Macdonalds got 2,000 Astaron-Bird shares from another client, Leonard Wiles, at 15s. 3d. and they paid 19s. 3d each for 1,500 shares in Caxton, a total investment of £1,458. Both shares immediately resumed their downward paths.

The fourth investment which worried the Macdonalds was a tiny clothing company, Philip Kunick. Stockbrokers Joseph Sebag had secured a quotation for Kunick in early 1964, after placing 260,000 shares at 9s. 7½d. By the end of 1965, as the company beat its prospectus forecast, the shares soared to over 16s. At this point Sebags again found buyers for blocks of Kunick shares, with the help of Investment Analysis. The Macdonalds were allotted 3,000 between them at 16s. 3½d.

It was shortly after this that the Macdonalds decided to remove their money from Investment Analysis' management. Slater claims there was a surplus of about £2,000 – about ten per cent – on their portfolio at the time, but on grounds of confidentiality did not produce the records on which he said this was based. This was, he said, achieved in very uncertain and on balance falling stock market conditions. My own information suggests that, while there may well have been a surplus of this order at the time, it may have been largely due to the Macdonalds' initiative in withdrawing some of the Lotery profits earlier on. In any event the legacy of Investment Analysis' period of management was to dog them for many years. They eventually realized a loss of £1,048 (plus £20 costs) on their Astaron-Bird in March 1970. At the same time they sold their James Halstead for a loss of £443, or eighty-five per cent. They finally got rid of their Caxton shares in the Pergamon bid, taking the 8s. cash alternative offer, to realize a loss of £858 or nearly sixty per cent.

The Kunick price managed to climb a little further after the Macdonalds had been allotted theirs at the end of 1965, reaching a peak of 18s. 4d. in early 1966. Then the company started running into trouble, and the price fell steadily to reach a low of 11s. in November that year. For the next two years the shares managed to stay a little above the 10s. level, but crashed again in 1969 to 3s. 3d. and again to under eight new pence in 1970. The Macdonalds had held on in the hope of seeing a recovery but they finally sold in the clear-out of their portfolio in March 1970 at 2s. 6d. to realize, after costs, another eighty-five per cent loss of £2,102 12s. 4d. Against these losses the Macdonalds were able to set a profit of £1,200 they realized on Shaw Carpets in 1967, and profits they also made on some other shares originally chosen by Investment Analysis, for example Grand Metropolitan Hotels, Croda International, William Press and Viyella.

Slater Walker was to come into Macdonald's life again when a paint company, Cementone, of which he was a director, became one of the first asset stripping victims of Slater Walker. The business, as we shall see, was sold to Beaver Paint in exchange for shares which were then placed with investment clients. It was the proposal to put him into Beaver that finally decided Willis, the client who had got 2,000 of Slater's own Astaron-Bird shares in April 1965, that he had had enough.

Willis' unease came to a head after about a year. He had made an excellent profit of £1,209 on Kenwood, but this had been almost completely offset by two big realized losses: £548 14s. on 1,000 of his Astaron-Bird sold in March 1966, and £654 18s. on another little electronics company, Derritron. This firm had been floated by Rowe Reeve in early 1965; then came the familiar story of a soaring share price on one good year's results followed by collapse of profits and price. Slater Walker was less heavily involved in Derritron than in, say, Caxton or Astaron-Bird, but Moss had a few shares which it sold, before the collapse, in the summer of 1965.

Willis had been taken in and out of two or three other shares at small profits, but the net position at the end of his first year was a realized loss of about £80. Including unrealized losses his portfolio showed a larger loss – five per cent according to Slater, but my information suggests more – against a small rise in the market over the same period. Willis at first merely asked Pendock to start switching him back into 'blue chips' but shortly afterwards decided to call off the deal. In the event, over the coming years Willis did very well out of two in particular of Investment Analysis' selections, trebling his money on contractors William Press and on a plant hire firm, Grayston Industries. In the final analysis these may have out-weighed the disasters but nearly ten years later, in addition to his Brocks shares (the legacy of Astaron-Bird), Willis still held Pergamon Press shares, exchanged for 1,500 Caxton Holdings bought by Investment Analysis for him in April 1965 at a cost of £1,581 8s. 9d. The Pergamon Press Stock Exchange quotation had been suspended since 1969 as that company's affairs were subjected to a long-drawn-out investigation.

Slater insisted I put too much weight on the shares' subsequent performance. He said it was unfair to attribute responsibility to Investment Analysis for the performance of shares of one-time clients once they had withdrawn their money, and especially years afterwards, 'an amazing ten years' in the case of Willis. The only relevant factor, according to Slater, was the performance at the moment they left. It is true that Stott, the Macdonalds and Willis could have avoided some of their losses if they had sold the bad shares quickly after leaving, but the suggestion that Investment Analysis can avoid all responsibility for shares it had originally chosen must be rejected, especially in the light of the manner in which clients' affairs were handled. Equally, Investment Analysis must be given credit for shares, like William Press, which turned out well. It is, of course, im-possible to say what would have happened had the clients remained, although Investment Analysis could no more have avoided some of the losses than the clients themselves. Also, clients like the three above felt that their capital was too small for Investment Analysis to be bothered with, and while Slater Walker may have been devoting much thought to the problems of managing such portfolios, as Slater claims, it was not until June 1967 that the solution of a unit trust was reached, and during the stock market boom of 1972 this and other Slater Walker trusts did enjoy a period of notable success.

While the loss of the smaller portfolios would not have been a serious blow to Slater Walker, a number of the more important clients also took their money away. Eric Knight removed Lombard Banking's funds – after they had been substantially reduced from the £100,000 starting figure – and Stein and Rabl, who had given Slater £70,000 and £50,000 to look after, also took their money away, although by then it had been considerably eroded by fiascos like Astaron-Bird, Caxton and Musical & Plastics.

Slater also lost the management of the Leyland and Standard-Triumph Pension Funds. It has not been possible to clarify exactly the circumstances in which this happened. When I went to talk to Lord Black in the summer of 1973, at Slater's suggestion, Black told me that the unions, who were represented on the funds' boards of trustees, did not always agree with Slater's investment policies. Slater had had most to do with the Leyland Fund, Black indicated, and when I asked Stokes about it, he said that Slater had not lost money for it, but that the management had been switched to Schroders following a review of the structure of the Fund. I understood from Stokes, however, that it had been felt that the type of investments that Slater favoured were not considered entirely appropriate for the Fund and Slater told me that on termination of the management contract, Slater Walker bought back some of the funds' smaller holdings, including for example the Tayside shares.

Following Black's remark, I attempted to contact the union trustees. Those on the Leyland Fund at the time have since retired, and I did not press inquiries because the Leyland Fund appears rarely in the registers of the Slater favourites of this period. But the Standard-Triumph Fund kept cropping up. We have seen that it invested £9,831 in 11,000 Astaron-Bird shares in April 1965, just as Slater himself was selling – shares which it later sold at a loss of about £6,800. We have seen how it lost money on Tayside. Slater also put Standard-Triumph into Bernard Wardle shares – 14,100 at a total cost of £5,260 – just before the price started to collapse in 1965. The Fund was also invested in Caxton, Halstead, G. & M. Power, and on the plus side, Kenwood.

So I asked Edward McGarry, the convenor at Standard-Triumph and one of the two workers' representatives on the board of trustees of the Pension Fund, about Slater's period of management. Slater, he told me, had had a free hand, and merely sent the trustees the contract notes to sign every month. The Fund, a new one, had started off with about £500,000 at the end of 1964, when Slater came to Coventry to explain his proposed policy. After a couple of years, the Fund was £100,000 down he said, and the workers' trustees felt that Slater Walker was 'not acting in our best interests'. He said they had something of a battle with the management trustees, who were in a majority before the management of the Fund was switched to Schroders.*

When I put the question of union concern to Stokes at the end of 1974, he told me that he was 'advised that the instances about which you spoke referred to a subsequent change-over from one merchant bank to another and had no connection with Mr Slater.' When I repeated what I had been told by a trustee Stokes replied: 'From time

---

* The union was not happy with Schroders either, McGarry told me, and the management was later again switched to Warburgs. As indicated Slater Walker had bought back some of the fund's smaller investments. But the fund's holding of Wardle was retained and later sold when the price finally recovered in 1968 and the fund probably only made a small loss. The Wardle price, incidentally, collapsed again in 1969 and 1970 and Stokes, who had sold 11,000 of his 36,000 holdings in early 1967 at just over 5s., disposed of the remainder in early 1970 to lose heavily on this second venture into shares.

to time the professional managers of the various funds are changed, at the discretion of the trustees, if in their opinion a change of manager is considered advisable. This is not necessarily any reflection on anybody who is currently giving us advice but merely that they must constantly be looking for the best that is available.'

The problems of the investment counselling arm of Slater Walker are reflected in the results of Investment Analysis: fees rose only by £9,500 in 1966 to £99,000 and profits were static at £65,000 – and included for the first time a substantial sum earned from giving financial advice to companies on takeover bids; it had not been the expected growth business. In early 1975 Slater wrote me:

> I think it is fair to say that the stock market turned extremely dull in the two years following the 1964 General Election and the market conditions were difficult for successful private client investments. As a result of this, and perhaps, inevitably, one or two unfortunate investments, we suffered not particularly good performance in the early days on the private clients' side. This, however, gradually became much better, as we improved and expanded our research department and market conditions improved. I think it is fair to say that we, ourselves, have taken on many clients from other financial institutions who felt that they had not received a satisfactory service in the past. Almost all financial institutions have some clients whose portfolios have not performed well and this is simply an inescapable fact of investment life.

I have concentrated on the affairs of Stott, Macdonald and Willis. Slater says that they are unrepresentative. Speaking from memory Slater said there were between 120 and 240 clients at this time; and he says he could show me a number of unprompted letters from his investment clients complimenting Slater Walker upon the investment performance of their portfolios. Presumably quite a number were satisfied although of the dozen or so clients of this period to whom I spoke, only a couple were enthusiastic. Apart from those who complained, the rest were for the most part noncommittal, including some of Slater's old Leyland colleagues.

It is difficult to discern any particular characteristic among clients which would explain why some fared better than others. None of the three whose affairs have been looked at in some detail had any particular 'pull' with Slater and there appears to be no pattern of favouritism in the transfer of shares from one client to another. We have also seen that while Slater's old Leyland colleagues often bought and sold at favourable prices, this was by no means always so, and Investment Analysis even lost money for Pendock's dentist.

His portfolio had been reduced by some forty per cent by late 1966 after two years with Investment Analysis, against a market fall of about ten per cent. After complaining he was partially placated with a quick in-and-out operation in Grand Bahama Development which recouped about £973. But he eventually recouped a great deal more on Slater Walker Securities shares, and an important factor behind client contentment was the gain many were able to make from an early investment in the master company: such an investment grew in value about ten times in five years and even at the bottom of the 1974 depression it would have still shown an appreciation of nearly $2\frac{1}{2}$ times. (But a couple of years later the investment would have been worth less than half its original cost.) Even in Slater Walker, however, there appears to have been no consistency of treatment: the Macdonalds, for example, were initially put into Slater Walker and then taken out. Kutchera, one of the few enthusiastic clients, on the other hand, still held most of his original Slater Walker investment when I spoke to him in early 1974. Yet John Hurst, another happy client, told me he was never put into Slater Walker itself. He had asked once why not, and he was told that the suggestion would have to come from the client, for it would not be ethical for Slater Walker to suggest the purchase of its own shares.

For most clients it was probably a case of swings and roundabouts; those who found themselves on the helter-skelter were probably just put there by some whim of office procedure. Slater argued that there was no 'ill intent' behind what he called the 'isolated instances' of transfers of shares between Slater Walker executives or dealing companies and the clients, claiming that the amount of money involved was minimal in relation to the several million pounds of investments that would have been bought for clients in 1964/66. He also reiterates that the portfolios of my principal examples of dissatisfied clients did not, in the period of Slater Walker's management, perform badly in relation to the market as a whole. But it is not so much their performance as the way they were managed upon which my criticisms are based; and there were not just one or two examples of bad luck or bad judgement, both among clients and investments, as Slater's arguments suggest. My investigations, carried out without access to the internal records of Slater Walker, reveal that the pattern was far too repetitive for that. In reality the customers' money was being used by Slater Walker for its own ends – a captive market which could be used either to realize profits at will, or to build up large, crucial holdings in industrial companies whose assets were ripe for 'liberation' – although Slater says this was never done when Slater Walker were contemplating making a bid.

12   *Some liberated assets*

It was John Bentley, the old Harrovian protégé whom Slater installed at Barclay & Sons, the former chemists, who gave asset stripping a bad name with some rather ham-fisted examples of the art. But that was not until 1972. Before then the general view was probably that there was something beneficial in 'predator' companies 'redeploying under-utilized assets' by selling them to those who would supposedly employ them more efficiently and profitably. Indeed in the early years of the Wilson government redeployment was all the rage, all part of building 'the new Britain'.

Slater was one of the earliest and best exponents of the technique, well described by John Ball in an article on Slater Walker in the American magazine *Fortune* in June 1973:

> Spot an asset situation, move in on it, cash some of the assets, and use the profit to bankroll the next deal. It was a mode of operation relatively new to staid British business. Its success, indeed, depended on a certain claret-grouse-and-port-induced somnolence in British boardrooms – failure to earn a reasonable return on capital employed, and indifference to the fact that many corporate assets, notably real estate, had a current value much higher than the figure in the balance sheet.

It should not be imagined that Slater carefully thought out the process of asset stripping. We have seen how the discovery that Lotery's Beaufort House lease could be sold profitably surprised Slater, and it was only with the onset of the bear market in 1965 that Slater began to put emphasis on the importance of asset backing in his investment strategy. But anyway Slater's development as an asset stripper was forced on him by circumstances.

The problem, as usual, was at Productofoam: it did not have any assets, or anyway none to write home about – let alone to the share-holders. At 30 September 1965 Productofoam's total net assets amounted to £504,570, of which almost exactly half – £253,072 – was represented, hopefully, by 'goodwill': net tangible assets per share were thus only 2s. 7d. - against a stock market price of 11s 6d. If that at least ruled out the possibility of anyone else spotting Producto-foam as an asset situation, it also meant that the share price was unlikely to rise any higher until it had some firmer backing. So just as important as the injection of dealing profits became the search for suitable assets for Productofoam.

The first company to have its assets 'liberated', as Slater liked to describe these operations, was an old established private paint firm in Wandsworth, South London, called Joseph Freeman - the firm for which, coincidentally, Macdonald, the Investment Analysis client, worked. Freeman had gained a reputation for its Cementone brand paints developed for use on exterior walls; it was what would have been called a nice little business, even if it was not particularly profi-table. But its owners wanted to get out and word had gone round that the business was up for sale.

Freeman was an attractive proposition because it had some cash and liquid investments in its balance sheet. Furthermore, in addition to a leasehold factory, it owned over fifty houses nearby which it had intended to demolish in order to expand the factory when their leases fell in. A number of offers were made for the company but Slater Walker secured it at the end of July 1965 for about £300,000: Despard was dispatched to see what could be done with it.

Freeman's paint business was resold on 22 September 1965 to Slater Walker's friends at Beaver, and Moss Securities played a leading role in the deal. For Freeman's working assets - stock, plant, machinery, laboratory equipment, and so on, valued at about £85,000 in the last balance sheet - were transferred by Slater Walker to Moss, who passed them on to Beaver in exchange for 150,000 new Beaver shares and about £12,000 in cash.

Moss, however, never took up these shares: they were 'placed' by Rowe Reeve and Investment Analysis at 13s. 6d., along with the Beaver shares that Moss had bought in the market, conveniently turning Freeman's assets into a further £101,250 of cash.

Freeman's cash, investments, properties and other assets belonging to Slater Walker realized over £250,000; and the surplus on the operation was thus probably getting on for £100,000, shared between Slater Walker and Moss, although the deal was not mentioned in either the Slater Walker or the Productofoam accounts.

While Freeman certainly had assets that were not being used par-ticularly profitably, as Slater pointed out, their effective transfer, via Moss, to Productofoam to help plug the holes in that ailing group's balance sheet can hardly be said to have been beneficial to the economy at large. Nor did the transfer of the Cementone business to Beaver produce any immediate, clear-cut advantages. Today Beaver is a successful paint company, of which Cementone is an important division. But it expanded too fast in 1965 and 1966, taking over a number of other companies besides the Cementone business. As a result it had itself to be completely reorganized in 1967, when profits dropped from £126,000 to £41,000: the results of Cementone were particularly disappointing that year. Beaver's profits recovered in 1968 but crashed again in 1969; that year the Wandsworth factory was sold and Cementone production moved to another Beaver subsidiary. It was not until 1972 that Beaver's earnings once more exceeded the 1966 level, or the sum of the profits of constituent firms before Beaver took them over.

Slater's operation on Freeman went unnoticed, but his next move, if it was not made in the glare of publicity that was to greet his later manoeuvres, at least commanded some attention in the press. For it was his first formal takeover bid for a public company.

It was made on Wednesday, 11 August 1965 – or rather that was the day Slater informed the rather discomfited board of the Cork Manufacturing Company by telephone that his firm, Productofoam Holdings, proposed to offer 24s. each in cash for Cork's 924,448 ordinary shares, and that if he was successful he would expect to put representatives on the Cork board.

Cork Manufacturing made, primarily, oil seals and gaskets for the motor industry out of cork and synthetic rubber. There was only one other leading British manufacturer, the much larger Engineering Components, and the two had been in amicable but tough competition for many years. Cork had however diversified into plastics, through Flexo Plastic Industries, and into the building trade through Flexo Plywood Industries. Its main factory was at South Chingford in East London, where it owned a freehold site of about 12½ acres.

Cork shares had risen from about 11s. early in 1965 to 19s. 6d. at the end of July. The company's performance provided some justification for the rise, for it had recently announced that profits in the latest financial year, which had ended on 30 April 1965, had increased by seventy per cent to £151,000. Furthermore, the board had had the freehold site revalued at an optimistic £1.3 million; this figure had not been included in the accounts, released just six days before Slater made his bid and in which properties were still listed at an old 1957 valuation of £374,000, but it had been circulated to shareholders.

The Cork board was well aware that there had been increased activity in the shares, although they had not been able to discover the identity of the buyer. It was Slater, using both clients' and Slater Walker's money; he was able to tell the Cork directors that holders of no less than 304,720 shares, or nearly one third of the total, were 'already committed to accepting the offer'. Ironically, Moss

Securities had just sold 5,000 shares, the gain of £150 or so helping to boost Productofoam's profits.

The directors of Cork formally rejected Productofoam's offer on 16 August 1965, saying that they regarded it as inadequate. Undeterred, Slater posted his formal offer direct to Cork shareholders on 18 August, using Investment Analysis as if it were a merchant bank adviser. As the offer was in cash, rather than in Productofoam shares, there was no need to tell the Cork shareholders anything about Productofoam – fortunately for Slater, as this might have proved somewhat embarrassing. Instead, Slater was able to point to the generosity of the offer and to criticize the Cork management's performance. As for the future of Cork if Productofoam secured control, Slater said that, apart from expecting to put its representatives on the board, 'at present Productofoam had no other concrete proposals which would lead to any change in the nature of the business carried on by Cork or in the terms of service of employees including Service Directors'.

The Cork directors gave their reasons for rejecting Slater's bid on 25 August 1965. They said that the outlook was 'most favourable' and promised a good dividend for the coming year. Of greatest significance, however, was the board's statement that it was 'most conscious' that the asset value for each Cork share was about 17s. 3d. above the 24s. offer price: 28s. 6d. of this asset backing was attributable to the revaluation of the Chingford site.

One of Slater's first moves had been to send an executive to make an estimate of the value of Cork's Chingford property, and he had said they might get £1 million for it. Although this fell short of Cork's own figure, some of Slater's co-directors thought it was still too high. Nevertheless, since the bid price of 24s. only allowed about £500,000 for the property, there was plenty of room for a margin of error.

Slater replied to the Cork directors' case on 4 September. He did not raise the question of asset values, but concentrated on attacking the directors' forecasts and their past record. He claimed furthermore that he now had acceptance for thirty-eight per cent of the shares. Acceptance had risen to forty per cent on 6 September; ten days later Slater had control and was appointed to the board. With sixty-five per cent of the shares in Slater's hands, the Cork directors finally withdrew their opposition to the bid, saying in their last statement that they had received assurances that the business would not be moved from Chingford and that employees' interests would be protected.

Although Productofoam thus secured Cork at below asset value with the help of client money, the deal was nevertheless most profitable for those clients – like Macdonald, for example, who had bought 1,500 Cork shares on 11 May 1965 at 15s. 10d. Cork was thus a clear example of clients' benefiting from having their funds invested in companies in which other arms of the group were interested, in contrast to Astaron-Bird. But Investment Analysis was advising both Productofoam and the clients, and I pointed out to Slater that investment departments of merchant banks are not supposed to trade even for the benefit of their clients on the basis of information obtained from their corporate finance departments. Slater explained that:

> Slater Walker invested clients' money in both earnings and assets situations. On occasions a bid would be made by Slater Walker itself subsequently and on other occasions other parties might bid for a company in which we had a substantial client share-holding. On other occasions no bid was made by anyone. Clients' funds were not invested in companies where a firm bid intention had been formed.

Just when Slater, as chairman of both Productofoam and Investment Analysis, formed a firm intention to bid for Cork is, of course, not recorded.

Productofoam itself had no cash to pay for Cork; in fact its own stock market valuation was rather less than the £1.1 million it was offering for Cork. But Productofoam had no problem raising the money, for both Slater Walker and swig had plenty of cash, the one from the sale of Beaufort House, the other from the initial subscriptions of its shareholders. So Slater Walker lent Productofoam £600,000 and swig lent it £511,000; the loans, Slater said, should be repaid by the spring of 1966.

If Slater had had no concrete plans for Cork back in August he quickly formulated some once he was in control. The selling-off pro-gramme started at once, to the accompaniment of a good deal of bragging about the coup. In the event however it ran into some unexpected problems and took rather longer than expected to complete, and the final composition of the surplus turned out to be very different from that originally estimated.

The first news of the Cork killing was released in December 1965, together with Productofoam's Moss-inflated profits for the year to 30 September. The *Sunday Times* reported that the deal meant a capital profit of 'well in excess of £500,000' and pointed out that this was a 'significant amount' for a company of Productofoam's size.

The good news helped the Productofoam share price up from about 13s. at the start of December to 16s. at the end of 1965. This was just as well, as without the rise swig's balance sheet at 31 December 1965 would not have looked too healthy. In its first year of operations swig had realized losses of £123,675 - a part of this would have been on Astaron-Bird – and its retained investments at the year end, at £1,826,488, were only worth £167,454 more than the group had paid for them. SWIG's Productofoam shares were valued at some £750,000 and without that last-minute rise which added about £140,000 to their worth, the net asset value of SWIG's shares would have fallen below their £1 nominal value. This might not have pleased Slater's important City backers, a further £511,000 of whose money had been committed to the little rubber company in loans.

Slater confirmed the £500,000 Cork capital profit in his annual statement to Productofoam shareholders released in January 1966. He explained how it was reached and how the £1.1 million loans from SWIG and Slater Walker would be repaid:

(1) The basic cork business was being sold to Engineering Components, Cork's main competitors, who had been anxious to buy them up for some time,* for about £850,000, the exact price to be finalized when accounts had been drawn up.

(2) The assets of Flexo Plastic Industries were to be sold to 'liberate' about £125,000. (Negotiations to sell the plastic subsidiary had, in fact, been started by Cork's previous management.)

(3) The sale of Cork's Chingford property for £1 million had been negotiated but was still subject to contract. (The factory would be leased back to Engineering Components.)

Even after all this, Flexo Plywood Industries, with assets of about £300,000, Slater said, would remain a profitable subsidiary of Productofoam.

Three weeks later, Slater modified his estimate of the Cork surplus; in a letter to Productofoam shareholders, he said it had been adjusted to about £450,000. Furthermore this now included the sale of the fixed assets and goodwill of Flexo Plywood as well, which it had been decided to pass on to the obliging Beaver Paint Company for £38,500 to be met by the allotment of 48,000 new Beaver shares: these were taken up by Moss, which wisely quickly resold them for £49,000 just as the Beaver price started on its descent – 4,000 shares being placed with Investment Analysis' clients at 23s. 4½d. The 'shell' of Flexo Plywood, however, would be left with £265,000 in cash and this, Slater said, brought the total cash available to Productofoam for 'internal expansion and reinvestment' to £696,000.

Shortly afterwards, Slater also told the shareholders of Slater Walker and of SWIG, in their annual reports for 1965, that the assets of Cork 'have since been sold off, realizing a capital profit of approximately £450,000 after tax'.

That was the last they heard of the matter. But a year later, in March 1967, Slater had a surprise for Productofoam shareholders.

---

*Turner & Newall, another large motor industry supplier, took over Engineering. Components a few months later.

The capital surplus on the reorganization of Cork, he told them, 'was below the level originally anticipated'. This was, he said, 'due in part to substantial pre-acquisition trading losses incurred by Cork up to the 31st December 1966, and in part to unforeseen expenditure arising from the reorganization'. This expenditure, Slater explained, was on construction work at the Chingford factory which had been necessary in order for the £1 million sale – to Prudential Assurance – to go through, and this had not been completed until 21 September 1966. These two factors, Slater said, had involved reductions totalling £177,282 in the realized surplus which, at 30 September 1966, had amounted to £254,367.

For a fuller account of what had gone wrong, however, one must turn to Slater's statement as chairman of the rump of the Cork company – a document, dated 19 May 1967, which would have had only a limited circulation. There it was revealed that Cork's subsidiaries had been sold for rather less than Slater's original estimates: the basic cork business had gone for £816,000,* Flexo Plastic had liberated not £125,000 but only £80,000, and Flexo Plywood had realized not £265,000 cash on top of the 48,000 Beaver shares, but only £151,000

But the most interesting part was Slater's explanation of the 'pre-acquisition' losses. Slater now said that interim accounts prepared shortly after Cork had been taken over had shown that the cork division was incurring 'serious losses' at the time. These, according to Slater, were due in part to disruption resulting from an explosion at the factory and in part 'to a deterioration in the Company's competitive position, aggravated by general economic difficulties'.

It had been the mainstay of Slater's case during the bid battle that the Cork directors were being over-optimistic, but this belated assertion, nearly two years later, that Cork had actually been losing money was a remarkable reassessment, especially as Cork had been earning record profits up to May 1965. The explosion, too, had happened almost exactly two years before, just after midnight on Friday 28 May 1965, in one of the gas ovens used in making cork blocks. Five employees on night shifts were injured, one seriously, and part of the roof was blown off. But Ian Coote, the old Cork chairman, had said in his last annual statement, released just before Slater made his bid, that stocks of cork blocks had fortunately been adequate, that production was already nearly back to its previous level, and that no customers had been seriously inconvenienced. The former Cork directors, too, were very surprised at the suggestion that the company had been suffering serious losses at the time of the

*The accounts of Engineering Components say that the final price for the Cork business was £805,713.

takeover, although they said that the bid battle itself caused some disruption.

Slater's revised surplus of £254,000 is the last official figure on the profit made out of Cork; but the £450,000 became fixed in the legend; Jonathan Aitken, for example, wrote in the *Evening Standard* in July 1968 that Slater bought Cork 'for £1.1 million and by selling off the unprofitable assets made a capital profit of £450,000 within six months'. Slater had in fact told Productofoam shareholders in March 1967 that the eventual surplus might rise above £254,000 as that figure did not take account of 'any insurance compensation in respect of consequential losses arising from the explosion', nor the possible recovery of some written-off debts. So I asked Slater if these had eventually brought the Cork surplus back up to £450,000. Speaking from memory, he said he did not think the insurance surplus on Cork was 'very substantial'; it was in the region of £100,000 to £200,000 he thought.

The Cork operation had been conducted from Hertford Street and had nothing to do with Productofoam's basic business – if Productofoam can be said to have had a basic business – and so we must now trace the fortunes of the rest of the rubber group, for it remained the largest single investment and therefore crucial to Slater Walker's survival.

The plan of Slater, Productofoam's chairman, and Meyer, its managing director, was to centralize the group's activities, and to this end in the early summer of 1965 they bought an old textile mill, Bedford Works, at Leigh, just a few miles away from Sebec's factory at Lowton-St-Mary in Lancashire. They paid about £50,000 for it, at a time, a local colleague commented, 'when you couldn't give mills away in Lancashire'. A man called Norman Humphrey was put in day-to-day charge of the northern operations, and Productofoam set out on the takeover trail.

The most important business acquired was called Cellofoam, owned by a financier called Douglas Ward and run by a Belgian, Lucien Leleu. It had two factories, one in Middleton, Lancashire, and one in Dover, which housed its main operations. Cellofoam was a distributor of Belgian-made foam, and was also in the laminating business, and Leleu had secured a promising contract with Renault in France to supply seat covers. But in the early hours of Sunday 23 May 1965 its Dover premises were completely burnt out, along with some neighbouring firms in the same factory complex, in a huge £1 million blaze. As a result, Ward wanted to sell out and so Leleu got in touch with Slater, of whom he knew as a competitor.

Cellofoam was attractive for two reasons: first, it had big tax losses to carry forward. Secondly, it had some important licensing rights to certain laminating processes whose patents belonged to American and Canadian firms. One of these had been showing a certain restlessness with British companies, including Productofoam – who it believed might be infringing these patents.

The deal with Cellofoam had hardly been consummated when, on Sunday 17 October 1965, Productofoam's own laminating factory at Lowton-St-Mary burned down. The cause of the fire was never established, but it was said to have been caused either by an electrical fault or by a cigarette end: a Sunday shift was working and the fire started during their lunch break. Anyway, the place was a write-off. 'All that remains of the works is a tangled mass of machinery buried under rubble,' the local paper reported.

So, suddenly, there was Productofoam without any laminating capacity. But fortunately, as Humphrey told the local press, the transfer to Bedford Works had already started; and they had a couple of laminating machines from Cellofoam's Middleton factory, although there was an argument – a foretaste of rows to come – between Humphrey and Leleu over whether to re-open Middleton or start at Bedford, which Leleu pointed out was not ready. (Meyer was away on holiday at the time.)

They started at Bedford Works and got the plant on stream within forty-eight hours, a considerable achievement. But Humphrey would be the first to admit it was a shambles: they had no telephone, no proper administrative offices or lavatories, and the mill floors were not strong enough for the heavy laminating machinery.

Slater himself was complacent about the fire in his chairman's statement for 1965. Dislocation was substantial, he admitted, but the company was insured, the move to Bedford Works would minimize any future risk of fire as there was a first-class sprinkler system and fire precautions were most stringently observed, and 'fortunately the loss of business experienced as a result of the fire has almost been recovered and we are now in a strong position to obtain additional business on a competitive basis'. He went on to forecast that Productofoam should make a profit of not less than £160,000 in the year to 30 September 1966.

But the situation of Bedford Works did not improve and the management structure was chaotic. Meyer quietly resigned as Productofoam's managing director at the end of 1965, leaving Humphrey in charge at the old mill: the latter had not just Leleu to cope with, however, but the managers of two other businesses that had been moved there, W. S. Heaton and Strene Development (making polyurethane tiles), all wanting to go their own way. In the summer of 1966 some sort of order was restored with the appointment as managing director of Bill Kenyon, a more experienced industrialist who had made a name marketing Turtle Wax polish for a company called Lloyd's Packing Warehouses.

But the arguments continued and one day, when Kenyon was on holiday, Humphrey sacked Leleu. The first Kenyon heard of it was when a very angry but agitated Slater rang him; Leleu, so Slater had heard, had written to Productofoam's auditors Roff Swayne & Co. asking for a list of shareholders. It seemed he was intending to call an extraordinary general meeting.

Leleu was in fact planning to tell his co-proprietors exactly what a shambles the company was, which would have blown the credibility of the whole SWIG structure. The recently-appointed Kenyon did not want to intervene – he got on little better with Leleu than Humphrey – and Slater rang Leleu himself, to be lectured for an hour and a half on what was wrong with Productofoam. The upshot was that Leleu was reinstated and Humphrey sacked – but with a generous settlement.

In his March 1967 chairman's statement Slater had to admit that the Lowton-St-Mary fire had had 'far more serious consequences than were initially envisaged'. Bedford Works, it had been discovered, 'lacked many of the facilities necessary to ensure satisfactory production'. Demand had been running at a record level at the time of the fire, and the company's subsequent inability to meet orders had lost it a substantial amount of business. Bedford Works had been modernized and re-equipped, but this had cost a lot of money and was still not finished at the start of 1967. A section had to be fire-proofed for the laminating activities to meet the requirements of the insurers. On top of this, demand had fallen again as a result of the general economic position.

In spite of its problems, Productofoam still managed to declare a trading profit of £199,721 in the year to 30 September 1966. Just how it was cobbled together, however, is far from clear. The breakdown this time was given as follows:

Textile, laminating and other activities	£114,532
Plastic consumer products	44,013
Rents, interest and sundry income, substantially arising from the Cork acquisition	53,896
	£212,441
Rubber gloves – loss	12,720
	£199,721

Slater explained the loss at Latex Surgical which was still producing rubber gloves in Hackney: a new semi-automated plant had been installed and 'we experienced an unexpected number of teething troubles'. The new plant, he went on to say, was now fully operational and providing a satisfactory increase in output with significant operating economies. This was to prove an over-optimistic statement.

The £53,896 item was principally made up of rent paid by Engineering Components and Beaver Paint to the rump of the Cork Company to cover their occupation of the factory at Chingford before the delayed sale to the Prudential went through. It was thus an unexpected contribution to Productofoam's profits. Cork's trading losses were not included in the Productofoam profit and loss account.

Three little concerns – a manufacturer of rainwear, P. & H. Bailey, a plastics firm called Coral, and a shopfitting business, Salisbury Parry, control of which had been bought during the year – made up some of the remainder. It had been a difficult year in the stock market and Moss Securities only made pre-tax profits of £19,592.

Some of the profit was also represented by insurance compensation. The Dover and Lowton-St-Mary claims were handled together and Tarling was appointed to the Productofoam board to negotiate with the insurers. Slater told shareholders in a letter in August 1966 that profits would be in 'excess of the forecast of £160,000', but said this would 'be subject to a reasonable settlement of the various fire insurance claims'. But the final insurance contribution to profits was never revealed. Former directors of Productofoam have told me that the loss of profits compensation alone was of the order of £150,000, but this was not all taken in one year. Productofoam's balance sheet however included a £217,000 item under current assets for 'estimated recoveries from the Group's Insurers for claims relating to Plant and Machinery, Stocks and Consequential Loss' and the Cellofoam accounts reveal that £25,000 of its £52,000 profit in 1966 was insurance compensation. Sebec Laminations (Northern), the subsidiary which traded at Lowton-St-Mary, turned in a loss of £6,250 after crediting an insurance surplus of £13,347.

There is nothing wrong in including consequential loss insurance payments in the profits and loss account without disclosing the amount. But the true quality – or rather lack of it – of the company's earnings did not emerge from Productofoam's accounts. The group was in a mess; there was no solid earnings base at all, the only profits coming from share dealing or newly acquired businesses. They used to joke in the old mill that they had no PE (price/earnings) ratio, only a PR (public relations) ratio.

But some things did show through the accounts: the 30 September 1966 balance sheet revealed that the benefits of the stripping of Cork had been whittled away. The diminished surplus of £254,000 was used to write off the previous year's £253,000 of goodwill; but an even larger intangible item – of £340,000 – took its place, representing the excesses over asset values that Productofoam had paid for its new subsidiaries. That £696,000 of cash, too, had evaporated and the balance sheet only contained £276,000 in spite of the fact that an investment company, Peak, with nearly £100,000 of liquid assets, had also been bought. Nor had the money been spent on acquisitions: they had been paid for by issuing new shares. As a result the net tangible asset value had only improved to just under 4s. This did nothing to help the share price: the stock market generally had fallen sharply in the second half of 1966 but the Productofoam share price had fallen even faster – from a peak of around 17s. on the Cork hopes of early 1966 to a little over 10s. at the end of the year. Clearly, Slater had some rethinking to do.

13   *Swallowing SWIG*

After the fire which destroyed Productofoam's Lancashire factory in October 1965, there was much talk in the company of the 'Phoenix Plan' for a new Productofoam to arise from the ashes. The new Productofoam never did arise, for from its chairman's point of view Productofoam carried within its history the skeleton of failure as well as the ashes of mishap. Both were best buried; it was only a question of finding the right grave. But Slater Walker itself did have the virtue of the Phoenix; it was able to renew itself. And by 1966 the time had come for such a renewal, or at least a metamorphosis. The grand design that Slater had set out in early 1965 had not come to fruition. That design was perhaps never more than an orderly façade for a distinctly opportunistic construction, but now the façade itself was in danger of crumbling.

The stock market was falling, and unless something was done the accounts for 1966 would reveal to SWIG's backers that their money had not been deployed with quite the skill Slater had promised. It was time for a rethink. And fortunately the year was to reveal a mechanism that would set Slater Walker firmly on a new route to fame and fortune. But first there was some tidying up to do. Failure could not of course be admitted, but it could be disguised as success, even as planned success.

In the summer of 1966 the stock market, which had taken an upturn in March after the election which returned Labour with a comfortable majority, started a disastrous slide. The seamen's strike in May marked the beginning of a collapse that was to take the FT Ordinary Index down by twenty-five per cent over the next five months. This was not helpful to either the investment advisory business or the share dealing companies. The surplus on the Cork acquisition was rapidly disappearing down the Productofoam drain and, perhaps worst of all, the value of SWIG's investments, on which a loss of nearly £124,000 had already been realized in 1965, began to fall even more dramatically. And SWIG was now a subsidiary of Slater

Walker, which had bought over 250,000 SWIG shares off the early backers – principally George Wiles – who had wanted to get out of the investment, to bring its stake to over fifty per cent. So SWIG's balance sheet would have to be consolidated with that of Slater Walker: it was Slater Walker's turn to need some more assets to make up the investment deficit.

If Slater had known little of City procedure when he left Leyland, he was learning fast. The Cork bid in 1965 had been a relatively unsophisticated affair, made outright with the SWIG cash subscribed by Slater's backers and the proceeds of the Beaufort House mortgage. But in early 1966, Slater had become involved in a rather more sophisticated takeover battle, for he had been asked by another emerging conglomerate, Cope Allman, to act as its adviser in a bid for Lloyd's Packing Warehouses. It was a 'paper' bid, that is Cope Allman proposed to pay for Lloyd's with a mixture of loan stock and ordinary shares, and after a twelve-week battle, in which a rival bidder was beaten off, Cope Allman was successful.

With some more takeover experience behind him, Slater was ready to attack again on his own account. He had been told by a stockbroker to look at a company called Thomas Brown and Sons: it was a British company with a London stock market quotation but all its business was in Australia, where it had a wholesaling concern, a rum distillery, some stores and one or two other odd interests. Horsman, whose job it was to find out about prospective victims, was sent out to look over the business; he had formed a little news service company just before joining Slater Walker and, according to Aitken in the *Evening Standard* in July 1968, he 'assumed the role of a journalist writing an article on the structure of the Australian grocery trade' – a rather curious apprenticeship for a future member of the Royal Commission on the Press.

Horsman returned with a satisfactory report, and a stake of about thirty per cent was quickly amassed before Slater announced his bid for Brown on 28 July 1966 at 23s. 6d. a share. Brown had made profits of less than £90,000 in its last financial year, and as the *Investors Chronicle* commented: 'Clearly it is not on earnings that Slater Walker Securities is making a share exchange offer.' The *Investors Chronicle* went on to point out that the net asset value of Brown shares was over twice the bid price and concluded that 'it is not difficult to see a dissecting operation taking place'.

Nevertheless, although the Brown directors rejected Slater's initial offer, he only had to increase the price to around 27s. a share before they agreed, and Slater was able to post his offer on 19 August 1966 with a recommendation from the Brown board.

Slater Walker's bid valued Brown at about £1,350,000. Even if Slater had wanted to offer cash, Slater Walker no longer had that sort of ready money. The bid was made in loan stock and Slater Walker ordinary shares, which, although they had fallen along with the market, were still at 12s. 7½d. – equivalent to 16s.6d. at the old rate after adjusting for a free issue of one-for-three made earlier in the year.

In spite of their board's recommendation the Brown shareholders were slow to accept; not only were there postal problems with the Australian shareholders, but some of those in the UK felt they should get a higher price. By the middle of September 1966, Slater Walker had control but only by a margin of eight per cent of the Brown ordinary shares. The offer was extended and the shareholders circularized again, with the emphasis on the time it would take to restore their company to reasonable profitability.

It was the Brown bid that provided Slater with the opportunity to restructure Slater Walker. The immediate effect of the paper bid was to make a nonsense of the plan Slater had outlined at the start of 1965, for, as he himself explained, Brown 'should logically be held by SWIG'. SWIG, being private, could hardly issue shares to make takeovers and, now that the £1.5 million it had enabled Slater to raise two years before from City institutions and other associates was spent, its usefulness was over. The simple answer was for Slater Walker to buy out the other shareholders, and an offer was duly made on 21 October 1966.

If the solution was simple, it was also convenient. For in October 1966 SWIG was in poor shape. Not only had SWIG realized another £16,000 of losses, but its remaining investments were worth £456,000 less than their value in the books. They had in fact been depreciating at a rate about double that of the market generally. The asset value of SWIG shares had dropped from the initial £1 to 17s. As one of the SWIG backers remarked, it had not been all roses.

Slater put a brave face on it in the SWIG offer document: many of the main investments were of a 'strategic nature', he said, and 'as a result they should be capable of eventual realization at substantially higher prices than present-day values as in most cases the size and nature of these holdings are such that they form a nucleus for a future acquisition or merger'. The outside SWIG shareholders were generously offered 21s. 3d. a share, in a mixture of Slater Walker shares, loan stock and cash.

This price at least ensured that Slater's important City backers did not lose on their decision to invest in his grand design. But Slater had to justify the premium over assets to the Slater Walker shareholders. He told them that a third of SWIG's investments were represented by Productofoam and George Wilson Gas Meters, 'both of which have currently forecast record profits'.

Strategic holdings in five unnamed companies, 'where the underlying assets represented by the shareholdings are considerably in excess of current market values', made up another thirty per cent and the balance was made up of further smaller 'strategic' investments. The board, he said, 'are confident that in the long term all these holdings are capable of eventual realization at substantially higher prices than present-day values'. He also mentioned that SWIG had investments in two private companies, Kintslaid Engineering and Young Chemical, which 'although not at present income producing, have considerable future potential'.

This description can hardly be said to have conveyed the true quality of much of the SWIG portfolio. It is true that Slater himself, as chairman of Productofoam, had forecast record profits two months previously, in August, and in due course the company announced it had made its £200,000 in the year to 30 September 1966. But we have already seen how they were got together and what the real state of that group was. Its importance to the whole structure – or rather the importance of its share price – can be seen yet again in the fact that Productofoam, at its October 1966 market price of around 10s. 3d., still accounted for over twenty-seven per cent of the value of SWIG's investments. But at that time Productofoam's own underlying assets were worth under 6s. 9d. a share or, excluding goodwill, under 4s. As it was, the fall in the market value of Productofoam had alone accounted for well over £120,000 of the depreciation in SWIG's investments, while the book value of the Productofoam holding exceeded its net tangible asset value by some £650,000.

George Wilson Gas Meters, of which SWIG also owned just under half the ordinary shares, was not a great deal better. Like Productofoam, it had been in the Slater sphere of influence since 1964, when he had joined the board. It had been selected as a suitable case for SWIG treatment but it retained at first a much greater degree of independence than Productofoam, which was essentially an integral part of Slater Walker. Wilson's profits in its last financial year, to 31 March 1966, had fallen from £51,000 to £33,000; its accounts, released in October 1966, showed net assets of just over £1 a share against a market price of 23s. and the chairman cautiously forecast 'satisfactory' results for the current year: in the event, profits recovered to £45,500 but that was after writing off the cost of reorganization – mainly the closure of a factory in Jarrow – against reserves.

It has not been possible to identify all of SWIG's investments. There was, of course, Astaron-Bird, which it had started to sell in the summer of 1966. SWIG also held almost thirty-four per cent of the little Scottish company Tayside Floor Coverings. Slater had first taken an interest in Tayside in early 1965 when Moss Securities and one of the dealing companies had bought shares. These had been resold to clients and to SWIG, which continued to build up its holding. SWIG had got its first shares at around 7s. 3d., but towards the end of 1965 it was paying around 8s.

Slater believed Tayside could be another asset situation, and an emissary was despatched to value the company's factory. He decided it was probably not even worth the figure at which it was carried in the books. On his return to London he bumped into Pendock, who asked what he thought of the company. The response was not enthusiastic and Pendock immediately sold out some of the clients' holdings: a broking firm was interested in Tayside too, and Pendock was able to get around 8s. 6d. to show good profits for the clients.

Slater, however, was angry that Pendock had got the information before a formal report was submitted. SWIG, of course, was still holding its investment and Tayside shares started to fall. In August 1966, with the Tayside price down to 6s. 6d., SWIG started to buy again, using nominee companies including Tiger Nominees, whose name Slater had kept after the Leyland executives' investment club had been wound up. By November SWIG had 339,350 shares at a total cost of over £121,000.

A buyer then emerged for Tayside. It was another new conglomerate called British Steel Constructors and it bid just over 7s. for Tayside, advised by Investment Analysis, which also underwrote the share offer in cash at 7s. 2½d., at which price SWIG just about broke even on its own investment.

The Slater Walker offer document for SWIG was essentially a formality, for its main shareholders had already agreed to the terms. But it contained the first published breakdown of the directors' shareholdings in Slater Walker. Slater's own interest was stated to be 311,866 shares, and I understand from Slater that he had sold a total of about 160,000 shares between April 1965 and July 1966 for a further realized gain of around £100,000. His holding had, of course, risen as a result of the free issue and Slater told me he had started buying back a few shares in August 1966.* Walker had 50,000 shares and must therefore have sold the equivalent of the free issue of April 1966, while Meyer and Despard each had 93,332 and Pendock 71,000.

In the summer of 1966 Slater Walker had acquired a small banking business called A. Rosenthal & Partners, which had about £1.4 million of public deposits. Around the end of the year, too, the group had bought two small private companies, an industrial painting contractor and a builder's merchant, and control of a little invest-

---

* There was an inconsistency between the figures Slater initially gave me, which indicated that he could not have had more than 300,000 shares in October 1966, and the SWIG offer document total. The latter, he later confirmed, was correct.

ment trust called Consumer Growth. But it was the consolidation of SWIG and of Thomas Brown, of which Slater Walker had finally by December got the ninety per cent acceptances to its offer, thus enabling it to compulsorily buy out the minority shareholders, that transformed the end-1966 accounts.

The key point was that with Brown, Slater Walker had acquired some £2,250,000 of assets, and their inclusion in the balance sheet minimized the impact of the sad state of SWIG's investments. The fall in their value during 1966 was also masked by an accounting change: in the 1965 accounts SWIG's investments had been included in the books at their market value, which was then considerably higher than their cost. Now they were inserted at cost, which was £166,000 *more* than their depreciated market worth. As a result of this change and the acquisition of Brown, Slater was able to claim a small increase in net assets per share of 8d. to 8s. 8d.

The dismemberment of Brown had started even before the end of 1966, however. Slater told his shareholders that they had decided that the 'possibility of restoring the wholesaling side of the business to a profitable basis was remote'; so this side of its business was closed down and its stocks sold. Altogether, Slater said, the disposal of the wholesaling assets should realize £1,600,000, and already £146,336 had been spent in buying a forty-five per cent interest in a quoted Australian coalmining company, Wancol. Slater Walker had in fact bought Brown's assets of £2,250,000 for a cost of only £1,350,000 and Slater reckoned that this £900,000 gain would be realized, and that Slater Walker would be left with the profitable trading activities of Brown.

But the closing down of Brown's wholesaling activities had been an expensive business, and in 1966 Brown turned in losses of some £600,000. These 'terminal losses', as was the custom, were charged to reserves and not allowed to impinge on the Slater Walker profits, which were declared to be £370,221 pre-tax.

It is hard to see how this figure was reached, not because the Slater Walker accounts were specially complicated, but rather because they were not sufficiently detailed. The group had been divided in two, with Slater Walker Ltd becoming the main holding subsidiary for the financial activities and SWIG for the industrial side, though the logic of this division was somewhat marred, since SWIG retained its own share dealing subsidiary, Dukersbrook. The only breakdown given was £270,228 for Slater Walker Ltd and £152,698 for SWIG, less £52,705 for parent company expenses, although Slater also provided an elaborate diagram showing 'all the operating subsidiaries and associated companies which made a material contribution to the profit of the Group'.

Yet the profits of the companies named, as drawn from their own

accounts, do not amount to anything like £370,221. Investment
Analysis' profits were still around the £64,000 mark in spite of a
much higher income as a result of its role as an adviser on takeovers;
and the two main dealing companies, Clamond and sw Industrial
Holdings, now renamed sw Equities, only managed about £60,000.
swig itself recorded a profit of £105,000, and its share dealing subsidiary, Dukersbrook, added a further £21,000; both swig and Slater
Walker Ltd had small contributions from the other acquired businesses during the year and there was interest on the loan to Productofoam. But just how the remainder of the profit was made is not clear.

An equally recondite accounting principle was applied to the
capital account. Brown's 'terminal losses' were written off reserves,
but these still managed to show a plus item of £458,459, which was
'the excess of net asset value of subsidiaries acquired during the year
over the cost of acquisitions after deducting losses' – the losses being
Brown's. Now Slater Walker had paid roughly £900,000 *less* than
asset value for Brown, which left a net addition to reserves of
£300,000 after the £600,000 terminal losses had been written off. But
Slater Walker had also paid £450,000 *more* than asset value for swig,
and about £200,000 *more* for the two private industrial companies.
How, then, an addition to rather than a subtraction from reserves?

The answer lies in an arcane accounting practice which served to
bolster the reputations of asset strippers. In the accounts, that part of
the price of acquired companies paid for by the issue of new shares
could be calculated either on the market value at the time of the
takeover – the so-called 'real' price – or on the more or less
meaningless nominal value of the shares, which in Slater Walker's
case was 5s. Slater Walker normally chose the latter course: it had
issued about 2,156,000 new shares as part-consideration for Brown
and swig, and this element of the cost was thus deemed to be some
£540,000 instead of the market value of about £1,250,000.

Now this practice, which, as we shall see, the accounting profession later tried to ban except in certain circumstances, did not
affect figures like earnings or tangible assets per share, which are the
commonly used indicators of a company's growth. But its effect was
to disguise the number of times Slater Walker paid more than the
asset value of its victims. For if it had chosen to account for the cost
of acquisitions on the market value of shares issued, an item of 'goodwill' would have crept into the balance sheet, which, it might have
been said, was not wholly consistent with its reputation as a spotter of
asset situations.

It will, of course, be readily seen that the higher the market price
of a bidding company's shares, the greater the discrepancy between
the true and the book cost of acquisitions. A high market share
quotation, however, had other, more important, accounting

advantages, as we shall see in the next chapter. To issue new shares to buy other companies was like printing your own money: in America they labelled it the funny-money game.

In a well-researched article on Slater Walker written in 1969, the magazine *Accountancy* commented on the group's 1966 accounts that 'the surprising thing, looking back, is that more doubts were not raised'. But when Slater Walker's 1966 accounts were released in May 1967 no one was in the mood to look deeply. The stock market was well into the two-year-long rise which took the *Financial Times* Industrial Ordinary Index from a low of 284.2 on 8 November 1966 to 521.9 on 19 September 1968. The balance of payments was improving, interest rates falling and the Budget had no nasty surprises: 'We are back on course,' Chancellor Callaghan concluded his speech. 'The ship is picking up speed. The economy is moving. Every Seaman knows the command at such a moment, "Steady as she goes".'

On top of this, takeovers were respectable, officially approved of and sometimes given government backing. Already in February 1967 Slater had made his biggest bid yet with a £3 million offer for the Greengate & Irwell rubber company. It was the start of the merger mania that was to help fuel the rise in share prices and to bring Slater to prominence and power.

But Slater had some last tidying up to do. In early 1967 his biggest early backer, Great Portland Estates, decided it wanted to pull out. As a result of the scrip issue and the buying in of SWIG it owned 1,200,000 shares, or about twenty per cent of the Slater Walker capital. The shares were placed in the City and with associates, but Slater and his co-directors bought many back themselves. Slater's slice was a block of 300,000, which doubled his holding and for which he paid 12s. 7d. each, or £188,750. On the sale, Samuel and his colleague Wallace left the Slater Walker board. The solicitor Walmsley resigned and Slater's original partner Meyer also quietly left – to run one of SWIG's private investments, the water purification company, Young Chemical – and Horsman and Tarling took their places. As Slater said, the effect was 'to make our Board fully executive', although deputy chairman Walker, of course, had many other demands on his time. It also meant the end of any restraining hand from outside advisers.

Finally, in July 1967, Slater Walker bought the outstanding shares in George Wilson Gas Meters and Productofoam, Slater's first two little industrial investments, still struggling along three years later. Slater recommended Productofoam's shareholders to accept the generous 11s. 6d. offer; their company had 'a reduced level of current profits' – reduced, that is against the 'record profits' the previous year which Slater had used to help justify the price paid to the SWIG shareholders – and, he said, benefits were likely to accrue 'from complete integration with Slater Walker'. One benefit to Slater was that the failure to turn Productofoam, the first public company of which he had taken control, into a successful industrial enterprise would be buried in the growing conglomeration of disparate concerns that the master company now was.

14   *The arithmetic of synergy*

The tidying-up process which occupied Slater during most of 1966 left his company poised on the brink of the three years of explosive growth that were to create for Slater Walker a charisma probably unequalled in postwar British business. By 1970, it was axiomatic that Slater and his imitators represented the white hope of the nation's industry – they were the men who could reconstruct old, tired companies and release under-used assets; the 'Mr Efficiencies' whom Tory policies, codified at Selsdon Park, would release from the trammels of socialist control and whose energy and ability a beneficent capitalism would harness for the national good.

During these three years between 1967 and 1970, Slater Walker took over seventeen companies and a dozen or so private firms. In 1966, Slater Walker's profits had been £370,000; in 1969 they were £10,443,000. The stock market value of the company's equity capital rose from about £4 million at the end of 1966 to some £135 million at the end of 1969. The value of one share, allowing for the two free issues during this time, increased by nearly 1,300 per cent. Earnings per share rose by 630 per cent and assets per share by 266 per cent.

As with the other turning points in his career as an entrepreneur, this growth seems to have been not the result of long-term planning but a consequence of Slater's talent for seizing opportunities. These were the years of takeover mania, when businessmen adopted the new fashion for mergers with uncritical fervour. In those years companies could be divided into two categories – those who took over and those who were their potential victims. To be on the winning side, one thing was necessary above all else – a high share price. With that weapon the puniest David could threaten the most invulnerable Goliath. During 1967 and 1968, the Slater Walker share price soared and gave Slater the weapon he needed: when I asked him early in my inquiry how planned the growth had been, he merely replied that it had seemed 'a pity not to use the shares'.

Later Slater insisted that while the strength of the share price was an important factor, it was not the sole rationale for expansion; he had seen the benefits accruing from the Cork acquisition and also from Cope Allman's acquisition of Lloyd's Packing, and was anxious for Slater Walker to benefit from an asset situation, as it did with Brown. In any event there appears to have been no preconceived design to build what it was then becoming fashionable to call a conglomerate; but the mechanism of taking over a company with a bid based on Slater Walker's own share price, first applied to a public company with the acquisition of Brown, must have appealed to Slater's instinct for the elegance of financial, as opposed to industrial, endeavour. Moreover, once set upon the takeover road the process became self-fuelling: takeovers demanded a high share price, but the maintenance of that price soon came in turn to depend on yet further takeovers.

Perhaps the greatest irony of all was that this growth took place under a Labour government, and was largely made possible by the policies of that government. The acceptability, indeed the desirability, of mergers as a means of promoting industrial efficiency became one of the main planks of the Wilson government's policy.

The origins of that policy can be traced back to Harold Wilson's speech to the party conference in October 1963. The main theme, as Wilson later described it in his memoirs, was 'the application of new scientific methods to industrial production', but at the time his words created a more dramatic impression: he had said that they were 'redefining and stating our socialism in terms of the scientific revolution', and 'there was no room for Luddites in a socialist party'.

The 'technological revolution', was, however, slow in getting going. It did not really gain impetus until Anthony Wedgwood Benn, then forty-one, succeeded Frank Cousins at the newly founded Ministry of Technology in 1966. Benn soon made it clear he was in favour of profits: the argument over the distribution of companies' incomes between shareholders, workers and customers 'can't even begin unless firms are profitable', he said towards the end of 1966.

Benn was also in favour of mergers, talking of the need to build giant British and European firms by welding smaller units together, a line he hammered throughout 1967 and 1968. It was, he said, the only way Europeans would be able to compete with the huge American and Japanese corporations in research and development in the era of 'high technology'.

Meanwhile the twin causes of profits and mergers had found another powerful advocate. In early 1966 George Brown, head of Wilson's other new ministry, the Department of Economic Affairs, had announced his plans for the Industrial Reorganization Corporation. It would have government money to invest directly in industry and, George Brown explained, it would actively persuade companies to 'rationalize', i.e. to merge: ordinary merchant banks, he pointed out, had normally to wait for their clients to come to them before they could organize takeovers. The IRC would take the initiative.

At first the idea of the IRC encountered a good deal of opposition from the Conservatives and the City, with charges of 'backdoor nationalization'. But by the time the IRC got going properly in early 1967, these fears had evaporated. Its first managing director, Ronald Grierson, was a conventional merchant banker, as was his successor Charles Villiers. They made it clear that the IRC's objectives were 'to promote industrial efficiency and profitability', and with only £150 million to invest it could not do much nationalizing. But it could promote mergers, which are good for share prices, so the City decided that on the whole the IRC was good for investment confidence.

It was also a far cry from the Labour government of 1945-51, which had introduced the Monopolies Commission to protect the public from exploitation by giant firms. With the profit motive firmly reinstated and with government backing for takeovers, the stock market took heart. It quickly recovered from the low point reached in November 1966 and in the next twenty-two months, the *Financial Times* Industrial Ordinary Index rose by nearly eighty-four per cent. Merger mania had taken hold, and even devaluation in November 1967 could but temporarily interrupt the market rise.

In theory successful mergers justify higher share prices: if the profits of two merged concerns will grow faster than the profits of the two if they remained independent, as a result of economies of scale and improvements in efficiency, then the shares should be valued more highly. In reality, however, the reason why share prices rise in a period of merger activity is largely due to pure speculation: investors know that a bidding company must normally pay well above the market price for the shares of the firm it wishes to buy, in order to secure control quickly and, hopefully, without a fight; so spotting the next likely takeover victims can be a remunerative operation. This in turn attracts more money into the stock market and so prices generally are inflated.

According to Board of Trade statistics, the total price paid for acquired firms more than doubled from 1966 to 1967 and again in 1968 to over £1,600 million. The Board's figures, strangely, record a fall in the number of mergers, but as Gerald Newbould of the Manchester Business School has pointed out,* because of the way the Board's figures were compiled they very considerably understated the full extent of takeover activity. Newbould's own figures, based on

* *Management and Merger Activity*, Guthstead, 1970.

daily reports in the press, show that the total number of mergers in 1967 was 1,068, valued at over £1,648 million, and in 1968 this rose to 1,433 mergers worth over £3,559 million. On top of this there were a substantial number of proposed mergers which failed for one reason or another.

Although Newbould did not give comparisons with earlier years, he concluded that 'it would seem safe to regard 1967 and 1968 as a period of significant boom in merger activity' – which is something of an academic understatement.

What both the Board of Trade's and Newbould's figures show is that the size of mergers was increasing. Newbould found that in these two years nearly seventy per cent of the UK's hundred largest firms were involved in mergers. The most significant of these was the government-approved consolidation of GEC, which under Arnold Weinstock had the previous year won control of AEI and English Electric to form a giant British electrical corporation.

This was the pinnacle of Labour's and the IRC's industrial rationalization policy. But although, as Newbould argues, the merger phenomenon was not receiving the attention its importance deserved, questions were beginning to be asked about the motives for, and the effects of, this wave of mergers among leading firms. Nor was the Monopolies Commission dead: in the summer of 1968, when even the usually cautious bankers got caught up in the scramble for size – simply, so many felt, for size's sake – and it was proposed to merge Barclays, Lloyds and Martins into one huge bank, the Commission said no.

The merger controversy came to a head in the first half of 1969 as a result of two proposed deals: Unilever, the huge soap, detergent, margarine and food manufacturer, and Allied Breweries, the country's largest brewery, decided they wanted to combine their operations; while the Rank Organization, in an attempt to reduce its reliance on the earnings of the Xerox photocopier, bid for an unwilling De La Rue, a group which combined, with no particular success, the manufacture of formica, banknotes and central heating boilers. Although attempts were made to rationalize the mergers, the arguments carried little weight and they were referred to the Monopolies Commission for judgement.

The Commission's recommendations were made in the summer of 1969: it could find little to be said for a merger between Unilever and Allied, but nor could it find much against it. So it was allowed, although by then the two companies themselves, in the changed conditions, had thought better of the idea and it was not pursued. On the other hand, the Commission accepted De La Rue's pleas that its efficiency would be impaired under Rank's management.

In both cases, the wisdom of the Commission's findings was open to dispute. Of greater importance were some general observations on mergers which the Commission produced at the Board of Trade's request. These concentrated on the growing trend, as demonstrated in both the Unilever/Allied and the Rank/De La Rue cases, for companies to want to merge with others in almost entirely different lines of business. By this time, too, the Board of Trade was clearly worried about something more than mergers of apparently disparate industrial concerns. With Slater in the forefront, a fashion was growing for the formation of what had been christened 'conglomerates' in the United States, where a similar merger mania had been raging. Frequently such concerns were founded on no discernible industrial base at all. Armed with a share price fostered more by energetic PR men than by facts, conglomerators bought companies at random; like magpies of the stock market, they collected companies with a compulsive acquisitiveness. Usually it was the gleam of profits already earned rather than the hope of profits to come that caught their eye.

The Commission defined conglomerate mergers as those 'between companies that do not produce similar products and where neither is an actual or potential supplier of the other'; and guidelines on mergers based on the Commission's report and later published by the Board of Trade pointed out that 'a pure conglomerate merger, by definition, cannot yield economies of scale in production or distribution'. The principal source of increased efficiency in horizontal mergers – those between companies 'that sell the same products (or products which can be easily substituted for each other)' – or vertical mergers – those between firms 'of which one is an actual or potential supplier of the other' – does not exist for conglomerates, the Board concluded.

This, however, did not mean that conglomerate mergers could not lead to increased efficiency. The Monopolies Commission stated: 'Typical efficiencies which a conglomerate merger can produce are in the field of management and finance (though there may sometimes be other efficiencies as well, e.g., in research and development or in marketing expertise).' These, the Commission said, may be more difficult to identify than other types of efficiency – as indeed it had found in the two cases it had just examined – 'but they can be equally real'.

As far as conglomerates were concerned, therefore, the issue came down to the question of who could make best use of resources – those in charge or those wanting to take over. The next part of the Commission's report expresses the views of Slater, and of others who were by then operating in a similar manner, like his old associate James Hanson, whose opinions had been among those canvassed but who were not named by the Commission:

Some companies which are active in acquiring diverse interests claim that their purchases of other companies produce considerable benefits to the economy by replacing bad management with good, ensuring that unprofitable units will be disposed of and providing finance for units needing it for fruitful development but previously unable to obtain it on such favourable terms.

The Commission did not attempt to evaluate these claims, merely saying that 'conglomerate mergers may well have these useful effects'; and it went on to point out, significantly, that 'it may also be worth a company's while to acquire another company for the sake of its current profits or its assets alone and without any particular plan for improving the use of its resources. In such the effect of a conglomerate merger may well be to reduce efficiency'.

The Commission went on to explain this in the most important section of its report which dealt with the financial effects of conglomerate mergers. The Commission had been concerned that the financial structure of a conglomerate could become vulnerable as a result of rapid growth, concern which resulted partly from the deteriorating position, and growing criticism of, conglomerates in the United States, where the first cracks had begun to appear in Ling-Temco-Vought, that country's fastest-growing corporate amalgam.

This vulnerability could stem from the fact that the bulk of takeovers were no longer paid for in cash, but by the issue of 'paper' by the buying company, mostly new ordinary shares or loan stock convertible into shares. In this currency, the cost of a takeover need hardly be noticed at the time, for, as the Commission explained, 'the higher the market value of the company's shares the better placed it will be to buy other companies'.

Now an important determinant of a company's share price is what investors believe, or are led to believe, about its future performance – 'the likelihood of high and increasing earnings per share'. The Commission continued:

> Thus future expectations play a large part in the financing of mergers. If these expectations prove to be exaggerated, it is possible that this, combined with the increase in company debt arising from the issue of loan stock in part-payment for acquisitions, could eventually lead to a situation in which the collapse of one or more large companies could have a serious effect on confidence in general and thus on the flow of resources into investment.

The Commission reported that several of those whose views it had sought had said that there was little danger of such a collapse in the United Kingdom. But the Commission's attention had been drawn to another danger, namely that the failure of a merger of conglomerate type to yield any efficiency benefits could be concealed from the shareholders and the public; indeed even a deterioration in performance could be hidden.

The Commission described how, after a takeover:

> The increase in reported earnings arising from the acquisition itself could to some extent mask an absence of earnings arising from real growth in the profits of either company. This could lead to a false appreciation of the results of the merger (in so far as earnings per share could increase, although the total profits of the two companies could remain the same or even fall) and an over-valuation of the shares of the company concerned, which in some cases might facilitate further acquisitions. Moreover, the ability to switch resources from one section of a diversified company to another could be used to conceal weaknesses in particular sectors.

The key section is the one in parentheses; the figure for a company's 'earnings per share' is one of the most frequently used indicators of its performance in stock market analysis. Yet effectively the Commission was saying that it was virtually useless as a tool for measuring the real benefits arising from takeovers.

A company's earning per share figure is calculated by dividing the profit available for distribution to shareholders as dividend by the number of shares in issue; and the price/earnings ratio – the P/E ratio – is obtained by dividing that figure into the current market price of the shares. Now a firm with a high earnings ratio may be no more profitable than one with a low ratio, but its higher 'rating' reflects, among other things, the market's expectation that its earnings will grow faster and therefore its shares are deemed relatively more valuable. Once it has got this higher rating, it can effectively pull itself up by its own bootstraps by acquiring low-rated companies, as the Commission demonstrated in an example tucked away in a footnote.

Rephrasing the Commission's example, this purely mathematical 'growth' is achieved as follows: say there are two companies, the Aggressives Corporation and Sleepies & Co. Ltd, each with one million shares in issue, and each earning £250,000 or 25 pence a share. Aggressives' shares are rated more highly by the market at £7.50 each, or a P/E ratio of thirty, because its managers spend a lot of time telling everyone how good they are at running companies. Sleepies' shares, on the other hand, are valued at only £3.75 each with a ratio of fifteen because its managers have not woken up to the fact that, in view of the importance of expectations in determining share prices, what you say you are going to do, and the confidence and frequency with which you say it, matter as much as getting on with the job of earning current profits as far as the stock market is concerned.

If Aggressives buys Sleepies by issuing 500,000 new shares in exchange for Sleepies' one million shares, the total profits of Aggressives will immediately double to £500,000. There will, of course, have been no real growth in earnings, but as Aggressives' issued capital will only have increased to 1,500,000 shares, its earnings per share will have risen to 33.3 pence.

In reality, Aggressives would have to issue more than 500,000 new shares to persuade Sleepies' shareholders to exchange their investment, for if they accepted one Aggressives share for two Sleepies, then they would simply be handing over part of their earnings to the Aggressives shareholders. But, because of its much higher share price, Aggressives would only have to issue about 511,000 new shares before the capital gain made by the Sleepies shareholders would start to exceed their lost income; and in practice Aggressives' bid would probably succeed with the issue of something like 600,000 new shares, giving the Sleepies' shareholders an immediate gain of about seventeen per cent. Aggressives' earnings per share would still rise to 31.25 pence, and only if it issued one million new shares to buy Sleepies - one-for-one - would there be no pure book-keeping increase in its earnings per shares; and exactly the same phenomenon happens to assets per share.

To deal with the possibility that shareholders - and for that matter the public at large - might be misled by such arithmetic, the Monopolies Commission recommended more detailed disclosure of financial information - just two years after Labour's Companies Act had already required firms to give a lot more facts and figures. The need to provide such information, the Commission hoped, might also 'deter companies from going ahead with mergers designed merely or largely to buy the assets and/or profits of the acquired company cheaply and without reasonable expectations, on the basis of positive plans, that they can use the acquired assets more effectively'.*

This recommendation has never been implemented; nor, in spite of the pertinency of its general observations, did the Monopolies Commission ever get the chance to examine in detail a fast-growing conglomerate of the Slater Walker type. This was partly because the report itself, and the growing criticism of conglomerates in the United States, led to some reduction in their activity, and in fact was one of the reasons Slater gives for changing the structure of his group

---

* It is interesting to note that in February 1962, at the time of the attempt by ICI to acquire Courtaulds, Walker had proposed in a speech in the Commons that in a takeover bid, both companies involved should prepare a prospectus on a similar basis of valuation.

yet again in 1970. But conglomerates were also not normally within the Commission's terms of reference, as they were not concerned with building dominant positions in one particular industry but with bidding for any company that took their fancy. Furthermore, for the most part they operated in industries not usually regarded as of the highest national importance.

In the United States, however, a Congressional subcommittee carried out a thorough examination of five of America's largest and most active conglomerates. Its report, published in June 1971, was a startling demolition of their claims.

In the first place, the committee concluded that 'financial considerations and not productivity goals were dominant motivating forces in the postwar merger movement'. It went on to say that this 'orientation of merger motivation in financial and securities transactions resulted in impairment in the financial stability of the sample companies'. In other words, not only was the prime aim of the conglomerate operators not the improvement of industrial efficiency, but also the paper pyramids they constructed were dangerous.

Still, even if the main motive was not the improvement of efficiency, there might have been some anyway. Not so, said the committee. The record, it said, 'does not support the contention that conglomerate mergers produced synergistic effects' – synergy, or synergism as the committee called it, having become the fashionable word to describe the supposed benefits of combining unrelated businesses in the same corporation. In fact, quite the reverse: 'Management difficulties with newly acquired companies indicate, if anything, that combination frequently had an injurious effect on efficiency, on productivity and upon corporate values.'

So, not only were these mergers not motivated in the way claimed, but they did not have the claimed beneficial effects either. The committee explained this damning conclusion more fully:

> In general, the major acquisitions by the sample companies were corporate organizations that were profitable and successful before acquisition. The main effect of the merger or acquisition was to transfer control and management of an already successful enterprise to a new group. Profitability ratios, which provide a measure of management performance, for some of the major acquired companies for the year immediately preceding acquisition when compared to the years after acquisition, indicate that in most instances the acquired companies operated less efficiently after acquisition. Only 7 of the 28 major companies analysed had a majority of its profitability ratios in the years after acquisition that were higher than the corresponding ratio in the year before acquisition.

So, it turned out, conglomerate operators were rather worse at running companies than those they ousted from control. Nevertheless the myth had grown up that they were a race of super-businessmen: how had this happened? Part of the answer emerges from the committee's detailed inquiries; it is, naturally, a great deal more complicated than the UK Monopolies Commission's simple example. But still the financing of acquisitions in such a way that there would be resulting increases in earnings per share was an important part of the fine art of synergy.

But the committee also found that the desire to emphasize earnings per share also caused some conglomerates to use other sorts of what it bluntly labelled 'accounting gimmickry'. This was stated most clearly in its examination of ITT, which had not at that time achieved notoriety for its political plottings. These gimmicks, which incidentally were within 'generally accepted accounting principles', arose from different ways of treating items like depreciation, research and development cost, and the capitalization of various expenses. Giving an example of the effects such gimmicks could have, the committee explained that 11.8 per cent of ITT's rise in earnings in 1968 had been the result of accounting changes made in three newly acquired subsidiaries.

Then there is the illusion of progress created by a corporation continually expanding by acquisition. Such 'external growth', the committee said, 'projects an image of growth and results in added value in the securities markets'. Internal, or organic growth, on the other hand, reflected in an increasing volume of sales and profits of an industrial unit, whether outside or inside a conglomerate, 'represents a net addition to the economy and reasonably provides a social benefit'.

The conclusions of the American survey cannot, naturally, be applied automatically to the UK. Nevertheless, the Monopolies Commission saw in 1969 that the sort of distortions that it was later established had occurred in the US could also exist in the UK. In 1967 and 1968 Slater Walker had become a classic conglomerate, 'with interests in everything from spectacles to window-frames', as Graham Turner wrote in the *Sunday Telegraph* in January 1972. In the early days Slater spoke out strongly in favour of American-style conglomerates – for example in a speech to the Northern Stock Exchange in May 1968 – but later, sensitive to the deteriorating conglomerate image, Slater used to deny the tag, although as he told Turner: 'It was no good saying we weren't a conglomerate because that just wasnt't true.'

Slater came to admit that conglomerates could be very bad, but a good one, he said, would be very good. He told *Accountancy Age*: 'It is not a thing you have greys in; it's either black or white. The

bads are very bad and the goods are very good – they have to be.'
But was Slater Walker a good conglomerate? That is, how much of
its profit growth was internal, or organic, as Slater called it, and
which parts produced any such growth? Did Slater Walker really
make better use of the industrial assets it acquired by improving the
return on capital? These are the questions that we are now going to
examine, stripping out accounting gimmicks or similar techniques –
like the inclusion of share dealing profits in Productofoam.

It was only at the start of 1967 that the Slater Walker share price
really took off. The initial impetus was given by the 1966 results, for
that year had been one of difficult economic conditions and Slater
Walker, as Slater pointed out, had been one of a relatively small
number of companies to announce higher profits. There was also the
expected surplus on Brown. But during 1967 the adulation of Slater
by the financial press started in earnest – on 15 January that year
John Davis of the *Observer* called him the 'man with the golden
touch' and wrote that he was 'today's leading exponent of buying
assets on the cheap' – and this helped push the share price up further.

The publicity was partly generated by Slater himself, who was
usually accessible and willing to talk with fluency about his
philosophy, his plans and his achievements. But it was also, like the
mergers themselves, a product of the climate of opinion. In the takeover boom, with its effect on stock market prices, spotting the next
victim also became a competitive business among City Editors: and,
as the *Sunday Times* said in August 1967, Slater was the 'trendiest
man in takeovers'. Then, too, in the general obsession about
industrial efficiency – the formation of the Ministry of Technology
and the IRC, not to mention the lectures from Swiss bankers – there
was a tendency to turn the limelight on those who claimed to be
doing something about it.

The share price then started to soar, not so much on past
performance but, as Slater has said himself, 'in anticipation of future
growth'. By the end of 1967 Slater Walker's price earnings ratio was
about fifty per cent higher than that of the market generally,
although the speed with which it took over companies and revised its
profits forecast meant that at any one moment the specific level of
this ratio meant little: all that mattered was that it was substantially
higher than that of other shares.

Slater Walker's first bid in 1967 was for the rubber company
Greengate & Irwell. This, together with remnants of Productofoam
plus two later acquisitions, P. B. Cow and Frankenstein Group,
formed one of Slater Walker's most important industrial involvements and will be examined in detail in the next chapter. But it
should be noted that on the terms of the takeover, in which Slater
Walker issued a mixture of ordinary shares and loan stock, and on the

profits forecast by both companies, there would have been a purely mathematical increase in Slater Walker's earnings per share of about 1½d. or nearly seventeen per cent.

After Productofoam and George Wilson had been absorbed in the summer of 1967, Slater Walker's next bid for a public company was not made until September 1967, when it paid about £750,000 – in shares and cash this time – for Constructors, which made office furniture, shelving and partitioning units and car seat slides from factories in Birmingham and London. Constructors had lost money in 1966 and the first half of 1967 and its chairman, in recommending acceptance, said that the restoration of the company to a proper level of profitability remained a 'long hard slog'.

Towards the end of 1967 Slater Walker bought another little public company, this time valued at only some £350,000, called Newman's Holdings, whose principal subsidiary made slippers. Newman's had made a profit in the first half of 1967 against a loss in the first half of 1966 and forecast that its total profits for 1967 would be not less than £80,000.

Slater Walker also bought a private printing firm, and two more private builders' merchants concerns which were welded together into a single division under the umbrella of a new holding company, Metropolitan Builders' Merchants.

As *Accountancy* remarked in its 1969 article it was 'a very mixed bag': and looking back *Accountancy* found it 'a little difficult to see why' the Slater Walker share price continued to rise. But at the time, the quality of the acquisitions was glossed over and, as the *Sunday Times* said in 1967: 'In response to any accusation that he is building up a rag-bag of interests he replies: "The only thing that fits in the group as far as I'm concerned is one I can make money out of."'

Making money he seemed to be, all right. Slater Walker's declared profits in 1967 were £1,158,848, against the £370,221 in 1966 and a forecast of £650,000 made just after Greengate & Irwell had been bought. Slater, conscious of the need to show that his company was earning as well as buying profits, told his shareholders that the improvement 'was partly due to acquisitions made during the year but there was also a substantial measure of organic growth within the businesses already controlled by your company'.

Slater did not reveal how much was 'organic' and the accounts only gave the breakdown between Slater Walker Ltd – £739,875 – and SWIG – £701,450 – less the expenses of the holding company – £282,477. The bulk of the industrial profits had, of course, been acquired during the year, the profits of taken-over companies being included from their date of acquisition. The largest contribution was from Greengate & Irwell with over £300,000. The remaining Australian business of Brown also now brought in £200,000, and this would presumably have fallen within Slater's definition of organic growth, as Brown was already – just – a subsidiary at the start of the year. The remains of Productofoam and of George Wilson Gas Meters, the two industrial interests which had been under Slater's influence for any length of time but which were only being consolidated in Slater Walker for the first time, both lost money in 1967.

The main organic growth, therefore, was on the financial side, although once again it is hard to see how the named active subsidiaries of Slater Walker Ltd made up its total profits. Investment Analysis' profits fell in 1967 to about £43,000, but this was to some extent accounted for by the fact that the licence to deal in securities had been switched to Slater Walker Ltd, which now handled the corporate financial advice division, leaving only the private client business to Investment Analysis. Slater Walker Ltd turned in a trading profit on its own account of £170,000 and the Rosenthal banking business made £74,000. But the largest element of organic growth was in three share dealing subsidiaries active during the year – sw Equities, Dukersbrook and newly-formed Bexwood Securities – which made nearly £400,000 between them, about eight times more than the previous year.

It is of course unlikely that the us Congress committee would have regarded internal growth in the form of share dealing profits as providing 'social benefit'; indeed, the committee described the practice of including such gains in the profit and loss account at all as 'questionable'.

The next deal, negotiated in March and April 1968, was the takeover of Keith Blackman, a public company manufacturing ventilating and gas oven equipment. Slater Walker opened with what Slater called a 'ranging shot' but had to increase the price by about £1 million to £4.3 million before the Blackman board would recommend acceptance – not that this proved much of a problem, as the increase was almost entirely financed by the soaring Slater Walker share price. But when Slater got a closer look at Blackman, he decided the job of reorganization was not for him, and within three months the company had been resold for £3.7 million cash. As Blackman had been bought with high-priced shares and loan stock it was, of course, only a loss on paper; indeed, it was not even that, for as far as the accounts were concerned, because the nominal value of the shares was used to calculate its original cost, the Blackman resale was actually deemed to have thrown up a surplus!*

---

* The cost of the last two of Slater Walker's six acquisitions of public companies in 1968 was calculated on the market value of the shares issued, but not that of the first four, and the accounts stated that if they had all been assessed on that basis 'the excess of cost of acquisition of subsidiaries over the net tangible assets acquired would have been £25,100,910'.

By then, Slater had a rather larger fish on his hook. At the end of May 1968 Slater Walker bought for around £18 million Crittall-Hope, the firm which dominated the metal window business in the UK. This was Slater Walker's most important industrial acquisition and will be examined in detail in a later chapter; but again the terms of the takeover would have led to an automatic increase in the Slater Walker earnings per share of about 1½d.

Later in 1968, Slater Walker paid about £6 million for TWW, the rump of the television company that had lost its licence for Wales and the West of England. Its principal asset was the opticians Dollond & Aitchison, and Slater Walker then bought two more firms with optical interests, Augustine Investments and Harrisons. Slater also forged a link with his old associate James Hanson by acquiring a large shareholding in the Wiles Group, now run by Hanson, after Wiles' departure, as another conglomerate. Slater Walker also bought control of an investment and banking operation in the Bahamas, Carden Withers – one of the few deals in which Walker was directly involved.

Towards the end of 1968 Slater Walker bought Drage's, a financial and industrial holding company which formed part of Sir Isaac Wolfson's empire. It was a huge, complex deal worth over £30 million, and was to form the basis of the next transformation of Slater Walker in 1969.

By the time that Slater Walker's 1968 accounts were being prepared the controversy over conglomerates had broken out and the government had asked the Monopolies Commission to produce its observations on this new type of corporation. Slater was the natural champion of the conglomerates and in February 1969 he wrote an article in the *Financial Times* in their defence. The controversy arose, he wrote, because of fears that conglomerates 'will grow too large without industrial logic and without organic growth in their underlying constituent companies'. Slater said he thought a great deal could be done to resolve this problem and to distinguish between real organic growth and growth by acquisitions alone. To make his point Slater used figures for his own company: total profits for 1968, he said, would be not less than £4,180,000 against £974,000 in 1967:* £2,128,000 of the increase, he said, was attributable to companies that had been in the Group at the start of 1968 and only £1,078,000 to those acquired during the year. Acquisitions, he claimed, had in fact slowed down the growth in Slater Walker's earnings per share.

Slater regarded his analysis as very important and suggested the best thing the Monopolies Commission could do would be 'to recom-

* Slater's figures in the *Financial Times* were reached after making certain technical deductions – minority interests and preference dividend – from the pre-tax profits, which in 1967 were £1,940,000.

mend legislation to ensure that all companies show the exact financial effect of acquisition in each year's accounts and give precise details of the profit performance of all companies under their control in an appendix to their accounts.'

Slater Walker's final pre-tax profit for 1968 came out at £4,868,213, an increase of £3,710,000: and in his annual report Slater now said that £1,940,000 accrued from companies in the group at the start of the year. But the accounts gave no more than the usual minimal breakdown of how the profits had been earned: 'financial and investment activities' were up from £739,875 to £3,617,930 and 'commercial and industrial activities' had risen from £701,450 to £2,014,561. The expenses of the parent company and loan stock interest – £764,278 – were again deducted from the total to reach the pre-tax figure.

This vague classification was considered by some hardly to accord with the greater disclosure requirements of the 1967 Companies Act, which demanded a breakdown of turnover and profits of different classes of business – let alone with Slater's own recommendations in the *Financial Times* – and in response to a Parliamentary question in July 1969 the Board of Trade said it would 'invite the company's directors to consider whether a more detailed breakdown should be given in the accounts for 1969'.*

Anyway, the bulk of the organic growth had been on the financial side. Some of this stemmed from the public launch in April 1968 of the Invan Unit Trust, which had initially been formed to accommodate private investment client portfolios of less than £50,000: the public put up a record £8 million and Slater Walker's slice of this in sales charge accounted for most of the £290,000 rise in the profits of Investment Analysis, now renamed Slater Walker Investments. Then there was a large increase in Slater Walker's banking profits, although the Rosenthal business had been sold at the start of 1968.

Further identification of the composition is almost impossible. But it is clear that share dealing profits again accounted for much of the increase in profits. Six share dealing companies alone which could be traced, including our old friend Moss Securities, contributed nearly £900,000, which was almost £500,000 more than their profits in 1967; and Thomas Brown, now effectively just an investment dealing company, made £356,000.

Slater told me that there 'is no dispute that investment dealing profits existed in 1967 and 1968, or that they were growing during those years', although he thought I was overestimating their importance. 'Equally,' Slater also said, 'there can be no argument that such

* When, a year later, the directors decided to comply, and gave comparative figures for 1968, over £160,000 of that year's profit had quietly been recategorized from commercial and industrial to investment and financial.

profits form and are correctly described as part of the organic growth in the overall profits of the group.'

But it was only retrospectively that Slater came to admit the full extent of the importance of share dealing gains in the profits of Slater Walker. Slater told me that it was absurd to suggest that he made any secret of the fact that he was a dealer as far as the Stock Exchange was concerned and that he had a considerable reputation to that effect. He points out that in the accounts for the year ended 31 December 1965 his chairman's statement named three companies in the Slater Walker group, saying 'these are all finance companies which trade mainly in quoted securities.' But in the later years 1967–68 his principal reputation was not as a dealer but as an asset stripper. On 8 June 1967 *The Times* did point to a dealing profit of £120,000 before tax which Slater Walker had made within the space of three weeks (and Slater points out that only six days later Slater Walker's pre-tax profits for the previous year were reported at £370,000); but not one word was said about dealing profits in the *Financial Times* article, or in his chairman's statements for 1967 and 1968 (or for that matter until 1973). Even a twenty-five-page eulogy of Slater Walker by brokers Sebags written in August 1968 ignored them. The only place they were mentioned was in the small print of offer documents when Slater Walker explained the basis on which profits forecasts had been made.

It is possible that the growth in Slater Walker's earnings per share would have been faster in 1967 and 1968, as Slater suggested in his article, if it had stuck to share dealing and not branched out into industrial takeovers. But this is not necessarily so, for many dealing profits stemmed from its activities in the shares of potential victims, i.e. as at the start, Slater Walker should not be regarded as two separate entities – a financial side and an industrial side – carrying on completely independently of each other.

Anyway, any increase in earnings from share dealing could also have further helped to mask a failure to improve the efficiency – or indeed an actual deterioration – of the industrial subsidiaries. So we must now take a closer look at Slater Walker's two most important industrial involvements.

15 *Rationalizing rubber*

One Thursday in the autumn of 1966 David Marshall, fifty-eight-year-old chairman and managing director of the Manchester-based Greengate & Irwell Rubber Company, called on Slater at his offices in Hertford Street in the West End. Marshall, in London for a meeting of the Confederation of British Industries, had telephoned to make an appointment and Slater met him in the hall.

Before he had taken his coat off, Marshall confronted Slater. 'I think you have got an interest in us,' he said. 'Yes,' Slater replied, 'as a matter of fact we have got quite a lot of money tied up in your company.'

Slater had had his eyes on Greengate for a long time, in fact since early 1964, when the *Sunday Telegraph* reader who challenged 'Capitalist' included the share in his rival portfolio. Since then, Slater had been learning, the hard way, about rubber through Producto-foam, but the problems of the industry were not confined to that company. For nearly ten years Greengate had made little progress. Marshall had himself for some time wanted to rationalize the industry by amalgamating three or four medium-sized firms, but had been unable to persuade his competitors. He outlined his plan to Slater and Slater said that he might be able to help. They had two or three further meetings over the following months and the two men found they got on well.

In early January 1967 Slater rang Marshall and told him he was proposing to bid for Greengate at about 5s. 3d. a share. Marshall replied straight away that the price was not good enough. But he agreed to talks and with the help of Greengate's advisers, the merchant bank of Hill Samuel, a fair price was agreed. Slater put out a 6s. 4d. offer, in Slater Walker shares and loan stock, on 15 February 1967. The price, which valued Greengate at about £2.8 million, was nearly forty per cent above Greengate's market quotation of a month before.

Once again Slater Walker investment clients and associates bene-fited from the bid. Walker Moate, for example, held 10,000 shares. I was unable to establish with either Slater or Walker exactly when these were bought: Slater told me he thought they would have been bought before the bid, while Walker assured me that no dealings were ever transacted by Walker Moate in the knowledge that a bid was to take place. As the acquisition of the shares was not registered until 10 April 1967, however, the timing was obviously close. Slater Walker itself had about sixteen per cent of Greengate at the time of its bid, and with this holding, the recommendation of Marshall and his board, and the premium over the market price, the Slater Walker bid went through quickly and smoothly.

The origins of the Greengate & Irwell business went back to 1867, but the company had not sought a Stock Exchange quotation until 1953. At that time its fortunes were closely related to those of the mining industry, for its most important product was conveyor belting for the Coal Board.

Profitability of this side of the business had subsequently fallen with the decline in coal, and the problem of steeply falling demand for belting was exacerbated by a high degree of competition. There were a number of other manufacturers, including some of the big tyre companies like Dunlop, who were prepared to sell belting at a lower profit margin than on their main product. On top of this, the Coal Board also started using belting made from PVC.

By 1967, therefore, the belting side of Greengate was effectively being subsidized by a whole range of other rubber-based products: cables, latex thread, rainwear and other coated materials – the latter being the sort of business at which Productofoam had been so singularly unsuccessful. Greengate also had a division making canvas and rubber footwear, which was not going well, and owned eighty-two per cent of a rubber company in Australia called Bramac.

The earnings from these other products had helped to check the rundown in Greengate's total profits, and in fact in the early Sixties there had been a recovery, with pre-tax profits reaching £432,000 in the year to 31 March 1965. But the following year they collapsed again to £307,000, and at the time of Slater's bid the Greengate board could foresee no real improvement for the year to 31 March 1967.

Once control of Greengate had been secured, Slater himself became chairman and Horsman went on the board, although he was quickly replaced by Tarling. But the man who was given the specific job of liaising with, and investigating and reporting on, the re-organization of the new subsidiary, also with a directorship, was Donald Saunders, who had joined Slater Walker from the American management consultancy firm of McKinsey. Marshall, however, was left in the post of managing director and was allowed to appoint two long-serving Greengate men to the board.

Marshall, like Slater, was a self-made man. He had started working for Greengate in 1924, when he was sixteen, and had gradually worked his way up to the top job, being made a director at thirty, sole managing director in 1959 and chairman in 1964. He did not reach this position as a result of family connections; indeed, the remnants of the old family control of Greengate presented obstacles to his progress. Although by the time Slater bid for Greengate Marshall had built up what was probably the largest individual shareholding, he did not feel that Slater was trying to expropriate a personal possession. In fact, becoming part of Slater Walker freed him from certain restraints and the shares he received in exchange for his Greengate holding made him a wealthy man.

In business Marshall was not a risk-taker. He had once told his shareholders:

> We believe it best to continue to apply ourselves to improving efficiency and developing products within our natural environment of knowledge and machinery, rather than explore where the grass may look greener, but which would be potential losers for those neither accustomed to nor understanding how to earn such apparently easy money.

On financial matters, Marshall displayed what would have once been called the virtue of prudence. He did not like his company to be in debt because he could see no point in trying to increase turnover merely to pay off the banks; in fact, he kept a good reserve of cash and easily realizable investments for emergencies. It was precisely these features that made any company both attractive and vulnerable to Slater.

The reorganization of Greengate was less dramatic than had been the operations conducted on Cork and Brown. But once again its primary purpose was to reduce capital employed, thus raising money for the use of Slater Walker elsewhere. By early 1968 Slater was able to tell his shareholders that they had been able 'to release £1,500,000 by better liquidity control, the sale of Bramac Limited and hiving off the elasticized thread division'.

'Better liquidity control' was a curious description of the way much of the money was raised. For Greengate's cash and securities had been disposed of for some £200,000 while the other assets had been used as security in the running up of a £674,000 overdraft by the end of 1967. As a unit, Greengate was considerably less liquid after the attentions of Slater Walker than it had been under Marshall's cautious financial policy.

Nor had the 'hiving off' of the elasticized thread division actually released any capital; for it remained a wholly-owned part of Slater Walker, being amalgamated with Latex Surgical, the rubber gloves subsidiary of Productofoam. In book-keeping terms, these Greengate assets were transferred to Latex Surgical – now renamed United Latex – for £334,000, which was then chalked up as a debt in the Greengate balance sheet. In physical terms, the rubber gloves business was shifted from Hackney to the Greengate thread factory at Melton Mowbray, where a huge Japanese machine for making lined gloves was installed.

The sale of Greengate's Australian subsidiary, Bramac, was not an 'arm's-length' transaction either: for it was sold for cash and shares, to Wancol Holdings, the coalmining company of which Slater Walker had secured effective control with some of the proceeds of the stripping of Brown, and which had been transformed into Slater Walker (Australia). Bramac was not doing well in 1967 – drought had affected its rainwear side and the Australian conveyor belting market was also highly competitive – and Bramac was sold at rather less than its book value. Slater Walker, however, was to make a huge profit on the deal (see Chapter 17 p. 246).

Slater Walker also closed or sold the canvas and rubber shoes divisions, but otherwise the basic structure of Greengate & Irwell remained intact. A review of overhead expenses was commissioned and Slater personally had a hand in altering Greengate's buying procedures. Prices were increased too, although this might have been done anyway. The most significant move, however, was that an outside management consultant, Peter Fatharly, was asked to look at Greengate's cable factory. He and Saunders agreed that they had to get new premises and persuade an initially reluctant Slater that the expenditure was unavoidable.

In its last year of independence, to 31 March 1967, Greengate had earned profits of £311,000. Its accounting period was then switched to the end of December, and in the following nine months its profits were £310,000, equivalent to an annual rate of over £410,000. In 1968, the Greengate accounts show a pre-tax profit of £583,868, but that was before £96,592 of expenses incurred in moving to the new cable factory at Trafford Park in Manchester, which was designed to serve in addition as a new head office for the group. Eliminating these costs reduced the profit to £487,276. Then in 1969 Greengate's pre-tax profits slumped to £291,656, recovering to £386,527 in 1970.

These figures suggest that there was an initial improvement in the profitability of Greengate after being taken over by Slater Walker, followed by a sharp deterioration. But the crude pre-tax profit figures need to be looked at in more detail to find out more precisely what effect Slater Walker was having on the efficiency of the rubber industry. The usual method of measuring industrial performance, used, for example, by the American Congressional subcommittee in its study of conglomerates, is to look at the movement in certain profit ratios, in particular the return on sales and on capital employed.

Since the purpose of the exercise is to discover the effect of Slater Walker on the profitability of the rubber industry, certain adjustments have to be made to the balance sheet figures. In particular, the capital removed from Greengate, which appears in its balance sheet as a loan to Slater Walker, must be eliminated, as it was used in some other activity, together with any interest paid on it. In the Greengate accounts this interest was lumped into trading profits and its extent was not revealed, but Slater gave me the following figures: 1967 – £6,264 paid on a loan of £857,000 outstanding for just one month. (This was the nine-month period during which the main financial rejigging of Greengate took place and this would make its inclusion in before-and-after comparisons of little significance.) In 1968 and 1969 a total of £152,054 and £75,727 of interest was paid on loans averaging £1,786,000 and £859,000, reducing profits in those two years to £335,222 and £215,929 respectively. In 1970 only £18,346 of interest was paid, bringing profits down to £368,181.

On the basis of these figures the following table of ratios compares the three full years after Slater Walker took control of Greengate with its last year of independent trading – the higher the ratio the better the performance:

	Profits/Net Assets	Profits/Sales
Year to 31 March 1967	6.9	4.7
Year to 31 December 1968	11.3	4.9
(Before the removal costs	14.5	6.3)
Year to 31 December 1969	5.0	2.7
Year to 31 December 1970	9.3	3.9

In early 1970 the *Moorgate & Wall Street Review** carried a study by a Cambridge economist, C. F. Pratten, of the before-and-after effects of Slater Walker on Greengate. It was probably the most thorough examination made of a specific conglomerate merger in this country, and Pratten concluded, albeit somewhat tentatively, that profits of Greengate were somewhat higher than they might have been otherwise; but he was only using results up to the end of 1968 and said that his was essentially a short-term exercise.†

---

* Published by merchant bankers Hill Samuel.

† Pratten was also using figures supplied him by Slater Walker. I have derived the figure for profits/sales in the year to 31 March 1967 from his article, as no turnover figure was given by Greengate for that year, its disclosure in company accounts only being made compulsory by the 1967 Companies Act. Pratten's calculations showed a rather greater improvement in ratios in 1968 than mine.

As Pratten pointed out, since average profits for manufacturing industry were rising strongly – they increased by about nineteen per cent from 1967 to 1968 – the immediate improvement might not have been entirely attributable to the change in control. It should be noted, too, that there had been an important accounting change. Once in charge, Slater Walker entirely wrote off from Greengate's books much of its old plant and machinery, financing the write-offs partly out of the company's ample reserves. In view of the age of the plant, the manoeuvre was not unreasonable. But its effect was to reduce the book value of capital employed and the depreciation charge on profits; in Greengate's last year of independence, depreciation had cost £156,000, but in 1968 it was only £94,000.*

Nevertheless, it can be concluded that there was an immediate improvement in profitability at Greengate followed immediately by sharp deterioration in 1969, and even by the end of 1970 profitability had not been convincingly restored to the pre-Slater levels.

The swig men involved told me that there had been major, unforeseen problems at the new cable factory. Slater does not agree, and told me that the main reason for the decline was that 'the major long-term orientated reorganization was taking place.' In any event, the cable division turned in a trading loss in 1969. By 1970, however, its profitability had been restored to pre-reorganization levels.

The cable division was not the only Greengate business to run into trouble after the takeover, for United Latex became a steady drain on Slater Walker's resources. Even before the amalgamation with Greengate's elasticized thread division Productofoam's rubber glove subsidiary had started losing even more heavily, recording a loss of £147,000 in the fifteen months to the end of 1967, including a £48,000 provision for the cost of moving to Melton Mowbray. Greengate's thread business had been in trouble a few years before the takeover, when corsets it was processing kept getting discoloured; but the situation had been retrieved and the small division was turning a few thousand pounds a year of profit when Slater Walker took control. Combining it with the rubber gloves was a disaster: in 1968, United Latex lost £189,000 after exceptional depreciation and write-offs of £138,000. This latter item did not make its way through to the Slater Walker profit record, where 'textiles', as United Latex was somewhat illogically categorized, were shown – in the comparative breakdown of profits given in the 1969 accounts – as having lost £51,000 in 1968.

By the end of 1968 United Latex was about all that remained of Productofoam Holdings, Slater's original industrial venture. The

* However, the rate of depreciation applied to Greengate's remaining plant was relatively higher than before.

group had been rapidly dismantled after Slater Walker bought out the remaining public shareholders in the summer of 1967. The laminating and related businesses at Bedford Mill had succeeded in losing over £250,000 by the end of that year and were mostly disposed of in early 1968, along with whatever subsidiaries could be sold or more or less given away, including profitable ones like Coral Plastics and P. & H. Bailey. The net loss on disposals of the subsidiaries and properties was some £300,000, and Productofoam's other odds and ends for the most part then ceased to trade or were eventually liquidated, with the exception of the stalwart dealing company Moss – but even that was losing money by 1969.

United Latex became a direct subsidiary of SWIG in 1968 – Slater then resigned from the board – and Slater Walker took over its inter-group debts, which by the end of 1968 totalled about £750,000. In 1969 it continued to lose money at over £10,000 a month and by the end of the year had turned in a trading loss of £156,000, without even any exceptional items this time, on a turnover of £857,000. Advances by Slater Walker and SWIG had risen to £1,174,000.

In 1970 United Latex lost another £206,000 on sales that had fallen to £659,000. On top of this, 'an exhaustive physical stock-taking and review' had revealed 'stock shortages, deterioration and obsolescence,' which should have been dealt with in earlier accounts, and an additional £46,000 had to be found to cover these. By the end of 1970 accumulated trading losses had reached £745,000.

In July 1969 Peter Fatharly had joined Slater Walker as Tarling's deputy at SWIG, with a special brief to look after the rubber interests including United Latex, and during 1970 negotiations to get rid of the company were concluded. The recalcitrant glove machine was sold to Dunlop and a huge stockpile of unsold gloves disposed of. Slater Walker's loans to its ailing subsidiary were then converted into £1.4 million of equity capital and these shares were sold for just £130,000. The deal came into effect on 1 January 1971, almost eight years after Slater had gone into the rubber glove business, and within a short time United Latex, now rid of this burden, and confined to elasticized thread, was trading profitably for its new owners.

Even SWIG men were amazed that such a little company as United Latex could swallow up such large sums. Small subsidiary though it may have been, in 1969 its losses amounted to over seventy per cent of Greengate's profits, but no mention was made of it in that year's accounts of Slater Walker. The losses were hidden by the fact that, as a result of the Drage's deal, Slater Walker had acquired substantial textile interests which allowed it to record a total 'textiles' turnover of over £35 million and profits of £1,271,000, while 'rubber and plastic products' were shown as contributing £268,000 of profits on sales of £8,709,000. But it is debatable whether the classification of United

Latex as textiles was appropriate. Indeed, arguably, to assess fully Slater Walker's performance in the rubber industry, the profits, assets and turnover of Greengate and United Latex should be combined. Slater says to do this is 'absurd' and that the bulk of the United Latex losses were attributable to the glove plant which had never been part of Greengate. I do not accept that it is absurd to combine the two, which produces the following ratios:

	Profits/Net Assets	Profits/Sales
1968	4.2	1.9
1969	1.2	0.7
1970	3.9	1.8

Slater commented only briefly on Greengate in his statement for 1969: it had, he said, 'achieved a further satisfactory increase in sales for the year although profits were below the level achieved in 1968, due mainly to start up costs associated witht the Cable Division factory at Trafford Park'; and for purposes of comparison the non-recurring removal costs had, uncharacteristically, been eliminated from the 1968 profits, which were shown at only £335,000 (thus minimizing the fall).

The construction of the new factory, and its problems, meant that the flow of money was reversed as capital was ploughed back. By the end of 1969 the loan from Greengate to Slater Walker was down to a little over £100,000 and there had been an increase in capital employed of about £1.3 million.

It must be said that Slater responded to the demands from the men at Greengate for the return of funds, and the money spent on the new factory and plant paid off in the end. But Slater himself did not like setbacks because he was concerned with the short run, in making money now, not tomorrow, so that each year assets and earnings per share would rise, pulling the share price up. 'The dramatic growth,' he told the *Investors Chronicle* in May 1969, 'comes from raising the performance of a Company from bad to reasonable, not from reasonable to very good'; and 'the faster the transformation, naturally, the more dramatic the growth of group earnings,' the *Investors Chronicle* commented.

The appearance of improvement can be achieved quickly by the use of accounting gimmicks or the 'hiving off' of loss-makers whose cost is charged to reserves. But genuine industrial turn-arounds can take up to five years and more, and there may be setbacks on the way, as indeed there were at Greengate. In 1969 it was clear that any improvement there was going to be a long job; there had been neither fast transformation nor dramatic growth and therefore, by

Slater's own criterion, far from being turned from bad to reasonable, Greengate had, if anything, been turned from bad to worse.

There were men at SWIG who were prepared to face such a long job. Some of them were good industrial managers – and others very bad – but they were not a special breed of supermen who could solve intractable industrial problems overnight, in the same way that Slater could make them vanish in the balance sheet. A process of disillusion set in at Slater Walker: on Slater's part it was disillusion with the industrial involvements of his company. Later he used a different version of the aphorism quoted in the *Investors Chronicle*: taking companies from bad to reasonable was easy, but taking them from reasonable to good was ten years' hard labour. Slater freely admitted he was not in the hard labour business. It was the realization of this that led to disillusion among the SWIG men hired in the first flush of enthusiasm for the technological revolution.

Slater's retrospective rationalization – that he was not in the hard labour business – for his decision to 'deconglomeratize' (i.e. to sell off the industrial subsidiaries) is parallel to his openly-expressed attitude to loss-making companies. In 1967 he told the *Sunday Times*:

> I believe that a business should be run like an investment portfolio – cut your losses and let your profits run – in other words concentrate your effort on the profit-makers rather than loss-makers. A lot of British boards seem to do the opposite: if they have a loss-maker on their hands, they work like fury to pull it round, while I would sell it.

While Slater Walker did often get rid of loss-makers, there is not much more consistency between Slater's adage for the stock market and his buying and selling of businesses than there was between it and his personal share dealing. Slater did not hold on to successful businesses any more than he let his stock market profits run: he sold them to reinvest the proceeds in new situations.

Nevertheless, the comparison was built in to the legend. 'The termination of unprofitable activities,' the *Investors Chronicle* said in May 1969, 'comes before backing winners in the batting order.' The article continued:

> It is sometimes argued that Slater's recipe of selling off loss-makers post haste is altogether too facile and that he will run out of buyers. The scantiest perusal of the evidence so far available is enough to throw this argument out of court. Take Greengate & Irwell whose loss-making footwear division was sold to BTR; take Productofoam whose Coral Plastics subsidiary was sold to Judge International and whose P. & H. Bailey subsidiary was sold to Cope Allman.

A somewhat deeper perusal of the evidence might have revealed not only that Coral and Bailey had actually been bought by Slater in the first place but also that they were almost the only profitable subsidiaries of Productofoam. Productofoam's laminating division was sold after four years of deterioration and the rubber glove business was allowed to lose money for five years before being sold; and one of the reasons they were held so long, Slater told me, was precisely the difficulty of finding buyers.

Selling profitable companies is clearly much easier than selling unprofitable ones. Greengate's problem in 1969, when the deconglomeration policy was in full swing – Slater has said that the decision to sell off the industrial companies was taken in 1968 – was that it was not making much money. The solution was to buy more rubber earnings, and Marshall's plan to rationalize the industry, which now had the backing of the IRC, was belatedly put into motion.

In November 1969, Slater Walker bid about £8.5 million for P. B. Cow, one of the rubber companies which Marshall had been trying to persuade to merge. Cow's main business was making a range of rubber components used in cars, commercial vehicles and consumer durables. But it also made various consumer items like li-los, hot water bottles, paddling pools and so on, and it had a plastics subsidiary. One of its main differences from Greengate was geographical: its factories were in the south of England. But it, too, had an Australian subsidiary.

Slater Walker's price for Cow was almost double the book value of its assets and over fifty per cent more than the value the stock market had put on the company a few weeks before. It was an offer the Cow board could not very well refuse. Charles Hawkins, the Cow chairman, told his shareholders that progress in sales and profits had been good, especially compared with other companies in the industry, and he expected the progress would be maintained. But the Slater Walker offer, he pointed out, was 'financially attractive'.

The key attraction of Cow was, of course, precisely that it was a strong, profitable company. It had made profits of £831,000 in 1968 and expected to make £950,000 in 1969. Its return on capital in those two years had been 20 per cent and 21.0 per cent and on sales 6.8 per cent and 7.7 per cent. But although the gap between the Slater Walker share rating and the rest of the market had ceased to widen in 1969, its price/earnings ratio was still a few points higher than Cow's, even at Slater Walker's high offer price.*

---

*Slater Walker forecast profits of £9 million for 1969 in the Cow offer document. The small print contains an interesting indication of the importance of share dealing profits: £818,000 of the £9 million was to come from gains expected to be realized between 24 October 1969 and the end of the year. The extent of gains already realized was not revealed.

There was not much point in messing about with the structure of Cow, and the only immediate change made by Slater Walker was to transfer its Australian offshoot, Leggett Rubber, to Thomas Brown, which had remained Slater Walker's wholly owned subsidiary in Australia. Nor were there many management changes. Slater left the Greengate board at the end of 1969, Marshall was reinstated as chairman and Fatharly was appointed to the board: these two went on to the Cow board, Hawkins was made a director of Greengate, and a management committee was formed 'with a view to obtaining maximum benefits from the association of these companies whilst at the same time retaining their separate identities'.

Slater Walker's next move in the rationalization of the rubber industry was made in June 1970 when it bought the Frankenstein Group. This company specialized in survival equipment – life rafts and jackets and protective clothing – through companies in both the UK and Australia, but it also had a textile laminating factory near Greengate in Manchester. Frankenstein was small and quoted only on the Northern Stock Exchange; in 1969 it had made profits of £80,000, about half of which came from Australia. Slater Walker paid £790,000 or 14s. 11d. in cash, about double the market price of three months before.

As with Cow, Frankenstein's Australian company, Beaufort Pioneer, was quickly transferred to Brown, providing it with another small but timely injection of industrial profits. Frankenstein's UK business was integrated with Greengate.

The acquisition of Cow transformed Slater Walker's performance in 1970. Even without its Australian subsidiary, which had been making around £160,000 a year, Cow cleared a profit of over £1 million in 1970. This represented over seventy per cent of the total rise in Slater Walker's declared profits that year, which, as we shall see, was one of many setbacks. As Cow had only been acquired at the very end of 1969, this contribution hardly qualified as 'organic' growth, but it at least helped to keep up the appearance that Slater Walker was still moving forward.

But equally important, the acquisition of Cow enabled Slater Walker to assemble an attractive package of its rubber interests, which it proceeded to resell to the public in July 1971, barely eighteen months after Cow had been bought.

Until the reflotation there had been little integration of Cow and Greengate. To effect their resale, a new holding company was formed called Allied Polymer, and Cow was relabelled the Southern Division while Greengate plus Frankenstein was called the Northern Division. Hawkins continued to be managing director of the Southern Division, but another SWIG man had replaced Marshall as managing director of the Northern Division. Fatharly became chairman and chief executive of Allied Polymer, while Marshall and Tarling were given non-executive posts on its board.

The accountants' report in the prospectus included a profit record going back to 1961 reconstructed from the independent performance of the companies welded into Allied Polymer. From 1967, the year Slater Walker bought Greengate, profits were shown to have risen from £906,000 to £1,354,000 in 1968, to have dropped to £1,103,000 in 1969, and then risen again in 1970 to £1,445,000. A note indicated that these figures did not allow for £704,000 of reorganizational costs incurred in those four years.

The bulk of the profits were, of course, provided by Cow, which had only been acquired by Slater Walker at the end of 1969 and whose previous record had owed nothing to the influence of the men at SWIG. But the most interesting aspect of the flotation of Allied Polymer was the financial manoeuvring that preceded it.

Allied Polymer itself acquired Greengate plus Frankenstein and Cow from Slater Walker, or more strictly SWIG, on 30 June 1971 by the issue to Slater Walker of 14,654,000 new shares and £500,000 of loan stock. It was 11,000,000 of these shares that Slater Walker was offering to the public at 75 pence each. But it emerged from the prospectus that Slater Walker was to get a further £3.5 million of the attractive ten per cent loan stock carrying rights to be converted into ordinary shares in Allied Polymer – £1 million 'for cash' and £2.5 million 'in satisfaction of the major part of the group indebtedness to SWIG'.

Now Greengate's own balance sheet for 31 December 1970 shows that SWIG at that point *owed* its subsidiary over £500,000. How then this sudden reversal? The answer was to be found in the small print of the accountants' report: the £2.5 million of loan stock, the accountants said more bluntly, had been issued to Slater Walker 'in settlement of special dividends totalling £2,500,000 declared on 10 June 1971 by Greengate and P. B. Cow, prior to their acquisition by the Company (that is Allied Polymer) out of reserves at 31 December 1970'.

In other words, the 'indebtedness' had been created by the declaration of these special dividends – £2 million from Greengate and £500,000 from Cow – and then settled the same day by the issue of the loan stock. It was in effect a free issue of loan stock to Slater Walker and there was no movement of cash at all.

I asked Slater why so much loan stock had been issued to Slater Walker, and he replied that this was done because Allied Polymer was ungeared and 'it obviously made it more attractive for it to have some long-term gearing'.* Slater went on to point out that this

* Gearing, in this sense, is the ratio between loan stock or preference stock and

helped the price earnings ratio and 'thereby the overall flotation price'.

While the loan stock may have had these effects, the decision to issue some of it in settlement of special dividends which were described as 'indebtedness' created the impression that this money had been borrowed from Slater Walker. Slater also argued that it was normal to restructure the capital of a company before flotation; but this transaction was not normal and Allied Polymer would obviously have been better off if the special dividends had not been declared.

The final £1 million slice of loan stock had been issued to Slater Walker for cash; but only £600,000 of this reached Allied Polymer, for £400,000 was deducted to cover the costs of the flotation. Slater said that everything that needed to be made clear to the public was made clear in the prospectus; but, quite apart from the 'indebtedness' point, how much of this £400,000 was the fee of Slater Walker as sponsoring bank was not revealed. (Slater points out that he was under no legal obligation to do so.) The £600,000 also proved a small burden, for shortly after it had gained its semi-independence Allied Polymer paid Slater Walker a dividend of £493,000 in respect of the first half of 1971 when Greengate and Cow were still subsidiaries.

The description of the special dividends as 'indebtedness' could well have created the impression that Slater Walker had been investing money in the rubber industry, especially as, elsewhere in the prospectus, it was stated that over the previous four years more than £3 million had been invested in providing new and improved plant and equipment. While this amount may have been spent in total, the actual net addition, for example, to Greengate's fixed assets – that is the difference between the cost of new factories and plant less the proceeds of disposals – during the four years it was under Slater Walker's control was £980,000, of which £160,000 was financed by government investment grants. The amount removed by Slater Walker on securing control of Greengate was enough to cover that with plenty to spare, and in addition Slater Walker had retained some £750,000 of Greengate's, Cow's and Frankenstein's assets represented by their Australian subsidiaries.

The stock market was rising strongly again in the summer of 1971 after the 1969/70 collapse, and there were plenty of buyers for the Allied Polymer shares even if there was not the mad rush that characterized some offerings. Existing Slater Walker shareholders and Allied Polymer employees were given preference in the allotment

ordinary shares. Since the interest on loan stock and preference shares is fixed, a highly geared company, will, if it makes good profits, have larger amounts available for its ordinary shareholders than one which is less highly geared.

procedure and when dealings in the shares started on the Stock Exchange they were quoted at 79 pence each.

So Slater Walker collected its £8,250,000 of cash from the public and was still left with 3,654,000 Allied Polymer shares, worth nearly £3 million, many of which it proceeded to sell on the market. On top of that it had the £4 million of loan stock, producing a steady income of £400,000 a year. In all Slater Walker picked up roughly the equivalent of £15 million for three companies which had cost it about £12,250,000, much of it paid in high-priced shares.

These manoeuvres demonstrate that while Slater Walker certainly had 'sophisticated financial control' – one of the qualities Slater extolled in conglomerates – it operated that control in favour of the conglomerate holding company itself rather than its constituent industrial parts. At a time when the great majority of economic opinion held that the rate of investment in UK industry was too low, Slater Walker did not raise any significant amount of fresh capital for its rubber companies, but was, on balance, taking money out.

Nevertheless, whatever its motives, Slater Walker acted as the catalyst for the rationalization of a part of the rubber industry, and Slater has asked me to point out that David Marshall, who was chief executive of Greengate & Irwell at the critical time and has also been president of the Federation of British Rubber and Allied Manufacturers Association, says: 'It would be wrong to close this chapter without making it clear that, in my view, the acquisition of Greengate & Irwell by Slater Walker was the catalyst for the formation of the successful and professionally managed Allied Polymer group. I have examined Slater Walker's industrial subsidiaries from a financial angle – for that was how Slater Walker itself looked at them – but Marshall adds: 'Throughout these operations where activities were terminated employees were transferred to other work. New developments created more jobs and labour relations were always given the highest priority and employees positively benefited from the progress of the group.' Marshall's view, therefore, is that Slater Walker's expertise brought about definite improvements in the structure of the general rubber goods industry. Indeed the Allied Polymer group that was created was a good one – in many ways the best to emerge from the dismantling of the Slater Walker conglomerate. It continued to grow fast, as did its profitability, as can be seen from the following ratios:

	Profits/Sales	Profits/Net Assets
1971	7.5	20.6
1972	9.3	26.2
1973	9.8	28.8

(The loan stock and its interest are excluded to make the figures more comparable with those given earlier for Greengate and Cow.)

How much of the improvement was directly the result of combining the three companies into one group is impossible to estimate.
Some of it may even stem from the fact that the SWIG men who stayed
at Allied Polymer established a degree of independence from their
old parent that many of the other so-called satellites may well have
envied. The mainstay of the improvement, however, continued to be
provided by the old Cow business, whose profitability was already
high and rising when Slater Walker bought it. But credit must be
given to the SWIG men's efforts to improve Greengate, which began to
pay off from 1970: the new cable factory, for example, averaged
profits of over £250,000 in 1971, 1972 and 1973, although Allied
Polymer subsequently sold it because they felt it had too small a share
of the market and could not continue indefinitely to expand in
competition with the large manufacturers. Still, if Slater Walker had
not been able to buy Cow with its highly rated shares at the end of
1969, it would not have been able to resell Greengate alone in 1971
on anything like the same favourable terms on its record under Slater
Walker's control. It was only through the acquisition of Cow that the
record could be made, quickly, to look respectable. The unappealing
and unwanted alternative was ten years' hard labour.

It is worth ending with an example of the absurdities that can be
perpetrated in the name of reorganization or rationalization. As
already noted, both Cow and Frankenstein had profitable Australian
subsidiaries called Leggett Rubber and Beaufort Pioneer. On the
takeover of their UK parents these firms were reorganized into
Thomas Brown, Slater Walker's Australian subsidiary (as opposed to
its associate out there, Slater Walker (Australia)). Slater Walker's
policy at this time was to extract the overseas companies acquired in
the course of taking over UK-based groups for later use in securing
local stock market quotations; and in due course, in July 1970,
Leggett was floated on the Sydney, Melbourne and Brisbane
exchanges as the principal asset of a new Australian vehicle called
Tagus. Later Tagus, Leggett and Beaufort were all shifted into
Slater Walker (Australia) to provide that company with some badly
needed profits after it had run into serious trouble (see Chapter 19).
Then, in the summer of 1973, Allied Polymer decided that 'in the
interests of the Group's long-term development' it was essential 'to
establish appropriate manufacturing facilities in selected countries of
the world'. So it bought back Leggett and Beaufort, together with
another local rubber company that had been acquired by Slater
Walker called Driclad, for over £7 million. It was perhaps not
surprising to learn that the activities of these Australian companies
were 'complementary and similar' to those of some companies
already in the Allied Polymer group.

16   *Accounting for profits at Crittall-Hope*

In May 1968 Slater Walker bought Crittal-Hope, the UK's largest manufacturer of metal window frames. It was to become the showpiece of the achievements of Slater Walker, a 'classic example of Slaterization' as *The Sunday Times* described it. It became Slater's own favourite example for use in defence of conglomerates. In an article in *The Times* in January 1973 he said:

> A great deal is written nowadays about asset stripping which is in fact a relatively rare occurrence and should not be confused with industrial rationalization and putting assets to much better use. There is no doubt that Slater Walker's catalytic action resulted in Crittall-Hope's assets being more profitably utilized and that this was in the national interest as well as in the interests of both Crittall-Hope and Slater Walker shareholders.

In December 1968, six months after Slater Walker had bought Crittall-Hope, *The Sunday Times* summarized that catalytic action: 'It took nearly 150 years to build Crittall-Hope into the world's biggest metal window business. . . . It took just 21 days this year to formulate plans to rip out the bad bits, bind the rest tightly together and jack up profitability by more than 150 per cent.'

The record of this, the most important of Slater Walker's conglomerate takeover, must be examined against the background of a five-year period of contraction in house building, for its fortunes were largely dependent on the building industry.

Index of Houses Completed (1963 = 100)

1963	100
1964	125.0
1965	127.9
1966	129.0
1967	135.3
1968	138.4

1969	122.7
1970	117.2
1971	117.3
1972	106.8
1973	98.4

In spite of the long history of its component parts, the Crittall-Hope group had only taken shape in March 1965 with the merger of the Essex-based Crittall-Manufacturing, which had started life in plumbing and ironmongery in 1849 and first made metal windows in 1884, and the Midlands firm of Henry Hope & Sons, which had been founded in 1818 and grew to fame making conservatories for Victorian mansions. The founding families were still in command on the merger but since the two companies had become public, neither had a controlling interest. It was an amicable arrangement, made on equal terms, and it was agreed that Michael Hope, the chairman of the Midlands company, should head the merged concern for the first three years, after which John Crittall, chairman of the Essex firm, would take over.

Crittall's and Hope's had merged for largely protective reasons. Hope's had been the mainstay of a price fixing agreement, the Standard Metal Windows Group, an arrangement which had been found by the Restrictive Trade Practices Court actually to operate in the public interest. But Crittall's had never joined the group and it had later broken up. Hope's believed that a merger with Crittall's would enable them, by virtue of their dominance of the market with more than sixty per cent of standard window sales, to raise prices. Crittall's were less concerned with this, but had had takeover approaches and preferred the alternative of a link with a partner on equal terms. At the time, naturally, less emphasis was put on these reasons for the merger than on the possibilities of economies of scale, principally in overseas sales and in research and development.

In fact, once merged, Hope and Crittall insisted that there would still be competition between them in the domestic market. The reason for this was that Hope believed that if the two did not continue to submit separate tenders for big contracts, overall the group would lose business to outside competitors, more of whom would be invited to tender in the first place.

Nor was there any rationalization of production. Hope's two factories in Smethwick and Wednesbury and Crittall's three plants in Essex were all kept going. Quite apart from the reluctance of the two families to shut down businesses with which they had been so long associated, Hope himself expected a good growth in the construction industry and wanted to keep the spare capacity in order to be able to accommodate it.

In the first full financial year after their merger, to 31 March

1966, the Crittalls and the Hopes achieved the opposite of synergy: the profits of the whole turned out considerably lower than the sum of the two parts in their last year of independence. A big increase in house building in 1964 had not been followed through and the resulting overcapacity at Crittall-Hope was the main cause. Nevertheless, the official forecasts were predicting a good rise in house building again in 1966, and production capacity was not reduced.

In the event this rise failed to materialize and 1966 proved a difficult year all round as a result of the measures taken to defend the pound. In spite of the economic conditions the profitability of Crittall-Hope's basic UK metal window business improved substantially in the year to 31 March 1967; but the improvement had been from a low level and the return remained poor, with the UK metal window companies contributing less than thirty per cent to the group's profits but accounting for nearly half its sales.

Crittall-Hope was kept going by its chain of overseas companies, which in that year contributed sixty-seven per cent of the group's trading profit of £1,498,000 on only thirty-nine per cent of its £30 million sales. The best business was in America, where Crittall-Hope owned three companies in the US, the most important of which, Hope's Windows, happened to have a portfolio of quoted American securities worth about £1 million. Crittall-Hope also had a Canadian subsidiary and it controlled a South African company which had minority public shareholders and a Johannesburg Stock Exchange quotation. The group also had subsidiaries in Zambia, Nigeria, Australia, New Zealand, Malaysia and Germany, and it owned half of two Irish companies and an interest in firms in India and Mauritius.

Nearly all these companies, like their British parent, made steel and aluminium windows and doors. In the UK, however, Crittall-Hope had some other sources of income. The Hope business had a heating subsidiary, dating back from the days when it built conservatories, which made oil and gas burners, while Crittall made agricultural equipment, including silos. Then in 1967 it bought a business which specialized in aluminium curtain walling for office blocks which considerably enlarged that side of the group's business. Crittall-Hope also owned fifty per cent of its main supplier of steel sections for its window frames, Darlington & Simpson Rolling Mills, of which the other half, after steel nationalization, belonged to the British Steel Corporation.

By August 1967, when Hope issued his chairman's statement for the year to 31 March 1967, the outlook for the UK business was better as there had been a revival in housing starts. But Hope could see trouble ahead in the overseas companies and told his shareholders that he would be 'agreeably surprised' if the results of the overseas subsidiaries for the coming year 'are anything like as good as those for the year immediately past'.

Some foretaste of the problems – intense competition in South Africa and a construction workers' strike in Canada – came with the interim results in January 1968, when it was revealed that profits for the first half of the year had fallen by thirty-seven per cent. By now the group was thinking seriously of more drastic rationalization, had sold one or two properties and had asked accountants Peat Marwick to make a study. But in the light of the recovery in construction at home, Crittall-Hope remained optimistic for the results for the second half of the year.

The optimism proved ill-founded: as the accounts for the year to 31 March 1968 were being drawn up, Hope got his surprise, but it came from an unexpected quarter. An accountant flew over from the German subsidiary to reveal the fact that the figures being fed back to the parent bore no relation to what was actually going on: they were being rigged.

On Thursday, 25 April 1968, as Crittall-Hope was trying to grapple with this unwelcome turn of events, another bolt came from out of the blue: Slater rang up Hope and told him that, after the Stock Exchange had closed, he would be announcing a bid for the company.

The Crittall-Hope directors knew that somebody was interested in the group; the share price had risen from 8s. at the end of 1967 to 13s. by 24 April 1968, an increase that would hardly have been justified by the interim results. They believed that a bid might come from one of the big aluminium companies. The name of Slater had been mentioned, but they thought that Crittall-Hope was too big for him, even though the inflated stock market value of his company, at £40 million, was more than twice theirs.

Slater's offer, mostly in shares then at the height of their 'glamour' rating, put a price of just under 16s. on each Crittall-Hope share, or about £18 million for the whole group. Since this was double the price of four months before and nearly twenty-five per cent above the market price before the offer was announced, the board knew, as they went into a huddle with their advisers, that it was going to be a difficult one to refuse.

The immediate question was whether or not the preliminary figures for the year to 31 March 1968, disclosing the full extent of the German disaster, should be released. It did not take long to decide that there could be no justification for holding them back, and on 7 May they were sent out.

Although there had been an improvement in profits compared with the first half of the year – excluding the German operation – the overall trading performance was still somewhat worse than the year before. But the blow lay in the £450,000 of losses that had been revealed in Germany: these cut pre-tax profits down by nearly forty per cent to about £950,000; but on top of this, £180,000 would have to be charged to reserves to cover Germany's losses in earlier years. An independent investigation of the position had been ordered, the announcement said, but was not complete.

Slater Walker's inquiries into Crittall-Hope before the bid, carried out naturally in secret and without the cooperation of the company, had thrown up that there was a problem in the German subsidiary, but the extent of the damage came as a surprise. Nevertheless Crittall-Hope's results 'could hardly have appeared at a better time for Slater Walker', as the *Financial Times* commented the next day, for they left the Crittall-Hope directors with virtually no chance of justifying independence. They soon started talks with Slater Walker and secured some slight alteration in the terms of the bid – reducing the amount of Slater Walker equity in the offer price, but not by as much as they wanted – before the formal offer was posted on 28 May 1968.

With the offer went a letter from Hope; he said that a three-year budget had been carried out and as a result he forecast that Crittall-Hope would make profits of £1,400,000 in the year to. 31 March 1969, and that they should increase further in the following two years. Nevertheless, Slater Walker's offer price was so much higher than any price the shares could possibly command in the market in the short term that Hope had no alternative but to recommend the offer. The Crittall-Hope shareholders accepted with alacrity, and on 18 June 1968 Slater Walker acquired its biggest subsidiary to date.

Before then – even before the offer went out – Horsman, with the agreement of the Crittall-Hope board, had been sent out to Germany to inspect the problem there. He quickly decided that this was no mess for Slater Walker to spend time sorting out, and on 12 July 1968 the German subsidiary was effectively given away. But the cost was enormous: a total of £1.4 million. On top of the £450,000 trading losses in the previous year, nearly £300,000 of trading losses relating to earlier years were uncovered. All these losses were financed by loans from German banks which had to be repaid, and by loans and capital injections from Crittall-Hope. Yet more capital had to be put up to persuade the local manager, whom the old Crittall-Hope board had recently brought in, to take over the German company, and there were further incidental expenses. All these costs, plus the original cost of the investment, had to be written off, all but the £450,000 being charged to reserves.

In early August 1968 Slater, who had become chairman of Crittall-Hope, issued his half-yearly report on Slater Walker in which he claimed that profits of Crittall-Hope were running at the rate of

£925,000 – and not the £1.4 million forecast by Hope in his letter recommending Slater's offer. There was, at the time, considerable controversy over profit forecasts made during bids as a result of the GCE/AEI battle and the apparent evaporation of the latter's profits after acquisition. The main reason for the shortfall in Crittall-Hope's profits was that Horsman had estimated that the German losses would be at least double the £150,000 allowed for by the old Crittall-Hope board in its £1.4 million.

The implication was that the over-optimism of the Crittall-Hope board had led Slater Walker into paying more than it need have done in the takeover. But the point was not pressed, and of course any allegation that the old board could not have met its forecast would have involved making assumptions on how they would have dealt with the German problem.

After downgrading the old forecast, Slater went on to produce one of his own: pre-tax profits of Crittall-Hope should be running at the rate of £2.5 million before the end of 1969: it was, as the *Daily Telegraph* reported, a 'jaunty' prediction.

Michael Hope was still a director of Crittall-Hope at the time that Slater was undermining the credibility of his figures, and it was clear that he could not remain much longer with the firm. His departure was announced on 1 October 1968, along with that of two other directors and of his eldest son, who had worked on research and development.

The new management structure created for Crittall-Hope was curious. Slater himself now handed the chairmanship over to Tarling. John Crittall survived the takeover and was made deputy chairman and chief executive. But a SWIG director, another ex-McKinsey man, Gordon Austin Davis, who had recently resigned from the board of the disastrous United Latex, was made managing director with responsibility for the reorganization.

The Hopes also had to go because it was their business which suffered in the reduction in capacity that Hope had himself so long delayed. Its two Midlands factories were to be sold, and all steel window production was to be concentrated in Essex. One half of the Smethwick factory, however, was to be leased back and the aluminium curtain wall activities would be centred there: this rump of Henry Hope and Sons was renamed Crittall-Hope (Smethwick Division). Hope's heating business, which had lost over £100,000 in the year to 31 March 1968, was also dismantled, although a part of it remained within Slater Walker as it was transferred to George Wilson Industries.

The decision to cut back in the Midlands rather than in Essex was inevitable. In the more industrialized area not only could the factories be more easily sold, but the 650 redundancies caused by the closures, out of Crittall-Hope's total workforce of about 7,000, could also be more easily absorbed than in the Braintree area of Essex where the local community was heavily reliant on Crittalls; indeed, Slater Walker said that an extra 420 people would be required there to handle the work to be transferred from the Midlands.

These plans were announced on 1 October 1968, and at the same time Slater Walker revealed some further changes. A few odd UK subsidiaries of Crittall-Hope, which were not making money, were being liquidated. (The decision to close a couple of them had been made by the old board.) Abroad, the Canadian company, which had lost £36,000 in the year to 31 March 1968, was jettisoned. The assets of the South African company, which had been making profits of nearly £100,000 a year, were sold to a local competitor; but Slater had plans for the corporate entity which retained its Johannesburg Stock Exchange quotation, and it was still a member of the Crittall-Hope group at the end of 1968.

This was the sort of 'dramatic knife-work' or 'drastic surgery' that impressed Slater's admirers, and by the end of 1968 the Crittall-Hope group was rather different from what it had been seven months before. This explains why the profits it turned in for the nine months to 31 December 1968 – its accounting date was switched to coincide with Slater Walker's – bore no relation to Hope's forecast of £1.4 million than to Slater's £925,000 figure; the recorded trading profit was £1,265,000 – equivalent to an annual rate of nearly £1.7 million – and this was lifted to £1.5 million before tax by capital gains that had been realized on the sale of the American subsidiary's quoted securities.

The overseas subsidiaries of Crittall-Hope, of which Hope's Windows in America was much the most important, in fact again provided the bulk of the profit – nearly £900,000 out of the £1.5 million. And while the elimination of the UK loss-makers had increased the total domestic contribution to Crittall-Hope's business, the profits of the basic window making business in those nine months declined by comparison with the previous year.

By the end of 1968 Crittall-Hope had been a subsidiary of Slater Walker for about six and a half months and it provided about £1 million – including the profit on the sale of the US stock market investments – of the group's £1.8 million of acquired profits that year. But Crittall-Hope was not the only window maker in Slater Walker, for in July 1968 it had bought a small private family business called S. Warner & Son which made metal windows – mainly aluminium – at Addington in Surrey. Slater Walker had first tried to get hold of this firm a couple of years before, for it was a highly profitable little business which made a £94,000 profit on sales of £870,000 in 1965 and £165,000 on a turnover of just over £1 million in 1966. Warner's was taking about fifteen per cent of its sales in profits and its return on capital was some fifty per cent, against comparable ratios for Crittall-Hope of four and seven per cent: as far as Slater Walker was concerned it provided an excellent model for what they thought could be done with its larger competitor.

The disposal of subsidiaries and investments can be carried out rapidly. Closing down plants and switching manufacturing facilities, on the other hand, takes time, and the reorganization of the basic Crittall-Hope businesses in the Midlands and Essex stretched well into 1969. While the decision to cut down capacity was taken when house building was at a peak, it was perhaps fortunate for Slater Walker that by the time it had been carried out, construction had started on its five-year slump, although Slater today claims that he saw it coming. One result, however, was that it was not found necessary to increase the workforce in Essex to the extent anticipated when the reorganization was announced; the average number of UK employees of Crittall-Hope in fact dropped from 6,025 in the last nine months of 1968 to 5,090 in 1969.

But in early 1969 Slater remained very optimistic about Crittall-Hope. He told Slater Walker shareholders in May that year that as a result of the reorganization of the window maker 'we estimate that profits before taxation which were running, on acquisition, at the rate of approximately £1,000,000 per annum will be more than doubled in 1969'. It was a forecast more or less in line with the 'jaunty' £2.5 million he had given the previous August.

By the end of 1969, however, there had been some further dramatic changes in the structure of Crittall-Hope. The most important was the sale in July 1969 of the American subsidiary, Hope's Windows, which had contributed nearly £500,000 of trading profits in 1968. It was sold for $7,740,000 or about £3.2 million cash. Slater claims it was sold because serious doubts had arisen as to its future viability in increasingly competitive conditions in the USA and that from a management point of view they would have found it very difficult to contend with problems in the USA similar to those they had experienced in Germany; but others involved say it was sold because Slater was simply not interested in the company's future and wanted to use the capital for investment on the stock market. Most of Crittall-Hope's remaining overseas interests were also disposed of, its Australian and Far East companies going to Slater Walker (Australia) while the South African shell company was floated off as Slater Walker (South Africa). The effect was to remove from Crittall-Hope's 1969 balance sheet subsidiaries which had contributed nearly £900,000 to 1968's nine-month profit figure of £1.5 million. The only overseas subsidiary retained was in Nigeria.

In the Slater Walker annual statement for 1969 Slater discussed the reorganization of Crittall-Hope in some detail. It had resulted, he said, in a fall of capital employed in manufacturing windows and allied products from about £21 million to £11.5 million, and over £6 million in cash had been redeployed within the Slater Walker group. He continued:

> Crittall-Hope's pre-tax profit for the year to 31 March 1968, immediately before joining the Group, was approximately £700,000 after deducting minority interests. In 1969 after eliminating the cost of reorganization, the profit from window manufacturing activities alone was £930,000, in an exceptionally difficult year for the industry. The liberation of capital started as soon as we acquired the company, but was not completed until mid-1969 which meant that less than half the anticipated profits from its redeployment are reflected in the 1969 accounts. In a full year, however, the £6,000,000 concerned could be expected to earn at least £960,000 at the Group's average rate of return on its assets before deducting loan capital. Thus the total annual rate of profits for Crittall-Hope would have been approximately £1,890,000 compared with £700,000 before its acquisition by the Group.

Just how Slater reached his £700,000 is far from clear: it was not altogether fair to the previous management. Crittall-Hope's pre-tax profits, after allowing for the German disaster, had been £934,000 in its last year of independence. Slater's proffered off-the-cuff explanation that the discrepancy was due to the Nigerian subsidiary, which was profitable, had minority interests and 'may have had a very high rate of taxation', hardly seems adequate.*

But it is worth looking at the 1969 performance of Crittall-Hope in rather more detail. In Crittall-Hope's balance sheet for 1969, its pre-tax profits were recorded as £1,263,100. Of this, according to a note, £324,061 represented interest on the cash extracted by Slater Walker, which appeared as a loan of £6.2 million at 31 December 1969 and which would have been outstanding for only about half the year. Again, since we are trying to assess Slater Walker's performance in the window making business, and since much of the money was 'redeployed' in the stock market, this interest must be eliminated, leaving profits of £939,039. As Slater said, these were in the main profits earned on window making, but the figure includes

---

*Later Slater said the Nigerian company did have a very high tax rate. It must have been very high. Minority interests represent that part of the profit which belongs to outside shareholders in subsidiaries. In the Crittall-Hope's balance sheet for 31 March 1968 minority interests of £57,000 were deducted from post-tax profits of £379,000. If pre-tax profits less minority shareholders' interests were only £700,000, then profits attributable to these shareholders must have been taxed at more than seventy-five per cent.

£32,123 of gains made on the sale of investments and £73,025 of income from investments, including dividends from Crittall-Hope's associated companies like Darlington & Simpson. Subtracting these items leaves £833,891.

But even this figure had benefited from some pure accounting changes. In the first place, Slater Walker had, according to Crittall-Hope auditors Thomson McLintock, standardized the 'bases of calculating depreciation and of evaluating capital projects' between the Hope and the Crittall businesses. The amendments 'resulted in a reduction of approximately £37,000 in the charges to profit and loss account for the year as compared with the bases adopted in previous years'.

This change was not unreasonable; but the next item, although again not in contravention of standard accounting practice, would certainly have been condemned as 'accounting gimmickry', by the US committee on conglomerates. In fact Thomson McLintock seem to have had some difficulty in trying to explain it:

> As a result of the acquisition of the company by Slater Walker Limited and the resultant reorganization, productivity was affected in the early part of the year resulting in a reduction of profitability. The measure of this reduction has been taken to be £162,000 which has been debited to the provision for reorganization expenses and credited to profit and loss account.

After a lengthy discussion with Crittall-Hope chairman Tarling in the autumn of 1973, I was little clearer as to how this item had been reached, although I was left with the impression that it was based on some specific expenses incurred in the reorganization, rather than being a purely notional figure. Three years later, however, Tarling clarified himself. The £162,000 he said, was perfectly straightforward and represented 'revenue as opposed to capital costs incurred during reorganization'. He elaborated:

> During the course of the year these costs were debited to normal expense accounts and thus ultimately to the profit and loss account in the usual way. At the end of the year exceptional and non-recurring expenses incurred as a result of the reorganization were analysed and the resulting total of £162,000 was then credited to the profit and loss account and debited to the provision for reorganizational expenses.'

It was, Tarling said, 'perfectly normal procedure'.

Tarling's explanation must be rejected, first because it is clearly inconsistent with what the auditors actually wrote in the note, and secondly because the very fact that they noted it, and repeated the note in the following year's accounts, indicates that it was not normal.

Reorganizing a company can be an expensive business: there are costs of transporting machinery and plant, expenses of contracting out orders already on the books which cannot be fulfilled as a result of factory closures, redundancy payments and so on. In the case of Crittall-Hope everyone agrees that the redundancy terms for all were fair and that Slater Walker treated special cases sympathetically, so that total redundancy payments must have been substantial. These costs totalled about £2.6 million over 1968 and 1969 and the hard cash to meet them came from the sale of properties and other assets. Crittall-Hope's properties were being carried in the books at only £4.6 million when Slater Walker took over – about £5 million less than their true value. By the end of 1969 Slater Walker had sold off £6.5 million worth, including much of a village which had been built by Crittall in Essex to house its employees. The surplus of sales over reorganization costs was, of course, the money available to Slater Walker to deploy elsewhere.

Although such costs qualify for tax relief, they are exceptional, and it was Slater Walker's policy – a normal one – to debit them to reserves, usually specially created for the purpose, rather than to the profit and loss account.

But the £162,000 was a very different matter. Brokers Sebags once said of Slater Walker that it was 'almost making money out of air' (they meant it kindly). This was going one better: they had credited the profit and loss account with money they had reckoned they had lost because of the takeover and reorganization. For the only interpretation of the £162,000 consistent with the auditors' note is that it represented profits estimated to have been lost as a result of the sort of disruption of production that often accompanies a dramatic event like a takeover and reorganization – as managers get used to new systems, workers hold meetings to discuss redundancies and so on. The £162,000 in fact represented profits Crittall-Hope might have made if it had not been taken over by Slater Walker and reorganized – for the purpose of improving profitability! This 'gimmick' – an excellent example of what Slater himself once called 'the Tarling school of accountancy' – was particularly misleading, for, as we shall see, the reorganization did not immediately result in a higher rate of profitability, and it was only this credit that allowed Slater to claim his profit from window manufacturing of £930,000 – 'after eliminating the cost of reorganization' – in his 1969 statement. Disregarding this credit, the depreciation change, the profit on sale of, and income from, investments and the dividends from associated companies reduces Crittall-Hope's 1969 profit to £634,891.

Crittall-Hope's profits continued to fall in 1970, and even Slater could not avoid a more subdued tone when commenting in his annual statement to Slater Walker shareholders delivered in May 1971:

Crittall-Hope made a worthwhile contribution to your company's profits last year, bearing in mind the very depressed state of the building industry . . . The reorganized Crittall-Hope group is now in a position where it should make marginal profits in the very depressed conditions at present prevailing, and produce excellent results when conditions improve.

The full extent of the decline was again difficult to discern after accounting changes. One of these was not the responsibility of Slater Walker: the Institute of Chartered Accountants had recommended that where one company owned more than twenty per cent of another and also played a part in its management, then the relevant proportion of this associated company's figures should be brought into the holding company's accounts.

The effect on Crittall-Hope's figures was substantial, for this new rule meant that the group could include half the profit of Darlington & Simpson Rolling Mills in its own profit, for Crittall-Hope men sat on the board of the steel firm. Darlington & Simpson had made record profits in its latest financial year, and Crittall-Hope was able to bring £470,457 of them into its accounts. This was brought up to £488,068 by the contribution from the Irish company of which Crittall-Hope also owned half the shares. In previous years only a relatively small dividend from these investments had been included in Crittall-Hope's pre-tax profits.

Crittall-Hope's share of Darlington's profits was included under 'metal windows' in the breakdown of profits given with the Slater Walker accounts and this category was shown as earning profits of £958,000 in 1970: the adjusted comparable total of £1,328,000 for 1969 included only £256,000 from Darlington.

To get the full picture of the decline in Crittall-Hope's fortunes one must turn again to its own accounts. Pre-tax profits of £1,585,000 this time included about £639,000 of interest (allowing for a small amount of interest payable *to* Slater Walker), and excluding this and the associated companies' profits leaves profits of about £457,000. But even this had been inflated by another accounting change. This time it had to do with whether profits were to be taken at the point of manufacture or on the fixing of metal windows. One side of the business had taken its profit only on the installation of the windows, while the other side had taken part of the profit at the time of manufacture and part at the time of fixing. The group system was standardized and again, in the words of the auditors, 'this resulted in an exceptional credit of approximately £57,000 to the profit for the year as compared with the basis adopted in previous years'.

Excluding this – the group anyway had later to change back to the other method as a result of a general recommendation on contract accounting from the Institute of Chartered Accountants – brings Crittall-Hope's 1970 profit down to about £400,000 to compare with the £635,000 earned in 1969: and even the £400,000 included some acquired profits, for during 1970 Crittall-Hope took control of an aluminium extruding and anodizing concern, Southern Extrusions, with which it had had a long association. A further indication of the extent of the deterioration is given by the figures for the old Crittall Manufacturing Company, now the main UK trading subsidiary: its trading profit, adjusted for the pure accounting changes, fell from £602,000 in 1969 to £123,000 in 1970.

In 1970, too, Slater Walker's other metal window subsidiary, Warner's, just disappeared.* Warner's had been run as an independent unit, according to Slater, because of profit warranties that had been given when it was bought. Initially it expanded rapidly under Slater Walker; sales in 1968 rose about a third to an annual rate of over £1.5 million and profits were about £180,000. In 1969, in spite of the contraction in the building industry, turnover fell only marginally to £1.4 million and profit to £150,000. But in early 1970 problems began to emerge, and the decision was taken to shut down the company. Trading was stopped and what remained of its assets, patents and contracts were sold or transferred to Crittall-Hope. Just who was responsible for what went wrong is hard to identify, for six years later acrimony lingered on. Slater blames the Warners, and says that only one executive was appointed to work there, and he by Warner himself. Slater and Tarling also say that the company over-traded and that as a result there were many complaints and claims over design and late delivery whose financial impact was often not felt for several years. The counter-argument of the old management is that these were exaggerated.

When I suggested to Tarling in the summer of 1973 that detailed examination suggested that there had been no real improvement in profitability at Crittall-Hope in the short term after its takeover by Slater Walker, he said that it was not right to use the figures for the limited companies from which the group was made up. One should, he said, compare the performance of the parts of Crittall-Hope that remained in the group after the reorganization, eliminating the records of those bits that had been sold; and Slater himself later argued that 'one must compare like with like' and that the comparison of the group as constituted before the takeover with its subsequent constitution was misleading.

* Tracing the fate of Warner's proved difficult at first: Slater Walker did not file accounts of this subsidiary for 1969 and 1970 at Companies House until February 1974.

I do not accept this: while it may not be possible to reach firm conclusions by comparing absolute totals of profits, turnover and capital
employed of a changing business, there is no objection to comparing
the profit *ratios* of one company with another, or of one company at
different times, however different the relative constitutions. Slater
amplified his argument by saying that, for example, the South
African subsidiary of Crittall-Hope, which had been earning about
£100,000 before the takeover, would, in my analysis, make no
contribution to post-acquisition figures since its assets had been sold
and its shares transferred to Slater Walker itself at book value of
£137,000. But since we are trying to assess the effects of Slater
Walker on the profitability of *window manufacture* it is necessary to
compare the group as structured before the takeover, which included
a South African manufacturer, with its later, altered form, which
did not.

In preparing the table below, the following adjustments have been
made to figures taken from the audited accounts of Crittall-Hope:
from pre-tax profits, all income from investments and associated
companies, profits on sales of assets, interest received and the effect
of the accounting changes has been eliminated. From total capital
employed, investments in associated companies and quoted securities
have been removed, but £5 million has been added back to net assets
for the three years before the group was taken over because of the
undervaluation of its properties. If this were not done there would be
a distortion in favour of the old management. The loans to Slater
Walker in 1969 and 1970 had already been excluded in the accounts.

CRITTALL-HOPE

Year to 31 March	Profit	Sales	Capital Employed
	£000	£000	£000
1966	1,015	20,742	20,143
1967	1,280	29,994	20,755
1968	649	31,629	20,550
9 months to 31 December 1968	1,157	21,240	16,043
(Annualized	1,543	28,230	16,043)
1969	635	16,256	10,314
1970	401	17,782	10,291

Year to 31 March	Profit/Sales	Profit/Capital Employed	Sales per Employee
	%	%	%
1966	3.3	5.0	n.a.
1967	4.3	6.2	4,278
1968	2.1	3.2	4,555

Year to 31 March	Profit/Sales	Profit/Capital Employed	Sales per Employee
9 months to 31 December 1968*	% 5.5	% 9.6	% 4,669
1969	3.9	6.2	3,194
1970	2.3	3.9	3,346

So, as with Greengate & Irwell, Crittall-Hope by 1970 was looking far from happy. It too had served its purpose of releasing money for Slater Walker to use in its financial activities, but it too would not be easy to resell. Slater Walker tried to tempt the big aluminium companies, but finally resorted, as with Greengate, to selling the business back to the public.

The flotation was achieved towards the end of 1971 by injecting Crittall-Hope into a public company, Butterley Engineering, which Slater Walker already controlled. Butterley was something of a hotchpotch of engineering businesses put together out of companies that Slater Walker had picked up at one time or another. It included George Wilson Industries, the old gas meter company in which Slater had first taken an interest in 1964 and which had yet again to be reorganized following the decision of the Gas Board to stop buying its basic product, a badly designed meter which had been introduced in 1966. Butterley even included a share and commodity dealing company, Priam Investments, once scheduled to be the 'vehicle' for fashion designer Mary Quant. It was included, Slater says, for the sake of its cash.

Slater Walker sold Crittall-Hope to Butterley for five million shares, worth about £4,850,000, and £4.4 million of loan stock. It was perhaps a rather humble consideration for the rump of the company that Slater had valued at £18 million three and a half years before. But apart from the 'organic' contraction, quite a lot had been squeezed out of it over the years. Anyway it became the most important part of Butterley, whose name was changed to Crittall-Hope Engineering.

The prospectus which had to be issued, under Stock Exchange regulations, on the amalgamation of Crittall-Hope and Butterley, provides a useful opportunity to examine the window maker's record as Tarling said it should be looked at, that is eliminating those parts of the business that had been disposed of. For it contained a profit record drawn up by Thomson McLintock, who made 'such adjustments as we considered appropriate; in particular, the profits and losses of those businesses carried on prior to June 1968, which have

*Profit and sales annualized.

since been discontinued or disposed of have, where practicable, been excluded'. It ran as follows:

	External Sales	Profit Before Taxation (£000s)
Fifteen months ended 31 March 1966 for Crittall Manufacturing and twelve months ended 31 March 1966 for Henry Hope	17,916	371
Year ended 31 March 1967	14,929	524
Year ended 31 March 1968	15,870	952
Nine months ended 31 December 1968	12,635	788
Year ended 31 December 1969	15,560	1,007
Year ended 31 December 1970	17,782	829

Thomson McLintock also excluded profits due to minority shareholders (which are included in my figures) but included Crittall-Hope's share of associated companies' profits. They provided, however, a separate table of these, and as they did not include a share of associated companies' turnover in their sales figures I have redone the table excluding associated companies' profits. I have also again eliminated the £162,000 special credit in 1969, which the accountants again noted separately.

	Profits £000s	Profits/Sales per cent
Period to 31 March 1966	185	1.0
Year to 31 March 1967	356	2.4
Year to 31 March 1968	734	4.6
Nine months to 31 December 1968*	454	3.6
Year to 31 December 1969	559	3.6
Year to 31 December 1970	341	1.9

This was a pretty sorry record on which to float a company, but the only explanation offered for the fall in 1970 was 'the lower level of housing starts experienced in that year'. But it was forecast that window makers' profits in 1971 would not be less than £1,200,000 'due to the substantially improved performance of the subsidiaries'.

Slater Walker retained considerably closer links with Crittall-Hope after it had been 'divested' than it did, for instance, with Allied Polymer. Tarling remained chairman and Slater Walker, after first reducing its holding in Crittall-Hope Engineering to less than fifty

---

*The accountants' adjustment on the profits for this period seems to have been particularly rigorous, much more unfavourable than mine.

per cent, later bought back control. But after the formation of this new group, the old window making company finally lost its financial identity and tracing its progress from the publicly available audited accounts becomes much harder. This is further complicated by the fact that the accounting date was changed back to 31 March, and so the next available figures for subsidiaries run for a fifteen-month period to 31 March 1972.

In his first statement as chairman of the new Crittall-Hope Engineering Group, made in May 1972, Tarling claimed that the £1.2 million forecast for the window making subsidiaries for 1971 had been 'comfortably exceeded'. The change in the accounting period makes it impossible to assess how big the margin was, although the sum of the profits earned by all the constituent companies in the fifteen months to 31 March 1972 suggests that it cannot have been all that comfortable. Tarling said of the main UK window making company Crittall-Hope Ltd, formerly the old Crittall Manufacturing, that it had produced 'reasonable profits in fairly depressed market conditions'. The trading profits* of this subsidiary in the fifteen months to 31 March 1972 were only £342,451 on sales of over £16 million, a ratio of only 2.1 per cent. Yet in its last year of independence this company had earned trading profits of £500,000 on sales of over £9 million, or 5.5 per cent.

Against this, however, Tarling was able to point to a new profit earner, Crittall-Hope Double Glazing. This company, he said, had had an excellent year and was continuing to expand to cater for 'substantial growth prospects'. The double glazing business had been started in August 1968, just after the takeover but following a decision previously taken by the old management. The development of this company, however, probably represented Slater Walker's most positive achievement at Crittall-Hope. They decided to sell direct to householders rather than through the building trade, and to produce a do-it-yourself version; and the marketing administration fitted in conveniently with a new line of aluminium greenhouses. It took nearly three years to get the project going but it started to pay off with profits of £375,000 in the fifteen months to 31 March 1972.

In his January 1973 article in *The Times*, however, Slater made the following claims for the growth of Crittall-Hope:

Overall, Crittall-Hope's turnover increased from £17.5 million in 1968 to £26 million in 1972 while the index for public and private housing starts fell from 100 in 1967 to 78 in 1972. The profits of the relevant parts of the business have increased from £1,265 million in 1968 to a forecast £2 million in 1972–73 with a

---

*Trading profits differ from pre-tax in that they exclude both interest receivable and interest payable.

much reduced capital employment, and turnover per employee has more than doubled from £2,520 to £5,150.

There is some ambiguity over the specific periods to which Slater was referring. Austin Davis, one-time managing director of Crittall-Hope, however, gave me the following figures for 'the relevant parts of the business':

	Pre-tax profits £000s	Turnover £000s	Employees
Year to 31 March 1968	1,265	17,426	6,944
Year to 31 March 1973	2,029	25,294	4,890

(Austin Davis would not give me profit and turnover figures for the intervening years.)

Slater maintains that these figures were adjusted 'to show a valid comparison of the organic growth of the UK business of Crittall-Hope'. Yet it is difficult to see how Slater reached the figure of £1,265,000 for 1968. The aggregate trading profits of the main Crittall-Hope subsidiaries and associated companies that made up the group in 1972 had indeed been of the order of £1.3 million in 1968; but Tarling said that it was 'difficult to be categoric' about how the figure had been compiled and Slater said he had asked the people concerned directly with the Crittall-Hope reorganization to prepare the figures for him before the publication of *The Times* article.

That neither Tarling nor Slater was able to say how the figure was reached is indicative enough of the credibility of the claims in *The Times* article. (Slater says: 'I was an extremely busy man at the time and obviously delegated to a considerable extent, but there was no attempt to mislead anyone.') Robert Heller pointed out in an article in the *Investors Guardian** in February 1972 that Slater was comparing 'what was left of Crittall-Hope today with what that same rump was in 1969' and concluded that even on Slater's figures – sales up forty-five per cent and profits sixty per cent over five years – 'a 10 per cent annual rise in sales and profits hardly adds up to proof' that Slater Walker had wrought 'great managerial wonders'.

Today Slater comments:

The decline in the main market for Crittall products from 1968 to 1973 was approximately 40 per cent. This inevitably made the market much more competitive, depressed selling prices and therefore profit margins were under severe pressure. To expand profits by 60 per cent during a five-year period such as this was in

*Heller is Editor of *Management Today*, which is published by the Haymarket Press, as was the *Investors Guardian* until it was closed.

my view a considerable industrial success, and in particular the efforts made in making Crittall sales dependent upon its less traditional markets were very worthwhile and profitable.

Detailed examination has shown that both this account and that in *The Times* gives a highly misleading picture of the profitability of Crittall-Hope under Slater Walker. But Slater has put forward two further justifications for the activities of Crittall-Hope. The first is that in a market which had declined by forty per cent, the only way to succeed was to rationalize facilities and to diversify into other products such as double glazing and greenhouses as quickly as possible. If the pure window manufacturing side is considered in isolation he accepts it shows a picture of poor profit, but says that the only way to obtain a fair picture is to examine the overall results of the business as a whole. Secondly he thought that the Crittall-Hope operation had been in the national interest. As he wrote in *The Times*:

> In particular, there has been a very substantial contribution to the balance of payments position arising from the repatriation of money from subsidiaries which were making a poor return, from the development of the South African company, the increased exports and the development of the Nigerian business from a profit of £55,000 in 1968 to over £600,000 in 1972.

Now to assess the claim that there was a benefit to the balance of payments it is quite appropriate to compare the reconstituted Crittall-Hope with its earlier form. Slater's claim should be read in conjunction with the following points:

- In the year to 31 March 1967 the overseas subsidiaries of Crittall-Hope, as a whole, were three times more profitable than the domestic companies. Their performance deteriorated in 1968, largely as a result of the German fiasco, but the American company in particular was still highly profitable when Slater Walker sold it in 1969; and whether a once-and-for-all capital repatriation is more beneficial than a continued stream of dividends is a matter than can be hotly debated.
- To talk of the 'development of the South African company' – that is Slater Walker Securities (South Africa) – which, according to Slater in his article, had 'created' £9.3 million out of the assets of Crittall-Hope's South African subsidiary, as if it had been an achievement of the management of Crittall-Hope was disingenuous. Slater says he tried to present it as an achievement of the way in which Slater Walker tackled the problem of Crittall-Hope, but the article did not mention that the profitable South African metal window business had been sold to a competitor within months of Slater Walker taking over. The fact that the stock market quotation

in Johannesburg was retained and the resulting shell injected with assets from other Slater Walker acquisitions to create Slater Walker (South Africa) was absolutely nothing to do with Crittall-Hope. While Slater's claim that the 'original investment had appreciated' to £10.5 million sounded good, this was not achieved by industrial growth so much as by takeover and stock market inflation; for the £10.5 million was the value of Slater Walker's stake in Slater Walker (South Africa) at the current market price and it quickly diminished again when the share price crashed.

• Total exports of the Crittall-Hope group, as constituted at the relevant dates, were £1,190,000 in the year to 31 March 1968; and they rose to £1,836,000 in 1970. Total exports of the Crittall-Hope Engineering Group, incorporating the old window business but with additional engineering companies, in the year to 31 March 1972 were actually lower than in 1968 at only £892,000 and in the following year they rose to £1,421,000. Slater's statement in *The Times* article, using only the Crittall-Hope 'rump' figures, that exports were 'increased from an admittedly low base by an average of fifty per cent', was hardly an accurate picture of what had happened to the foreign exchange earning power of Crittall-Hope after Slater Walker's reorganization. Slater today says that his comment in *The Times* was not meant to give a picture of the additional engineering companies but to give a picture of what happened to Crittall-Hope's companies after the takeover.

There is little problem in seeing where Slater's £2 million-plus profits for Crittall-Hope in the year to 31 March 1973 came from. The double glazing subsidiary turned in trading profits of over £600,000, as did the Nigerian subsidiary. Even the basic UK metal window business started to grow again with the main UK company producing trading profits of £871,000 on sales of £15.6 million – a return of 5.6 per cent, just 0.1 better than in its last year before the Slater Walker takeover.

Rough though the analysis unavoidably is after 1970, there is no evidence that Slater Walker's reorganization had any effect on the profitability of Crittall-Hope until five years after its takeover. Even then, it was far from startling, and certainly not enough to justify the basic claim that the extraction of capital from British industry for use in the sort of financial activities in which, as we shall see, Slater Walker engaged from 1970 onwards, was in the national interest.

There is, too, an end to the Crittall-Hope story that casts further doubt on Slater's claims. In early 1974 Slater Walker sold its interest in Crittall-Hope Engineering to an independent industrial holding company, Norcros, after declaring that the whole group had made £2,650,000 in the nine months to 31 December 1973, against a total of £4,240,000 in the previous year. Shortly afterwards Norcros announced that, using their accounting standards, Crittall-Hope Engineering had only made £1,150,000 in the whole year to 31 March 1974. What had happened? Well, in the first place, an investment in a French engineering group called Voyer, made in 1972 during Slater Walker's rule, had turned sour: instead of contributing profits, large provisions had had to be made to cover both trading losses and the cost of the investment. Secondly, it seems that the main British window making business had been losing money – about £1,630,000, Norcros decided. The three-day week had, of course, intervened and this had apparently affected the profitability of Crittall-Hope more seriously than most other industrial companies. But it cannot have been anything like enough to account for the loss of over £2 million subsequently recorded in the accounts of Crittall-Hope Ltd, which included a £250,000 provision for 'loss from trading activities discontinued in earlier years'. Slater, in the course of my inquiries, gave me two further explanations. The first was that it was the policy of Norcros that all freehold premises should be owned by a group properties company which then charged rentals to operating companies with the result that Crittall-Hope profits would have been transferred as rentals to Norcros group profits. Unfortunately there is no evidence at all that such rentals were charged in the accounts in the year ending 31 March 1974 and when I specifically checked this with Norcros' finance director he informed me that no such charges had been made. Secondly Slater said that a number of important profit making subsidiaries of the former Crittall-Hope group had been separated out into other Norcros divisions and that these included in particular Adamson Alliance, Darlington & Simpson and the Nigerian company. Again unfortunately there is no evidence that these had been separated out for the purposes of the relevant accounting period.

As the *Daily Telegraph* commented, it was 'a sad indictment of Slater Walker's stewardship'; or, as Slater wrote me, albeit in the summer of 1973, the profit record of Crittall-Hope speaks for itself. By 1976 however Slater felt that he was able to draw comfort from the fact that by 31 March 1975 the profits of the reduced Crittall-Hope group amounted to £1,995,000, but by this stage it had been under Norcros' management for a full year.

17   *The Tokengate concept*

In November 1971 Slater was invited to address the conference of the Institute of Directors, held annually in the Albert Hall. 'Profits,' he told the assembled businessmen, 'are without doubt the lifeblood of our existence. Until this is recognized a general apathy will continue to adversely affect the British economy. Increased profits – that is, an increased return on capital employed – must be the objective.'

The Crittall-Hope story demonstrates the elusiveness of industrial profits, and indeed of the very concept of 'profit', and Slater's basic formula for improving the return on capital employed in any industry was not to increase the level of profits earned on the existing resources but to remove some of the capital in the hope that the remaining assets would be made to earn more than before. In the case of Crittall-Hope it turned out to be a vain hope; though accounting changes and the complexity of the reorganization ensured that that fact was thoroughly obscured.

Nevertheless, it is curious that Slater persisted in using it as his prime example of the benefits of 'Slaterization'. Allied Polymer in the end proved a much more viable company, and some of Slater Walker's other industrial involvements turned out well.

The various builders merchants, for example, that Slater Walker had bought through 1967 and 1968 were welded into a single unit, Metropolitan Builders Merchants, with a turnover of about £5 million, and this was sold at the end of 1968 to a large independent public group, Mercian. The optical group, too, that Slater Walker forged out of three companies bought in the second half of 1968 was a successful operation. Manufacturing and administration were centralized and the group, which had about eight per cent of the UK spectacle market, was resold to Gallahers, the cigarette firm, in the autumn of 1970 for £10.2 million cash.

There were also some successes from the old SWIG 'strategic stakes' days. Slater Walker used a twenty-three per cent holding in a leather firm, Barrow Hepburn & Gale, to secure the appointment of Horsman to its board. On his advice the firm closed a plastics division that was losing money and began on a period of profitable expansion. The directors went so far as to vote Horsman an ex-gratia payment of £5,000 when he left the Barrow board at the end of 1969.

But none of these was particularly significant in terms of the economy, certainly not as important as the investments in rubber and metal windows. There were, too, more failures. The slipper business, Newman's Holdings, turned out to be a poor deal, and Slater Walker's attempt to reorganize the manufacturers of shelving and runners for car seats, Constructors – or Chapman Constructors as it had been renamed – was a noted disaster. It will not be examined in detail but it provides an interesting example of the uncritical praise that met every move made by Slater Walker. In preparing their lengthy study of Slater Walker in August 1968, brokers Sebags sent an analyst to look at Chapman. Sebags then reported that it was a highly efficient unit 'achieving impressive operating results', described it as one of the 'three major UK subsidiaries representing the best examples of the Slater Walker method of making money', and estimated that it would make a £50,000 profit in 1968 even after substantial reorganization expenses. In fact Chapman lost £129,000 in 1968.

Nothing more clearly exposed the lack of really serious purpose behind Slater's hastily constructed conglomerate than the reasons he gave for abandoning the enterprise within two years of its inception. In April 1973 Slater explained the decision to a Canadian audience:

> By 1968, and particularly in America, the word conglomerate was becoming bad news, and rightly so in many ways, because there are very few well-run conglomerates. They are the exception rather than the rule and it definitely needs a genius to run one well. So we had a good think about the situation and we decided as a Board to divest ourselves of our various industrial interests and to concentrate our activities in five main areas. These areas were banking, investment, insurance, property and overseas interests.*

Slater has said that he embarked on the series of takeovers because 'it seemed a pity' not to use the high-priced Slater Walker shares. Now it appeared that the decision to sell off the industrial companies again was taken for almost as apparently casual a reason: it was a question of image! Of course, this reasoning was not as trivial as might at first appear, for since the success of the whole structure depended on the price of Slater Walker shares, and since that price

---

* Slater Walker had in fact formed a property subsidiary called Dryber in 1967, which by the end of 1968 had spent £400,000 on properties. These were sold in 1969, some to other group companies, some elsewhere, for a total loss of £223,000.

depended more upon public relations than upon industrial talent, the image was indeed crucial.

Slater need hardly have worried about his image. For in the controversy over conglomerates, the first whispers of which were only just being heard in 1968, the press placed Slater firmly among the geniuses who could successfully run conglomerates. Indeed in February 1969 the *Investors Chronicle* concluded that his role as a conglomerator was why 'a place in history' should be allotted to Slater: it was because he had 'regenerated and enhanced the holding company idea in this country that he will command a special place in the annals'.

But perhaps it was the image of Slater Walker, rather than the collective image of conglomerates, that worried Slater. Did he think Slater Walker was one of the 'very few well-run conglomerates' in danger of being painted with the same brush as the bad, or was he concerned that people might discover that Slater Walker was no better at running industrial companies than anyone else?

In January 1972 Graham Turner wrote in the *Sunday Telegraph*: 'The weaknesses of this Third Empire' - as Turner called the industrial conglomerate phase - 'slowly became apparent to Slater - fortunately long before they became apparent to the market. The twilight of the great American conglomerates helped alert him to the dangers, but it was already clear that it would take a genius to run as scattered an empire as he had accumulated - and he didn't feel up to the job.'

Nevertheless, even by the end of 1968 the problems, for example, of running Greengate & Irwell and Crittall-Hope had not become apparent. Their difficult years were 1969 and 1970. The truth was that there was no sudden transition within Slater Walker; Slater, the dealer, had always been prepared to resell companies at the right price, and more were acquired in 1969 and 1970. But by the end of 1968 it was clear that Slater Walker could not continue to go on issuing shares at the same rate in order to buy still more businesses, for the giddy rise in their price since early 1967 had already started to falter. The two-year rise in share prices generally also came to an end and in the first seven months of 1969 the stock market dropped about thirty per cent in the face of government measures to restrict the money supply and curb home demand. In these conditions ordinary share dealing gains were difficult to achieve.

But where then was the profits growth to come from? Whatever their importance to the economy, profits were the lifeblood of Slater Walker, and Slater would not be satisfied with the normal rate of increase in industrial profits: that would not 'measure up to our ideas of what I would call super-growth', Slater told *Accountancy Age*. As it turned out, anyway, the profits of Slater Walker's main industrial investments deteriorated for the next couple of years rather than grew. This reinforced the urgency of finding other ways of making money.

The solution evolved also helped deal with another problem, namely how to dispose of the less saleable bits and pieces acquired in the two-year period of indiscriminate acquisition. The answer was the satellite system, and Slater himself explained how it worked in his speech in Canada:

> This was where we sold a firm we owned into a public company, usually a small one, for shares in that public company. We installed as Chief Executive a very able young man, who in some cases had been trained by us. We kept a substantial stake in that Company and it became an active banking client, and thirdly it enabled us to offer excellent positions and exciting opportunities in these client companies to people from our central team.

Slater Walker's first satellite had in fact been launched in 1967: it was Slater Walker Securities (Australia) and the history of the take-off of that operation had clearly demonstrated all the advantages listed by Slater, plus another even more important one – the way the value of businesses could be blown up by shuffling them from one company to another within the Slater Walker orbit.

The origins of Slater Walker's Australian operation lay, as we have seen, in the takeover at the end of 1966 of Thomas Brown. With the proceeds of the sale of some of this company's assets Slater Walker had bought a forty-five per cent interest in the coalmining company Wancol, which retained its quotation on the local Australian stock markets. Now in June 1967 Slater Walker sold to Wancol one of Brown's remaining subsidiaries, a manufacturer of jute and calico bags called Tunleys, in exchange for more Wancol shares. These were valued at £162,550, of which no less than £146,410 was recorded in the books of Brown, which remained a wholly owned subsidiary of Slater Walker in London, as 'capital profit'.

Then in December 1967 Slater Walker sold to Wancol, this time for shares and cash, Greengate & Irwell's Australian subsidiary Bramac, which made rainwear and conveyor belting. Wancol's name was then changed to Slater Walker (Australia), of which Slater Walker now owned, through its subsidiary Brown, 68.5 per cent, and of which Tarling was chairman and in overall command.

In early 1968 Slater Walker reduced this holding to about thirty per cent by 'placing' blocks of shares with institutional investors both in the UK and Australia. The shares were sold for a total of £984,954, resulting in a capital gain of £502,152. It was a remarkable reward for a year's shunting around of companies.

The process continued during 1968. Slater Walker passed on to its

Australian associate the remainder of Brown's old businesses, which included a rum distillery, a manufacturer of food essences and what was left of its stores interests. Slater Walker (Australia) also set out on the takeover trail on its own account, buying another colliery and branching out into plastics. But it really started to move at the end of 1968 when an Australian named Ian Murray was dispatched to take over the managing directorship. Murray had spent a year with Slater Walker in England during which he had been involved in the Chapman Constructors reorganization. It was an inauspicious training, although the full extent of the Chapman failure was only uncovered after his departure.

Slater Walker's big coup in Australia was the takeover, at the end of 1968, of Drug Houses of Australia, a major chemists suppliers. But the brashness of Slater Walker's tactics in securing control, which helped to fuel the outcry against the buying up of Australian businesses by foreigners, was to have repercussions.

On 14 November 1968 Slater Walker (Australia) announced a bid of $2.26 a share for Drug Houses – about twenty-seven per cent above the ruling market price. Then the following day Slater Walker itself, via Thomas Brown, rushed into the market and started buying Drug Houses shares at $2.40; it also bought a block of about ten per cent of Drug Houses shares directly from Slater Walker (Australia) which that company had previously built up at prices ranging from $1.40 to $1.75 a share, the transaction providing a much needed boost of about $1 million to Slater Walker (Australia)'s flagging 1968 profits.

The Drug Houses shares came out thick and fast; by 27 November Slater Walker told the Drug Houses board they had fifty-one per cent of the entire ordinary capital. The Drug Houses directors had lost control of their company before they knew what had hit them. They tried to persuade Slater Walker to offer cash for the rest of the shares, but Slater Walker refused, only conceding a small increase in the price, to be paid in Slater Walker (Australia) shares and loan stock, to $2.52 – not a matter of great hardship to the whole Slater Walker enterprise as Brown thus made, in its turn, a paper profit of about £200,000 on its investment in Drug Houses. But it also ended up with a pile of unwanted loan stock, partly because it also agreed to swap outside shareholders' loan stock for ordinary shares, and this became a cause of future friction between Slater Walker in London and its Australian associate. So too did a huge $1 million (£470,000) fee that Slater Walker exacted from its Australian affiliate for the advice and help it gave in the takeover. Slater says the fee was justified by the substantial risk Brown took: 'If the bid had failed, Brown would have been locked in to a minority position of say 35 per cent in Drug Houses involving an investment of over $10 million at $2.40 per share, nearly double the level of the market price when Slater Walker

(Australia) started picking up the stock.' But the fact is Brown bought a controlling interest, not a minority one, and this ensured the success of the offer. The only risk Brown ran was during the brief period it was buying control in the market.

The Brown/Slater Walker (Australia)/Drug Houses formula was one worth using again and 1969 saw the launching of a number of satellites both in the UK and abroad. But the businesses that were re-sold quickly in this way were not those that had been bought back in 1967 and early 1968, like Greengate & Irwell and Crittall-Hope. They had for the most part been bought only months before their resale. A number of them came from Drage's, the holding company that Slater had bought from Sir Isaac Wolfson in the autumn of 1968.

It was the Drage's deal that really marked the turning point in Slater Walker's development. It was a complex deal, the precise motives for which – on both sides – are still unclear, although no doubt the fascination of both men for doing deals for their own sake played a part.

It had been consummated in the middle of October 1968 when it was announced, after some weeks of hard negotiation and much market speculation, that Slater Walker had bought a large block of Drage's shares from the Wolfson Foundation for about £11 million in cash and was bidding nearly 34s. each for the remainder, to be paid for by the issue of Slater Walker shares.

The deal put a value of about £33 million on Drage's. It was thus the largest acquisition that Slater Walker ever made, although not a particularly big deal by Wolfson's standards; indeed, Slater has told a story of how, once the negotiations, which had been conducted at Wolfson's flat and which had been tense, were over, Wolfson had taken him up to another room – much larger than the one in which they had been bargaining – and had told him gently: 'This is where we do the big deals.' The £33 million was, however, considerably greater than the company's net asset value and furthermore, as part of the deal, it had been agreed that Slater Walker would sell back to Wolfson interests £10.3 million worth of Drage's assets for only £9.5 million. As a result market observers felt that Slater had been out-witted by Wolfson, and many Drage's shareholders took the cash alternative to the Slater Walker share offer which had been under-written by Rothschilds. The effect of this was that over the coming months blocks of Slater Walker shares issued to the underwriters instead of the public overhung the market, acting as a further brake on the meteoric rise in the share price.

But Slater Walker had nevertheless been left with some valuable assets in Drage's, even if their true worth was not immediately appreciated. The most important of these was Drage's fifty per cent stake in yet another holding company, Ralli. Now Ralli in its turn had three major subsidiaries, a commodity trading company, Ralli Brothers & Coney, a manufacturer of artificial fibres and textiles, Philips Brocklehurst, a minority of whose shares were held by the public, and a bank, Ralli Brothers (Bankers).

It was this last company that was to provide Slater Walker with the cover for its new-found profession of bankers. Slater Walker had, of course, always had a banking company within the group, having first formed Slater Walker Acceptances in early 1965 to do the job, then acquiring Rosenthal, and later transferring the function to Slater Walker Ltd. But Ralli Brothers (Bankers) was a proper bank; that is to say it had all the appropriate licences and privileges which banks are accorded under company law and Bank of England regulations. It even had the highest distinction of being a 'schedule 8' bank, which meant that it need not reveal its true profits nor the true extent of its reserves – adding a further complication to the problem of analysing Slater Walker's progress.

Whether or not Slater foresaw the importance of the bank at the time he did the deal with Wolfson is a moot point. Slater claimed to me that the acquisition had been 'far-sighted' but Graham Turner wrote in the *Sunday Telegraph* in January 1972 that: 'Slater did not buy Drage's because of Ralli – indeed, he admits that if he had had a very good offer in the early days, he would have been tempted to sell his half-share – but within months he had realized that he had a golden opportunity to become a banker by buying the other half.' Slater bought the other half in two stages – and with some difficulty. In January 1969 Slater Walker succeeded in prising out another twenty-five per cent of Ralli to gain control but it was not until later in the year that it became a wholly owned subsidiary.

Ralli Brothers (Bankers) was rechristened Slater Walker Ltd – the old Slater Walker Ltd becoming Slater Walker Holdings. Ralli also provided Slater Walker with a new home, more appropriate to its latest adopted role, for in 1969 they moved out of Hertford Street to Ralli House, in the shadow of St Paul's in the City. (The suggestion by an insufficiently reverent member of the staff that the building should be renamed Lottery House – adding a 't' to Slater Walker's original name – was not thought to be amusing.)

Before the Slater Walker share price started to fall sharply Slater made a last bid, offering £10.5 million in shares and cash for the Forestal Land Timber & Railway Company. Like Brown its attractions lay in the use that Slater Walker thought it could make of its chain of overseas subsidiaries.

The basic business of Forestal was the supply of tanning extracts for the leather industry. The demand for these had fallen as a result of competition from synthetic products and this posed problems for

Forestal's most important subsidiary, Natal Tanning in South Africa, and its extensive wattle estates in East Africa and Rhodesia and quebracho plantations in Argentina, which supplied the raw material for the extracts. To try to offset this decline the company had acquired a string of unrelated businesses in the UK and Germany.

Almost before Slater Walker had secured control of Forestal the East African and Rhodesian subsidiaries had been sold to Lonrho, in exchange for a large share stake in that company. The European assets were also quickly disposed of. The Argentine business proved more of a problem. The subsidiaries there were left in the Slater Walker books at their cost of nearly £5.9 million because Slater Walker reckoned they could resell them at at least that amount, after reorganization. The auditors, however, felt that it was 'not practicable' for them to assess their value and said they were 'unable therefore to form an opinion as to whether or not the company's interest in the shares of these subsidiaries' were worth the £5.9 million. As it turned out, as we shall see, the auditors' caution was sounder than the views of the Slater Walker directors.

But the key to the Forestal operation, as Anthony Vice points out in *The Strategy of Takeovers*, lay in South Africa. There the share price of the old shell of Crittall-Hope's subsidiary had more than quadrupled merely on the revelation that Slater Walker intended to develop it on the same lines as Slater Walker (Australia), with a similar high-flying price/earnings ratio: 'The magic was to put Natal Tanning, with its substantial assets and sizeable profits, into Slater Walker (South Africa) and so valorize the former Forestal company on the same appealing basis as its new parent.' The effect was to double Natal's book value to over £7 million; and similar wonders were worked on a South African textile company, Berg River, which Slater Walker had picked up with Drage's and which was simultaneously injected into Slater Walker (South Africa).

Meanwhile, back at home, suitable pilots were being recruited for a UK satellite programme and their launching pads made ready for blast-off. First to go was twenty-nine-year-old John Bentley. He had never joined the Slater Walker staff but he had been in and out of the offices for three or four years, ever since he had proposed to Slater that they should take over an asset-rich insurance company – an idea that had not enthused staid insurance circles but which had yielded a useful dealing profit.

Bentley's rocket was the Brighton chemist's business, Barclay & Son, of which Slater's early mentor, Freddie Cheshire, had been a director many years before. Slater Walker had acquired sixty per cent of the company in the Drage's deal but it retained a separate stock market quotation. At the outset of 1969, however, it was still a minute company with a paid-up capital of £150,000 in 1,500,000 2s.

shares. Its 1968 profits were only £63,000 and at a share price of 3s. 3d. the whole company was valued at under £250,000.

By April 1969, however, word had got around that great changes were afoot, and the share price had reached 6s. 6d. Then on 7 May, when the price had risen almost 1s., the quotation was suspended following the announcement that Barclay was proposing to buy a Swansea firm of clothing, furniture and hardware wholesalers, J. T. Morgan & Co., for the issue of 2,500,000 new shares, and that John Bentley was to take charge.

On 4 June 1969 the deal was approved by Barclay's shareholders, John Bentley was appointed chairman and some further details of the transformation were revealed to the world in a prospectus. Morgan was hardly a startling little business, having made only £111,000 of profits in 1968. Indeed the prospectus actually disclosed that the profits of Barclay plus Morgan were expected to fall in 1969. What the prospectus did not say was that Morgan, like Barclay, was another subsidiary of Slater Walker – but without a separate quota- tion – and had also been acquired with Drage's. Remarkably, in fact, the prospectus did not even mention Slater Walker, although it revealed that Ralli Brothers (Bankers), Slater Walker's newly acquired banking subsidiary, would own about 1.3 million shares, or about thirty-five per cent, of the enlarged Barclay capital.

This meant that Slater Walker had in fact succeeded in selling some two million Barclay shares in the process of transforming Barclay. Most of them – 1.4 million – went to John Bentley at 7s. each; 200,000 were sold to the Invan unit trust, and further blocks were allotted to other investment clients, as we shall see.

While the relaunch of Barclay was conducted with a minimum of fanfare, it was no secret to shrewd market operators that Slater Walker was behind the deal and when dealings in Barclay shares resumed on 10 June 1969 they were changing hands at over 8s. 'From that moment onwards the prime object of the Company was and will continue to be to increase earnings and assets per share to the maxi- mum amount,' Bentley later declared. By early 1970 the Barclay share price had passed the £1 mark as Bentley set out to emulate the man who had put him in business. Thus the value of Slater Walker's initial investment more than trebled, although the profits of Morgans, the injection of which had started Barclay's share price rise, actually fell in 1969.

Bentley, however, was no more than a cheap firework compared with the big shot of Slater Walker's 1969 satellite programme – the November launching of Malcolm Horsman and Ralli International.

The shell of Horsman's rocket was forged from a company called the Oriental Carpet Manufacturers. Formed originally in 1907 to make carpets in Turkey, by 1969 its main manufacturing units were in India and it had distributing companies in London, New York and Canada; it also had an investment subsidiary in Luxembourg. By comparison with Barclay it was quite a substantial business with a turnover in 1967 of £5.75 million and pre-tax profits of £193,000. There had been considerable improvement in 1968 but OCM was slow in releasing figures and did not announce the results for the first six months of 1968 until 14 March 1969. These showed that profits had more than doubled, but so rarely traded were the shares that not even this disturbed the stock market quotation of 42s. 6d. - against a 1967 balance sheet net asset value of £6 13s. 3d.

Such a plum could hardly escape the attention of Slater Walker and indeed they were first told about the company in 1967. But OCM was controlled by two families who did not want, at the time, to sell. Then in early 1969 Slater Walker heard that one of the families might be willing to part with its shares. Slater Walker pounced and on 24 April 1969 became the owners of a block of 74,714 shares, or nearly thirty per cent of the capital, for which it paid £300,000 - £4 a share.

Slater Walker had some trouble prising out the second family's shares – it had to pay £6 a share this time – but by 22 May its holiding had increased to 124,000 shares, effective control at 49.6 per cent - and, anyway, as we shall see, Slater Walker also acquired shares through its 'investment clients'.

Naturally this operation was conducted discreetly: there was no point in causing a rush for the shares by advertising Slater Walker's interest. But the market in OCM shares was very narrow and by early June the quotation had already crept up to 65s. On 3 June 1969 - the day before Bentley joined Barclay - most of the old OCM board quietly retired, to be replaced by Horsman and other Slater Walker men.

Their appointment was spotted by the *Sunday Telegraph* on 6 July 1969. 'Can it be,' the paper asked, tongue in cheek, 'that this cash-rich, overseas-based company is being took over by thrusting Mr Slater?' By then the shares were being traded at over £6 each.

The price continued to surge on up as the cleverer operators scrambled for the almost unobtainable shares. It was like the good old days. By the end of August they had touched £10 10s. Then on the 29th of that month OCM requested that the Stock Exchange suspend its share quotation. The reason: it was having talks with a company called Ralli Brothers (Trading) which might lead to a merger.

Ralli Brothers (Trading) was, of course, a subsidiary of Slater Walker, acquired with the rest of Ralli as a result of the Drage's deal. It was a holding company for the group's commodity merchanting interest: cotton from throughout the world, jute from Pakistan, India and Thailand, sisal from East Africa and coffee from Kenya. It was a substantial business with a turnover of £63.5 million in 1968 on which it made profits of £1,125,000 – including an exceptional item of £235,000 resulting from the sterling devaluation.

The reflotation of the Oriental Carpet Manufacturers under its new name of Ralli International took place on 14 November 1969. The prospectus forecast that the combined group's profits in 1969 would be not less than £1,290,000 – actually lower than the sum of its two constituent parts the year before even if the exceptional devaluation profit is eliminated. No attempt was made to argue that the two would actually benefit from being joined together. It was clear that the group was going to rely on acquisitive rather than organic growth, and it was only the magic of the Slater Walker connection that justified the remarkable flotation price earnings ratio of 15.8, compared with about 9 for other commodity groups. The *Financial Times* was moved to comment that the offer was 'speculative' and even Horsman himself later admitted that the financial fundamentals of his new vehicle were weak: 'It had no liquidity other than banking facilities and overdrafts necessary to sustain its existing profit level,' he told an international investment conference in 1972, and eighty per cent of the forecast earnings were to come from cotton broking, 'which was not every investor's idea of quality earnings', he said.

The fascinating aspect of the offer, however, was again the financial manoeuvring that preceded it. In September, Slater Walker shifted some of the Ralli Brothers (Trading) shares around within the group and sold some to an associated – but not subsidiary – dealing company, Bion Securities,* at a price which put a value on the commodity merchants of £7,125,000.

On flotation, however, the value of Ralli Brothers (Trading) plus Oriental Carpets was set at £10,875,000. So the worth of the OCM half had been judged to be £3,750,000. Yet when dealings were suspended back in August, the total market value was only £2,500,000 at £10 a share and even this was nearly £2 10s. above the 1968 net asset value, the audited accounts of OCM for that year having been belatedly released by Slater Walker in early September although they had been signed by the accountants on 13 May 1969.

What this meant was that Slater Walker had decided to put a price tag of £15 on each OCM share. But it did not appear that way in the issue, for OCM's 250,000 £1 shares were split into ten 2s. shares to increase the number to 2.5 million, and this was then doubled by a one-for-one free issue of shares. The price to the public of the old OCM shares, renamed Ralli International, was thus 15s. (i.e. £15 divided by 20) against a net asset value per share of less than 4s.

Slater Walker offered 1,812,500 to the public at this price. Ralli

* See Chapter 19.

International's total capital was 14.5 million shares, of which, before the offer, Slater Walker (and Bion) owned 10,871,520. It had got 9,025,000 of these in exchange for Ralli Brothers (Trading), while the remaining 1,846,520 represented the OCM shares acquired for the most part earlier in the year as increased by the split and free issue – less some shares which Slater Walker had resold, as we shall see. The recipients of these shares and any old OCM shareholders who had been sensible enough to hold on owned the bulk of the remaining 3,628,480 shares.*

The deal was thus a marvellous windfall for any members of the public who still happened to own OCM shares, and extremely profitable for Slater Walker – and for a select band of favoured Slater Walker investment clients who were allowed a share of the gravy.

When I first asked Slater about the way the original stake in OCM had been distributed he replied: 'Approximately 160,000 shares in OCM appear to have been acquired, before 9 September 1969, and this holding was divided about equally between Slater Walker and investment clients.' The average cost of the whole, Slater said, was about £5 a share.

Slater Walker itself, as we have seen, had built up a holding of 124,000 OCM shares by 22 May 1969. The only 'investment client' to buy OCM shares at the same time was the Tokengate Investment Company, which bought 19,098 shares in late May for which it paid £6 each.

Like OCM itself, Tokengate was very small, with only 274,940 shares of 10s. nominal value outstanding, of which 35,845 were in bearer form. It too had a stock market quotation – although the market was extremely narrow and there had been literally only half a dozen deals in the shares in the previous two years. Formerly called Argentine Lands and Industries, Tokengate was a classic shell; on 9 May 1969 three Slater Walker men, including Anthony Buckley, quietly replaced the old Tokengate board, which had been composed mainly of representatives of bankers Hill Samuel, the previous managers of the company. Although little attention was drawn to the change, Tokengate's share price jumped from about 17s. 6d. to over 25s.

Tokengate's existing investments in the Argentine and London were immediately sold off and the proceeds reinvested in Slater Walker's new favourites; for in addition to the OCM shares, Tokengate bought 200,000 Barclay shares at 7s. These two holdings in fact accounted for all of Tokengate's investments in quoted securities in

---

* Lord Carrick, managing director of Ralli Brothers (Trading), had had a small minority interest in that firm which he had bought for £12,187 10s. in November 1968; for this he received 475,000 Ralli International worth £356,250 at the flotation price.

its 30 June 1969 balance sheet, which, with OCM's middle market quotation at £5 and Barclay's at 8s. 9d., had a value of £182,990. This was just a little below their total cost of £185,000 – the immediate gain registered on the Barclay shares on that company's reflotation nearly offsetting the paper loss still just being shown on the OCM shares.

Thus in the early summer of 1969 Slater Walker and Tokengate had between them 143,098 OCM shares, and on 12 September, in a purchase that must have been outside the market, Slater Walker brought this up to 160,424 by the acquisition of a further 17,326. But before market dealings were suspended on 29 August Slater Walker had started to *reduce* its own holding: it sold 900 OCM shares on 31 July 1969, 16,000 on 5 August, 25,000 on 15 August, and 7,100 on 26 August – just three days before the suspension.*

As a result of these transactions Slater Walker was left with 92,326 shares, which were converted into the 1,846,520 Ralli International shares after the split and the free issue. As Slater Walker had paid the equivalent of 4s. each for the bulk of this holding, its profit on reflotation was of the order of £1 million on these Ralli International shares alone. Because of the complexities of the Drage's deal it is more difficult to say exactly how large was the appreciation on Ralli Brothers (Trading) as a result of the £7,125,000 value placed on it, for which the equivalent value of Ralli International shares were issued, but this was probably nearly ten times the book cost.

The realized gain was, of course, only on the shares sold, but in addition to the 1,812,500 shares offered to the public Slater Walker disposed of a further 1,480,000 at the time of the relaunch. Of these 800,000 were sold to Malcolm Horsman at a discount of 1s. 6d. on the issue price – and Slater Walker lent him the money to buy them.†

Slater Walker's profit would, of course, have been even greater if it had not resold those 49,000 shares to investment clients in July and August. Identifying these lucky clients was made particularly difficult by the fact that OCM shares were in bearer form, which meant that the company did not keep a register of the holders. However a register had to be compiled in the course of the capital reconstruction and from this and other sources it was possible to trace and identify most of those clients.

* Details from the register that had to be kept of Slater Walker's dealings in OCM shares because its holding exceeded ten per cent of the capital.

† The directors' dealing register of Ralli also reveals that two other directors, Lord Carrick and Mr A. K. J. McBride, acquired 500,000 Ralli shares between them on 14 October 1969 at the even more favourable price of 6s. each. The entries are confusing, however, because at that date Ralli/OCM still only had 250,000 shares in issue. The 6s. price is, of course, equivalent to £6 for the old 'heavy' shares. Apparently this sale was part of an executive incentive arrangement and further such sales to executives could have accounted for the whole 1,480,000.

The 900 shares sold by Slater Walker on 31 July 1969 almost certainly went to a nominee account, Founders Court Nominees D 2649. This account represented Edward Heath, then Leader of the Opposition, whose investment affairs were at this time being handled by Slater.

Founders Court is the nominee company of Brown Shipley, the merchant bank for which Heath worked at the start of the Fifties and to which he returned in October 1964 as a director after the defeat of the Conservatives. Heath had owned some shares of Brown Shipley itself for many years, and 3,125 were registered in his own name when he was appointed to the board. But shortly afterwards, in January 1965, 2,625 of Heath's Brown Shipley shares were transferred to Founders Court D 2649, leaving only 500 registered in his name. (The articles of Brown Shipley require a director to hold at least 500 shares in his name.)

Heath resigned from Brown Shipley in July 1965 on being elected leader of the Conservatives, but he continued to hold 500 shares in his name; D 2649 also continued to hold 2,625 shares. Then in early 1968 Brown Shipley announced a one-for-five rights issue, entitling the holding in Heath's name to another 100 shares. No new shares were, however, credited to this holding but two lots – 100 and 525 – were credited to D 2649. A few days later the 500 shares in Heath's name were also transferred to D 2649, which thus held 3,750 Brown Shipley shares worth over £12,000.

In May 1968 Heath disposed of 2,750 of his Brown Shipley shares – but D 2649 continued to hold the remaining 1,000 – and shortly afterwards, in August 1968, D 2649 became the holder of 4,210 shares in Slater Walker itself, of which the price was then about 50s. each – an investment of about £10,500. The holding was increased to 5,613 in June 1969 by a one-for-three scrip issue and had risen in value to some £12,500. Heath's 900 OCM shares would have cost about £6,000, assuming, as is likely, that he paid the market rate, which was between £6 11s. 6d. and £6 15s. on 31 July 1969. As a result of the split, the free issue and the reflotation the D 2649 holding became 18,000 Ralli International shares worth, at 15s., £13,500.

Slater, of course, would not comment on the question of his management of Heath's money, and nor would Heath. Walker told me he did not know about the arrangement. A Slater Walker executive closely involved, however, told me that Heath left his money with Brown Shipley and that Slater Walker gave advice to them. Heath, therefore, would not necessarily have known what shares he was being put into.

The 16,000 OCM shares transferred by Slater Walker on 5 August 1969 were sold to the Tokengate Investment Company, and Tokengate almost certainly paid the market price of about £6 17s. 6d.

Together with the block bought by Tokengate back in May, this brought the little company's holding up to 35,098 shares which had cost £222,500.

The 25,000 OCM shares sold by Slater Walker on 15 August 1969 went to Invan, the unit trust Slater Walker had first set up for its private investment clients in 1967 and then offered to the public in April 1968. On 15 August the OCM share price was around £7 but Slater told me that Invan only paid £6 a share.

By selling these OCM shares to Invan Slater was, of course, sharing the benefits of the Ralli International reflotation with several thousand unit holders. But the fact that this was done at the expense of Slater Walker shareholders, aggravated by the fact that the sale was at a discount on the market price, demonstrates the difficult conflicts of interest that arise when a unit trust management company starts acting as a principal in transactions with the trust it runs. But Invan was, at this precise moment, presenting Slater with a serious problem: in the early part of 1969 Invan's performance had been poor and redemptions had started to pile up. Then the August issue of the magazine *Planned Savings* – published at the end of July – had scathingly told Invan unit holders to sell: 'The best course of action for an investor is to place his money with managers who attempt to balance the claims of their own profit with the unit holders' expectation of performance.' The sale of 25,000 OCM shares to Invan appears to have been an attempt to implement this advice to the managers.

There remains the 7,100 block sold by Slater Walker on 26 August 1969, just three days before the 'merger talks' between OCM and Ralli Brothers (Trading) were announced and dealings on the stock market were suspended. I have not been able conclusively to identify to whom these shares were sold and Slater maintains he does not know who the recipients of this 'relatively small parcel' – worth over £55,000 at the 26 August price – were. In fact, on a number of occasions before the summer of 1976 Slater said he could not give precise answers to questions about these August 1969 transactions on the grounds he no longer possessed the records of Tokengate, although, as I pointed out, these were sales by Slater Walker and so the answers should be found in Slater Walker's own records. (As a licensed dealer in securities Slater Walker should keep relevant records for seven years under the licensed dealer regulations: these sales, by Slater Walker acting as principal to its own investment clients, would have been covered by the regulations.)

There is, however, evidence which suggests that 5,000 at least of the 7,100 shares were also sold to Tokengate, among the evidence being the fact that the same nominee account in which Tokengate's other OCM shares were later registered contained entries equivalent to an extra 5,000 shares.

With or without this last block, Tokengate was thus the 'client' to benefit most from the Ralli/OCM operation. Its original investment of 35,098 OCM shares had turned into 701,960 Ralli International shares worth £526,470 at the issue price, and by March 1970 this had increased to over £1,050,000 as the Ralli share price more than doubled in just over three months. (The extra block, which appears to have been resold quickly after the reflotation, could have yielded a further realized gain of £50,000 to £60,000.)

But who then owned Tokengate? Well, a large part – at first forty-four per cent but later over fifty per cent of the capital – was owned by Slater and other directors of Slater Walker personally, and much of the remainder was owned by Slater Walker itself or was allocated at various times to favoured clients and other executives, friends and relations.

Tokengate was, in fact, designed to 'give the boys a bit more', as one of the boys frankly described it. Another one explained more fully that what had happened was that as a result of the fall in the Slater Walker share price after the autumn of 1968 and of the Labour government's penal taxation measures on conventional stock option schemes, the Slater Walker share options were no longer attractive: Tokengate was designed to overcome these problems.

Slater himself first put it rather differently when I broached the matter of Tokengate with him in October 1974. He said that Tokengate's purpose was to stop Slater Walker executives from dealing in shares on their own account in the market. I asked Slater if he had personally held shares in Tokengate and he said yes, he had. I then wrote to Slater in April 1975 that I would be delighted if he would be prepared to give me a full breakdown of Tokengate's investments from 1969 to 1973 and of his own dealings and those of other Slater Walker directors in its shares. Slater replied: 'I really do not think you can expect me, nor do I feel prepared, to request information from all past and present directors of Slater Walker as to their personal dealings, if any, in Tokengate shares going back over a period of six years.'

Nevertheless, as a result of my own continuing investigation into the available records of Tokengate I was able to build up a fuller picture of the history of the company and to put further questions to Slater, the answers to which, although far from complete, at least confirmed what I had come to suspect.

As we have seen, Anthony Buckley and two other Slater Walker executives, Richard Eldridge and Stephen Maltz – both at various times Slater's personal assistants – were appointed to the Tokengate board on 9 May 1969. But it was not until late June that the old shareholders actually transferred their shares, for the records state that Slater Walker itself acquired 44,964 shares on 26 June 1969.

About the same time a further 199,999 shares were transferred into the name of Midland Bank (Stock Exchange) Nominees – and subsequently increased by one share to 120,000 – making a total of 164,964 or exactly sixty per cent of Tokengate's 274,940 shares in issue.

The question was, then, to whom did these 120,000 shares belong? The first clue was to be found in the directors' dealing register of Tokengate, which said that chairman Buckley had acquired 20,000 Tokengate shares at '90p.' on June 1969.* Then examination of the register, and in particular of later transfers out of the Midland Bank nominee account, strongly suggested that the 120,000 represented separate individual holdings of 20,000 each.

So I asked Slater in February 1976, in a letter accompanying the draft of the book as it then stood, if he could confirm that about 120,000 shares in Tokengate were acquired by himself and other directors or executives of Slater Walker in May or June 1969 at about 18s. each. Slater's solicitors replied in March 1976: 'On 20th June 1969, 120,000 shares were placed at 18s. 6d. each. Mr Slater received 20,000 shares and other directors of Slater Walker received the balance of 100,000 shares.'

There were seven directors of Slater Walker in June 1969: Slater, chairman; Walker, deputy chairman; Simon Pendock, Malcolm Horsman, Richard Tarling, Anthony Buckley and John Ford. Walker had told me in early 1975 that he had never invested in Tokengate shares and Slater confirmed that he had not been allocated any since he was not an executive director. (Walker bought 7,000 Ralli International shares in the November reflotation.) Slater said his own interest was no greater than that of any of the other directors, which means that the six executive directors had 20,000 each – although it should be noted that Malcolm Horsman denied to me that he had ever held Tokengate shares.

Slater Walker's intervention in OCM was spotted by the *Sunday Telegraph*, but its association with Tokengate remained unpublicized. Nevertheless the Stock Market quotation of Tokengate's shares, which had stood at a somewhat academic 17s.-20s. in the first four months of the year, rose to 21s. 3d.-25s. on 12 May following the appointment of Buckley and his two colleagues and then to 23s. 9d.-27s. 6d. on 20 May. It dropped back to 21s. 3d.-25s. on 18

---

* Throughout this inquiry the slackness with which Slater Walker kept its records was always a serious obstacle. The details on the directors' register had been 'taken from previous records' and did not include, as required by law, the date on which the acquisition had been notified and the date on which it had been entered on the register. The 'register' of Slater Walker's own holdings, which had to be kept while in excess of ten per cent, consisted of a series of letters from Slater Walker giving details of transactions that had taken place. The letters contained errors – for example, stating that Tokengate's shares had a nominal value of £1 when in fact it was only 10s. These inaccuracies did not increase the credibility of other information on the files.

June, but then in early July it started to move steadily upwards, reaching 28s. 9d.-33s. 9d. at the end of that month and 32s. 6d. at the end of August.

During the latter two months there were still relatively few transactions in the shares, only about 15,000 to 16,000 of Tokengate's registered shares changing hands. Of these, 8,200 went into Heath's Founder's Court Nominees D 2649 account on 28 August; this means they were probably acquired a month or so earlier. These shares did not come from Slater Walker's own holding and, although it is difficult to be precise, their cost was probably in the region of £12,000

In the autumn of 1969 the Tokengate share price began to rise much faster, as dealings in the extremely narrow market became more active – and because of the huge investment in ocm/Ralli International. Slater Walker itself initially bought a few more shares and then began to reduce its holding. On 6 October 1969, just as the market price jumped from £2 to £3, it sold a block of 20,000; Slater told me they were probably sold to Roland Rowe, who was appointed a director of Slater Walker at the end of that month.

At about the same time, Slater Walker sold 500 Tokengate shares to the Royal Yachting Association. Slater had been approached by the Association – quite independently of Heath – to help raise money for the Olympics. He agreed to take part of its capital and invest it, undertaking to make up any difference himself should he fail to make several thousand pounds. Slater also put the Royal Yachting Association directly into Ralli International with the purchase of 650 shares at the reflotation.

By the end of October the Tokengate share quotation had reached 70s.-75s. and by the end of November 85s.-90s. Tokengate's 10s. nominal value shares were now split into five 2s. nominal shares and when dealings started in the new form on Christmas Eve 1969 they were quoted at 17s. 6d.-20s. But by the end of the year they had reached 23s. 9d.-26s. 3d., equivalent to some £6 5s. in their old form. The seven executive directors now each had 100,000 Tokengate shares worth £125,000, an appreciation of 576 per cent on the cost of £18,500 to the original participants just six months before.

Around the end of 1969 Slater Walker appears to have distributed the remainder of its own holding in Tokengate to about forty different investors. Much the largest single block – 9,000 shares – went to Heath's D 2649 account, and would have cost over £9,000 at the current market rate. Heath's total holding, adjusted for the share split, was thus now 50,000 shares, or 3.6 per cent of the capital of Tokengate – an interest of sufficient size to be declarable under the disclosure rules covering MPs' business interests that came into force in 1975.

About the same time the Royal Yachting Association acquired a further 8,475 Tokengate shares – but not from Slater Walker this time – to bring its holdings to 10,975. They were sold again within a few months, as were its shares in Ralli International.

When I first discovered that Tokengate had invested in OCM shares shortly before it was refloated as Ralli International, I thought there could be no question but that Slater knew perfectly well that this would prove a highly profitable investment. So in early 1975 I asked Slater what reason there had been for giving the profits on the OCM shares to Tokengate, a company in which the directors of Slater Walker were personally interested – although at that time I did not know to what extent. Slater replied: 'I utterly reject the idea that Tokengate was "given" a profit as you suggest. Only with the benefit of considerable hindsight could this possibly be said and the invest-ment could have proved to have been an unsuccessful one. Indeed, Tokengate held the bulk of its shares for some time at a substantial loss on the market value.'

As Slater himself later pointed out, Tokengate had bought its first OCM shares in May 1969. That month the market price was mostly only a little above £2 and so it is true that Tokengate was for a short period showing a paper loss on its initial investment in OCM at £6 a share. But it was only a matter of six weeks or so, as the market price had surpassed £6 by the first week of July.

Slater continued:

> It is always possible to look back upon any successful investment and argue that, at the time, it was a 'gift'. It is very different making an investment judgement without the benefit of hind-sight. Tokengate had an aggressive investment policy and, in buying its OCM shares, took a risk, as indeed did other purchasers at that time. The main reason for OCM's subsequent price rise was the injection of Ralli which was not envisaged until several months afterwards.

Tokengate in fact got its second tranche of OCM shares not several months but only just over three weeks before the announcement of the plan to inject Ralli Brothers (Trading). Slater said later that he had been referring to the first tranche when he had given me his answer, but I continued to question him to try to establish when the plan had been first 'envisaged', and in March 1976 I was told: 'The idea of injecting Ralli Brothers (Trading) into OCM was first thought of as a vague possibility in June 1969 but did not firm up to become at all tangible until several months later. As soon as the possibility became a strong probability the shares were suspended at our request on 29 August 1969.'

So the plan to inject Ralli had not, after all, been envisaged even several months after Tokengate bought its first block of OCM shares in late May but at most a few weeks afterwards; and Tokengate, forty per cent owned by Slater and his colleagues, had been sold its second block of ocm – from Slater Walker's own holding – in the full knowledge that this injection was on the cards.

Four years later, in July 1973, Walker, in charge of the Heath government's promise to reform company law as Secretary of State for Trade and Industry, published a White Paper setting out his plans. It stated:

> The Government's view is that dealing in a company's securities by anyone who, by reason of his relationship with the company or with its officers, has information which he knows to be price-sensitive, should be a criminal offence unless he can show that his primary intention in dealing at that particular time was not to make a profit or avoid a loss.

It seems to me, but not to Slater, that Tokengate's activities – in particular the purchase of its second tranche of ocm shares from Slater Walker – fell clearly within this definition. But in 1976 Slater amplified his explanation in the following words:

> You should realize that there was rarely a time when we were not considering several different types of scheme for the many quoted companies in our orbit. It was, however, only when the nebulous idea of a scheme became a tangible probability that in our view the shares became price sensitive and we requested a suspension. For every ten vague possibilities of a scheme on average only one would come to fruition.

Indeed he went further and said:

> At that time literally every week there were up to as many as twenty deals to be considered, the vast majority of which were abortive. Slater Walker only requested suspension and positively stopped dealing in those shares when a deal became a strong possibility.

Slater's case, however, rested on his argument that at the time the various investments in ocm were made during the summer of 1969 the purchasers were taking an ordinary investment risk – indeed, he went so far as to suggest that 'many would have said it was an extra-ordinary risk'. Slater quoted various figures to support his contention – that, for example, the £6 price at which Tokengate bought its first tranche of ocm shares valued the company at the very high price/earnings ratio of 23 and was also close to the net asset value of £6 13s. 3d. But these were based on the out-of-date 1967 accounts and ignored the fact that the interim figures for 1968 had been published and these indicated that profits were likely to be double 1967's, making the prospective price/earnings ratio half Slater's figure. Slater went on to say that Tokengate's second purchase at £6 17s.'6d. in August 1969 was on a price/earnings ratio of over 11, which is fair enough as the full 1968 profits had been announced in early July – although this was not now a comparatively high ratio. But Slater then said that Tokengate this time had paid in excess of the 1967 balance sheet asset value, ignoring the fact that in August 1969 Slater Walker was in control of OCM and would have had access to the 1968 balance sheet, signed by the auditors on 13 May 1969, and this showed net assets of just over £7 11s. Any reliance by Slater Walker on this balance sheet, which was not published until early September, in making investment decisions for Tokengate would itself have been a misuse of 'inside' information. (It is also, of course, possible that Slater Walker had had access to these 1969 figures during the negotiations to purchase OCM in the spring.) Slater now says that in the light of the fact that OCM's assets included inventories of nearly £8 a share as well as net overdrafts of around £3 a share, he considers that 'investors were taking a calculated risk'.

But Slater's whole argument is quite unreal. Slater Walker was not buying into OCM because it particularly liked the prospects for the oriental carpet trade, and Horsman was not interested in devoting himself to selling carpets. Slater Walker wanted a base on which to build a new group, and the main reason for the rise in OCM's share price before the suspension was not, as Slater claimed, the injection of Ralli: it was because the stock market knew full well that Slater Walker had not moved into OCM without some plans for it, and anyway, as everyone knew, the mere news of an association with Slater Walker was always enough on its own to drive up the price.

Nor was the higher price put on the shares when they were refloated in November due to the injection itself of Ralli Brothers (Trading). It was due to the decision, taken by Slater Walker, that they would get away with refloating OCM as Ralli International at the even higher relative P/E ratio of nearly 16 – relying on the 'glamour' of the Slater Walker connection.

It was thus again disingenuous – at best – of Slater to suggest that when one company – Tokengate – whose fortunes were controlled by Slater Walker, invested in another company – OCM – also controlled by Slater Walker, it was taking an ordinary investment risk, let alone an extraordinary one; and anyway, if an investment in either Tokengate or OCM in the summer of 1969 was really so risky, what sort of money manager would have committed a large part of the wealth of the Leader of the Opposition to them?

But Tokengate did run a risk – that someone would find out that Slater Walker directors personally owned large blocks of its shares. This was kept as quiet as possible. It was not disclosed, for example, in the Ralli International prospectus in which one would have expected the directors of Slater Walker to declare their substantial indirect interest in the company they were promoting. Nor was it disclosed to the shareholders of Slater Walker itself, some of whose assets the directors were effectively selling themselves just before they themselves determined a much higher value for those assets. Relatively senior executives of Slater Walker did not know about it – even Walker seemed ignorant of its true purpose. In July 1977 Slater offered the following two further explanations which I quote in full: 'There was nothing illegal about the non-disclosure of the Slater Walker directors' Tokengate shareholdings. It would, of course, only have been in the interests of the directors if the fact had been made public because it would presumably have had the effect of driving the price up further.'

The function of Tokengate Slater had amplified to me in the summer of 1976:

> Tokengate's investment policy was directed towards investment in Slater Walker associates such as Barclay and Ralli and in this way enabled the Slater Walker executive shareholders to participate directly in their growth. It represented a simple and practicable way of granting an incentive to top executives, and restricting them from dealing directly in the market. Obviously, other more direct and safer incentive schemes could have been utilized. In particular in this way executives' funds were obviously entirely at risk.

'Incentive' to do what? Slater Walker already had its own share option scheme, under which all the directors, with the exception of Slater and Walker, had had options to subscribe for substantial quantities of Slater Walker shares, many of which were still outstanding in early 1969. As already stated, the attractions of such options had been considerably reduced by the fact that the Slater Walker share price had ceased to rise so fast – and because of tax measures introduced by the Labour government; and it is true that Tokengate was to some extent a way round these, because, while Tokengate was only liable to corporation tax at forty per cent on short-term dealing profits, Slater Walker directors would have had to pay tax at their own individual top rates on such gains if they had invested directly.* But other ways round the tax obstacles to ordinary options were devised based on partly-paid shares, and Slater Walker itself introduced such a scheme in early 1970.

---

* Tokengate had a share dealing subsidiary called Plate Securities which made short-term gains of over £58,000 in the year to 30 June 1970 on sales of just £113,000 worth of securities. It is possible that much of this represented the profitable resale of that final block of OCM shares transferred on 26 August 1969.

Why then did Slater Walker directors need something more? None of the directors were executives of Ralli International, with the exception of Horsman, and he was sold a very substantial extra slice of Ralli shares. Slater says it was a practicable way of restricting the directors from dealing directly on the market. Could not they be relied upon not to deal in the shares of Slater Walker's associates – its banking clients – on the basis of confidential information?* Was Tokengate merely an incentive to stop them abusing their position? Slater regards the following as an adequate explanation: 'Slater Walker had a very large equity base and therefore the equity and option stakes in it were much less meaningful than those in the smaller satellite companies. Many of the central executives such as Malcolm Horsman became restless and wanted to leave to do their own thing and it was essential to try to retain a strong central team. Many of the executives were stock market orientated and needed a quid pro quo for not being able to deal in the stock market. To illustrate the risk of investment in Tokengate Michael Booth [one of his later directors] lost money on his investment in it. Ian Wasserman [another later director] did not have any of the shares.' The reality remains that Tokengate was just a way of making more money – an organized insider dealing operation.

As for the 'obvious' risk, that has been dealt with: there was no real risk of loss and Slater's claim must be further qualified by the fact that Slater Walker probably lent the directors the money to buy their Tokengate shares in the first place, as Slater has subsequently stated that this was usually done in these circumstances. Naturally, however, the extent of gains made by the directors depended to some extent on the level of stock market prices at the time they chose to sell their shares.

Slater finally – in March 1976 – gave me details of his own dealings in Tokengate. He said that he sold his original stake on 18 September 1970 for a profit of £50,381. By then, as we shall see, a storm had blown through the securities markets around the world, and prices had dropped back from the high points reached in early 1970: much of the profit represented the fat built up behind the Tokengate share price as a result of the Ralli operation the previous summer and autumn.

Stock markets surged forward again in 1971, however. Slater told me that in May that year he reinvested in 137,250 Tokengate shares – 9.98 per cent of the capital and so fractionally under a disclosable interest – for which he paid £136,866, and these, he said, were sold in November 1973 for a total of £321,083 – a profit of £184,217.

* It is interesting to note that the Slater Walker 'Conditions of Employment' contract around this period merely stated that 'private trading is not permitted within the premises of the company'.

Buckley, who had slightly increased his holding in the autumn of 1971, sold out at the same time for a profit of £215,000. We shall be looking at some of Tokengate's later investments in following chapters and also at the possibility not only that Slater Walker itself financed some of the directors' realizations of Tokengate shares, but also that it bought back some of Tokengate's investments. If, however, all the directors made gains similar to Slater's and Buckley's, the total they made out of Tokengate would have been over £1.5 million.

Heath naturally required his portfolio to be liquidated when he became Prime Minister in the summer of 1970. It was not a favourable moment to sell. His Slater Walker shares, for example, were sold in the market around 20 July 1972 at about 36s. - a price about equivalent to what he had paid for them in the first place, adjusting for the intervening free issue. He may, of course, have held other shares on which he also did not do well.

There was however still plenty of room for profit on the Ralli and Tokengate shares. The transfer of Founder's Court Nominees D 2649's 18,000 Ralli shares - to a Slater Walker nominee company - was registered on 28 September 1970: the Ralli price was, in fact, rising quite strongly that month after earlier falls - from about 14s. to over 17s. - and Heath could have got about £13,500 and a profit of £7,500. The transfer of D 2649's 50,000 Tokengate shares - also to a Slater Walker nominee company - was registered on 2 October 1970. In the preceding weeks the price had been mostly around 14s., although it had briefly fallen as low as 13s., and so Heath could have realized about £35,000 and a profit of around £14,000.

As a result of its new policies the profits of Slater Walker soared to £10.4 million in 1969 – well over double 1968's £4.9 million – in spite of the problems being experienced by its industrial subsidiaries. The revelation of the increase in early 1970 drove the share price, which had been as low as 37s. in 1969, up to over 61s. in April 1970 – only a little below the peak reached in 1968.

Almost before it was launched, Slater Walker's new satellite, Ralli International, had embarked on its own takeover programme, buying up another jute merchants, Willcox & Co., and Millars Timber and Trading, with saw milling interests in Australia and South Africa. Slater Walker's own acquisitive phase was drawing to a close, although it was at the end of 1969 that it bought the Cow rubber company: and in early 1969 it moved into a completely new field by acquiring Walker's insurance broking business, Walker Young. The deal was worth over £188,000 to Walker and was the largest single addition to his wealth.

As we saw in Chapter 5, in the first three years after the merger of Walker Moate and Rose Thomson Young, the profits of the merged concern made little progress. Walker Young's broking profits in 1963, the first year after the merger, were £6,629; in the fifteen months to 31 March 1966 they fell to £5,239, although the firm made a further £5,138 on investment dealing during that time.

In December 1965 Slater was appointed to the board of Walker Young; there was, according to Walker, an arrangement whereby Walker Young would give Slater Walker a rebate from the brokerage commission on business introduced by Slater Walker. Then, at the end of 1965, Walker parted with another two of his early colleagues, Roger Moate – the younger brother of his original partner David Moate – and David Clarke. Both had become Parliamentary candidates and Walker felt that this was not compatible with their jobs as heads of department with his firm. So he offered to buy them out with enough money to set up in some other business. They also set up in insurance broking on their own.

The most important development, however, was the acquisition in early 1966 of an associated company, Rose Thomson Young (Reinsurance). This had been formed in 1964 by Walker and Clouston as a vehicle for a Lloyd's reinsurance expert they had recruited called Derek Collins; it was now integrated in the main group and helped to push total profits of Walker Young to £21,000 on a brokerage income of £255,000 in the year to 31 March 1967.

The following year broking profits crept up to £26,000 and commission income to £265,000. But in this year Walker Moate, Walker's original company, was turned into an active share dealing subsidiary and made £32,000 on a dealing turnover of £429,000. The Walker Young group therefore was able to chalk up total profits of £58,000 in the year to 31 March 1968 – its first rapid growth. It was also able to increase its gross dividend payout from £7,750 to £19,375, of which Walker's share would have been about £2,670, against £1,040 the previous year. His pay as chairman rose to £3,850.

In the autumn of 1967 Slater Walker, via a subsidiary, SWIG Developments, bought 45,252 shares in Walker Young, representing about twenty-nine per cent of the capital, at just over 30s. each – a total investment of nearly £70,000. The terms valued Walker Young at £240,000. About half of Slater Walker's shares came from Walker's colleague at the Rodwell property group, Sefton Myers, who sold out and retired from the Walker Young board. Some of the rest came from Young, whose stake in the business was gradually declining. Walker himself now held about fourteen per cent of the capital of his broking firm, valued, according to the price paid by Slater Walker, at about £33,000. Walker says this deal was done at a discount on the true market value, and that the reason for allowing Slater Walker to have an equity on advantageous terms was because it was designed to replace the brokerage commission rebate agreement and to encourage Slater Walker to send more introductions to Walker Young. He says the selling shareholders, who were nonexecutive, agreed amicably to the discount, Sefton Myers in particular because he recognized that, contrary to the original purpose behind his shareholding, he had not been able to make much contribution to the firm.

As a result of the relationship with Slater Walker, Walker Young naturally got introductions to the companies that Slater Walker took over. They were not given the insurance business automatically, however, but only if they could quote better terms than the companies' existing brokers. David Marshall of Greengate & Irwell told me that after his firm had been taken over a young man turned up from Walker Young expecting to get the business automatically, but Marshall sent him packing and only reinsured through Walker Young once lower premiums had been quoted. But Walker Young was getting many non-Slater clients, the most important of which was probably Sir Isaac Wolfson's mail order company, Great Universal Stores.

It was in the year to 31 March 1969 that Walker Young's insurance profits began to advance. Its main Lloyd's subsidiary, Rose Thomson Young, that year recorded profits of nearly £37,000 against only £4,753 the previous year. The contributions from the reinsurance and other subsidiaries, plus a good growth in interest and investment income – a standard source of profits for insurance brokers, who normally put the premiums they receive from their clients on deposit for a few weeks before passing them on to the underwriters – brought insurance profits to nearly £68,000. But Walker Moate had been very active in the stock market that year, and turned in a profit of £71,000 on a dealing turnover of £1.7 million. That brought Walker Young's profits to £139,000. Walker had become a full working member of Lloyd's in 1968, for which he would have had to show he was worth at least £15,000 – against the £75,000 of an ordinary underwriting member – and his salary as chairman of Walker Young went up to £4,350 while his share of the dividend for 1969 would have more than doubled to £5,525.

It had always been the hope of Walker and his colleagues that they might one day be able to cash in on their work in building up Walker Young, and in the summer of 1969 the first rumours of a proposed public flotation were heard. In July *The Times* reported: 'Peter Walker, the 37-year-old Shadow Housing Minister, is preparing the ground for bringing his Walker Young insurance broking group to the market, and probably with the aid of Ralli Brothers, the banking subsidiary in the Slater Walker Securities stable. Autumn is the time now set for the flotation.' The issue, *The Times* said, would clearly identify Walker 'in the millionaire bracket'.

Walker had always put the emphasis at his firm on expansion at the cost of current profits. This means that brokerage income was spent on hiring more staff to get more business rather than taking it into profits. Profits were further depressed by the cost of issuing new policies, as opposed to renewing existing ones. It is only when a sufficient backlog of renewal business is built up that profits begin to come through. That point had not really been reached by 1969 and the *Times* announcement was premature. Walker Young was just not big enough to command a Stock Exchange quotation on its own. But Walker had a problem: towards the end of the year he knew that the Conservatives had a chance of being returned at the General Election that was now looming up, and that if they were, he might well be appointed to the Cabinet, in which case he would have to resign from Walker Young. He had therefore to think about the future of his firm.

Walker says that he told his colleagues and co-shareholders at Walker Young that they had a number of alternatives. One was to continue expanding the firm and eventually to float it as a public company in its own right. A second was to merge with one of a number of other Lloyd's broking firms which, Walker says, were interested in teaming up with Walker Young. A third was to become part of Slater Walker and in so doing to continue to benefit from the connection with and expansion of Slater Walker – a proposal which carried the added attraction, compared with the second alternative, of ensuring a continued degree of independence.

The takeover was announced on 9 January 1970, but received scant coverage in the press. It was not formally signed until 4 February and next day the *Daily Express* briefly reported: 'Shadow Housing Minister, Mr Peter Walker, has sold his insurance broking group Walker Young to Slater Walker – headed by colleague and business partner Jim Slater – which already has a 28½ per cent stake in the company. Price: £975,000.'

Walker told me that he warned his colleagues that if they were to sell out to Slater Walker it would have to be at a price 'below the proper market price so that there could be no criticism'. Walker and Slater say that the terms were vetted by Rothschilds who said they were favourable to Slater Walker, and that this vetting was disclosed to the Stock Exchange and in the press statement. Nevertheless a detailed look at the transaction reveals that, largely because the price was paid in Slater Walker shares which were rising strongly at the time, the terms were not ungenerous to the Walker Young shareholders. Slater Walker was to issue 421,411 new Slater Walker shares for the 71½ per cent of Walker Young it did not already own. The day before the deal was announced the Slater Walker share price had reached 51s. 3d. and at this level Walker Young was valued at £1,509,000 and Slater Walker was paying £1,080,000 for the 71½ per cent of Walker Young – not the announced £975,000. This latter figure, it seems, was determined on the basis of a Slater Walker share price of 46s. 3d., the level of a couple of weeks before, valuing Walker Young at £1,360,000. By the time the deal was formally signed on 4 February the Slater Walker share price had risen to 55s. 6d. and the price of Walker Young to £1,635,000.

The terms of the deal stipulated that Walker Young should make profits of at least £170,000 before tax in the year to 31 March 1970, and Slater pointed out to me that on this basis, at the value of £1,509,000, the price/earnings ratio of Walker Young was 16.15 against the *Financial Times*-Actuaries Index ratio for insurance brokers of 18.81. The Index, however, is compiled from the figures of large, leading and quoted insurance brokers which would normally command a higher rating than a small unquoted firm like

Walker Young – and the average price/earnings ratio of *all* insurance brokers quoted in the *Financial Times* on 8 January 1970 was just 16; and another, larger Lloyd's broking business which changed hands at about this time was sold on a ratio of only 9. Furthermore, using a multiple of 2½ times brokerage turnover, which Walker had previously told me was the appropriate way to value a broking firm, would have produced a price for Walker Young of only about £1.1 million. Against this, Walker Young's asset backing was probably relatively high – but this was largely because of the huge appreciation it was showing on the Slater Walker shares it had bought right back at the outset in 1964 at a cost of little more than £20,000: at 51s. 3d. they were worth over twelve times that amount.

Walker later said that the main expansion of Walker Young was in the highly lucrative reinsurance business and that therefore it would 'enjoy a substantial premium above the general market rating', and that there was no doubt that they would have done better financially to merge with or be taken over by another broking firm. Comparisons with other brokers, he said, were also not justified because they were not going through the 'dynamic growth' of Walker Young at the time. Still some of them were not only growing but also in the reinsurance business and it is hard to see just what Walker Young shareholders were giving away to put the deal above any possible criticism.

Walker also argued that the 'further fluctuations' in the price of Slater Walker shares after the price had been agreed should not be taken into consideration. I see no reason why not, since the continued rise made a big difference to Walker. He was the largest shareholder in Walker Young and received 81,511 Slater Walker shares worth, at 46s. 3d. each, £188,494; at 51s. 3d.- £208,872; and at 55s. 6d.- £226,193. Clouston got 52,274 Slater Walker shares, Collins 44,546, Longbottom 34,998 and the nominee company of Alan Beaumont Dark's Birmingham stockbrokers, Smith Keen Barnett, 29,166. Young received only 17,991 and the rest were divided among twenty-five Walker Young shareholders who were mostly employees.

Although it was presumably fairly well known that Walker, deputy chairman of Slater Walker, was also chairman of and a shareholder in Walker Young, Slater Walker shareholders in the UK were not told that he had a personal interest in the deal, either in a special circular or in the annual report. Normally the Stock Exchange requires at least a circular to be sent out when a director has a personal interest in a proposed acquisition, but exemption can be granted: so it was on this occasion, on the grounds that Walker's interest in Walker Young was only fourteen per cent, and that the total addition to Slater Walker's assets was less than five per cent.

Walker says that for this reason, because the deal was vetted by

Rothschilds and because of the expense to shareholders, he did not insist on a circular – although I pointed out to him that this would have helped put the deal above all criticism. However small in relation to Slater Walker's total assets, the deal was important from Walker's point of view, providing the single largest contribution to his readily realizable wealth; and Walker Young had benefited over the years from the association with Slater Walker – although to what extent it has been difficult to assess. Clouston told me that only seven per cent of Walker Young's business at the time resulted from the Slater Walker connection, but I was not told how this figure was reached.

Walker Young had forecast that it would make £170,000 in the year to 31 March 1970: there would, naturally, have been no point in Slater Walker buying a lot of share dealing profits, which had amounted to over half Walker Young's pretax profits of £139,000 in the previous year, and only £10,000 were allowed for in this figure. Making money in the stock market was anyway considerably more difficult in 1969 – Walker Young had even started dealing in pictures – and at 31 December 1969 the group was showing dealing losses of over £14,000. But in the first three months of 1970 it managed to recoup this, thanks mostly to an Australian subsidiary, and turned in a final dealing profit of nearly £18,000. Other profits came out at £167,000, of which more than half had arisen in the first three months of 1970.

Walker said that this was because all reinsurance accounts and the principal UK accounts come in then; and indeed it is obvious enough that many premiums are likely to fall due at the beginning of the year. But, given the talk of dynamic growth, it is odd that in the last nine months of 1970 Walker Young's profits were not outstandingly better than in the same period of the previous year. Excluding dealing, profits were £117,000 against £69,000; but interest and other investment income accounted for £87,000 of this, against just £36,000, and so profits from broking alone had fallen slightly in spite of a rise in brokerage of over £100,000 to £388,000. Walker's explanation appeared to be that expenses had risen because Walker Young was re-equipping an additional floor of office space and also continued to expand its staff. The interest itself mainly came from Walker Young's new parent, for Slater Walker had treated Walker Young like its other acquisitions and had squeezed more than £1 million out of it to put on deposit with its own bank – a good part of it raised by the necessary sale of Walker Young's shares in Slater Walker.

In 1971 Walker Young's growth potential became evident, with profits rising to £345,000 on a brokerage of £880,000. But in the summer of that year Slater Walker resold the business in a typically complex share deal. On 17 May 1971 Slater Walker announced that it was to sell Walker Young to the much larger firm of Wigham-Richardson & Bevington's in exchange for shares, and that it would simultaneously bid for the rest of Wigham's stock. The announcement pushed the Wigham share price up from 180 to 220 pence. In the event Slater Walker bid 222 pence but did not secure full control, ending up with about sixty-nine per cent of the Wigham capital. But at 222 pence each the 1,235,000 Wigham shares that Slater Walker got for Walker Young were worth £2,734,000. Slater Walker promptly reduced its holding in Wigham to under fifty per cent by 'placing' shares. Finally Slater sold the remainder in the autumn of 1972 to Anglo-Continental Investment and Finance, a group run by his friend James Goldsmith.*

Walker argues that the high resale price of his old firm is another reason why the original price to Slater Walker was cheap, although, as we have seen, part of the difference merely reflected a rise in the Wigham share price. By the time of the resale Walker was, of course, in the government and he was not consulted. He says that he had no idea that Slater would resell Walker Young. Slater explained at the time that he resold it because the insurance broking business was causing a conflict of interest with the insurance underwriting companies that Slater Walker had started or acquired in the previous two years. Given the much more serious conflicts of interest that had existed within Slater Walker since its inception, it is not an explanation that carries much weight.

Before returning to the mainstream of the Slater Walker story, we must pause to examine what had become of Walker's other business associations. As we have seen, he had parted from Unicorn and du Cann – there was never much love lost between the two – in 1967, when the unit trust company was bought up by Martins Bank. But Walker remained closely involved with the Myerses and the Rodwell Group, of which he continued to be director, up to the start of 1969, when the property company was also taken over.

The Myerses, however, did not confine themselves to property development. Bernard's son Sefton had inherited some of his father's enthusiasm for new ventures, and Walker was drawn into a couple of these. The first was a little company called Computaquants, which had been started by a surveyor with the idea of providing a computerized billing service for quantity surveyors. In the summer of 1962 the Myerses and Walker each took up 4,000 shares in the company, and Walker became chairman and Sefton a director.

In September 1962 the *Evening News* reported: 'Mr Walker fore-

---

* Wigham-Richardson later merged with another group to become Wigham-Poland, and in early 1976 Walker was appointed to the board.

casts that in the second half of this year projects worth more than £45,000,000 will go through his machines. By 1964 work expected to be handled may well run into hundreds of millions of pounds, he says.' But if the contracts handled by Computaquants were counted in millions, the fees it charged never amounted to more than a few thousands, and by 31 March 1966, after some four years' trading, Computaquants had accumulated losses of over £75,000 and its directors and others, including Walker, had lent nearly £53,000 interest-free to keep the company going. But the men who ran the business still believed the corner was about to be turned.

At this point, in May 1966, Computaquants became a subsidiary of Rodwell, which acquired a sixty-two per cent interest in the firm, including the 12,000 shares of Walker and the Myerses. The decision by Rodwell, a public company, to take over the investments of its directors in a loss-making private company was unusual. Walker explained:

> I transferred the shares to Rodwell at no cost because Rodwell were interested in this company for its future potentiality and the reason they considered that this was a venture which they should develop was that the majority of the development cost seemingly had already been met but it needed a property company with its connection with developers and builders to use the systems of Computaquants which were all linked with the construction industry. It also made sense for the company to be administered by a larger entity and it was one of the full-time executives of Rodwell who thereafter did this.

Later Walker added that at the same time as he and the Myerses gave Rodwell their shares, it was also agreed that there would be no repayment of the loans they had personally made to Computaquants. He said that neither he nor Sefton had voted on the question of the takeover and that the board had decided to acquire the company for nothing believing it would become a profitable investment.

John Cohen, however, told me that Computaquants was 'wished on to us for nothing'; and the balance sheet reveals that interest-free loans from 'others' of £55,600 were still outstanding a year later. Nor were the hopes that the business would become profitable under Rodwell's wing ever fulfilled: it was finally disposed of in September 1968 and the venture cost Rodwell some £20,000.

The second venture was a firm called Kintslaid Engineering which Sefton Myers backed in 1964. It had been formed by two young men in the textile trade to develop a machine they had invented and named 'Kraftmatic': this, they hoped, would make pile cloth for towelling and suchlike much better and faster than conventional looms. Myers brought his friends and associates into the project in

1965 and Rodwell, Slater Walker and Walker Young made modest investments in the business. The following year the main backers put up more money, Slater Walker and Rodwell ending up with twenty-eight per cent and fourteen per cent of Kintslaid respectively, and Tarling joined the board. (Walker himself was never on the board or involved in the management of Kintslaid.) The new machine was then announced to the world: it would 'revolutionize' textile production, the newspapers reported.

But the revolution never happened, and in 1968 Slater, who once said that inventors were dangerous people, told Tarling to get Slater Walker out of the investment and to take a loss of over fifty per cent if necessary. Tarling had by this time become good friends with Sefton Myers and feared an embarrassing interview; but Myers said at once that he would buy the Kintslaid shares back at cost to preserve Slater Walker's goodwill. Kintslaid, however, remained indebted to Slater Walker for substantial sums it had borrowed.

Other Kintslaid backers were not so lucky and Rodwell, which had also lent money in addition to its equity stake, was still holding the loss-making investment in 1969.

These little extraneous investments did nothing to help the fortunes of Rodwell, or to ease the relationship between the Cohens and the Myerses. The Myerses, father and son, had built up their private property business in the lush times of the Fifties, and had effectively taken their rewards in the merger with the already public Lombard London in 1962. In the more hostile environment in which property 'speculators' found themselves operating by the mid-Sixties, and with the added responsibilities of running a public company, the Myerses soon found the going a lot harder.

Many of Rodwell's development projects were sound. Sefton Myers, who had been made managing director of the group on the amalgamation with Lombard, had considerably better business judgment than his father Bernard, who became chairman, as well as a more developed sense of financial responsibility; and at the time when the excess of office building in central London was beginning to be apparent, from the consequences of which a number of property companies were only saved by George Brown's ban in 1964, Rodwell's concentration on suburban and provincial development proved fortunate.

Rodwell had built itself a new head office in Duke Street, St James, in the West End of London, where it moved in 1964, leaving its old Hertford Street offices to be taken over by the embryonic Slater Walker. West London, however, continued to be its most important development area, with, in particular, a large office block at Gunnersbury which was let to the American computer firm IBM when completed. Sefton Myers also formed an association with the Lex

Garage chain to develop some of its sites, and the first completed was an office block on the Great West Road. In addition, however, under the Myerses' direction, Rodwell built up an ambitious programme of office and shop developments throughout the country, including schemes at Archway in North London, in Croydon, Staines, Farnborough, Luton and Manchester.

The tensions between the Myerses and the Cohens, however, began to build up from the outset. The first sign, perhaps, had been the resignation of Richard Cohen from the board in 1963. But it was between the fathers, rather than the sons, that the contrast was greatest, and it was inevitable that the immense conservatism of John Cohen would clash with the recklessness of Bernard Myers. By 1965, anyway, Bernard Myers was yet again in personal financial straits; he had already sold many of his Rodwell shares, and the Cohens now agreed to buy about two thirds of his remaining holding. But Bernard had to go.

John Cohen now once more started to take a more active role in the management of the company: he and Sefton Myers became joint chairmen. But Sefton Myers remained in day-to-day charge as managing director, and relations between the two gradually became more strained. Not only did Cohen disapprove of the diversifications into Kintslaid and Computaquants, and of the prices that Myers was prepared to pay for sites, but also Rodwell's liquidity position began to deteriorate.

The problem was due to planning and licensing delays on some of the developments, and to difficulties in letting others that had been finished. As a result Rodwell was rapidly using up a £9 million loan facility given by two insurance companies and the Electricity Supply Pension Fund, and it had mortgaged properties to banks, including Brown Shipley and Singer & Friedlander, as well as using other properties as security for substantial short-term borrowings.

On top of this, Sefton's passion for the stage led Rodwell into one costly white elephant – the New London Theatre. The scheme was devised with the help of Myers' friend, stage designer Sean Kenny, and the development, once permission had been given in 1966, took place on the site of the old Winter Garden Theatre in Drury Lane. Commercially, it was a wild venture, with no prospective tenants for the theatre, nor indeed for any other part of the development, which included a huge restaurant, shops and showrooms, flats and an underground car park. With an empty Centre Point just round the corner, no lucrative office space could be included.

The first step taken by the Cohens to strengthen the company's position, in December 1966, was to arrange for Rodwell to take over a small private property company of theirs, Monarch Securities, which Richard Cohen had been running since he left Rodwell. This had some properties which had not been mortgaged and the deal improved Rodwell's balance sheet.

The Cohens were naturally not disposed to sit back and watch the benefits of this deal being eroded by Sefton Myers' imaginative but extravagant plans. Walker had to some extent been able to keep the peace between the Myerses and the Cohens, and to keep Sefton's feet on the ground, but by the autumn of 1967 matters came to a head. Sefton Myers was replaced by Richard Cohen as managing director, the deputy managing director, a Myers man, left the company, and John Cohen became executive chairman, spending all his working time on Rodwell's affairs. Although Sefton Myers remained joint chairman for three months more, before being demoted to an ordinary director, the reversion of control to the Cohens was complete.

The Rodwell share price had been in almost continuous decline since the formation of the group in 1962. To some extent this reflected the problems of all property companies after the introduction of corporation tax and the office building restrictions. But it was also the result of Rodwell's particular difficulties – and of the tendency of the Myerses to sell their shares. Sefton sold nearly two million in early 1967 and the price reached a low of 2s. 1d.

The price then fluctuated until July 1968, when it began to rise sharply, reaching 3s. 6d. by the second week of September. This was partly the result of an improvement in the company's affairs, but a new factor had started to affect it: the rumour of takeover.

In the late summer of 1968 talks started with J. Lyons, the catering group. The rationale was that Lyons needed property expertise to develop its own sites; but there was also a family connection: another son of John Cohen's had married a Salmon, one of the Lyons ruling families. News of the negotiations leaked out after a few weeks of talks, and the companies were forced to make an announcement on 10 October 1968. This pushed the share price up another $2\frac{1}{4}$d. to 3s. 10$\frac{1}{2}$d.

In the event Lyons decided there was no attraction in a deal and the news that the talks had been called off at the end of October knocked the share price back. Again it was only temporary, for now Rodwell had become a firm takeover prospect. There were a number of suitors, and the Cohens even asked if Slater Walker might be interested. By the end of the year the share price had reached 4s. 6d. Then on 7 January 1969, Star (Great Britain), now called the English Property Corporation, announced that they had agreed takeover terms with Rodwell; these valued the group at £11.5 million – 5s. 1d. a share in Star stock, or 4s. 9d. in cash.

The deal was worth little to Walker personally, for he had sold the bulk of his holding back in 1962 immediately after the merger and held only 5,000 Rodwell shares at the time of the takeover. However, Walker Moate, his insurance firm's dealing subsidiary, became the registered holder of 12,500 on 8 July 1968 and Walker's mother of 13,000 on the same day, to add to 15,990 she had acquired earlier in the year. These 15,990 were transferred simultaneously to a Brown Shipley nominee account, bringing the total number of shares in that account to 350,000.

I asked Walker about his mother's shareholding and he replied: 'I vaguely remember that Brown Shipley provided a facility at the time to lend money against Rodwell shares and it may have been that I recommended her that she bought some shares under this facility – but I really cannot be certain.' It is thus not possible to say to whom the Brown Shipley-held share belonged, although, in addition to those transferred from Mrs Walker, many of them were transferred from Bernard Myers' holdings and 5,000 came from Alistair Goodlad, Walker's one-time personal assistant. They were, of course, like those of Walker Moate, acquired before the takeover talks with Star, or indeed those with Lyons, had started; but the investments were well timed, for nearly everyone who bought Rodwell shares in the first half of 1968 must have doubled their money in less than a year.

So Rodwell disappeared into Star. Sefton Myers continued his career as a property developer until his death from cancer in 1971, but financial troubles continued to dog his father Bernard. He had spent a great deal of money on Walton Manor and his racing stables and stud farm in Buckinghamshire. They lay, however, in the area designated for the new town of Milton Keynes, and were compulsorily purchased in 1970. Myers asked for nearly £800,000 in compensation; the development corporation offered £230,700. The Land Tribunal decided in December 1972, after a lengthy case, that the corporation's figure should stand; but Myers was unlucky for only a point of law prevented him being awarded, not his whole claim, but at least £636,000. It emerged during the hearings that Myers was, in early 1970, once again in a state of 'impecuniosity'. The settlement, unfavourable though it may have been, at least helped to restore his position.

Walker had been as insistent as any of the Rodwell directors in demanding that Bernard Myers resign the chairmanship at the end of 1965; indeed he had taken on the job of ensuring that Myers went. One of Walker's co-directors told me that Walker had expressed concern about his public position. But Walker says this was not so and that he acted purely out of public duty to the shareholders as an outside director. Indeed, he has recently stated: 'When Bernard Myers started to sell shares because of his horse racing activities it was I and I alone who went in and told him he had to resign as chairman otherwise I would personally resign from the board. John Cohen supported this action on my part but did not himself take it.' Apart from that he says that his involvement with Rodwell affairs was 'limited to one board meeting a month'.

But Walker was rising to political prominence in 1965. He had been appointed by Home to the front bench as a spokesman on financial and economic affairs and his first job, along with Barber, was to help Heath, the shadow Chancellor, attack Labour's first finance bill in the early summer of 1965. This was the bill that included the major innovations of corporation tax and a full long-term capital gains tax, and Heath and his lieutenants fought it clause by clause.

Labour did not back down on any important matters of principle and Walker, who handled the capital gains tax side, failed in his attempt to prevent the extension of the Conservatives' own high-rate six months speculative gains tax to cover resales within one year. But it was an efficiently organized campaign which caused the government, with its small majority, some embarrassing moments. The tactics were regarded by some as schoolboyish, but they also resulted in a number of technical improvements in the Act.

Walker originally supported Macleod for the leadership of the Tory party in succession to Sir Alec Douglas-Home. Nigel Fisher, in his biography of Macleod, says that when Walker 'realized that Iain had no chance, he went to see him in the most straightforward way and told him he was transferring his support to Heath. Macleod, who had already decided not to stand, fully endorsed Walker's decision and there was no hard feeling between them.' Walker, however, says that this is incorrect, and that he only switched to Heath when he and Macleod together decided he had no chance, and that he would have supported Macleod had he decided to stand. In any event he was a prominent organizer of the Heath campaign which led to his victory over Maudling in July 1965. Heath initially left Walker in his position as spokesman on economic and trade affairs, but Walker was now firmly established in the Tory hierarchy.

For his London base, Walker moved into a flat in Gayfere Street in Westminster, which also served as offices and which he shared with Ian Gilmour, then proprietor of the *Spectator*, and Charles Morrison, son of Lord Margadale, whose victory at a by-election in 1964 he had helped organize. Uncharacteristically, he even bought a half-share in a racehorse with Morrison's wife.

Heath promoted Walker to the shadow Cabinet after the Conservatives had lost the 1966 election and when morale in the Heath camp was low; Walker, at just thirty-four, was the youngest member and his brief was transport. This provided him with his next major Parliamentary campaign – the attack on Barbara Castle's transport bill in early 1968. Again he emerged with an enhanced reputation, his tactics having forced the government to drop a number of clauses. Later in 1968 he was moved to housing, land and local government, and he then took back transport, in addition to these, in 1969.

By then the new 'abrasive' Tory party ideology was well on its way to final enshrinement at the Selsdon Park conference in May 1970: confrontation in industrial affairs, law and order at home, laissez-faire in business with high rewards for the strong and successful, no government support for the ailing.

In business, Slater Walker seemed to embody this philosophy: it was the self-made enterprise challenging the industrial and financial establishment, promoting mergers and efficiency not through state intervention but through market forces and managerial talent. Walker has recently said that his own political career shows that it is 'total nonsense' to describe him as a great advocate of laissez-faire policies beneficial to financial operators. But these were the policies set out at the Selsdon Park Conference; and it is another of the ironies of the story that the return of the Tory government in June 1970 coincided with what was little short of a crisis in the affairs of Slater Walker, the first major setback in its rise, as the inner, un-revealed weaknesses almost broke through the facade.

19   *When bulls were bears*

In November 1972 it was Walker's turn to address the annual conference of the Institute of Directors. Walker had just been moved from the Department of the Environment to Trade and Industry, and he chose the occasion to announce his plans for a major reform of company law. 'We need,' he told the directors 'to have a framework which encourages the good firms and clobbers the rogues.'

Disclosure was to be the theme of the new legislation. 'Company law needs to be reformed so as to see that the activities of commercial concerns are clearly known to all. We must decide what needs to be disclosed and then we must take the necessary steps to see that it is disclosed,' Walker announced. 'Certainly, I am not going to tolerate a situation where there is a law that states certain returns and certain information should be provided publicly and a great sector of commerce ignores that demand,' he continued.

Walker's threat was to those companies that were not even fulfilling the disclosure requirements of the Labour government's 1967 Companies Act. This Act, intended originally as the first of a series, was hurried through to deal with two urgent problems – a spate of failures among motor insurance companies and a legal quandary that had arisen over the distinction between money lenders, hire purchase companies and banks. Nevertheless the Act contained a number of important disclosure provisions: many private companies which had previously been exempt from filing public accounts at Companies House were required to do so; any public company that owned more than ten per cent of the shares of another had to reveal that fact; and in an attempt to curb 'insider trading' – the use of confidential information by directors and others privy to company secrets to make money on the stock market – every public company was required to keep a register, open to inspection by all, containing the details of dealings in its shares by its directors.

Presumably what Walker had in mind when he spoke to the

directors was that thousands of private companies were either not filing their accounts or sending them in so late as effectively to make the requirement useless. But in the circumstances it was perhaps somewhat ironic that Slater Walker had itself failed to register some of Walker's own dealings in Slater Walker shares while he was still deputy chairman of the company.

The directors' share register of Slater Walker recorded that on 20 June 1970, the day that Walker resigned to join the new Heath Cabinet, he owned 148,177 shares, the last entry being the addition of the 81,511 shares he received from the sale of Walker Young. But the main share register of Slater Walker shows that the transfers of about 23,000* shares out of Walker's name were registered between 28 May and 19 June 1970. The main share register does not record either the exact date of sale or the price paid: the directors' share register must, under the 1967 Companies Act, show both. But this transaction was not recorded in the latter.

However, when I asked Walker about this he told me that he had sold 23,000 shares between 5 and 8 May 1970 at 50s. each. He said he had sold them 'in order to obtain funds for purchasing a farm which had become available in my constituency'. This transaction had fallen through, Walker told me, and 'the funds were thereafter kept on deposit', until nearly a year later when, in March 1971, Walker bought a 267-acre estate at Martin Hussingtree, near Droitwich, as a family home. He had married Tessa Pout, secretary of Ian Gilmour, daughter of a former treasurer of BOAC, and sister of a stockbroker with the firm of Rowe Rudd in February 1970, and by then their first son had been born. At the time it was reported that the price Walker paid for the seventeenth-century Martin Court was about £100,000. He had also acquired a house in Cowley Street in Westminster, and in early 1972 he bought another farm in Shropshire for a reputed £50,000.

Slater Walker had, of course, been a very profitable investment. When the Slater Walker directors' share register was opened in November 1967 Walker owned 50,000 shares. If, as he says, he had only acquired 50,000 at the outset in 1964, he must have sold the shares he received in the first scrip issue in the summer of 1966; the price ruling at the time suggests he would have only realized a little over £10,000, but this would have gone some way towards covering the original cost of £25,000.

Walker sold the 16,666 shares he got in the 1968 free issue over the ensuing months for a total of just under £56,000, but held on to the 16,666 he received in the 1969 scrip issue, to bring his holding to 66,666 at the end of that year. To this were then added the shares

---

* The register was very untidily kept in the summer of 1970 and the exact total of shares transferred by Walker in that period is not clear; it looks like 23,400.

issued for Walker Young to bring his holding to 148,177, of which 110,177 were registered in his own name and the remainder in nominees. The 23,000 sold in May 1970 would have realized a further £56,637 10s. gross; so by the time he was appointed to the government Walker had probably realized a total of about £125,000 from Slater Walker shares.

The sale of Walker's 23,000 was finally entered on the directors' register on 28 October 1974 – over a year after I had first pointed out the omission. The entry stated that the shares had been sold for an average price of 49s. 3d. – not the 50s. Walker had given me – between 4 and 8 May 1970. Walker told me that Slater Walker had been informed by letter of the sales on 8 May 1970, but he said he 'was unable to check whether or not they had entered this information into the register as naturally I was very quickly thereafter involved in the General Election campaign'. I was then given the following reason for Slater Walker's failure to enter the information:

> It so happens that there was no further meeting of the directors prior to his resignation as a result of his becoming a minister. The person responsible for up-dating the directors' share register, instead of checking as to whether there had been any change since the last board meeting as far as Mr Walker was concerned entered into the directors' register the correct information that he had resigned as a director.

I pointed out that this was both unintelligible and misleading: the Companies Act simply requires a company to 'inscribe' the details of any director's dealing within three working days of the notification by the director; there is no need to wait for a board meeting. To this Walker replied that in practice the requirement to enter within three days was not carried out. The explanation on the belated entry itself said that Walker had sent the details to Charles Harris, who was personal assistant to the chairman, and the 'information was not passed to the Company's Secretarial Department until after Mr Walker's resignation as a director, dated 20th June 1970'.

The failure of Slater Walker to register the details of these sales at the time is naturally not the most serious of transgressions, although unfortunate in view of the fact that Walker was in his own Companies Bill later to rely on disclosure as an important deterrent to financial misbehaviour. It is, however, worth taking a closer look at the dealings by Slater Walker directors in the company's shares in 1970.

It was a year of crisis for the company. For the first time its headlong growth was halted, the share price fell dramatically, and there was a major disaster in one of its most important offshoots. By the year's end, Slater had managed to produce a set of accounts that was respectable, though not up to the 'super-profit' standards of previous figures. Part of the trouble was due to the general decline in stock markets around the world that year; but a more detailed examination reveals that Slater Walker came perilously close to suffering a major setback. It was a period when his company's problems called for all Slater's adroitness and skill, yet he and his fellow directors found time to indulge in some intricate and, on the basis of the explanations Slater has offered, somewhat mystifying dealings in Slater Walker shares. While Slater Walker survived the critical year and went on to new heights before effectively succumbing to a repetition in much more drastic form of the 1970 crash, Slater had himself realized, before the outcome was clear, enough capital by selling shares in his firm to ensure that his financial security was no longer directly linked to Slater Walker's future.

The Slater Walker accounts for 1970, dated 23 April 1971, revealed that during the year the five directors had reduced their total holdings of Slater Walker shares by 391,738 to 1,595,868 on 31 December 1970. Slater accounted for most of the reduction, the holdings of himself, his wife and children – which must all be included under the terms of the 1967 Companies Act – having fallen by 306,664 to one million shares. Tarling's stake had dropped from 95,000 to 35,000 and that of John Ford, another former Leyland executive who had joined Slater Walker as finance director a couple of years before, was down from 55,999 to 25,000. One director, Buckley, slightly increased his holding while that of the fifth, Rowland Rowe, who looked after Slater Walker's growing property dealing side, was unchanged. Walker's holding was not listed as he had resigned, and nor were those of Horsman, who had left the Slater Walker board in March 1970 after the Ralli launch, and Pendock, who had resigned in December to run another quasi-satellite, Southern Pacific Properties, formed to develop a holiday resort in Fiji.

Slater gave the following reason for the sales in his accompanying chairman's statement:

> You may recall that in the 1969 Finance Act certain categories of interest payments were disallowed for tax purposes. This abrupt legislative change imposed a severe and unexpected tax burden upon me and certain of my colleagues and as a result it was necessary for us to reduce our shareholdings in the Company. I would emphasize that in each case your Director's shareholding represents his principal personal asset and none of us has any intention of reducing his present shareholding in the foreseeable future.

The inference was that Slater and other directors had sold shares in order to pay off loans, the interest on which was no longer to be allowable against tax.

In fact this 1969 taxation change had been neither unexpected nor abrupt. Slater explained that his statement to shareholders was not misleading because the change 'was not mentioned generally in the press in advance or expected by most people in the investment world' and that it could, for example, have applied to fresh loans only. But this explanation is itself misleading. It was widely reported in the run-up to the Budget that year that Chancellor Roy Jenkins wanted to curb the growth in personal loans made by the banks, and also that elements in the Labour government could not accept that stock market operators, for example, should be entitled to claim tax relief on the cost of the money borrowed to finance their activities. The removal of tax relief was the 'obvious way to tax personal borrowings', as the Conservative *Economist* put it in its pre-Budget issue in 1969. But more important, it was obviously not abrupt because those who already had loans on 15 April 1969 were given plenty of time to rearrange their affairs. In the first place, interest on fixed-interest loans outstanding at that date was to continue to qualify for tax relief until, at the latest, 6 April 1975; while those with other loans or bank overdrafts at that time could continue to claim tax relief for nearly one full year – until 5 April 1970. The removal of tax relief only applied immediately to new loans to new borrowers. (Slater said later that he considered that a tax on *fresh* loans was likely because it was the *growth* of personal loans that the Chancellor wanted to curb, and repeated his view that, while it might have been mentioned in the *Economist* pre-Budget issue in 1969 that the removal of tax relief was the obvious way to tax personal borrowings, this 'was not mentioned generally in the press in advance and nor was it expected by most people in the investment world'.)

British shareholders and commentators might also have thought that Slater's explanation sounded rather odd if they had discovered, as was possible if they knew where to look, that on 7 May 1971, the day the accounts and Slater's statement were released, he was borrowing more than £450,000 from Slater Walker itself, at an interest rate of ten per cent, repayable on 11 June 1971. If he could afford to borrow over £450,000 at this rate without tax relief in the spring of 1971, then a year before he must have been borrowing very substantially in excess of that, from sources other than Slater Walker, for a 'severe and unexpected tax burden' to have forced him to sell Slater Walker shares.

So I asked Slater about his borrowings in 1970 and 1971. He replied:

I have managed to find out that the £450,000 loan was advanced by Slater Walker Limited in April 1971 as a temporary loan for the purpose of setting up a Jersey settlement. My total borrowings in April 1970 were £1,220,904. The borrowings were mainly from banks and I do, of course, have a detailed schedule of them. I do not, however feel that it would be appropriate for me to give you the individual names of the banks in question. My borrowings in April 1971 totalled £275,440 but in addition to this there was also the £450,000 loan from Slater Walker.

I had, however, already established that Slater had had a large *interest-free* loan in 1970, as we shall see, and he said that this accounted for £346,000 of the 1970 total. Thus his interest-bearing borrowings in April 1970 were only £874,304, while a year later they were £725,000, including the £450,000. Slater said that he looked on the interest on the £450,000 loan simply as part of the one-off cost of setting up the trust and not an annual ongoing cost, like the interest on his other short-term borrowings.

Accepting Slater's explanation of the £450,000 and his figures for his borrowings from other banks, for which I have no independent evidence, it would appear that Slater personally did substantially 'degear' between April 1970 and April 1971, and he maintains today that his tax position became very unfavourable on 'an annual basis' as a result of the 1969 tax change, and that he waited the full year of grace. But, as we shall see below, the tax change itself was unlikely to have been solely or even primarily responsible for the precise timing of his sales of Slater Walker shares.

The fact that Slater Walker was in the habit of lending generously to its own directors was the revelation which caught most public attention when it finally emerged in the investigating accountants' report in the autumn of 1976. The details of these loans have, however, been available for some years in circulars sent out by Slater Walker to its Canadian shareholders.

A British company is not normally allowed to lend money to its directors unless its ordinary business is that of making loans. Slater Walker Ltd was by 1970 a fully-fledged bank, and so its directors were fully entitled to borrow from it. Their loans did not even have to be revealed to shareholders under British law as long as they were made 'in ordinary course of business'.* But in 1969 Slater Walker had secured a quotation for its shares on the Toronto Stock Exchange, and Canadian law requires such quoted companies to reveal their directors' indebtedness.

Excluding Slater's £450,000, other Slater Walker directors had reduced their loans from Slater Walker between April 1970 and May

---

* This, the government indicated, would be reviewed in the light of the Slater Walker revelations.

1971: Tarling from over £30,000 to under £15,000; Rowe from nearly £61,000 to about £37,000; while Ford had completely repaid one of £5,000. Pendock, who resigned during the period, had been borrowing £21,000 at 30 April 1970. The only indication that directors were lent money to appear in the main Slater Walker balance sheet was a note to the accounts for 1969 which said that a loan, of unspecified size, had been made to Horsman, who had just resigned. This was disclosed, according to Slater Walker, because at the time it was considered to be a 'significant contract with a director' and was to help Horsman buy his shares in Ralli International.

As with Walker, Slater's personal wealth was often exaggerated. After I had attempted to reconstruct Slater's dealings in the shares of Slater Walker before 1967, Slater told me that by 5 April 1967 he had 'realized overall capital profits of approximately £125,000' and that he was 'left with 600,000 shares which had an in-cost of £305,200 and were then worth just over £380,000'. In fact figures given for Slater's shareholding in takeover documents in 1967 suggest that he had about 15,000 more shares at that time, but his holding stood at 600,000 when the directors' register was opened in November 1967.

Slater's holding rose to 799,997 shares at the start of 1968 as a result of the one-for-three free issue, and Slater brought this up to a round 800,000 by buying three shares for just over £4. Then, in December 1968, shortly after Slater Walker shares had passed their first peak, Slater – or rather a family trust – bought 180,000 shares at just under 62s. 5d. and 20,000 at 60s. each for a total of £621,000

Slater bought these 200,000 shares from Despard, his first deputy managing director, who left Slater Walker at the end of 1968 to form another quasi-satellite, Cannon Street Investments (which was to become a victim of the banking crisis of 1974/5). Despard had a total of 300,000 shares and his other 100,000 were taken up by Pendock, Horsman, Tarling and Buckley at 64s. Despard, however, did not require immediate full payment from his erstwhile colleagues, but gave them interest-free credit until the end of 1970. Hence Slater's interest-free loan of £346,600 in April 1970, indicating that he had paid nearly half the total consideration for Despard's shares by then.

In June 1969 Slater received a further 333,330 shares in Slater Walker's third free issue, bringing his holding to 1,333,330. Then in December that year he sold 26,666 at 43s. 6d. to realize £58,000. Slater did not engage in any further dealings before May 1970, so in spring of that year he and his family held 1,306,664 shares which had cost about £870,000.

Because of the credit from Despard, less than £525,000 of this cost had to be financed elsewhere. The total proceeds of Slater Walker shares sold by Slater since 1964 amounted to about £425,000 and on top of this Slater had realized about £148,000 from Productofoam. Slater, of course, did not have to use this money to pay off loans although he indicated, in the context of Astaron-Bird, that he had paid off much of his original borrowing in 1965. He may well also have used Slater Walker shares later as security to raise money for other investments, or – less likely – just to spend. But it is clear that only a small part of Slater's non-Despard interest-bearing borrowings of £874,000 in April 1970 was strictly needed to finance his Slater Walker shares, 'his principal personal asset'. With Bank rate at seven per cent, the interest, without tax relief, would have been a substantial burden, although in addition to his pay as chairman of Slater Walker of £14,500, Slater would have had a dividend income from his shares of about £80,000.

It is only possible to give a rough idea of what other investments Slater may have had. There was Tokengate, of course, the details of which were given in chapter 17. He had built up a collection of paintings by a minor Victorian artist, F. W. Watts – not to be confused with the superior G. F. Watts – but some of these would appear to have belonged to Slater Walker itself. He also later acquired many acres of farmland in Sussex. The only other investment of Slater's at this time of which details are known was his holding of British Leyland shares.

Slater had been asked to rejoin the board of his old employers in April 1969, his only major appointment outside the Slater Walker group. On his appointment he already owned one million British Leyland shares; these, he told me, he bought for an average of 14s. 1½d. each and the finance was, he said, arranged through a firm of stockbrokers. Towards the end of 1969 Slater resold 750,000 of these for, he said, an average of 11s. 1½d. each. The directors' register of British Leyland actually records that he resold the whole million, 750,000 at 11s. a share and 250,000 at 11s. 2½d., and then bought back 250,000 at 11s. 3d. a share. Either way, he sustained a loss of about 3s. a share on 750,000, or about £112,500. These shares were also sold, it was said, because of Slater's tax problem; as far as British Leyland was concerned he told the *Sunday Telegraph*: 'I am very, very confident in the long-term outlook for the company.'

The price of Slater Walker shares was, as we have seen, rising rapidly during the first three months of 1970, and it reached a high point on Friday 3 April and Monday the 6th, when shares changed hands at just over 61s. At this level Slater's 1,306,664 shares in the company he had created were worth just under £4 million. Horsman, who had left the Slater Walker board in March, shrewdly chose this moment to sell out his holding of about 130,000 shares.

But since the second week of January 1970, the Slater Walker share price had been rising against the trend for the stock market as a whole. Share prices had staged a brief recovery towards the end of 1969 but the downward path that had started at the end of 1968 was resumed towards the end of January 1970 and by 6 April the FT Index had fallen 7.7 per cent since 14 January to 391 against a rise of 11.6 per cent in the Slater Walker price.

In the spring of 1970 share prices on both sides of the Atlantic were facing difficult economic conditions; tough monetary policies were holding back growth but costs had soared, catching company profits in between. Then, on 9 April, a new factor emerged: the crisis in the affairs of Bernard Cornfeld's Investors Overseas Services. Its spectacular collapse through April and May of 1970 was the final straw for stock markets around the world, for the Geneva-based complex of offshore funds held some £1,000 million of investments, many of them speculative stocks whose prices had been forced up by IOS buying. Now these shares were being thrown wholesale on the market in desperate attempts to raise money, and the already weakened stock markets could not easily absorb them.

IOS had two investment vehicles in the British market, the International Life Insurance company and the Sterling Fund of Funds. Slater Walker had become one of their most important investment advisers, managing some £16 or £17 million pounds for them. With IOS emphasis on 'performance', it was an ideal captive market, and Slater Walker shares found their way in large numbers into the funds until they became one of their largest single holdings. Just what proportion were bought for the two funds by Slater Walker itself is not known, but at the end of 1969 they owned nearly 580,000 Slater Walker shares bought at a cost of over £1,055,000 and then worth £1,365,000. On top of this, they had invested £350,000 in Slater Walker's Australian and South African offshoots, which had appreciated to £553,000: and one of IOS's main Geneva-run dollar funds, the International Investment Trust, had backed Slater Walker, buying 440,000 Slater Walker shares at a cost of about £1.2 million. But IOS's largest single investment in Slater Walker companies was a 1.4 million share stake in Slater Walker (Australia) bought for ITT at a cost of over £2.6 million.

ITT's investments in Slater Walker had actually fallen in value by the end of 1969, and they were among the first to go as the liquidity crisis gripped Cornfeld's empire: the whole lot had been cleared out by the end of March 1970 and Slater Walker itself, albeit without enthusiasm, bought back the 1.4 million shares in its Australian affiliate. It was perhaps some consolation that the Sterling Fund of Funds poured another £100,000 into the shares of Slater Walker itself as the price rose in the first three months of the year.

On Monday 20 April 1970 brokers Rowe Rudd put out a strong

'buy' recommendation for Slater Walker shares at 59s. 3d.: 'Whereas in the past the group had tended to be regarded as a "go-go" conglomerate, it has now become an investment banking group. We are convinced, however, that Slater Walker is in no sense "ex-growth",' and the brokers concluded that the shares 'should command sustained investment support over the medium to the longer term'.

The last two weeks of April 1970 were a terrible time for shares around the world. In London the FT index dropped from 390.2 to 359.1, nearly eight per cent. The Slater Walker share price fell twice as fast, to less than 50s. on Friday 1 May.

It was a tense time for investment managers and those at IOS, faced with massive redemptions of the group's open-ended mutual funds, were particularly jumpy. Towards the end of April they had a row with Slater Walker over the handling of a particular investment and Slater Walker was abruptly sacked as investment advisers. Slater was told on 1 May that IOS had already started dumping the shares held by its two sterling funds: on 30 April and 1 May 1970 it disposed of 225,000 shares at between 46s. and 49s. That still left them with over 390,000 shares the bulk of which were thrown onto the market in the following weeks.

On 30 April the stock market lurched through 1969's low point, but next day, Friday 1 May, Slater Walker shares were firm. The Slater Walker report and accounts for 1969 had been released the previous day and Slater was optimistic: 'For 1970 your Board anticipates another excellent year. Your Board can clearly see very substantial scope for improving profits by the further development of our banking, investment and insurance activities.' The report was picked up by the *Daily Mail*'s deputy City Editor and he also spoke directly to Slater: 'Talking to Mr Jim Slater and seeing Slater Walker's full figures suggest that the shares of this old favourite are cheap.' 'Jim's a bargain' sang the headline to brighten the prevailing gloom; and the following day the influential *Economist*, speculating on who had 'sold Jim short', concluded the shares must be 'highly attractive to those who have confidence in Mr Slater's ability to bump up profits by 25 per cent'.

In spite of dire predictions in the Sunday newspapers on the general theme of 'was it to be another 1929 crash?' the stock market remained reasonably steady on Monday and Tuesday 4 and 5 May 1970. On the 6th, it had its best day for nine months, the FT Index rising ten points to 368; the main reason was a belief that Wall Street, the main US stock market, would revive following the easing of credit there.

It was, of course, on 4 May, four days after the publication of the report and accounts for 1969, that Walker started selling Slater

Walker shares to raise money for the farm he hoped to buy. On the 6th Slater started to tackle his tax problems, about a month after the year of grace given by the Labour government to those with outstanding loans had run out: he sold 150,000 Slater Walker shares at 50s. each to raise £375,000.

Wall Street did not rally as hoped and by the end of the week, Friday 8 May, London share prices were almost back where they had started. The next week, beginning 11 May 1970, was another terrible time: the FT Index fell twenty-seven points to 333.7, or 7½ per cent. But Slater Walker shares dropped from 50s. to 37s. 6d., a sickening fall of twenty-five per cent.*

On Monday 18 May, the Slater Walker quotation improved slightly to 40s. and Slater sold 80,000 shares that day at 40s. 10½d. On 20 May, the stock market dropped nine points, but then started to fluctuate and by 2 June 1970 the FT Index was back to 339.7. The Slater Walker price, however, had fallen further to 37s.6d. and in this two-week period Pendock, the head of the Slater Walker investment department, sold 48,777 shares at an average price of 39s. 6d. and Slater – or more accurately, a Slater family settlement – sold another 220,000 shares at an average of 38s. 6d. each. Slater told me that he was not personally involved in the decision to sell these shares, and could not recall for certain why the trustees had sold.† It would seem, therefore, that nearly half the shares sold on behalf of Slater's interests in 1970 were not sold because of any 'severe and unexpected tax burden' on Slater personally.

Slater – and his family – had thus sold a total of 450,000 shares, and the proceeds came to £962,000, enough to cover the whole cost

---

*Prices used are middle market quotations from the official Stock Exchange list. The *Financial Times* closing price for Slater Walker dropped from 48s. 4½d. to 39s., or 19.4 per cent.

† The directors of Slater Walker had to file reports of their dealings in Canada as well as in London as a result of the Toronto Stock Exchange quotation. Ontario law, however, differs from British law in that insiders there need report only dealings in shares over which they have 'control or direction'. These do not necessarily include shares held by a wife or by children's trusts, which must be included under British law on the more realistic grounds that they are unlikely to be completely outside the influence of the director. The sale of the 220,000 was not reported in Canada but a further transaction, the sale of 24,000 shares by Slater on 11 May at 48s. to his wife, was listed. My analysis of Slater's dealings makes some use of the Canadian reports but after lengthy attempts to reconcile them with the UK returns, Slater Walker admitted that a number of them were just wrong. It should also be noted that after an initial inspection of the UK directors' register, Slater Walker completely revised it on the grounds that it originally included information only required in Canada, where a director must also give the names in which his shares are registered. Slater was continually switching shares from one nominee to another, often at the market price; for example on 7 May 1970 80,000 shares were switched out of various nominees at 49s. 9d. into NCB Trust, a subsidiary of the First National City Bank of New York with offices in Moorgate, which handled Slater's family settlement. The First National City Bank also administered a private company, Esher Investments, that Slater had formed in the Bahamas a year before.

of Slater's investment in Slater Walker and to repay any loans financing it, although he only repaid £150,000 to Despard on 7 July 1970, leaving the balance until its due date at the end of the year. Slater was left with 856,664 shares 'free': they were still worth £1.6 million – even if they had dropped by an alarming $38\frac{1}{2}$ per cent in value in just six weeks. As Slater wrote to me, the fall gives 'some idea of the pressures of a bear market particularly if one is heavily geared and having to pay large sums in taxes and interest at the same time!'

Slater would, presumably, have been liable to considerable capital gains tax, possibly of the order of £200,000. But he would have had the loss on his British Leyland shares to set against this.

On Thursday 4 June 1970, Slater Walker held its annual general meeting of shareholders. Slater remained optimistic: 'I am pleased to report that the profits of your Company for the first quarter of the year were again a record,' he told shareholders. 'During the last two months stock market conditions have obviously been unhelpful to some of your Company's activities. In spite of this there has been considerable progress made in further developing our merchant banking business and your Directors are confident that this will be a major source of profits for your Company in the future.' Slater Walker also had strong liquid resources, Slater said, 'which put us in a favourable position to take full advantage of any improvement in the economic climate.'

On 19 June 1970, the day after the Conservative election victory, the stock market celebrated and share prices, including Slater Walker's, jumped. They relapsed again slightly the following week, and then drifted sideways: Slater Walker remained at a level of around 36s. to 38s. until early August. Pendock had sold another 42,000 shares in the second half of June for an average of 37s. $11\frac{1}{2}$d. and it was during this period that the Slater Walker shares held in Heath's Founders Court Nominees D 2649 were disposed of, while Walker says he also gave instructions, on being appointed to the Cabinet, that all his remaining Slater Walker shares should be sold. He then held about 125,000 shares of which 86,777 were registered in his own name. Of these, 68,727 were transferred out of Walker's name on 20 July and put into a Slater Walker nominee company without any change in beneficial ownership, while the transfer of the remaining 18,050 was not registered until April 1971. I was told that the transfer into the nominee name was made shortly before delivering the stock, which had already been sold, to the market, and that the reason for this procedure, which was done without Walker's knowledge, was 'to avoid the appearance of Peter Walker's name on the share transfer as a substantial seller and the possible resultant rumours' – an odd precaution, as Walker had a perfectly good reason for selling. The late registration of the remainder was not explained;

Walker says all his shares were sold between 29 June and 2 July 1970. With the market price at that time around 37s. to 38s. he could have realized more than £230,000.

Just after midday on Friday 7 August 1970, Slater Walker announced its results for the first half of the year, revealing that the second quarter had been 'disappointing due mainly to exceptionally difficult stock market conditions which meant that our merchant banking and investment activities were operating at a reduced level and some underwriting losses were incurred'.

In fact profits for the full six months showed a small rise over the comparable period of 1969 and the share price did not immediately fall. As a result, Tarling, who sold 45,000 Slater Walker shares that same day, was able to secure an average of 38s. 4½d. each.

But the analysts did their sums and on Saturday 8 August Lex of the *Financial Times* commented: 'After the cheerful talk of the first quarter, the market slide in the second three months seems to have temporarily put paid to earnings growth.' Lex went on to the nub of the matter: 'Thus for perhaps the first time the question is not how much earnings growth sws can produce, but whether it can produce any at all. The answer hangs largely on the state of the stock market.'

Early the following week the shares dropped by 2s. 6d. but the real blow came on 21 August 1970 when the *Investors Chronicle*, commenting scathingly that 'Mr Slater has attracted to himself a personal following which one suspected looked only passingly at the fundamentals and bought the shares regardless of price whenever they had the money,' committed the ultimate heresy of actually advising that the shares should be sold. The price dropped to a low of under 28s. and the value of Slater's investment to under £1.2 million.

The market in Slater Walker shares remained difficult in September with the price hovering around the 30s. mark. But on the 19th of that month it received some support: the Slater family trust bought back 100,000 shares at 31s. Slater told me he was not involved in the decision to buy these shares. The price improved over the next week with the stock market, and again in the first week of October, when Tarling sold a further 14,000 shares at 39s. 6d. to bring his total sales proceeds to over £114,000, and John Ford sold 29,000 at 39s. 7½d.

By the end of that month the market had turned down again, and November was another difficult month for Slater Walker shares. There were, it seems, still a number of holders who wanted to get out and at the end of November Slater Walker arranged for a block of 500,000 shares to be sold to the Hong Kong public. Who the sellers were was not revealed in the prospectus, which merely described them as 'major institutional and other holders, most of whom will retain substantial shareholding in the Company'. I asked, at the end of 1974, who they were: Colin MacInness, Slater Walker company secretary, told me that the shares 'came from a mixture of investment clients of Slater Walker and friendly holders whom we knew wanted to sell'. They were clearly anxious enough to do so, for they accepted a price slightly lower than that ruling in London and the wily Hong Kong dealers immediately resold most of the shares back in London for a quick profit.

In fact the principal seller of Slater Walker shares in the Hong Kong issue was a £100 company called Jaydean Securities which was so structured that it was not technically a subsidiary of Slater Walker but was nevertheless totally controlled and managed by Slater Walker, or rather Slater personally. (I shall consider Slater's explanation of the function of Jaydean in the Hong Kong issue later in this chapter.)

Jaydean was one of four such little companies. Their existence was first publicly revealed in the summary of the independent accountants' report published in September 1976, and their names – Bion Securities, Euroglen, Jaydean and Petershill Trust – then emerged in the Guildhall Magistrates Court hearing in February 1977 when charges brought by the Department of Trade against Slater under Section 54 of the Companies Act in respect of the activities of Bion in 1973 and 1974 were dismissed. I had myself discovered the existence and odd status of the first three companies long before* and had first asked Slater what their function was in November 1974, pointing out that one effect of their status was that their investments did not have to be consolidated with those of Slater Walker (either for the purpose of the accounts or under the 1967 Companies Act requirement that a ten per cent holding in a third party be disclosed). Slater merely replied: 'It was useful to have companies outside the Slater Walker Securities Group such as Euroglen, Bion and Jaydean as they could, within certain rules, hold shares in companies without these being aggregated with Slater Walker Securities for consolidation.'

Just what the rules were, Slater did not explain; nor did he mention that these companies had another major function – to deal in the shares of Slater Walker Securities itself. Slater later explained to the investigating accountants that these companies' purchases of Slater Walker shares were 'related to a number of business objectives including the listing of the shares on certain foreign stock exchanges and the development of associations with several major commercial groups'. He went on to say that 'management believed these objectives to be in the general interests' of the Slater Walker group.

I had discovered that Euroglen had played an important role in the listing of Slater Walker shares on the Toronto Stock Exchange in

---

* I have not been able to trace Petershill Trust at Companies House.

the autumn of 1969, for the prospectus had disclosed that it had sold nearly half the 300,000 shares offered to the Canadian public – although no details about Euroglen had been given. Euroglen had started trading on 20 May that year and its £100 capital was held by sw Equities, the main Slater Walker dealing subsidiary, Tokengate and two small investment trusts controlled by Slater Walker, Consumer Growth and Unex. Bion, which we have already met in the flotation of Ralli International, started operations on 31 July 1969, and its capital was distributed in much the same way. The accounts of both were audited by Roff Swayne, the little firm that had been Productofoam's auditors, rather than by Slater Walker's own auditors, Arthur Young McClelland Moores, but the latter were auditors of Jaydean, which was formed on 31 March 1970.

Between 20 May 1969 and 30 September 1970 Euroglen dealt in over £9 million-worth of securities; and Bion sold over £2.5 million worth between July 1969 and 31 August 1970, although this must have reflected almost entirely its intervention in the Ralli flotation – the reason for which, Slater told me, could not be recalled. Jaydean's turnover is not given, but from incorporation to 30 June 1971 its total income was nearly £173,000 and in the following period to 31 October 1972 over £650,000 – the major part being dealing profits. But the income of these companies was always almost all eaten up by interest payments, for, having no resources, they had to borrow – from Slater Walker naturally.

Thus another effect of the status of these companies was that dealing profits were converted into bank interest in the hands of Slater Walker. Nevertheless there is no question that the objective of securing stock market quotations in Canada and Hong Kong was most useful to Slater Walker because it familiarized local investors with the group before it embarked on massive expansion in both places in 1971 and 1972. But equally, after the years of takeover in the UK, there was an enormous number of Slater Walker shares in issue and there can be no doubt that one of the advantages of these little 'floating' companies was that they could buy up Slater Walker shares when the price was relatively low, thus helping the market, store them and then resell them either when the UK market had improved or in new markets abroad.

The summary of the accountants' report states that they had 'found no evidence that either Mr Slater or any other sws director derived any personal benefit from any of the transactions' in Slater Walker shares by these companies. But the fact is that Jaydean, which had been formed in March 1970, had accumulated a holding of some £500,000 worth of Slater Walker shares by the end of November that year, when it resold all but a few thousand pounds' worth to the Hong Kong public. Therefore it had apparently been buying in a period when Slater Walker directors had, on balance, been heavy sellers. I asked Slater in early 1977 whether any of Jaydean's shares in Slater Walker had been acquired either directly or indirectly from his own or his family holdings or those of any other directors of Slater Walker, but he would not answer on the grounds that the matter was sub judice.* In July 1977, however, Slater said Jaydean only acted as a conduit to collect the shares which came from investment clients and institutions. He said that 'between August and November 1970 the investigating accountants found that Jaydean acquired 404,000 shares from sources that could not be identified. These would, however, have included institutional holders. The balance of Jaydean's holding came from sources and friendly holders.' In any event, the support given to the market by Jaydean's intervention would clearly have lessened the impact of the directors' sales on the share price.

From October 1970 Slater's own dealings in Slater Walker shares become even harder to follow, largely because of the intervention of two charities, the Slater Foundation and the Helen Slater Charitable Trust, which had been formed earlier in 1970. There was a complex series of transactions involving these two bodies, the upshot of which was that by the end of 1970 Slater's interest in Slater Walker shares had increased again by a further 43,336 shares to exactly one million; but 53,336 of these were owned by the Slater Foundation, about whose operations we shall hear more.

The FT Index did not reach its 'low' of 305.3 until 2 March 1971. But the Hong Kong flotation marked the turning point for Slater Walker – the end of the 'bear raid' that never was, for sales by IOS, Slater, and his co-directors were quite enough to explain, in the conditions of 1970, the collapse in the share price – and from that point the shares started on another eighteen months of giddy rise.

But 1970 had been a bad year. The new Heath government was not, at least in its initial phase, hostile to takeovers, but the reputation of conglomerates had reached a nadir. In the US Ling-Temco-Vought, to which Slater Walker had been compared, had collapsed, along with several smaller conglomerates. Slater Walker had declared its change of nature, of course, but it still retained many subsidiaries. We have already seen just how badly some of them, like Crittall-Hope, were doing in 1970; the appearance of improvement in the rubber companies was only achieved by the purchase of Cow at the end of 1969, and the disasters of United

---

*The Department of Trade decided to appeal the Magistrates' dismissal of the Section 54 charges concerning Bion and the appeal had not been heard while this text was being finalized. Slater argued that the affairs of all four companies were relevant to these charges.

Latex added to the problems experienced by Slater Walker's main textile interests acquired with Drage's.

Overseas, the only major interest to do well in 1970 was the South African subsidiary whose profits rose by over fifty per cent to more than £1.9 million. In North America, the Canadian offshoot did not really get going until 1971 and a Los Angeles firm, Creative Capital, in which Slater Walker had taken an interest, disappeared in the crash; and in the Bahamas Carden Withers ran into trouble and was sold to Security Capital Corporation and Butlers Bank, two companies which became intimately involved with Robert Vesco, the final 'looter' of ios. There was also a problem with the Argentinian subsidiaries of Forestal Land, the tanning group bought in 1969. It had proved impossible to resell these companies for their cost of £5.9 million as Slater Walker expected, and £2.3 million had to be written off Slater Walker reserves on that account. But the worst disaster area was Australia.

Australia had been a rich source of profits in 1969. It was the year of the great mining boom – Poseidon shares were still on their way up at the end of 1969 – and Slater Walker's wholly owned subsidiary out there, Thomas Brown, made profits of £1.7 million before tax, the bulk of it on a share dealing turnover of £17 million. Slater Walker (Australia) itself made over £2.6 million, after floating off its own satellite, Mining Finance Corporation, based mainly on its old coalmining subsidiaries. As its share price soared, Slater Walker in the UK was able to make another killing, selling a $7\frac{1}{2}$ per cent holding back to Slater Walker (Australia) at more than double the price it had paid.

But already by the end of 1969 problems were beginning to arise. Ian Murray, Slater Walker's Australian managing director, had ambitions of his own and there was, anyway, a basic conflict of interest between Slater Walker and its Australian affiliate. Quite simply the more money Slater Walker made out of Slater Walker (Australia) the less there was for the local company to put in its own shop window. The one million dollar fee for the help given in the Drug House battle had to come from its own coffers, and there was a rather more complex dispute about the redemption of some debentures that Slater Walker (Australia) had issued to finance that takeover. Slater says that each fee had to be agreed on its merits by the board of Slater Walker (Australia) and they always had the right to use other advisers if they preferred to do so and that this did in fact happen. The situation, however, was further exacerbated by the general anti-foreign business climate that was still growing in Australia.

Murray flew back to London in December 1969 to sort out the problems and it was then that the policy of 'Australianization' was hammered out. Early the following year, Tarling was replaced by Murray as chairman of Slater Walker (Australia) and Slater also resigned from the board, and the company's name was changed to Australian Industrial & Mining Corporation (Austim). Slater Walker through Brown retained a substantial interest in Austim, but as part of the deal Murray and other Austim executives agreed to buy personally some of Brown's shares in Austim. Brown obligingly lent them the money to do this – a total of over £770,000.

Having let Murray loose on his own – which some Slater Walker executives believed was an unwise move – Slater Walker itself quickly started to build up yet another Australian affiliate through another quoted company called Tagus. Into this would be injected other bits and pieces which Slater Walker had picked up in its takeover spree, like, for example Leggett Rubber, the Australian subsidiary of P. B. Cow.

Meanwhile, under Murray, Austim was quickly heading for calamity. The reorganization of Drug Houses had been carried out too abruptly, its traditional wholesaling activities being switched almost overnight to cash and carry to the annoyance of much of the chemists trade who turned elsewhere. Then Austim bought stakes in a number of quoted industrial companies which turned out simply to be bad investments. But, most seriously, it speculated heavily in the stock market, became over-extended and got caught when the fun went out of the Australian stock market just as it had out of those in London and New York. The spirit in which Austim had brashly chosen for itself telegraphic and telex codes of 'Swingin' and 'Swagman' soon turned sour.

It is hard to understand how Slater Walker in London could have gone through most of 1970 without an inkling of what was happening in Australia, but that is what Slater says happened. The problems only came to light, he told me, in September 1970. 'The point here is that it is, of course, easy to recognize a problem with hindsight, but in practice, a problem can exist for some time before one realizes that there is a problem at all,' he said.

Slater Walker, however, did not take up shares that Austim offered in a rights issue in July 1970, aggravating its associate's problems. The Austim shares price had soared to a high of over $A12 as Murray had got to work: on the failure of the issue it collapsed. But Slater Walker was in too deep to let its Australian affiliate crash completely, for although it had sold shares on the way up, taking a profit of over £450,000, it was still left with a huge investment, much of it the remains of the 1.4 million block of shares it had had to buy back from ios the previous March for about £3.4 million.

The way that repurchase had been financed caused considerable problems in the sorting out of the mess that Austim had got itself into, for Murray maintained it had contravened the law. There was also the problem of the loans to Austim executives to buy their shares. Not surprisingly it was only after a 'very difficult' board meeting in November 1970 that Murray resigned as chairman and managing director of Austim, ousted by his colleagues at the instigation of Slater Walker in London.

When Slater Walker came to assess just what Austim's position was, it was decided that there had to be write-offs and provisions of about £5½ million to cover capital losses and the fall in the value of investments and subsidiary companies. In spite of these losses, Austim's profits were still declared to have amounted to over £1.9 million. But Slater Walker had to pay off some short-term borrowings whose repayments had not been 'adequately planned'. Tarling rejoined the board, it was decided to merge Tagus and Austim, and relabel it once again Slater Walker (Australia). Slater Walker was 'facing up to its responsibilities', as Tarling described it to me.

But it really had little alternative. At the end of 1970 Slater Walker owned 23.6 per cent of its tottering Australian affiliate, the large majority of it – twenty-two per cent – via Thomas Brown, an investment which had cost over £6½ million. On top of this Brown had advanced over £800,000 to Austim. But at 31 December 1970 the market value of the shares was under £3.9 million and the unrealized loss was considerably more than Brown's total capital and reserves. The shares were left in the Brown books at cost. By 5 March 1971, when Brown's auditors, Arthur Andersen, signed the accounts, the value had dropped to £2.8 million. Arthur Andersen decided to qualify the Brown accounts: the most recent audited financial statements of Austim, they pointed out, were for 31 December 1969. They had, they said, 'insufficient other information' to enable them 'to form an opinion as to the present prospects for the ultimate recovery of this investment'; and 'because of the significance of the investment' Arthur Andersen were 'unable to express an opinion on the accompanying financial statements taken as a whole'.

The accounts of Slater Walker itself for 1970 were the first prepared following a recommendation by the Institute of Accountants that any group which held between twenty and fifty per cent of another company and exercised a significant influence in that company's management should include a proportionate share of its results in its own figures. Although Austim clearly qualified as an associate – as companies which met this definition were called – at the end of 1970, Slater Walker nevertheless decided to treat it merely as a long-term investment, as it did all its other satellites, no doubt on the grounds that it had only just brought the erring offspring back onto a tight rein. Such long-term quoted investments had, since

1966, been carried at cost in the balance sheet and this was the first year since 1966 when their market value had fallen below cost – by some £3.2 million out of £22.5 million.

So Austim was in the main Slater Walker balance sheet at a cost of £6.6 million, but there was no mention of the qualification of the accounts of its subsidiary Thomas Brown by Arthur Andersen. Slater told me that 'quite different considerations applied in the consolidated accounts where the entire group reserves were available to meet any deficiency which might ultimately arise on the realization of the Austim investment'. He added that anyway the 'board were satisfied, after careful consideration, that no permanent diminution in value had occurred'.

In his chairman's statement Slater said briefly that Austim had 'suffered a major setback due to severe stock market conditions and management problems'. There was, he said, a 'long and hard job ahead to bring the company back to full profitability'. Tarling was already engaged on the task and was, no doubt, in a better position by then to assess the chances of recovery than Arthur Andersen had been some six or seven weeks before. But still Austim's own accounts, the absence of which led Arthur Andersen to qualify the Brown accounts, were not finalized until a week after Slater Walker's, and they revealed that a further £4.9 million had had to be written off.

Slater went on to argue that 'the major improvement in the value of the investment in Austim in 1971 justified the decision of the directors in respect of the 1970 accounts'. In reality the recovery of Austim, or Slater Walker (Australia) as it was now again renamed, was slow and it was not until 1972/3, when it was allowed a share of the huge Far Eastern dealing profits then being made, that its viability was secured. In spite of the measures taken in late 1970 and 1971 its profits fell again and there were further write-offs in the 1971 accounts. During that year Slater Walker increased its stake to over thirty-six per cent, largely because of a merger with the other Australian vehicle, Tagus, whose principal business was P. B. Cow's former Australian rubber subsidiary, Leggett. In spite of the fact that the share price had revived to some extent by the end of 1971 and that Slater Walker's new shares had for the most part been acquired at the nominal price of $A1 each, the cost of Slater Walker's total investment still exceeded its value at 31 December 1971. This time, however, the gap was little more than £250,000 and, Slater Walker having now decided that the Australian company was an associate and that it would carry associates at market value in the balance sheet, this was written off reserves.

Slater's justification of the decision not to write down the value of the investment in Austim in the 1970 balance sheet depended on the use of hindsight. In early 1971 it was obviously most important that

Slater Walker should persuade its auditors, Arthur Young, that the investment in Austim was recoverable, and that Arthur Andersen's qualification should not be repeated. The 1970 accounts already had to carry a note to the effect that the Slater Walker directors had been wrong in anticipating that the Argentinian subsidiaries could be sold off at cost, a decision they had reached in spite of the fact that the local auditors had said they could not form an opinion of their value. Another note indicating that the directors of Slater Walker were again prepared to reach an opinion when a leading firm of accountants were not might have raised considerable scepticism; and the possibility that Slater Walker might have to write down a substantial part of the £6.6 million investment could have had a serious effect on the Slater Walker share price. If the investment had been written down to its March 1970 market value, then Slater Walker's net asset value per share would have fallen for the very first time.

In early 1971, too, Slater Walker's method of accounting for the cost of many of the companies that it had taken over, using the nominal rather than the market value of new shares issued, was being challenged by the accounting profession. In January the Institute of Chartered Accountants proposed a formal change in accounting practice which would have forbidden the use of the nominal value except in the case of genuine mergers of companies of roughly equal size.

If Slater Walker had changed to the recommended basis its total assets in the balance sheet at 31 December 1970 of £182 million would have been increased by a further £35.5 million of 'goodwill', balanced on the other side by a similar increase in 'reserves'. What it meant was that Slater Walker had paid £35.5 million more than the net tangible assets of the companies taken over, even after allowing for the revaluation of those assets where appropriate.*

Slater Walker declared a pre-tax profit for 1970 of £12,161,000, an increase of fourteen per cent over 1969. It was much the smallest percentage increase since Slater Walker had been formed. Ironically much of the rise was provided by newly acquired industrial companies, the most important of which was Cow, taken over at the end of 1969. But there was also a selection of engineering companies

---

* The accounting guideline was not implemented at the time partly because of controversy within the profession and partly because of legal objections, but the issues remain under consideration. Slater Walker was not alone in using the nominal value, but the discrepancy between book and real cost was the greater, the higher the market value of the shares used; in fact, the change would have been most effective in preventing the use of inflated shares to make acquisitions. The practice of using the nominal value is not allowed in Canada and Slater Walker had to file additional financial information in Toronto stating the element of goodwill there would have been in its balance sheet if Canadian rules had been used.

which were later amalgamated with Crittall-Hope to form Crittall-Hope Engineering, and, of course, Walker Young.

On the financial side, the fastest growing source of income lay in the fees that Slater Walker charged its 'banking clients' – its captive satellites – for the advice and help it gave them as they started their own forays, under Slater Walker's supervision, into the world of takeovers and asset stripping. As a result the profits of Slater Walker Ltd, the group's bank, jumped to £1,792,000 in 1970 from £387,000. Although as a fully authorized bank it was entitled not to reveal its full, true profits, it is unlikely that this figure was struck after anything more than a nominal transfer to inner reserves.

As for its stock market activities, in spite of the difficult conditions of 1970 Slater Walker still managed to make some impressive gains. These could not, however, all automatically be credited to profit and loss account: for tax reasons, only the realized gains of subsidiaries specifically designated as share dealing companies could be consolidated in total profits. When I suggested that the distinction between what Slater called capital and revenue profits was arbitrary and that investment losses were debited to reserves whenever possible Slater objected:

> Long-term investments were purchased by and held in capital companies whose objects clauses in their Memoranda of Association were purposely designed so that the Inland Revenue would be satisfied that any disposals were treated as capital and taxed as such. Conversely dealing stocks were bought by and held in trading companies whose profits were subject to corporation tax. Thus the purpose of the investment determined what company made the purchase and on disposal the treatment of the profit or loss arising depended on whether the holder was a capital or revenue company.

Thus, when in 1970 Slater Walker repatriated the dollar proceeds of the sale of Hope's Windows in America and so picked up a windfall gain of £360,000 on the investment dollar premium, this was credited to reserves. But in most cases there was no clear-cut distinction of the sort that Slater suggested: Slater Walker, in reality, did not invest in some companies for their long-term potential and in others as short-term speculations. On the contrary, a seemingly arbitrary part of nearly every major investment in quoted associates or subsidiaries was put into the dealing companies, for realization as and when necessary or possible; and when the supply of dealing stocks ran dry there were ways of transferring more. No mention was made of any distinction in Slater Walker's accounts, where, as already stated, no indication was given at this time of the existence of dealing profits; and on at least one occasion Slater Walker publicly announced that a recent, important investment was long-term – when all the shares were put into a dealing company.*

At the end of 1969, for example, Slater Walker's holding in Ralli International was about equally divided between dealing and investment companies. The shares sold in the reflotation had come from one of the main dealing companies, sw Equities, and they had thus contributed to about half that company's huge dealing profit of £2,278,000 in 1969. But the next year dealing in Ralli International shares was taken over by Status Change Investments, to which over three million shares had been transferred (via Bion – another use of the 'floating' companies) at the end of 1969. These no doubt helped Status Change, which had lost money in 1969, turn in a dealing profit of over £1 million in 1970. Meanwhile sw Equities' profit in 1970 dropped to £974,000: a good part of this was no doubt made by selling off shares in Slater Walker's quoted South African subsidiary, of which it had owned about twelve per cent out of Slater Walker's total stake of 77½ per cent.

But Slater's best coup in 1970 was clinched right at the end of 1970. In a matter of weeks he had built up a 12½ per cent stake in Hay's Wharf, a company that was developing a huge site on the South Bank of the Thames. The idea had been brought to him by two property men who had secured some key development rights, but suddenly Slater sold out to another developer for a gain of about £1.5 million – much to the annoyance of the original promoters of the scheme. Slater says that only £300,000 of this went into the profit and loss account and he claims that this clearly indicates that profits for the whole year could have been substantially increased if there had been any strain to do so.

This deal was symptomatic of the improving investment climate and by the time the Slater Walker accounts for 1970 appeared, in May 1971, the stock market had recovered, and, as the *Financial Times* had foreshadowed the previous August, so had the prospects for Slater Walker. The problems of 1970 could now be forgotten, but it had been a shock. Slater's personal financial position had been safeguarded at least against the failure of Slater Walker by the sale of his shares at the start of the year, but nevertheless, as Graham Turner later graphically described it in the *Sunday Telegraph*, Slater had 'lived through his own dark night of the soul'.

* Haw Par International: see next chapter.

20 *The 'Dustbin' and other trusts*

The City and industry had naturally welcomed the return of the Conservatives to power in June 1970 and were pleased with the appointment of a businessman, John Davies, formerly director general of the Confederation of British Industries, as Secretary of State for Trade and Industry. But they soon found that the Heath laissez faire policy towards business entailed some fairly uncomfortable consequences. The government's refusal to bail out the Mersey Docks and Harbours Board in November 1970 cost City investors dear, and it looked as if the same was going to happen with Rolls Royce.

It was the failure of British industry's most famous name in February 1971 that pushed the stock market to its bottom. But the government now began to compromise on its 'lame duck' policy, agreeing, in the name of defence, to rescue the main aero-engine business. The policy was effectively buried in August 1971 with the salvage of Upper Clyde Shipbuilders.

By then share prices had risen by some forty per cent from their lowest levels. The market was given plenty of encouragement in Barber's expansionary 1971 Budget which cut personal and corporation taxes and created expectations of large increases in company profits. Interest rates were also reduced and, to the delight of stock market operators, the punitive short-term capital gains tax was abolished.

When these measures did not seem to be having the desired effect a further boost to the economy was given in July 1971, with the announcement of a public works programme and the lifting of hire purchase restrictions. In September interest rates were again lowered and then in October the Bank of England's new competitive credit control - or rather non-control - policy for the banks was put into effect. With that the stock market took off, rising some twenty per cent in the following three months; it went on to reach a high of 543.6, as measured by the FT Index, on 19 May 1972 - a rise of over seventy-eight per cent from its 1971 low.

Just as Slater Walker had made its name in the bull market of 1967 and 1968, following its shaky start in the difficult 1965/6 period, so it was now hauled out of its 1970 troubles by the resurgence of the stock market and its reputation restored. The Slater Walker share price, however, did not this time outstrip the market by the same margin, rising ninety-five per cent between the FT Index low in March 1971 and high in May 1972. Still, when Slater Walker shares reached their own all-time high of 412 pence on 1 May 1972, they had risen 194 per cent since those dark days of August 1970.

So by January 1972 when Graham Turner was writing in the *Sunday Telegraph*, Slater had recovered all his old confidence. His standing was, in fact, at its peak. This was the period of 'Slater Walker government' as Kenneth Fleet, then *Daily Telegraph* City Editor, had called it. Slater Walker was a large contributor to the Conservative party, giving £40,000 in the five years 1969–73 plus another £19,000 to various Tory pressure groups. Slater, of course, knew Heath and, along with other industrialists, was consulted by the government on policy matters, and while the lame duck policy in its extreme form might have been dropped, the emphasis was still on creating a climate in which the strong and efficient would prevail.

As already noted, Slater had been asked to talk at the Institute of Directors' annual conference the previous November. This itself was a signal honour, as businessmen are only rarely invited to address their fellows, the speakers being mainly chosen from other professions.

The guest list was especially eminent in 1971. It was headed by Anthony Barber, Chancellor of the Exchequer, and included Christopher Soames, then ambassador to France, Lord Goodman, then chairman of the Arts Council, Lee Kuan Yew, Prime Minister of Singapore, and Dr Billy Graham, the American evangelist.

As Parliament had just five days before the conference approved the government's decision to join the Common Market, most speakers made some sort of reference to the 'great opportunity' or the 'new challenge', except for Billy Graham who preached to the directors on the need for integrity. Barber also pointed out that he had already cut the top rate of tax on earnings from over ninety per cent to seventy-five per cent, as the Institute of Directors had previously urged him to do.

But the Conservative government had not yet reversed all the measures taken by Labour to make the accumulation of capital more difficult, and Slater, who chose as his main themes the importance of profits and of adequately rewarding managers, put in pleas for stock options, for further reductions in surtax, and for the restoration of tax relief on the interest paid on borrowed money. 'I hope that the next Budget will allow interest on capital as a charge against income for both taxation and surtax. This is particularly essential where the funds borrowed are applied by a manager in buying shares in the company for which he works,' Slater argued, for there was strong evidence 'that managers are at their most efficient when they have some form of stake in the companies they are managing'.

The restoration of tax relief on interest, in particular, was a matter of some controversy. The Conservatives had promised it in their 1970 election campaign but many felt, even in the City, that it was a dangerous and unnecessary sop to financial interests and that the promise would have been better forgotten. But in his second Budget in 1972, Barber duly implemented all three of Slater's recommendations – and soon seven Slater Walker directors, including Slater, were borrowing between them about £1 million from their company, 'in the ordinary course of business'. But it was not until the autumn of 1972 that Slater Walker reintroduced stock options, having only in early 1970 adopted a partly-paid share incentive scheme. This latter type, possible under Labour legislation, suffered from the disadvantage that the executives could lose as well as gain, for they were committed to pay up the full market price at which the shares stood on the day they were issued, for a nominal down-payment, at some future date, when the price might be lower rather than higher.*

With the revival in the share price Slater was once again lauded in the press, and he freely predicted that the stock market value of his company, around £200 million in early 1972, would grow to £1,000 million in the following ten years, putting Slater Walker among the ten largest British companies. Graham Turner encapsulated Slater's claim to economic importance and power: 'When Slater Walker gets to £1,000 m., Slater believes, it will own "a significant percentage of every major asset situation in Britain" and will have a profound effect on British (and subsequently European) industry "by helping transfer assets from the inefficient to the efficient",' and John Davis wrote in the *Observer*: 'Slater needs Europe and Europe needs Slater. There is no one on this side of the Channel who has a better grasp of how the Continentals should start restructuring their finance and industry if they are to get the most out of Britain's entry into the Common Market in 1973.' Slater had, it seemed, at last found the right formula for himself and his company: 'Now I know what I am and Slater Walker knows what it is,' he told Turner. 'Watch out.'

But what had Slater Walker become? In March 1972 Patrick Hutber, City Editor of the *Sunday Telegraph*, wrote: 'Slater of course started as the great industrial renovator, almost a one-man IRC. But he quickly found his true role to be that of an investment

---

* But when this eventuality threatened Slater Walker executives in 1975, a 'stop-loss' provision was passed.

banker, someone who I think is cleverer with money than anyone else in the world.'

International investment bank was the popular tag, favoured by Slater himself, for the new Slater Walker to emerge after 'one of the most fundamental and successful business reorganizations to have been achieved in the commercial world', as one stockbroker described it. It was not a merchant bank in the traditional City mould, for such banks, as their name implies, had their origins in the financing of trade – not an activity that would have met the 'super-profit' qualification. But investment bank, it was felt, was appropriate because Slater Walker held investments in a series of industrial companies – the satellites – which it advised in return for a continuing fee income.

But this was only part of the picture. Slater Walker was founded on share dealing, not on industrial renovation, and by 1972 it had reverted to type. For the Slater Walker that arose from the 1970 crisis was basically a machine for generating stock market profits around the world.

Slater Walker had erected a mammoth paper chain of companies in the UK, Australia, South Africa, Canada, Singapore and Hong Kong, each with its own stock market quotation; and this was matched by a string of investment vehicles, its dealing companies, unit trusts, investment trusts, life assurance companies. Shares were then churned around this complex, with the effect that the value of the investments once again lost contact with any growth in the underlying businesses, but was determined only by the malleable forces that rule share prices and the eagerness of investors to join any promotion bearing the Slater Walker imprimatur. As the *Sunday Times* financial editor Graham Searjeant perspicaciously wrote, in May 1972: 'The whole circus has become a machine that earns a lot of its profit by generating the premiums that boost its own apparent assets – a seething pyramid of escalating paper.'

To finance its dealing activities, Slater Walker could use the proceeds of the sale of its industrial interests as well as the capital extracted from them. But in addition, just as Slater had borrowed in the early Sixties to augment his own resources, so Slater Walker now also borrowed heavily on the home and international money markets, raising some £50 million.

The amount of money that Slater Walker managed for other people had also grown fast, after the initial problems of 1965/6. Slater Walker ceased to be interested in handling small private portfolios individually, and it found that it could much more effectively attract smaller investors by promoting unit trusts and, later, life insurance bonds. Also, as it built up the industrial conglomerate there was a useful captive market in the pension funds of the companies taken over. By 1972 the funds under Slater Walker's management had risen to £250 million from £50 million in 1968. It was not large by City standards, but coupled with the magic of the Slater Walker name and the uncritical press acclaim, it was enough to exert a considerable influence on share prices.

With the intensification of Slater Walker's own dealing activities and the increase in the money it managed for others, as well as the widening variety of its clients' requirements, all the old conflicts of interest assumed greater complexity and proportion. In order to chart some paths through the jungle of interlocking companies we must go back to the origins of some of Slater Walker's financial activities on which the fortunes of the group were now based.

When Slater Walker had first offered the Invan units to the public in early 1968, assurances were given to questioning journalists that the trust would not invest in Slater Walker's own shares. But such idealism was abandoned in 1969, when it became important to find firm homes for the large amounts of Slater Walker paper that had been issued, and by early November that year Slater Walker itself had become the trust's third largest investment.

The performance of Invan had been poor throughout the first half of 1969: the price had dropped and repurchases by investors were heavy, forcing Slater Walker to sell investments at bad prices to redeem the units. This culminated in the sell recommendation by *Planned Savings* in August. (See Chapter 17 page 257.) But steps were being taken to improve its record. New management was brought in – in particular Brian Banks, who rose to be director in charge of the investment management division – and, as we have seen, Invan was awarded some Oriental Carpet before its reflotation as Ralli. It had also got some Barclay Securities at the time of the 'injection' of John Bentley. Invan's largest investment, however, in early November 1969 was P. B. Cow, the rubber company that Slater Walker was in the process of trying to buy. Slater suggested to me that the investment in Cow had been made by the managers of Invan acting quite independently of Slater Walker's intention to bid for the company. I asked the manager concerned if this was true and he said he could not remember; in any event it is not credible that he should have stumbled across Cow, which it had always been Slater Walker's intention to bid for in order to rationalize the rubber industry, purely as an independent investment on its own merits. The fact is that it was useful to Slater Walker to use the trust's money to further its own ambitions – not that the unit holders could complain, for the high price that Slater Walker was prepared to. pay for Cow naturally helped the trust's performance. Still, once again the operation smacked of pulling oneself up by one's own bootstraps.

Slater Walker launched its second unit trust, the Slater Walker trust – later renamed Capital Accumulator – in early 1969. The timing was wrong as the stock market immediately fell, but it attracted another record response. In April that year, too, Slater Walker started an International Fund based in the Bahamas – and therefore not authorized by the Board of Trade – designed to minimize tax and exchange control problems for wealthy investors. Both proceeded to invest in Slater Walker shares. Invan, now renamed the Growth Trust, also increased its holding in Slater Walker shares, until they had become, on 5 May 1970 – just before the market collapse – its largest single investment at over five per cent of the portfolio. Ralli and Barclay Securities accounted for a further seven per cent, and these two also turned up in the portfolio of Slater Walker's fourth unit trust, the High Income fund, started more auspiciously in August 1969.

Slater Walker's next unit trust was not started until the autumn of 1970, after the worst of the market crash, and it was not until that year that the Slater Walker life insurance company first became really active. It had been formed at the end of 1968 to handle the pension fund business of Slater Walker's subsidiaries and associates, but it was also intended that it should develop on its own. The idea of launching an equity-linked life policy in association with the unit trusts – like the Equitas policy that Walker had helped start in 1957 – was rejected because it would not yield the obligatory 'super-profit'. Instead Slater Walker opted for annuity business, which became the basis for insurance 'bonds'.

The great attraction of these was that they required only the backing of fixed-interest securities. The key to the operation – not, incidentally, used exclusively by Slater Walker – was to invest in fixed-interest securities which carried conversion rights into ordinary shares, for then all the capital profits on conversion accrued to the proprietors of the life company, rather than to the policyholders. But there was a further advantage: the fund could invest in convertible loan stocks issued by associated companies and it could be arranged that these loan stocks were issued at high enough interest rates to enable the advertised yield on the bonds to be extremely attractive to investors when compared with, for example, the return on building society deposits. Thus more money could be attracted.

Slater Walker's third main method of raising public money was through conventional closed-end investment trusts. 'We entered the investment trust field initially by becoming investment advisers to Flag Investment Trust,' Slater announced in early 1971. Flag was a small quoted company control of which had been acquired towards the end of the previous year, whose capital Slater Walker had doubled and whose shares it was now reselling to the public and to investment clients, including the unit trusts, so that unit holders were now having their money twice managed by Slater Walker.

Slater Walker had in fact bought its first investment trust, Consumer Growth, back in 1966 and had acquired a second, Unex, the following year. But Consumer Growth had, at the end of 1969, been turned into a satellite, Sterling Guarantee Trust, the vehicle for a young property dealer, Jeffrey Sterling; and Unex was later sold to Despard at Cannon Street Investments. Of course Slater Walker had also acquired Tokengate in 1969, but that had the special function of making money for the boys – or, as Slater would have put it, 'incentivizing' himself and his co-directors.

The Tokengate share price was badly hit by the market crash in May 1970, as were the prices of its two main investments, Ralli International and Barclay Securities. These two still constituted the bulk of its portfolio at 30 June 1970 – although half the Barclay holding appears to have been sold for a relatively small gain of £11,500 – and in spite of the recent price falls Tokengate was still showing unrealized gains of over £360,000 on these two investments. These gains were to some extent offset by a paper loss on a new, unidentified investment, and Tokengate's total unrealized gains at 30 June 1970 were £338,000 on investments which had cost £383,500. In addition, the share dealing subsidiary had made a profit of £59,000 and as a result, even allowing for tax on the unrealized gains, the asset value of the shares had risen from the equivalent of 3s. 10d., adjusting for the share split, to 7s. 8d. As Tokengate chairman Buckley modestly pointed out in his annual review, this represented 'an increase of 100 per cent over the year which compares very satisfactorily with the decrease in the *Financial Times* Ordinary Share Index over the same period of 12.7 per cent.'

Tokengate appears to have sold its Ralli International holding shortly afterwards, the transfer of its 701,960 block being registered on 26 August 1970. The price of Ralli was fluctuating sharply that summer, not only because of the stock market collapse, but also because of a controversial bid it had mounted for the Fordham property and investment group. In June the price had fallen as low as 12s. but by the end of July it had recovered to about 15s.9d. and so Tokengate's total profit on the holding could have been of the order of £330,000.

How did Tokengate dispose of such a large block in a weak market? It has not been possible to identify conclusively to whom it was sold, but there is evidence to suggest that Slater Walker itself was closely involved. Slater Walker was itself a major shareholder in Ralli International and an active dealer in its shares; and it declared that on 18 May 1970 it sold an amount exactly equal to the Tokengate holding – 701,960 shares.* Then, after a number of intervening transactions, it repurchased 656,960 Ralli shares on 29 and 30 July.

Whatever the exact mechanics of the sale, the relationship between Slater Walker's own dealings in Ralli shares and those of Tokengate, in which the directors of Slater Walker had such large personal interests, was clearly fraught with conflicts of interest; and then there is the further question – how did the directors of Slater Walker dispose of their large blocks of Tokengate shares when they wanted to realize their investments?

As we have seen, Slater told me he sold his original stake in Tokengate, now 100,000 shares, on 18 September 1970. In spite of the fact that the Tokengate price had dropped from the high levels of over 30s. in early 1970 to about 13s. 9d., Slater still made a profit, he said, of over £50,000. It is unlikely that such a large block could have been sold in the market on a single day, and anyway the register suggests that they were not sold in this way because blocks of 100,000 shares can be traced passing intact from one nominee name to another.

One clue could lie in the fact that one of those useful little companies, Jaydean Securities, turned up about this time owning 170,000 Tokengate shares, having, it declared, acquired 100,000 on 16 November 1970. Jaydean bought another block of 100,000 on 29 January 1971, which after a few other small purchases and sales left it with 266,500 shares. It then sold 249,000 on 3 February 1971: where did they go? Again it is difficult to trace them, but the Flag Investment Trust, which Slater Walker had recently acquired and whose shares it was now busily selling back to the public, declared that it bought 243,000 shares in Tokengate on 26 February. It went on to build this holding up to over 300,000 shares by the early summer, an investment of over twenty-two per cent of the Tokengate capital. It then resold 250,000 shares on 15, 16 and 23 June 1971, and as the price had increased by about twenty-five per cent, this gave the Flag net asset value a flying start. The Tokengate share price was, however, to outstrip Flag's by far and among the beneficiaries was Slater himself, for he had rebought, as he told me, 137,250 Tokengate shares in May 1971 at just under £1 each. The records suggest that a Slater family trust may also have bought a similar holding, for the NCB Trust acquired 137,250 at about the same time. The NCB Trust also dealt heavily directly in Ralli International shares in 1970/2.

In the year to 30 June 1971 Tokengate realized total gains of £667,000, its dealing subsidiary made £95,000 and there were

---

* This deal was not notified, according to the ten per cent register, until 24 July, although the 1967 Act requires such transactions to be notified within fourteen working days.

further unrealized gains of £171,000. After tax the net asset value had jumped from 38p. to 67½p. Just how the proceeds of the sales of Ralli and Barclay were reinvested is not fully clear, although Tokengate had acquired a big holding of some 200,000 shares in another Slater Walker satellite called Drakes, run by a young promoter, Christopher Selmes. But Tokengate had also acquired a large stake in the brewers Watney Mann, the subject of much takeover speculation. Since Watney Mann was not an associate of Slater Walker, this investment further undermines Slater's explanation of Tokengate as an 'incentive' scheme directed towards companies associated with the main group.

In the summer of 1971 Tokengate was let in on the ground floor of Slater Walker's next overseas satellite, Slater Walker of Canada. This same technique was applied to the launching of this company as had been used so successfully in Australia back in 1967. In April 1971 Slater Walker bought control – fifty-seven per cent, or about 53,500 shares – of a small company, listed on the Toronto and Montreal Exchanges, called Stanley Brock, whose main business was a laundry and dry cleaners in Winnipeg. The cost was $15 a share, a total of $803,000 or about £330,000.

In July 1971 Brock's name was changed to Slater Walker of Canada and its shares were split into three, so that Slater Walker now had some 161,000. But even before then – before the new offshoot had done anything – the magic of the Slater connection had driven the shares up fourfold from Slater Walker's original purchase price of $5, adjusted for the split, to over $20. Slater Walker of Canada now decided to raise more capital by offering its shareholders the right to subscribe for two new shares for every one held: the price was appealingly set at only $5, the same price that Slater Walker had paid for its initial investment.

Slater Walker itself was entitled to subscribe for 323,133 of the new shares, but it immediately resold 166,969 of these, at the $5 price, to three of its 'investment clients': Tokengate got 56,268 costing $281,340 (about £117,000); Flag 43,200 for $216,000; and the International Fund 67,500 for $337,000. Tokengate, the Canadian public was told shortly afterwards in a section of a prospectus purporting to give the 'interest of management and others in material transactions', was 'a listed English investment company, the shares of which are beneficially owned by Slater Walker Securities and associates to the extent of 35 per cent': not a word about the directors' personal interests.* Furthermore Slater's claim that

---

* It is impossible to say what was included in this percentage. There is no evidence that Slater Walker itself had bought any Tokengate shares since it disposed of the rest of its holding at the end of 1969. If the 'associates' are in fact the directors, then this means that some of the directors had sold out during 1970 and 1971, as previously they had held over fifty per cent.

Tokengate provided a simple and practicable way of restricting the directors from dealing directly on the market should be viewed in the light of the fact that he personally, in addition to his indirect interest via Tokengate, had bought 1,000 Brock shares on the way up in June, which had multiplied into 9,000 Slater Walker of Canada shares. Their cost had been $60,000, but by the end of 1971 they were worth double that. Slater says that he bought the shares because he was chairman of Slater Walker of Canada at the appropriate time, and 'obviously had a shareholding in the company to demonstrate his confidence and involvement in it.'

Slater Walker of Canada had started on its own series of takeovers and Slater Walker's investment in the new satellite, which had cost less than $1.6 million, was valued at over $4 million by the end of 1971. Slater Walker of Canada first bought a large holding in Peoples Department Stores and then, in December 1971, proposed a merger with a quoted investment company called Unas. Slater Walker in London had already bought up twenty-two per cent of Unas in the market, on behalf of itself and certain unnamed investment clients, and the terms of the deal not only produced an immediate gain of over $200,000 on the investment but also yielded an underwriting fee for Slater Walker of a further $265,000. This was the lucrative satellite system at work again.

The merger with Unas became effective in June 1972, and shareholders in the original Slater Walker of Canada received two shares in a new Slater Walker of Canada for each one they previously held. The share price had nearly doubled again, so that now Tokengate had over 112,000 shares valued at $1.12 million against their original cost of $281,000. The International Fund however chose this moment to sell; already by the end of 1971 its holding of Slater Walker of Canada represented over twenty-one per cent of its total portfolio – and Slater Walker satellites in the UK and overseas represented more than two thirds of the fund's total investments of £1.9 million in one of the more striking examples of the incestuous interdependence between the performance of Slater Walker's trusts and the share prices of its satellites. The fund wisely 'felt that the investment should be disposed and the proceeds invested elsewhere', as they told the Canadian authorities, and the line of stock was sold for a profit of $1,282,500 or about £540,000 – straight back to Slater Walker itself.

The Slater Walker of Canada share price reached a peak of nearly $20 in early 1973, a rise, after adjusting for all the splits, of about eight times on Slater Walker's initial purchase price. The price then started to fall back almost as fast as it had risen. Tokengate was still holding a slightly enlarged stake in September 1973, but again there was so much fat behind the early rise that the investment was still the largest single holding in value and the price still four times what Tokengate had paid for it in the first place.

Just what happened to Flag's investment in Slater Walker of Canada is not clear; it was probably still holding it when James Goldsmith's Anglo-Continental Finance bought the trust in the autumn of 1972. But the investment had contributed much to Flag's remarkable performance in 1971. Its market quotation had risen by about eighty-six per cent that year, against thirty-nine per cent for the FT Index, and Slater wrote in his annual statement that Flag, 'we are pleased to report, was the best performing investment trust in the United Kingdom in 1971.'

Slater was being unnecessarily modest, however, for Tokengate far outstripped Flag, rising no less than 340 per cent in 1971. Indeed, as we have seen, part of Flag's rise was due to the fact that it had been allowed briefly to share in Tokengate's privileges with a twenty-two per cent stake. Tokengate did not pay dividends to its shareholders and was not, therefore, approved as an investment trust for tax purposes; that, Slater initially said, was the reason he did not mention it in his statement.* But Tokengate described itself as an investment trust in its own annual reports, and later Slater said I should make it clear that it would have been wholly inappropriate for Tokengate to be classified as an investment trust for the purpose of comparing its performance against other investment trusts. That, of course, I do not dispute because Tokengate was not an ordinary investment trust: it was an insider dealing operation for the benefit of Slater and his co-directors and other favoured clients, masquerading as an investment trust. Its price reached a peak of about 500 pence in the early summer of 1972, a rise getting on for 2,450 per cent from its adjusted starting level of less than 20 pence when the Slater Walker directors made their initial investments. At that point the shareholding of its chairman Buckley was worth some £500,000 and Slater's new holding of 137,250 shares was worth over £685,000.

In the autumn of 1971 Slater Walker floated off a new investment trust on the London market called simply the Slater Walker Investment Trust, or SWIT for short. Its purpose was to raise £22.5 million to invest in 'companies whose underlying asset values are in excess of their quoted market price and where substantial medium-term appreciation on the market price can be foreseen as a result of takeovers, mergers or internal reorganization'. This was a familiar Slater formula that everyone could recognize, and the issue went well. But with his second launching of a newly-formed investment

---

* Tokengate later altered its tax status after the 1971 and 1972 Finance Acts had removed some of the advantages referred to in Chapter 17. It also alleviated some of its tax liabilities by buying 'tax loss' companies.

trust Slater went just a little too far, and the first serious crack in the refurbished image appeared.

It happened, ironically, just as Slater reached the height of his public acclaim, in January 1972. That month, Slater offered his eager followers a creature called Dual Trust. The basic principle of the trust, that one half of the shareholders should get all the income and the other half all the capital appreciation, was neither new nor of Slater's devising. What was unique was that Slater Walker was proposing to sell to the trust, i.e. to the public and its investment clients, £17.7 million worth of securities at a potential gain to itself of £4,652,000. It was precisely the same technique that Slater had used – but less openly – in the 1964 to 1966 era.

The investment policy of Dual, Slater announced, 'will be concentrated on young, financially-orientated aggressive companies. A particular emphasis will be placed on companies which are investment banking clients of Slater Walker Limited' – a fairly transparent euphemism for the satellites. The shares that Slater Walker was proposing to sell off in this way included many of the old favourites – Allied Polymer, Crittall-Hope Engineering, Wigham-Richardson, Ralli International, Cannon Street Investments, Barclay Securities, Drakes, Hanson Trust. The price at which they were to be sold to the new trust was to be two per cent below the lowest level the shares reached in the market between 7 and 26 January 1972.

The reception that Dual received was distinctly cool by comparison with the usual enthusiasm displayed for any Slater project. 'One of the most sophisticated ways of selling off large lumps of stock the City has seen for a long time,' remarked the *Sunday Times*. 'Those who are uneasy say that London's lack of rules could have allowed Slater Walker, which is a giant operator in the market, to massage the market in these shares: so that when they are transferred from the company into the investment trust the company would realize a healthy cash profit that it could not have obtained by selling the shares into the market,' the *Economist* observed circumspectly, 'massaging' having become the polite term for share rigging.

The *Investors Chronicle* dismissed Dual as 'an exercise in pyramiding', pointing out that in addition to the capital profit, Slater Walker was proposing to collect an underwriting fee on the issue and a management fee of £150,000 a year for running the trust; it advised professional speculators to steer clear. In the City Dual was nicknamed the Dustbin.

Dual's capital was thirty million shares priced at £1 each, half of which would get the income from the investments and half of which would get the capital growth. Slater Walker itself subscribed for 7.45 million of each class of share, so that its net cash surplus on supplying Dual with its initial portfolio was £2.8 million. Slater Walker's investment clients put up £4.6 million and 10.5 million shares were offered to the public. In the face of the criticism there was not the usual overwhelming response of which a Slater Walker issue could normally have been assured at the height of a bull market: the capital shares, the more risky ones, plunged to a discount when dealings began.

Slater could not accept such humiliation, and support for Dual was organized. 'Pride then also entered into it,' he told John Davis of the *Observer*, and Davis went on to describe Slater's action: 'With typical panache he waded into the market and bought every share he could lay his hands on. It produced the desired effect. The shares have now revived . . .' The brokers, Sebags, produced one of their eulogies, recommending Dual principally because 'it can be seen that Slater Walker's investment reputation rests to a large extent on the success of this company and so no effort will be spared to ensure that success'. Slater Walker itself bought up another four million of the Dual Income shares but found the Capital shares no more to its liking than did others and sold four million of them to that useful company Euroglen, which also waded into the market for a further 900,000. By the end of 1972 the Slater Walker unit trusts also held over £800,000 worth of Dual shares.*

In many ways the spring of 1972 represented the true turning-point in the fortunes of Slater Walker. Apart from the Dual fiasco, there was the little-noticed departure of a series of executives from the Slater Walker insurance company. The reasons were complex; there were, for example, fears for the actuarial stability of the fund. Managing a guaranteed bond fund requires delicate matching of surrender and maturity terms with the yields of the fund's investments. Because Slater Walker effectively controlled the issue terms of the convertible loan stocks of its associated companies, it had no difficulty in ensuring that plenty of investments were available to enable its insurance subsidiary to offer highly competitive terms on its bonds. But there was a fear that if the fund had suddenly to go liquid to meet surrenders, it might then find it difficult to maintain sufficient income to meet the maturity values on the remaining bonds. But more serious were the fears that the fund might anyway have difficulty in going liquid because of the very heavy investment in companies associated with Slater Walker. The

---

* Brian Banks defends the purchases on the grounds that Dual was 'at an above average discount compared with other investment trusts and proved to be a successful investment'. Nevertheless the reason Dual stood at such a large discount was that the rest of the market thought it was a bad investment because of its portfolio of Slater Walker-connected companies – of which the unit trusts already had more than their fair share; and the only reason it proved a 'successful' investment was that, as we shall see, Slater Walker itself bought Dual back at a premium – pulling itself up by its bootstraps again.

investment policy of the insurance company was dominated by Slater personally and in April 1972 he had invested some seventy per cent of the total fund, then valued at £13.6 million, in loan stocks of associated companies – for example, £842,000 worth of Ralli International, nearly £1 million of Barclay Securities, £600,000 of Drakes, £600,000 of Allied Polymer, and so on. They were all showing substantial profits at that moment because the Slater magic was at its most powerful. But after the launching of Dual, the lack of any real connection between the market values of Slater Walker's associates and the 'fundamentals' of those companies was gradually but increasingly being realized: what if sanity should return? To allay such fears Slater gave an assurance in April 1972 that the life company would not invest in any firms in which the group itself owned more than twenty per cent of the capital, not a particularly onerous undertaking since by then Slater Walker had already reduced its holdings in many associates to below this level – although it is possible that the purpose of the Dual flotation was in part to ensure that Slater Walker's stakes in its associates was not in danger of exceeding this limit.

So Slater Walker's business methods had come under serious attack, both from within and without, and the question was being asked whether this 'seething pyramid of paper', with all its inherent conflicts of interest, did not pose a threat to the reputation at large of the financial community.

The stock market, furthermore, had risen over seventy-five per cent in about fifteen months and to many it was becoming clear that this rate of growth was bound to have its repercussions. But in the spring of 1972 there were other stock markets around the world that had only just started to move, notably Hong Kong, and Slater Walker was able to keep the paper chase going for a few months longer yet with a last Far Eastern fling.

Slater Walker had embarked on its Far Eastern adventures at the end of 1970, when a young executive called Donald Ogilvy Watson was dispatched to Singapore to see what he could find. He succeeded in purchasing control of one of the most important local firms, Haw Par Brothers, and the deal was announced in June 1971. Haw Par in turn controlled a bank and a newspaper, but it was known mainly as purveyors of a popular panacea named Tiger Balm. Slater Walker immediately sold the bank and the newspaper and farmed out the management of the balm business – causing resentment among the local establishment, as it had done in Australia, by the brashness of its tactics.

Slater Walker was thus left with a useful 'shell' with quotations on the Singapore and Malaysian Stock Exchanges. It quickly set about buying up other companies, the first of which was a local insurance group, Motor & General Underwriters, which also had a quotation on the Singapore Exchange.

In March 1972, Slater Walker and Haw Par set the Hong Kong stock market alight with the announcement of a phrenetic series of deals. First, Haw Par bought seventy per cent of a Hong Kong pharmaceutical company, Kwan Loong, whose shares were quoted on the local stock exchange; then, a week later, Haw Par bought sixty-five per cent of a small but quoted property business named King Fung and announced that into this shell would be injected Pendock's Fijian holiday resort venture, Southern Pacific Properties, in exchange for the issue of seventy million new King Fung shares. Southern Pacific was valued at about £13.7 million for the purposes of the deal, but when the stock market heard the news the price of King Fung soared, driving the paper worth of Southern Pacific up to £21 million – not bad for a day's work, considering that the Fijian resort was still in early stages of development.

The shares of Kwan Loong had also 'taken off for the blue azure', as the financial editor of the *South China Morning Post*, presciently grasping for his copy of Galbraith's *Great Crash*, put it. On top of all this, Slater Walker also announced a link-up with Hutchison International, a trading group with established Hong Kong connections; and Ralli, under Slater's colleague Horsman, was simultaneously announcing its own series of deals in the colony.

In this heady atmosphere it was not surprising that when Slater Walker proposed the flotation of a new investment trust in Hong Kong, which, like Dual, was to be fed with its initial portfolio of securities by Slater Walker itself, no voices of dissent were raised.

By comparison with Dual, Slater Walker Overseas Investments Limited, alias SWOIL, was a small affair. Slater Walker was only asking for about £3.2 million from the Hong Kong public and the portfolio it passed on to SWOIL was only valued at about £2.6 million. This time, too, Slater Walker allowed a discount of ten per cent on the market value and also exchanged the securities entirely for forty-five per cent of the capital of SWOIL without taking any cash.

The portfolio included shares in Slater Walker's Australian, South African and Canadian offshoots as well as Haw Par itself. SWOIL was also sold a line of shares in Slater Walker itself, but the Hong Kong public were not told who the sellers of these were. The local investors were in no mood to be worried by matters like that: SWOIL shares jumped from $HK5 to $HK6.35 (about 44 pence) on 17 March 1972, the day dealings started, and the financial editor of the *South China Morning Post* again aptly summed it up: 'All in all, Slater Walker made the Hong Kong stock market yesterday'; and, of course, overnight Slater Walker had not only recovered the ten per cent discount on its investments but made a further seventeen per cent gain.

In the following months, Hong Kong share prices soared to absurd heights: between the end of March 1972 and its peak eleven months later, the Hong Kong stock market rose about fivefold. Slater Walker reshuffled its interests there at the end of 1972, putting them all under the umbrella of Kwan Loong, which was then renamed Slater Walker (Hong Kong). Included in the deal was Slater Walker's investment in SWOIL, which it had by then reduced to thirty-five per cent; nevertheless this had jumped in paper value to well over £6 million.

Back in the UK, Slater Walker had, by the summer of 1972, launched three more unit trusts, one of which was based in Jersey, and two new investment trusts which Slater Walker had floated in London – the Slater Walker Australian Investment Trust and the Slater Walker Far Eastern Investment Trust.

The flotation of the latter, designed to allow British clients and other investors to join in the Far East upsurge, nearly ran into a last-minute disaster. The prospectus, offering £6 million worth of shares, was filed on 7 June 1972, but no money had been subscribed before 23 June when the Bank of England announced 1) that the pound was to float, and 2) that the sterling area was to be abolished and that all new investments in the old sterling area countries would henceforth have to go through the investment dollar market. If the Far Eastern trust had had to pay the premium on such currency, now fluctuating wildly around twenty to twenty-five per cent, the whole operation would be threatened. Slater Walker hurriedly started negotiations with the Bank of England and on 29 June Slater told Tarling: 'We are free to invest all the funds before 31 July 1972 in normal exchange and then when we sell obtain the benefit of the premium.' Justifiably jubilant, Slater added: 'This is wonderful news.'

More significant, however, is how, with the deadline set for its investments, the new trust went about selecting its portfolio. The trust had only three directors, Brian Banks and two other executives of the investment department, and the prospectus stated that these three:

> . . . believe that opportunities exist to achieve capital growth through the investment of the Company's funds in the Far East and propose to create an investment portfolio which is well diversified both as regards geographical location within the Far East and as regards areas of business activity. They intend that the Company's portfolio should be concentrated on the securities of leading companies incorporated in the Far East and quoted on the Stock Exchanges of the Far East.

The initial proposals for the portfolio, however, were not drawn up by the directors of the trust but by Richard Tarling, main board director of Slater Walker and chairman of Haw Par. He listed a portfolio for Banks and sent it to him with the comment that it would 'absorb the total £6,000,000 solely from stocks already in house', i.e. already owned by Slater Walker group companies, in particular Haw Par.

The following day, 30 June 1972, there was a meeting between Tarling, Banks and Ogilvy Watson, Haw Par's managing director, at which it was agreed that Banks and Ogilvy Watson were to liaise to finalize an initial portfolio of 'house stocks' based on Tarling's list 'but amended as necessary

i) in the light of Haw Par's profit realization and strategic requirements.

ii) in the light of the Far East Trust's general investment requirements.'

The portfolio was finalized at a meeting on 3 July 1972 at which Slater was also present, and the shares, in six companies associated with Haw Par (including 800,000 Kwan Loong), were sold to the trust out of Haw Par's own holdings on 7 July at ruling market prices – and a profit of over £1.4 million to Haw Par. Shortly afterwards Slater Walker also sold the Far East trust 600,000 shares from its own holding of Haw Par itself – at a profit of over £350,000 – while Slater Walker Australia sold it a further 400,000 Haw Par shares.

The episode demonstrates clearly enough the order of priority at Slater Walker. Slater commented:

> The key factor was quite clearly that investment had to be made quickly by the Far Eastern Investment Trust to meet the deadline date of 31 July 1972. To invest through the market would have been difficult if not impossible in the time. Shares were therefore made available from within the group and, as the principal Far Eastern company, Haw Par naturally supplied most of them. Obviously they would only supply shares that fitted their own profit requirements. The fact that an instant portfolio could be made available was a great financial advantage to shareholders in the trust, as was subsequently tangibly demonstrated when it was sold to Anglo-Continental.

There were, however, many other examples of 'house stocks' being sold directly to trusts both in the Far East and elsewhere, and, while the dollar premium deadline may have added a special urgency to the transaction, the transfers by-passing the market were in no way exceptional at Slater Walker. More specifically it also turned out that Ogilvy Watson had been under the illusion that Haw Par would have to provide the stocks at a discount of perhaps ten per cent on the market price and when Tarling – not, it should be noted Banks – told him that this would not be required he was naturally 'quite happy'. It is true that when the Far Eastern trust was bought by James Goldsmith's Anglo-Continental in early 1974 the net asset value per share still stood at more than fifty per cent above the launching price, but a good part of this simply reflected the generosity of the Bank of England in handing out an imediate appreciation equivalent to the dollar premium on the entire portfolio. In any event, the main significance of the episode is that it shows that the claimed independence of the investment department was a myth.

All the unit trusts, of course, invested in Slater Walker associates and investment trusts; but if the whole operation was beginning to lose touch with any real underlying values and to look dangerously self-supporting, at least while markets were still going up Slater Walker was able to make money for everyone, even if some, like Tokengate, made more than others. All the unit trusts appreciated by a comfortable margin over the FT Index in 1972, and the *Observer* twice selected Slater Walker as 'Manager of the Year' in the early Seventies.

Slater also turned to dealing in shares for charity. We have seen that in 1970 two charitable organizations were formed, the Slater Foundation, which invested in a block of Slater Walker shares, and the Helen Slater Charitable Trust. Slater started the Foundation off with an initial gift of £25,000, but by early 1973 its resources had risen to nearly £800,000. These had largely been accumulated from donations made to the Slater Foundation by the Helen Slater Charitable Trust out of profits made by two investment dealing subsidiaries, Canossa Securities and Duovale, and two property subsidiaries. Slater explained that this arrangement had been made to meet the tax requirement that a registered charity must donate all its income each year – fulfilled by the Helen Slater Trust donating its income to the Slater Foundation, which received it as capital – and in order to allow a period during which the Foundation's resources could be built up. 'Now that a substantial capital base has been established in the Foundation, it is intended that the Foundation will make donations not only of its annual income as it arises, but also out of the accumulated profits which have been built up,' he told me. Indeed, it was the main sponsor of the First World Games for Multi-Disabled.

Slater Walker shares hit their next high point of 412 pence on Monday 1 May 1972. By the end of the week they had fallen back slightly, and on Friday Slater bought 100,000 shares at 390 pence each. That Sunday John Davis quoted Slater in the *Observer* talking about his own company: 'The fundamentals will show through in the end, and the fundamentals are good. We are building a formidable platform for the future.' As for UK shares generally, it was time for 'cautious investment', Slater told Davis. Slater, Davis wrote, thought that the *Financial Times* Index could hit 700 (it was then 531.6): 'But that sort of rise is not for me,' Davis quoted Slater. 'I want more than that.'

Three days later the well-informed City Editor of the *Daily Mail*, Patrick Sergeant, advised his readers: 'On the whole, why not stick to the old saw: "Sell in May and go away". Cash is unfashionable but, before too long, you may be awfully glad you've got it.' The *Mail* even suggested it might be wise to keep a gold Krugerrand under the bed.

The FT Index continued to rise for a few days more, reaching its high of 543.6 on 19 May 1972. There was no sudden collapse as there had been two years before, but share prices began to fluctuate. That summer's foreign exchange crisis, the deterioration in the balance of payments aggravated by another dock strike, the tightening of monetary control, all helped to establish a gradual downward trend.

In the summer of 1972, too, a new, strange factor began to affect share prices: a growing, general public reaction against the activities of financial operators.

The 1971/2 stock market boom had been accompanied by a new wave of takeovers. Slater Walker had only made a few bids itself, mainly for financial purposes, like the acquisition of insurance companies or properties. But the Slater Walker satellites had been active once again in the industrial field, and it was the depredations of John Bentley, Slater's acolyte at Barclay Securities, in Britain's toy and film industries that brought the public antagonism to a head and earned Bentley the title of No.1 asset stripper.

Concern, too, was once again aroused over mergers which appeared to have no industrial logic to justify them. The prime example of this was the merger, in the autumn of 1972, of Horsman's Ralli International and the Bowater Paper Corporation. Absurdly vague reasons were given for this marriage in the official documents, and Rober Heller succinctly commented in the *Investors Guardian* that: 'Any resemblance between flogging commodities, which is Ralli's stock in trade, and making paper, which (for its sins) accounts for virtually all of Bowater's profit, is strictly coincidental.'

Heller also pointed to the 'prodigies of self-denial and secrecy the Slater camp must have had to perform' in the course of the Ralli/Bowater negotiations arising from the fact that Slater Walker controlled fifteen per cent of the shares of Ralli and twelve per cent of those of Bowater, many of them held in the unit trusts, and was acting as financial advisers to Ralli. One of Slater Walker's main objectives during the boom was to seek out potential takeover targets in this way and 'to build up a holding that would make its cooperation vital in case someone else made a takeover bid', as the American business magazine *Fortune* described it. Slater would direct all the available money into the shares of potential victims, using unit and investment trust funds as well as Slater Walker's own resources. The use of the latter brought the added advantage of surprise, for the trusts' holdings did not have to be aggregated with Slater Walker's own when it came to declaring interests in excess of ten per cent – one variation of the practice that was labelled 'warehousing' in the City.

Slater objected to this suggestion that he used the trusts under Slater Walker's control in this way, and Banks, the investment director, told me that: 'There was never at any time a conscious policy to warehouse stocks but if we were offered a particularly attractive stock we would always be prepared to invest substantial amounts in order to get the fullest return.' Slater also said that Banks could have rejected any stock if he had thought it appropriate to do so, that in many cases Slater Walker itself bought shares that were not in the unit trusts and vice versa, and that Banks had the final say on unit trust investment. He says: 'There were many instances of Brian Banks refusing stocks. Far Eastern Trust, for example, was an exceptional happening. Even in this case Banks could have rejected any stock if he thought it proper to do so. In this case there was an overriding requirement for an almost instant portfolio.' But the conclusion of my investigation is that this is not an accurate picture of the relationship. Certainly the investment department was free to deal as it wished in shares that were of no interest to Slater, but when it came to the shares of Slater Walker satellites, associates or other chosen targets, the investment department had to do what it was told. If Slater offered the department a line of stock, it had to be attractive: it was an offer that could not easily be refused.

By the autumn of 1972 there was widespread concern over the issue of warehousing, which in its extreme form meant simply paying a friendly institution a straight commission for holding shares for you, shares either in a third company while you built up a stake of over ten per centt, or even in your own company when you wanted to prevent large blocks hitting the market. Concern too had grown over nominee names, which could be used both in warehousing and to cover the abuse of 'insider trading' – the use of confidential or privileged information to make secret dealing profits. It was this concern that led Walker on his appointment to the Department of Trade and Industry to promise a reform of company law in November 1972.

That same month Slater himself entered the controversy. In an article in the *Financial Times* he advocated wide changes in the law himself: he recommended in particular stricter control of insider trading and a broader definition, in law, of what constituted control of ten per cent of a company. He was, in fact, suggesting that warehousing should be stopped, and to make his proposed changes effective Slater went so far as to recommend that the use of nominee names should be banned. 'If the City of London is, as I hope, going to become the financial centre of Europe, it is vitally important that we strengthen our company law now so that it will be an example to all and become respected both nationally and internationally,' he concluded.

The article was another misjudgement on Slater's part. At the time it was written, Slater Walker was busily building up, through its trusts and associates as well as itself, and using nominee names – including Tiger Nominees, which had acted for the Leyland executives' investment club in the old days – an undeclared stake of about twenty-five per cent in a glass manufacturing company called Rockware. When this came to light, first in an article in the *Guardian* in December 1972 and later by admission, Slater's failure to practise what he preached could hardly be described as setting a good example. When a correspondent to the *Financial Times* wrote that it seemed Slater's thinking might have changed since he had published his article, Slater replied: 'Any new law would apply equally to all professional and other investors. In the meantime I am not prepared to penalize our Investment Department and ask them to act in isolation in accordance with my own personal view of what the law ought to be.' It was a lame excuse.

By the end of 1972 the FT Index had only fallen about seven per cent from its May peak. The first sickening slump in share prices took place in the first few weeks of 1973. On 23 January, when the Index was down to 478.2, the *Daily Mail* spread more gloom: 'Jim Slater says shares are still too high,' warned the City Page headline, but Sergeant reported that Slater was 'happy at the posture of Slater Walker who have been going liquid ever since we agreed last May was a month to sell in and go away'. In 1972 in fact Slater Walker had reduced its investments in UK companies, excluding its own direct associates, by some forty per cent, and in doing so had realized – it was later revealed – £9.2 million of dealing profits, of which no less than £8.1 million had been taken in the first half of 1972, as the market reached its peak.

But Slater Walker was still asking for public money to invest. (Slater said that so were many other similar organizations; but their chiefs were not publicly declaring it was better to be liquid.) At the end of November 1972, Slater Walker had launched its latest investment vehicles on the public, the Whinsparken Investment Trust, which was to invest in smaller quoted companies, and the Status Change unit trust. It was like a voice from the past as the promotional literature announced:

We believe that there are many companies with below-average

price/earnings ratios which, in view of their past records. and future prospects, are sounder investments than shares with more glamorous ratings. Fuller acknowledgement of the excellent prospects of these companies could result in considerably higher ratings by the stock market and consequent capital appreciation.

By the middle of February 1973 Status Change had invested a slice of the rather meagre sum the public had subscribed in the shares of Slater Walker. That Slater Walker should have to categorize its own shares, once the most glamorous of them all and now down forty per cent from their peak, as a 'candidate for an upward status change' was humiliating enough. As it was, Slater Walker was due for a status change all right, but it was not in an upwards direction.

21   *Retreat into cash*

On the morning of Thursday 26 April 1973 discreet telephone calls were made to selected financial journalists summoning them to 100 Wood Street, the City headquarters of the banking firm of Hill Samuel, to hear 'something big'. By the time they arrived, the news was out: Hill Samuel and Slater Walker were to merge. 'Together they will form a comprehensive international banking group with a market value of £250 million and capable of challenging the big American, Japanese and European banks. It will be easily the biggest British merchant bank,' reported the *Daily Telegraph*.

Hill Samuel's chief, Sir Kenneth Keith, and Slater together explained the deal to the journalists, and perhaps the first signs of the coming fiasco were to be seen at the briefings: which man was in charge?

Sir Kenneth Keith, at fifty-six against Slater's forty-four, was naturally the senior. He had the social background and urbane appearance associated with a typical member of an 'Establishment' family merchant bank. But Keith had not inherited his job: like Slater he had trained as an accountant and had built up the business of which he was head. He, too, had in his time been called a buccaneer.

The growth of Hill Samuel had also been to some extent based on takeovers. Keith had joined a small West End bank called Philip Hill Higginson just after the war, and it was not until 1959 that he broke into the City proper by merging Philip Hill with a small City accepting House, Erlangers. But Philip Hill's big step forward was in 1965, when it merged with one of those typical family merchant banks, M. Samuel & Co. The merger resulted in considerable friction between Keith and the Samuels, especially Lord Melchett, Samuel's most important executive. Keith came out on top, after Lord Melchett had resigned to run the British Steel Corporation. Keith's ambitions had received a severe setback in 1970, however, when a plan to merge Hill Samuel with the giant Metropolitan

Estates & Property Corporation failed mainly as a result of City opposition.

Unlike Slater, though, Keith had been accepted into the City establishment. His bank was, in the first place, a member of the Accepting Houses Association, the coveted inner ring of banks whose credit is almost underwritten by the Bank of England. Keith had also come to be regarded almost as the spokesman for the City following his appointment to the National Economic Development Council; and he had joined the boards of many important and diverse companies, including Times Newspapers, Eagle Star Insurance, the National Westminster Bank and Beechams, while leading businessmen like Sir Charles Clore and Lord Kearton of Courtaulds had been invited onto the board of Hill Samuel.

Nevertheless in the subtle rankings of the City, Hill Samuel was rated slightly differently from the old family houses and, while a merger proposal with one of these would have caused considerable surprise, the immediate reaction to the announcement of the talks with Hill Samuel was that this would be an appropriate, almost pre-dictable merger, a reaction which explains why the talks had got so far.

Later, however, after Slater's resignation from Slater Walker in the autumn of 1975, it was reported that Slater had in fact tried to go into partnership with other leading accepting houses on two previous occasions. The first talks, it emerged, had been more than three years before with Lazards. This bank, part of Lord Cowdray's exten-sive empire which included the *Financial Times*, had been one of the original backers of the Slater Walker Industrial Group in 1964. But like Schroders, another original backer, it was very different from the bank that Slater Walker itself had grown to be: it was a true 'blue-blooded' establishment bank, headed at the time by Lord Poole, former chairman of the Conservative party, who had succeeded Lord Kindersley, a leading City figure and a member of the Court of the Bank of England. It would have been a most unlikely union, but the talks nevertheless apparently reached an advanced stage, only breaking down, it is said, after objections from Lazards' sister bank in Paris – although what should have led the French branch to oppose the merger remains a mystery.

The second more recent merger proposal was in its own way just as unlikely. It was to have been with Warburgs, the merchant bank created by Sir Siegmund Warburg, the pre-war immigrant to the City from Germany. Although Sir Siegmund had, like Keith, secured his entry to the charmed circle of the accepting houses by acquisition, his bank had never had a 'buccaneering' image and its reputation, at its peak in the second half of the Sixties, was founded on the one hand on its success for its clients in hard-fought takeover battles, and on the other on its management of international loans. This merger is said to have been turned down by the Slater Walker board, against Slater's personal wishes, although such action would have shown an uncharacteristic independence of mind on the part of Slater's directors.

In spite of these two previous attempts, the negotiations with Hill Samuel did not stem from a continuing quest by Slater to team up with an established City House. They originated in talks that Slater had been having with his old colleague Malcolm Horsman, who was now co-managing director and deputy chairman of the Bowater Corporation. Horsman's Ralli International had been absorbed by Bowater, as recounted in the last chapter, at the end of 1972 under the aegis of Slater Walker – and with Hill Samuel acting as Bowater's advisers. That merger accomplished and Horsman's expanded but still fundamentally weak commodity trading and dealing group safely lodged in with Britain's cyclical but sound paper manufacturing giant, Slater and Horsman planned to bring Slater Walker itself into the fold. The deal was all ready to go to the Bowater directors for final approval when to their surprise they were told it had been called off and that Slater Walker and Hill Samuel were going to merge instead. At the time the Bowater directors were somewhat annoyed to find that their financial advisers had taken their place and Robert Clark, Keith's number two at Hill Samuel, who had a seat on the Bowater board, in consequence resigned this directorship; but in the event the Bowater board should have been grateful for the narrow escape their company had, for writing off Horsman's ill-guided attempts to emulate his former chief's reputation cost the paper group dear enough.

For Slater the superior attractions of a deal with Hill Samuel were clear enough, quite apart from the fact that the alliance was, on the face of it, a more natural one. But it was a common characteristic between the two which led to doubts about its ultimate success – the dominance of the man at the top. In reality Hill Samuel was much less of a one-man operation than Slater Walker, with greater depth of management and, in Robert Clark, a man who was quite capable of succeeding Keith. Nevertheless, there was no question who ran the bank and Keith's position was a great deal more than the *primus inter pares* status of many merchant banking chief executives. The immediate question that everyone asked was, would Keith and Slater be able to work together?

Or rather the question was, who was going to get rid of whom? Under the formal arrangements Keith was to be chairman of the new bank and Slater his deputy. But, although Hill Samuel had greater total resources than Slater Walker because of its much larger conventional banking business, in terms of net assets Slater Walker was more than 2½ times as large. Therefore the merger was to be effected by Slater Walker taking over Hill Samuel by a new issue of shares and this would leave the old Slater Walker shareholders with a much bigger stake in the new bank than those of Hill Samuel. Slater, the younger man, it was said, could afford to wait a year or two, when Keith might be willing to cede full control.

Considerable significance, on the other hand, was attached to the fact that the new bank was to be called simply Hill Samuel: Slater's and Walker's names were to disappear completely from the full title. It was noted that Slater looked thin and had had a gall bladder operation earlier in the year. Could it be that it was he who was intending to bow out and was merely trying to assure a safe home for his group?

When Slater's earlier attempts to merge his company with established banks came to light, they were interpreted as evidence that he had for some years been trying to withdraw gracefully. But the fact that Slater may have wanted to merge his company with another does not mean that he himself intended subsequently to fade from the financial scene. In retrospect it is clear that Slater Walker needed a merger in early 1973; for Slater Walker was then essentially a façade for share dealing, and with stock markets around the world starting to fall dramatically, share dealing profits were going to be much harder to make. Indeed it was soon to be revealed that Slater Walker's profits were falling, for the first time ever, at the time the merger was proposed.

Slater naturally disputed this, and argued that less than ten per cent of the Slater Walker group's assets were employed in share dealing. But Slater's explanation is yet again misleading. In the first place, no less than forty per cent of Slater Walker's profits in 1972 came from share dealing – although this was to fall to just under thirty per cent in 1973. Slater says that although dealing profits of £9,205,000 were made, so that on this basis 40 per cent of profit arose out of dealing, for accounting purposes £5,385,000 of this was transferred to inner reserves (see page 335). But furthermore, even in 1973, it was later revealed, £33 million of the group bank's loan portfolio of £123 million to companies *outside* the group were for the purpose of share dealing, and so an important part of 'commercial banking' profits were also dependent on this activity. There was also a £3 million loan to Bion – neither in nor outside the group, so to speak – and then the 'major proportion' of the bank's loans to companies in the group were also for share dealing (and a certain amount of property), according to the former chief accountant of Slater Walker. So clearly the group's reliance on stock markets needed bolstering with some real business, whether it was Bowater's paper making or Hill Samuel's real commercial banking. But equally if Slater had pulled the deal off, there was no ostensible reason why he should not have continued onwards and upwards to positions of even greater influence from a more secure base. As for the Slater Walker name, it no longer exerted quite the same old magic – and it was becoming increasingly embarrassing to Walker.

It is the last great irony of the Slater Walker story that it was Walker who was the minister charged with the task of dealing with the growing public antagonism towards big business. Already in his time at the Department of the Environment Walker had established a reputation for being reasonably tough with property companies. His only serious political setback had been the affair of the 'inspired', or planted, Parliamentary questions at his ministry in the autumn of 1971. As we have seen, within days of his move to the Department of Trade and Industry in November 1972 he had promised a reform of company law and by January 1973 he was preaching a 'New Capitalism', in which the old ideals of 'laissez faire' had been abandoned and a new role found for government intervention. He told the London Graduate Business School:

> It is the task of government to see that the impetus of capitalism is harnessed to the interests of all the people. Capitalism should not be regarded as the means for a few to get rich without regard to the needs and hopes of the majority of people. The government must see that commercial activities are fair, open and just. The framework of company law must be correct. Practices which give an unfair advantage to a few to the detriment of the many, such as the practice of insider dealing, must be stopped. If major sections of the economy are to merge or the efficient firm is to take over the inefficient, it should be done on the basis of full information about the likely advantages and disadvantages for the interests directly concerned and the community as a whole. I cannot overemphasize the importance for the working of capitalism that it should be open, free and based on integrity.

There could be no room for the old Slater Walker in the new capitalism. The whole story is full of examples of non-disclosure and the use of privileged positions to make money which have not been adequately explained – dealing in shares that were being tipped in the *Sunday Telegraph*, selling shares at a profit to investment clients without telling them, boosting Productofoam's profits with secret stock market gains, failing to disclose the full extent of share dealing profits of Slater Walker itself, keeping quiet about industrial disasters like United Latex, directors borrowing large sums from the company without telling shareholders, making money by being in on the ground floor of promotions like Oriental Carpets and Tokengate, building up effective control of more than ten per cent of the capital of other companies without declaring it. Walker has, of course, said that he did not know all that was going on at Slater Walker, but the fact remains that if he had wanted to give one example of what was wrong with the old capitalism, he had but to name the company he had helped to found.

Over the past four years, Slater and Walker have had – and taken – every chance to put to me their own explanations of their activities. Those explanations have been incorporated in this book, more than 13,000 words of them. Slater and Walker do not agree with my conclusions, nor have they agreed the text of this book. I invite readers to return to these explanations and form their own views. In addition readers may wish to consider Peter Walker's most recent description of his involvement in Slater Walker:

I never owned other than a small part of the equity. My period with the company ended in June 1970 and during the period with the company I received a remuneration of £2,500 per year. I never on any occasion had an office at the company or even a desk. I was never involved in any press conference given by the company, nor directly in any of its publicity. From memory I never once wrote a letter on the company letter-heading. I was never a director of any of the company's main subsidiaries either at home or abroad. I was never involved in any of the negotiations for acquisitions made by the company. In the days the business was at Hertford Street I would perhaps call in on average once a week and have a half-hour talk with those who were there and I would attend a monthly board meeting. From the time the firm moved to the City I normally attended a two hour management meeting on Monday morning. I was made deputy chairman on the basis that the main shareholders and directors considered that it would be appropriate if I took the chair at the board meetings in the event of Jim Slater being absent. In fact he never was absent from a board meeting that I attended and therefore at no time did I perform any duty as deputy chairman. My relationship with this company was therefore never one of being involved in the detail of the company but one of being a person who admired the abilities and talents of Jim Slater and appreciated his friendship. I was able to give him advice and comments in a totally objective way. We frequently saw each other during this period on a social basis when business discussions would take place, and we frequently conversed on the telephone. It was therefore the case that on certain issues my advice would be sought as someone independent of the detailed occurrences within the firm. It was always made clear that I intended to leave the firm altogether and devote my future life to politics and throughout the whole of this period the great majority of my working time was spent building up my insurance broking office.

The reputation of the old capitalism sank even lower with the Lonrho affair, with its revelations of extravagance, tax avoidance and the intertwinement of directors' private affairs with those of the public company. The timing did nothing to help Slater Walker, for it was on 15 May 1973, just as the controversy over the Slater Walker/Hill Samuel merger proposal was building up, that Heath branded the Lonrho business as the 'unpleasant and unacceptable face of capitalism'.

Naturally, in view of the size of the Hill Samuel/Slater Walker merger, there were demands that it should be referred to the Monopolies Commission for further examination. Walker, obviously, could not play any part in the government's decision, and the matter was left to Sir Geoffrey Howe, Minister for Consumer Affairs under Walker. He decided against referral, but only after Sir Kenneth Keith had given three undertakings which indicated quite clearly that the Department of Trade officials had themselves formed a pretty clear opinion of the desirability of Slater Walker-type operations. They were:

a. It is our intention to develop on the lines of a European Banque d'Affaires and our policy will be directed to the long-term improvement of profitability, with due regard to the interest of employees, rather than to the realization of short-term gains;

b. We shall not without previous reference to your Department enter into any transactions which indirectly or through de facto control of companies create a situation that, if it had been created directly, would be within the terms of the Monopolies and Mergers legislation;

c. In respect of disclosure of shareholdings of 10% or more of the voting capital we shall adopt a broader definition than that contained in the Companies Act 1967: we shall include in calculating the aggregate holding falling for disclosure shareholdings of investment clients together with our direct holdings.

The *Sunday Telegraph* fiercely attacked the conditions as being 'in the interests of the Government's pathetic anti-capitalist strategy', but pointed out that they suggested a further reason for the merger: 'Did Slater feel that the Government climate was getting so hostile to any remotely vigorous operator that it was as well to settle for corporate status?' Clearly, a merger with Hill Samuel would not only bring Slater respectability and security but would also allow him to swap power based on publicity and charisma – power that was in decline – for power being the scenes; and Hill Samuel had £670 million of other people's money under its management against Slater Walker's £250 million.

Meanwhile opposition to the merger mounted. Slater had never really been accepted in the City, but this was not just the defensive rejection of an interloper. The City likes to be left to police and discipline itself: Slater's activities had helped swell the chorus of demands for outside government intervention. Even the City Takeover Panel, set up to deal with the problems and abuses of takeovers, had come to believe, for example, that insider trading could only be dealt with by legislation. Many were alarmed at the prospect that Slater might gain control of such a huge sum of money.

In the press, the opposition campaign was led by the *Sunday Times*, whose financial editor Graham Searjeant and reporter Lorana Sullivan had been engaged on a worldwide inquiry into Slater Walker. The *Sunday Times* had already in early 1972 described Slater Walker as a 'seething pyramid of escalating paper'; it now repeated its warnings of the 'dangers of a system where Slater Walker's dealing in shares dominated by Slater Walker produced a major part of its profits, while at the same time, the price of some of those shares, inevitably influenced by the dealings, constituted a major part of its assets'. In a series of articles, the *Sunday Times* raised a number of questions concerning the complexity and interdependence of Slater Walker companies, and the lack of information on which to make a firm judgement. It concluded: 'There must be serious doubts over the true earnings and assets of Slater Walker and whether a combination of the two operations will really benefit Hill Samuel shareholders.'

On the other side of the fence, Slater's old supporter at the *Daily Mail*, Patrick Sergeant, argued that the deal was not in the interests of Slater Walker shareholders, because it would just be giving away some of its enormous unrealized profits. But what clinched Sergeant's opposition was the belief that Slater and Keith could not work together: 'Both of these men are householders and masters of their houses to boot. They wouldn't get on and their staffs wouldn't get on.'

Sergeant came out against the bid on 18 June 1973. By then the Slater Walker share price, which had stood 240 pence just before the merger had been announced, had dropped to 185 pence. In the face of the mounting tide of dissent and a growing disquiet among the Hill Samuel men as they tried to disentangle the web of Slater Walker associates to get some idea of their worth, Keith and Slater decided to call the deal off on 19 June, announcing briefly that discussions had 'revealed fundamental differences of workstyle and personalities, which both boards now consider could prejudice the successful implementation of the merger'.

The whole affair badly damaged the reputations of both banks: here were two supposed experts in the art of merging companies that had made a mess of merging themselves. But Slater Walker suffered far more than Hill Samuel. This was to some extent the result of the *Sunday Times'* criticism: was it not clear, asked Mr Benn in Parliament the day after the merger had been called off, that Slater Walker 'had engaged in operations which called for further inquiry'?

But furthermore, while Hill Samuel could go on much as before, it suddenly became clear that Slater Walker was left without any obvious line of development. In theory it could continue with its complex dealing activities. For, in the first place, the undertakings to the Department of Trade lapsed with the dropping of the merger; and, secondly, Walker's White Paper on company law reform, published in July 1973, hardly presaged the sweeping changes that had been foreshadowed. To be sure it proposed legislation to deal with insider trading and warehousing, but it pointed out the complicated problems of definition in the former, and relied mainly on reducing the ten per cent limit to five per cent to deal with the latter, without trying to bring in the holdings of 'associates'. On top of this, the chances of effectively policing any new laws were somewhat reduced by the Department's view that there was 'nothing inherently wrong in the practice of holding shares through nominees'.*

But in practice there was no going back, especially in the deteriorating stock market conditions, and Slater was shrewd enough to see that. Indeed, in order to try to restore his company's standing, Slater decided on what in the circumstances was a brave move: he would meet the criticisms of complexity and lack of information with fuller disclosure.

On 4 July 1973 he announced that Slater Walker would in future not only reveal its true profits, forfeiting its banking privilege of hiding a part in 'inner reserves', but also give a fuller breakdown of their composition, which would include the contribution from share dealing. On top of this, Slater Walker would give fuller details of its investments, including the size of substantial stakes in public companies held both on its own account and for its trusts and other investment clients.

But the accompanying breakdown of Slater Walker's 1972 profits

---

* If all shares were held through nominee names there would be little point in requiring companies' share registers to be made public. The reason that they are public dates back to the Companies Act of 1844: it is 'so that the public would have the means of knowing with whom they are dealing'. Walker's Companies Bill was finally published in December and gave companies – but not the public – some power to get behind nominee names on their share registers. It also made insider trading, by directors only, a criminal offence. The Bill became a casualty of the Conservatives' defeat in February 1974.

did little to bolster confidence. The true figure, it emerged, was £22,977,000 against the previously declared £17,592,000; but the startling point was that no less than £9,205,000, or forty per cent, had been made by share dealing.

Slater explained that the 'very substantial' transfer to inner reserves of £5,385,000 in 1972 had been made 'in view of the high overall level of investment dealing profits and in particular the fact that substantial dealing profits amounting to £2.7 million arose from supplying the initial portfolios on the formation of Slater Walker Dual Trust Limited and Slater Walker Overseas Investments Limited, both of which could be regarded as exceptional transactions'. Indeed they were exceptional, but Slater Walker's total gain on the flotation of Dual alone had been £4.6 million. Slater explained that £1.9 million of this had been capital as opposed to revenue profits; this had been credited to the ordinary disclosed reserve, and Slater Walker's total capital profits, after tax, from the sale of investments in 1972 came to £3.3 million.

The revelation of the importance of dealing profits did nothing to help the Slater Walker share price, which continued to fall much faster than the stock market generally. It was given a further sharp push downwards when Slater Walker announced on 9 August that in the first half of 1973 it had only made profits of £11.9 million against £16.3 million in the first six months of 1972. Furthermore, it now emerged that £8,135,000 of 1972's £9.2 million of dealing profits had been made in the first six months of the year. In the first six months of 1973 share dealing had only yielded £4.8 million.

Slater Walker also tried to improve its image by buying back, at prices which showed a small profit to the original subscribers, the outstanding shares in the abortive Dual Trust. Later, too, it bought back swit, and sold off or merged the other investment trusts, none of which had met with a popular reception. But by now the speculation throughout financial circles was, what was Slater going to do now?

One theory was that Slater Walker would turn again to direct investment in industry, and in July 1973 Slater told John Davis of the *Observer* that 'it is true that we are going back into industrial companies'. It would be on a longer-term basis than before: Slater had already in the interview accepted 'as fair criticism that in the past we have dealt too much in the stock of our client companies and should have taken a longer-term view in many instances'. In other words, the Slater Walker of the future, like the Slater Walker of 1965, would hold long-term investments of substantial size in industrial companies whose boards it would furnish with advice.

Whether or not Slater really believed that he could revert to the original blueprint at this stage, it was not to be. Even before 1973 had ended, rumours were circulating that just about anything that Slater Walker owned was up for sale. Slater maintains that certain investments, for example in Rockware Glass, civil engineers Richard Costain and traders James Finlay, were intended to be 'longer-term subject to liquidity requirements'; but when the much publicized programme of raising cash – 'the optimum investment' – began in earnest in early 1974, the selling seemed indiscriminate. The first big industrial investment to go was Slater Walker's holding in Crittall-Hope Engineering; sold, then, were two insurance companies; sold were Slater Walker's South African interests, and its investment in Slater Walker (Hong Kong) – to its own associate Haw Par. The investment in Haw Par was then in turn sold to independent buyers – and so were sown some of the seeds of Slater's own demise.

Sold, too, was Thomas Brown, Slater Walker's Australian investment banking subsidiary. Its main investment was still a thirty-four per cent stake in Slater Walker (Australia), and this first overseas offshoot, which had nearly brought the whole operation down in 1970, had had another disastrous year in 1973. The total cost of Brown's investment in Slater Walker (Australia) had been $A19.7 million (£11.8 million); $A11.7 million (nearly £7 million) had already been written off reserves at the end of 1973. Now, in May 1974, the whole of Brown was sold off for just $A1,160,000 (about £715,000) and the return of $A4,750,000 (£2,930,000) of loans.

Sold also was Slater Walker of America – at a loss of £2.2 million. This, the famous Slater Walker assault on the US which had been foreshadowed as far back as 1968, had only been set up in May 1973; and just two weeks before it was dumped Slater told the *Wall Street Journal* that he was still trying to expand in the US. 'We thought we could do a Slater Walker in America. But we failed,' a director sadly explained.

There were naturally many reasons for the change of mind, for the decision to abandon the plan to go back into industry in favour of a 'reversal into cash': the miners' strike, the three-day week, the rejection of Heath and the Tories by the electorate and the return of a considerably more socialist Labour government than the one under which Slater had risen to fame, the slump in share prices, the onset of world inflation – they had all radically changed the outlook.

But still everyone wanted to know what the great financial wizard had up his sleeve. Two rival schools of thought developed: one said that Slater Walker was not nearly as liquid as it appeared and was raising cash in desperation. This school was able to point to the fact that the 1973 balance sheet was not as strong as it looked at first sight, for the massive £107 million investment in associated companies had been entered at cost rather than, as previously, at its stock market valuation of only £75 million – the same change that had been made back in 1966 when the market value of the Slater Walker Industrial Group's investments fell below their cost. Slater this time explained that they had changed the basis of accounting 'to that now used by the majority of companies'. But the great majority of companies had in reality entered their associates at cost in their balance sheets ever since the Institute of Chartered Accountants had issued their standard accounting practice instructions, which allowed either method, in 1971. The school might also have pointed to the note of unreality which had crept into Slater's statement that, because of an excess of net assets, in the opinion of the board 'these investments were worth more than their market value'. Assets are normally only worth what they can be sold for.*

The second school held that Slater was preparing to sell out, making his company attractive by filling it with cash to encourage a bid from a big bank like the National Westminster – perhaps hoping, too, that he would be invited to join its board. This theory prevailed and the Slater Walker share price, reacting as many a share had done in the past on the expectation of a bid from Slater Walker itself, held up rather better than most through the difficult days of February, March, April and May.

The chance at last to hear from the Master himself came on 30 May 1974; it was the eleventh annual meeting of shareholders over which Slater had presided, held just a month short of ten years after he had bought control of H. Lotery. At the Connaught Rooms in Great Queen Street several hundred people crowded in not just to hear what Slater had to say about his company but to glean whatever advice they could from the words of the Master in these gloomy times. Even his 'satellites' were there – Horsman, Despard, Hanson – as curious about Slater's intentions as the rest.

The meeting was no anticlimax. For an hour and a quarter Slater lectured his shareholders and the world at large on the merits of cash, the 'optimum investment'. Slater was relaxed and, as always, spoke fluently and confidently. The shareholders applauded: they loved him still, and had he not reminded them that he retained his Midas touch by revealing that Slater Walker had invested heavily in gold shares and had made profits of £6 or £7 million on them? But, as the *Financial Times* reported: 'His own question, "Where do we go now?" was never really answered.'

With Delphic skill Slater had covered all possibilities: he wanted to

---

*Slater commented: 'In the event all the investments were subsequently sold at prices in excess of market values at the time of sale which demonstrates that sizeable shareholdings have an additional strategic value.' But the market value *at the time of sale* was on balance considerably less than either cost or market value at the end of 1973: hence Slater Walker's plight.

be 'flexible'; to be 'in a uniquely strong position to take advantage of favourable investment opportunities when they arise'; he was ready to sell out, and indeed there had been 'tentative, nebulous bid talks'. He even hinted at disaster: 'The name of the game is survival.'

But he assured shareholders he would not abandon them. While he could not 'say to you in all trust that I look on capitalism with the same joy as in 1964', nevertheless he was 'feeling very well, feeling energetic and have never been as involved in the business as I am now'.

Financially this was true. We have seen that Slater had bought 100,000 Slater Walker shares near the top of the market the previous May to bring his holding to 1.1 million shares. This had been increased by a further one-for-three scrip issue in July 1972, but in addition Slater and his family interests bought on balance a further 283,337 shares at a cost of about £711,000. Furthermore Slater had acquired a slice of convertible loan stock for £221,250. So Slater had reinvested over £1.3 million in the company since the 1970 crisis year, although part of the cost of this could have been met out of an earlier in-and-out operation in the convertible loan stock in 1971/2 which had yielded a profit of some £300,000. Slater converted the second slice of loan stock the day after the 1973 annual meeting at 147p. a share against the market price of about 205p. to bring his holding to two million shares; a year later they were worth £2,680,000.

But Slater had realized considerable gains elsewhere. He had, he told me, sold his second investment of 137,250 Tokengate shares in two tranches in November 1973 for a total of £321,083 – 234p. each – and a profit of £184,217. Buckley, according to the directors' register, also sold 110,000 Tokengate shares in November 1973, on the 19th at 230 pence each – a total of £253,000 and a profit of £215,000. Tarling also appears on the main share register as holding 90,000 at this time, the transfer of which was registered in early 1974.

In the autumn of 1973 Slater Walker had arranged for Tokengate to take over, by an issue of new shares, another investment company which had been launched by Slater Walker's South African arm some three years before and called simply the Slater Walker Investment Trust of South Africa. As a result of this deal Slater Walker Securities (South Africa), in which Slater Walker in London then still held a substantial interest, acquired 835,000 new Tokengate shares on 16 November 1973 when the takeover became effective.

When this deal was first proposed in early September the Tokengate share price had been about 255p., but by 19 November 1973 it was down to around 225p. and by the end of the month it had fallen further to 195p. - and the Official Stock Exchange List records no deal at over 227p. a share during the whole month. The price continued to drop like a stone in the first half of December and on the 19th it was down to about 145p. That day Horsman bought 940,435 Tokengate shares on behalf of the Bowater Corporation.

In the autumn of 1975 Horsman told me that he had heard that I alleged that Bowater had bought its Tokengate shares to get Slater and 'the boys' out. I had, in fact, made no such suggestion, but I told Horsman that the thought had occurred to me that their Tokengate shares might have ended up with Bowater via those free-floating companies like Jaydean. Horsman replied, inconclusively, that he did not know from whom Bowater had bought its Tokengate shares. He said that he had acquired them for Bowater because he thought they were a good buy and he got them under the market price.

Just what the paper group was getting, however, was far from clear. At the time of the deal with the South African investment trust, Tokengate's portfolio consisted of holdings in Slater Walker itself and in fourteen other Slater Walker trusts, associates or satellites, nearly all of them long past their prime. In the event this portfolio was liquidated before the end of the year and proceeds reinvested in gold shares; but this change of policy was not announced to shareholders at the time – and it did not prevent Tokengate's net asset value from falling from 248p. on 30 September 1973 to 118p. a year later.

I asked Slater himself on 3 April 1976 if any of his Tokengate shares or those of any other directors of Slater Walker were sold to the Bowater Corporation, but he never replied. The evidence, however, indicates that the profitable exit of at least some of the boys from their Tokengate 'incentive' was facilitated more directly by Slater Walker (South Africa): for in addition to the 835,000 new Tokengate shares which it received as a result of the investment trust takeover, it went on to buy 100,000 Tokengate shares on 28 November 1973, 45,000 on the 29th and 110,000 on the 30th, according to the Tokengate register of substantial interests.

Reaction to Slater's peroration in favour of cash was mixed. The stock market took heed of his advice and dropped, reaching shortly its lowest levels since 1959. Slater Walker shares fell too. *The Times*, in a leading article exemplifying the awe in which Slater, in spite of everything, was still held, asked: 'If Mr Slater values cash so highly, how can any of the rest of us dare to own anything but money?' *Punch* declared that: 'If everyone followed Slater's lead (and quite a few companies are doing just that) the slump he predicts would come a good deal sooner.' More pertinently, John Gordon of the *Sunday Express* pointed out that at the same time as Slater Walker was selling up investments, including his American company, Slater was inviting the public to subscribe for a new North American unit trust.

'If cash is good for his company,' he asked, 'shouldn't Mr Slater explain why it is not also good for small investors whom he invites to part with their savings?'

The Slater Walker unit trusts had in fact been going liquid too, but the Slater Walker companies were for the most part the last to be sold. For example, at the start of October 1974 the Slater Walker Financial Trust, which had been started in 1971, was seventy-one per cent cash, but 23.5 per cent was in the shares of companies associated in one way or another with Slater Walker. Its largest investment – 6.79 per cent – was in that investment trust Slater Walker had floated in Hong Kong, swoil, which had shortly before quietly announced that in the year to 31 March 1974 it had realized losses of over $HK95 million (about £7.8 million) and had made further provisions of $HK10.5 million (over £860,000). In November 1974 Slater Walker sold out its interest in swoil, too, completing its withdrawal from the Far East, having in the summer already disposed of its interests in Haw Par and Southern Pacific.

By 20 August 1974 Slater Walker shares had disappeared out of the Status Change unit trust, but an interesting new holding, representing 7.36 per cent of the portfolio, had taken their place. It was a little company called Lubok Investments, and this one was scheduled for an upwards rerating: for on 2 September it was announced that Slater personally was to take over as chairman of the company and that he and some associates were to inject nearly £700,000 into Lubok, which would give them control of about half of its capital. The price was 10½ pence a share.

Simultaneously it was announced that Lubok had been buying gold shares since May and was going to use much of its new money in the same way. It was also going to buy up stocks of Krugerrands, the South African gold coins. Suddenly, everyone wanted to do the same and the premium over the actual value of gold in a Krugerrand shot up from around ten per cent to twenty per cent.

The Lubok share price also shot up as it started on its own series of takeover deals, tiny though they were by comparison with the heyday of Slater Walker. By late November the Lubok price had reached 33.5 pence, and Slater admirers were being overcome by fond memories; even the *Financial Times* was moved to comment that Lubok 'continues to evoke a delightful nostalgia by the way it is exploiting its share price'.

But the Slater Walker share price now tumbled; and not just because of the second great storm blowing through stock markets. For it seemed that in spite of the assurances given Slater Walker shareholders just a few months before, Slater was abandoning them. Indeed, as the *Guardian* pointed out, his shareholding in Lubok had become worth as much as his shareholding in Slater Walker. 'It is only fair to ask what plans Mr Slater has for Slater Walker,' commented the *Daily Telegraph*.

'Slater Walker is still the one to back as far as I am concerned,' Slater replied through John Davis in the *Observer*. 'There is no question of my abandoning it. It is my main responsibility and 90 per cent of my effort is devoted to it. I happen to have an investment in Lubok because I feel everyone ought to have in these uncertain times some of his money in gold. A proportion of my assets is in gold, that is all.'

But was that really all there was to it? Or was it the other old Jim Slater at work again? Since the annual meeting of May 1974 Slater had been urging one and all to get into gold. But, as the half-year figures had shown, Slater Walker itself had long been in and out of gold shares: in the first six months of 1974 the 'major proportion' of Slater Walker's £6 million of dealing profits – sixty per cent of total profits of £10.1 million – had been made in gold shares. By early 1975 the gold price rise had faltered; Slater even admitted to the *Sunday Times*, that, while he 'would be cautiously bullish about gold', he would 'trade it rather than hold it'. Slater Walker had got much the best of the rise.

In March 1975 Slater announced that Slater Walker had survived 'the year of the hurricane', as he described it to the *Guardian*: 'Survival is what it was all about. Look at the rest of the financial conglomerates – there aren't very many of them left. Through our cash disposals and determination we have emerged from 1974 with assets of £80 millions still intact.'

That Slater Walker had survived the crash so far was essentially the result of Slater's decision to start liquidating the group before the market had reached its peak in 1972 and to take the profit on gold while its price was still climbing. The gains on gold, indeed, accounted for about half the £14.5 million profit that Slater Walker still managed to record for 1974, against 1973's £23.4 million. But the cost had been high: some £30 million had been written off the value of the group's investments as a result of the sales and the fall in share prices, although the impact of the damage was softened by financing these losses from reserves.

But the speculation continued: what was the shape of the Slater Walker that had survived, and where, still, could it go? In the summer of 1975 the only discernible pattern was that Slater Walker was intent on keeping a lot of other people's money under its control; for it had bought about thirty-five unit trusts from former rivals Jessel Securities and Triumph Investment Trust (which had already absorbed Sir Denys Lowson's National Group), which had not managed to keep themselves from being eliminated in the storm. To Slater 'the shape was irrelevant to its surviving,' as he told the *Sunday*

Times: 'It was a question of making absolutely certain of survival. But if Slater Walker had survived, Slater's days as head of the financial phenomenon he had created were numbered.

22   *Mr Slater tendered his resignation . . .*

In late October 1975 a party of financial journalists from Europe, including a number of British City Editors, was on a press 'facility' trip to Indonesia for the opening of a branch of an international bank. On the way back there was a scheduled stopover in Singapore on Friday 24 October, where a press conference with Prime Minister Lee Kuan Yew had been arranged for Saturday afternoon.

Back in London a rumour spread that Lee was to take the opportunity to make a statement about the conduct of Haw Par when it had been Slater Walker's Far Eastern associate, perhaps reinforcing the charges of 'serious wrongdoing' first made in July 1975 by Singapore's finance minister. In the event Lee told the journalists nothing of significance; but if he had ever intended to try to force some reaction back in London, where his government's allegations hitherto seemed to have made little impact, he had been forestalled: for late that Friday afternoon Slater abruptly announced that he was resigning from Slater Walker and retiring from the City.

The Singapore newspapers and the *Far East Economic Review*, published in Hong Kong, had for weeks carried extensive and critical reports of a series of investigations that had been started by authorities in both Singapore and Hong Kong; but, oddly enough, the British newspapers that had been most alert to their potential import were normally Slater's staunchest supporters. It was the *Sunday Telegraph* that first highlighted the news that the investigations involved Slater personally, back on 10 August; but more important, Patrick Sergeant of the *Daily Mail*, who had visited Singapore before joining the Indonesian party, had published an article on Monday 20 October in which he concluded that 'one cannot see Slater shares as a buy until they get the albatross off their neck – and that could be a long time'.

That article and the Lee conference were important in determining the timing of Slater's departure, but nevertheless the news took everyone by surprise, and the share price dropped 11 pence to

35 pence in 'after-hours' dealing on the news. Such was the particular reputation that Slater had created for himself that most newspapers automatically led their front pages with the story the following day, and his going dominated them for a further three days. In a personal statement Slater said:

> Matters connected with the recent inquiry into the affairs of Haw Par in Singapore have received adverse publicity which is damaging to Slater Walker Securities. In addition to this, a newly constituted Board, not connected with the original development of Haw Par, will find it easier to resolve the outstanding problems with Haw Par and the authorities in Singapore.

But Haw Par was, to Slater, essentially an opportunity for retiring, not the underlying reason; for he spoke of having wanted for two years to retire from the City to devote more time to his family and other interests and concluded: 'I find therefore that my wish to retire from the City and the interest of Slater Walker Securities are now identical.'

Patrick Hutber, Slater's friend, wrote in the *Sunday Telegraph* that Slater 'had lost his zest for the game, or, to be more accurate, today's game is not one he found he could enjoy'. But Hutber suggested that my own book was also a factor, for he wrote that 'on top of the Singapore tension there was the added possibility that sudden newspaper serialization would turn the danger of a run of some sort on the bank into actuality.'

The danger of a run on the bank, and on the unit trusts and insurance companies controlled by Slater Walker, was what worried the Bank of England, and it went to considerable lengths to ensure that newspapers did not suggest that Slater Walker was in any real financial straits. A Bank spokesman told the *Financial Times* that: 'There never has been, and is not, any necessity for "lifeboat" support for Slater Walker.' (The 'lifeboat' was a mechanism by which the big banks provided special credits to help selected ailing 'secondary' banks survive the 1974 crash.) And *The Times* wrote that the Slater Walker problems were 'not of the sort that overtook the secondary banks in the City', which were for the most part 'the result of throwing away common banking prudence'.

Slater had forewarned the Bank of his intention to go, and to minimize the blow to 'confidence' the Bank had arranged that the reconstituted board should contain leading City names: Lord Rothschild, former head of the Think Tank, who had moved to his family bank, was appointed, and so was Charles Hambro, head of another leading City acceptance house. Each was accompanied by another director from his bank, and Sir Ronald Leach, senior partner of accountants

Peat Marwick Mitchell, was to be a consultant to the new board. But the man who took Slater's place as chairman was his close friend and business associate James Goldsmith.

Goldsmith's first transaction with Slater Walker had been as long ago as 1965 when his infant Cavenham food company bought an interest in a tobacco wholesalers, Singleton & Cole, from Slater Walker. There then appears to have been little business between the two until 1972, when there were a number of complex transactions between Slater Walker and Goldsmith's financial arm, Anglo-Continental: Anglo acquired Slater Walker's interests in the insurance brokers Wigham-Richardson, incorporating Walker Young, in three investment trusts, including Flag, and in a property group, Argyle. The following year Goldsmith became involved in the negotiations by Slater Walker to sell its Far Eastern interests, but in the event only took over the London-based Far Eastern Investment Trust. In 1974, however, the association between Slater Walker and Goldsmith became particularly close.

After the collapse of the Hill Samuel merger plan in the summer of 1973 it had been vital for Slater Walker to try to secure the backing of a large public company, and by the autumn of that year Slater had been negotiating with three unidentified parties, of which two were possibly Lonrho and the Middle East middleman, Adnam Kashoggi. But these came to little, and the following year Slater and Goldsmith developed an unusual plan under which a French consortium, composed of Goldsmith's French holding company Générale Occidentale and the nationalized motor manufacturer Renault, was to buy a stake of twenty to twenty-five per cent in Slater Walker.

An agreement was signed on 16 July 1974, and the French consortium acquired some 1,250,000 Slater Walker shares, and later a further block of similar size – some three per cent of the Slater Walker capital.* But by the autumn it became clear that the French government was not going to allow the plan to proceed. Goldsmith was thus left controlling a substantial holding in Slater Walker: indeed, in addition to the three per cent, it was reported that his companies owned a further four per cent of Slater Walker.

So clearly one motive for Goldsmith's taking over the helm at Slater Walker was to protect his investment. But his familiarity with

---

* The consortium bought its shares from Bion Securities, which had acquired them in the market with loans from Slater Walker. The initial block was bought by the consortium at cost, but the second block had to be sold by Bion at a loss. In all Bion – and thus Slater Walker – lost some £1.3 million on its dealings in Slater Walker shares. It was Bion's dealings in the 1973 and 1974 negotiations that were the subject of the Department of Trade's prosecution of Slater under Section 54 of the Companies Act. This prohibits companies from financing the purchase of their own shares, with the exception of banking companies that lend for this purpose in the ordinary course of their business.

the business and friendship with Slater also made him a suitable successor, in the eyes of the Bank of England, because they wanted to ensure that Slater's departure would cause the minimum of disruption. There were already the inevitable public demands from Labour MPs that the government should appoint inspectors under the Companies Act to carry out a thorough investigation of Slater Walker – as Heath had ordered of Lonrho in 1973 – and the Department of Trade was being privately pressurized by some leading City figures to do the same. But the Bank was against it, concerned again with the effect on 'confidence' of a prolonged inquiry which might, they felt, reveal nothing warranting further action. In any event, calls for an official inquiry were forestalled by Goldsmith's announcement on Tuesday 27 October 1975 that he was asking two leading firms of accountants, Price Waterhouse and Peat Marwick, to report fully on Slater Walker's current financial position. The results, he said, would be made available to the Department of Trade, thus giving the government a good reason for refusing an inquiry of its own.

Goldsmith's main reason, however, for taking over at Slater Walker was, as he put it to the *Sunday Times*, 'to take the emotion out of this Far East affair'.

That affair has, of course, now been thoroughly aired both in the newspapers at the time and in the coverage of the subsequent litigation. In my original inquiries I did not go into the Far Eastern activities of Slater Walker in great detail – a line had to be drawn somewhere – and so the revelations were as new to me as to anyone else, if less surprising. It is now not possible for me to explain them at length, partly because the litigation was still dragging on when this text was being finalized – and likely to for some time to come – and partly because to do so would only further delay publication.

But it must be said that what Slater Walker did in the Far East was in essence no different from what it did in the UK and other parts of the world, although it was exaggerated by the absurd rise in the Hong Kong stock market. The now famous 'incentive' dealing company, Spydar, through which Slater, Tarling and some executives of Haw Par made nearly £1 million, was in principle the same as Tokengate – indeed Tarling called it the 'Tokengate concept' when it was being set up. The importance of the Far East was rather that the huge dealing profits made by the Slater Walker group there in 1972, and the accounting device of storing those profits in various Hong Kong 'unit trusts', helped postpone the inevitable day of reckoning for the whole Slater Walker operation.

In the autumn of 1975 the immediate threat to Slater Walker, apart from the bad publicity, was that Haw Par would refuse to repay some £14.5 million that it owed Slater Walker, of which over

£6 million was due on 22 January 1976. Much of the debt resulted from the sale of Slater Walker (Hong Kong) to Haw Par at the end of 1973 and the new government-appointed board of Haw Par was claiming that, in the light of what the investigations were uncovering, the price had been too high. Various proposals for settling the matter had been put forward before Slater's resignation, and Goldsmith put out new feelers. These resulted in a trip to Singapore in December, and after five days of negotiations Goldsmith and the chairman of Haw Par jointly announced that the discussions 'could lead to a positive solution to the difference between the two groups'. But the official investigations ground on, and in late 1975 and early 1976 the Singapore Stock Exchange released five volumes of their findings while the inspector appointed under the Singapore Companies Act produced two.

On 17 June 1976 it was announced that Slater Walker and Haw Par had settled their differences. Haw Par would repay at once to Slater Walker some £10¼ million and Slater Walker agreed to the 'discount' of some £4¼ million, partly because the second tranche of the loan had not been due for repayment until 1979 and partly to reflect claims made by Haw Par, including those for the return of the near £1 million profit made by the participants in Spydar; and the participants in Spydar agreed to repay their profits to Slater Walker, although they were given until 30 June 1981 to do so. The settlement of the civil dispute no doubt raised hopes that the Singapore government might now drop the matter; but it had no intention of doing so, as the *Sunday Times* reported three days later.

The illusion created at the time of Slater's resignation, that Slater Walker was financially sound, was rudely shattered eleven months later when, on 14 September 1976, a summary of the report of accountants Price Waterhouse and Peat Marwick was published along with the company's 1975 report and accounts. Slater Walker, it turned out, had needed a lifeboat all to itself: the Bank of England, it was now revealed, had made a standby facility available to Slater Walker on Slater's resignation which had been formally renegotiated a month later with a maximum of £70 million – of which £45.2 million had been used by 31 July 1976. On top of this, the Bank had, on 11 December 1975, guaranteed and indemnified Slater Walker against losses from bad debts on loans its banking subsidiary had made up to £40 million over and above Slater Walker's own provisions of £9.6 million.

Slater Walker, it had been decided, had lost £4,354,000 in 1975; then on top of this there were 'exceptional' items of £3,894,000 (including £443,000 of fees to Rothschilds, Hambros, the investigating accountants and others) and tax to pay of £2.4 million, bringing the loss to £10.6 million. But then there were a further £31.7 million of 'extraordinary' items, making a total loss of £42.3 million. Of this, £28 million represented provisions against the fall in the value of investments, of which the biggest single loss – of £5.8 million – was on Equity Enterprises, the satellite that Slater had formed for David Frost.

The accountants prefaced their report by pointing out that they had been asked to carry out their review to help the new board in planning the future direction of the group: 'They did not, therefore, regard it as part of their terms of reference to inquire into the circumstances of past transactions, except to the extent that these might have a bearing on the current and future position of the group' as it was constituted at the time of Slater's resignation. It was not therefore an historical investigation and the accountants' judgements were based on what they found in Slater Walker in the autumn of 1975. Nevertheless, they were critical of most aspects of the group, in particular the bank, where they found that there were a 'small number of very large loans, whose size appeared out of proportion to the resources' of Slater Walker. But the investment management division 'appeared to the Accountants to be well run and managed in an orthodox manner'.

The Slater Walker share price, already languishing at 16 pence, halved to 8 pence on publication of the report. In the newspapers there was much editorializing about the City's 'fallen idol', or the 'Icarus of the City', although the item in the report that hit the headlines hardest, at least in the more popular press, was the revelation that at the end of 1975 four directors had been borrowing nearly £1.4 million from Slater Walker. Buckley, who had resigned just before Slater, accounted for £773,000 of this, and Slater – or rather his wife – it was a house mortgage – for £118,000. (But unnamed 'companies controlled' by Slater had repaid £352,000, it was stated.)

The one area in which the investigating accountants had clearly looked at past transactions concerned the activities of the four 'floating' companies, Bion, Euroglen, Jaydean and Petershill – although they were not named. Their further report on these had been submitted to the Department of Trade which then conducted its own investigation under Section 109 of the 1967 Companies Act:* and on 22 September 1976 the Department issued fifteen summonses against Slater.

The following day the *Guardian*, picking up the *Sunday Times* report of the previous June, splashed the story that the Singapore government had applied to the Home Office for leave to start extra-

---

* Unlike investigations under Section 165 of the 1948 Companies Act, these are carried out in secret by the Department's officials. Their existence and findings usually only become public knowledge if further action, such as prosecution, follows.

dition proceedings against Slater, Tarling and former Haw Par executives. On 8 October Home Secretary Merlyn Rees gave the go-ahead, and the hearing, which lasted three weeks, took place in early 1977. On 27 January Chief Metropolitan Magistrate Kenneth Barraclough cleared Slater on the six charges he faced but ruled that Tarling should be extradited to be tried on all but two of the seventeen charges brought against him, including four of the same charges on which Slater had been cleared. The Singapore government then tried to have Barraclough's decision on Slater reviewed by the Divisional Court, but the application failed. At the time this text was being finalized the results of Tarling's appeal, by means of an application for habeas corpus, were not known.*

The Department of Trade's prosecution of Slater under Section 54 of the Companies Act lasted two days, and on 4 February, in the Guildhall Magistrates Court in the City, he was cleared of all fifteen charges. Slater had only faced a maximum fine of £1,500 and after the presiding magistrate, Sir Hugh Wontner, chairman of the Savoy Hotel, had refused his application for £3,000 of costs, Slater agreed this 'reflected the fact that there were areas of criticism of the company'. The Department of Trade also decided to try to get the decision reversed, but again its appeal had not been heard when this text was being prepared.

Meanwhile in October 1976 various newspaper reports appeared to the effect that the Department of Trade had started a Section 109 inquiry into Tokengate, some details of which had been published in the *Sunday Times* a year before, after Slater's resignation; and then in February 1977 it was reported that the inquiries had been completed and a report submitted to the Trade Minister, Edmund Dell. Since no more has been heard, it would appear that the Minister decided that no further action should be taken.

On 27 September Slater broke a year-long silence since his resignation and appeared on the BBC television programme Tonight. The Home Secretary had not at that point given the Singapore government permission to proceed with the extradition application, and Slater's principal purpose was to gain publicity for his cause: he accused the Singapore government of carrying out a vendetta against him and claimed he would not get a fair trial there. But Slater also discussed his personal affairs: he told interviewer Ludovic Kennedy that he was 'almost a minus millionaire'. The same day he explained to Kenneth Fleet, then still at the *Daily Telegraph*, that he owed £900,000, his debt after selling all his assets, including 3,000 acres of

---

* On 29 July the Divisional Court also cleared Tarling on the Spydar charges but decided he should be extradited on six of the other charges. Leave to appeal to the House of Lords was refused but both the Singapore government and Tarling said they would petition for leave.

Sussex and Surrey farmland. 'I was highly geared and heavily invested in Slater Walker shares. It was the result of errors of judgement. I lost money with the other shareholders,' he said; and on 18 October 1976 the American magazine *Newsweek* published an interview with Slater: 'Have you anything stashed away?' he was asked. Slater replied: 'All my assets were invested in Slater Walker shares. I also bought some land and some pictures. With the land I broke even. I resold the pictures at considerable loss; everything else I had was in Slater Walker shares.'

Slater was later to estimate that he had been worth £8 million in 1972, of which about £4.5 million must have been his holding in Slater Walker itself. Slater still held two million shares at the time of his resignation. He sold these a few months later to his successor, Goldsmith, at 23 pence a share, or a total of £460,000. My calculations suggest that at the end of the day Slater had lost about £930,000 on balance from his dealings in Slater Walker shares since he started the company. One error of judgement was the heavy reinvestment he made in 1972 after the big reduction in his stake in 1970.

Slater had also invested heavily in other Slater Walker companies in 1972: he had bought 100,000 shares in both the Slater Walker Investment Trust and Dual (and his non-beneficial interests a further 100,000 in the latter), although he would have made little out of these. But he had also acquired holdings in Slater Walker's four European associated companies which he resold in 1973 for a total profit of some £135,000. He bought some more shares in Slater Walker of Canada in May 1973 to add to his original investment made two years before and then, strangely, resold the bulk of the holding a matter of weeks later. He realized more than enough to cover the whole cost of the holding, leaving him with a gain of about £8,000 and 5,000 shares which he may have sold later in the year for about £14,000. It was also later revealed that he had shares in Slater Walker (South Africa), but what he made out of these, or investments in other Slater Walker associates, is not known. His personal profit on Tokengate was £235,000, but of course his share of the Spydar profit – approximately £175,000 – is repayable to Slater Walker in 1981.

Then there were Slater's shares in Lubok: he had sold 2,257,000 of these in September 1975 for a total profit of £507,825, to be left with three million (of which 250,000 belonged to the Slater Foundation). Slater resigned from Lubok at the same time as he retired from Slater Walker – also to be replaced by Goldsmith – and the Lubok share price was affected both by this and the devaluation of the South African rand, where it still had considerable investments. However, in the spring of 1976 when the share price had fallen back to its starting level of 10.5 pence, Lonrho bid for the company in Lonrho shares: Slater's paper profit was another £188,794, of which £7,607 went to the Slater Foundation.

At the time of his resignation Slater had said that he wanted to devote more time to his other interests. Apart from Lubok, it was not widely known what those other interests were – or indeed that he had any. In about 1972, however, Slater appears to have started, in conjunction with two or three young men at Slater Walker, a number of private enterprises. That year, for example, Slater briefly became chairman of, and took shares in, a toy company, Good-Wood Playthings. But more important he and his personal assistant Charles Harris formed a partnership to acquire farms in South Wales, and Slater's 'other interests' were principally in property. A group of companies were formed to handle these interests, the principal one being Strongmead, which had been registered in the summer of 1972. Strongmead had first become active in the year to April 1974, however, when it made over £500,000 profit, and then the following year Slater's various property interests appear to have been consolidated into it.

The news of Slater's new business first broke in March 1976: 'It's a property comeback by Jim Slater,' said the *Evening Standard*, while the *Guardian* revealed that a Strongmead subsidiary, Elmrise, was offering the 'top holiday investment tip for 1976' – holiday homes near Carmarthen Bay in South Wales. Then, in April 1976, at the time of the Lubok deal, Lonrho went into partnership with Slater, putting £100,000 of cash into Strongmead. With that, and the backing of other old friends, like James Hanson – like Goldsmith, knighted in Wilson's retirement honours – and Oliver Jessell, the new property concern branched out into the more controversial 'break-up' business – the selling-off of individual flats in large blocks to their tenants.

But in the summer of 1977 it was not clear whether Slater was attempting a real comeback. Strongmead's offices are in a quiet mews in Wimbledon, and according to one of Slater's assistants quoted in the *Evening Standard*, Slater's personal involvement would not be on a day-to-day basis: he would be coming in 'two or three days a week perhaps'. Slater is not even a director of Strongmead. Slater has said that when he decided to leave Leyland at the end of 1963 he contemplated retiring quietly to an office in Staines to run his investment advisory business: perhaps at last Slater has realized his true ambition.

It is in itself, perhaps, a verdict on Slater Walker that few of the former 'whizzkids' emerged from the crash with enhanced reputations. Some appear, like Slater, to have been left in financial straits: Buckley, for example, who, after leaving Slater Walker in the autumn of 1975, made a brief but disastrous foray into a company called Lamont which ended in calls for a Department of Trade probe. But others appear to have emerged financially secure: Malcolm Horsman, for instance.

Horsman was the most important 'product' of the Slater Walker era, for he had become deputy chairman and joint managing director of Bowater, Britain's tenth largest industrial company. But in 1975 it emerged that Horsman's policy of diversification, often into new financial ventures, had rebounded on the paper group and it was abandoned at considerable cost. Horsman resigned his executive positions, although he remained on the board. Then in the autumn of 1975 it was revealed in the *Sunday Times* (as a result of my investigations) that in 1971, before the merger with Bowater, Ralli International had started its own 'Tokengate concept' in the Far East. Under this two companies, Grove Securities formed by Horsman and St Georges Square Securities formed by Alastair Goodlad, Conservative MP and Walker's one-time assistant, who had later moved to Ralli, had made about £750,000. Unlike Slater's scheme, however, Horsman's should clearly have been disclosed in the UK directors' register, for Ralli's Far East companies remained subsidiaries, not simply associates. Bowater ordered an internal investigation and the entries were eventually made in early 1976: Horsman declared that five months after Grove had been formed he had sold his beneficial interest. He told me, in 1975, that the proceeds were intended to go to charity.

In October 1973, however, Horsman had started reducing his 1,200,000 holding of Bowater shares and by the end of 1975 he had only 25,000 left. He had realized a total profit of over £1 million on his dealings in Ralli and Bowater shares since he was launched out on his own by Slater in the autumn of 1969.

The most tangible remnant of Slater Walker itself was the investment management division, and at the end of 1976 the unit trusts were 'relaunched' under a new banner – Britannia, the name of one of the groups taken over in 1974. Whether or not the managers can produce a successful record without the whole battery of satellites and the background of bids and warehousing remains to be seen. But the emergence of one rather scarred investment manage- ment company is hardly enough to justify the effects of Slater Walker's influence on a decade of financial practice.

In the summer of 1973 John Davis of the *Observer* asked Slater what he thought he and his company had contributed to the country's welfare: Slater chose the 1967-8 period, the industrial conglomerate phase, to justify his activities in the context of the economy as a whole:

> In our early conglomerate phase I think we stimulated a lot of boards of sleepy industrial companies to look at their underlying

assets and the efficiency of their business a lot more seriously than might otherwise have been the case.

We ourselves took over quite a number of these sort of companies and in most cases dramatically improved their profitability. In addition our associated companies also took over quite a large number of inefficient companies, and I am certain that our high activity in this field stimulated many boards to improve their efficiency. It is important to realize that in the 1960s British industry was relatively inefficient, and I think that it is now very much better. I think that Slater Walker played its part in this reformation and to this extent we have certainly contributed to the country's welfare, as well as in the more direct material sense.

Walker, too, interviewed by the *Evening Standard* shortly after Slater's resignation, chose the early period to justify Slater Walker:

> When Jim Slater decided to start up on his own after leaving British Leyland, he shared my view that a lot of British industrial management needed improving. It was exciting to start him off. I thought that he would make an impact on improving some British industries, although I never thought that he would get as far as he did.
>
> There were a number of industrial firms that would have gone to the wall but for the better management and new capital and the improvement that took place when Slater Walker took them over. I think that what was done had the good effect of making firms all over the country use their assets more fully. I'm only sorry that it has all ended the way it has.

This was the 'the role of the marauders', as the *Financial Times* headlined its leader on Slater's resignation; or as Hutber wrote in the *Sunday Telegraph*: 'There was a time when the directors of almost every company in Britain, short of ICI and Shell, looked nervously over their shoulder, and worked a little harder, for fear of a Slater bid. To my mind that was a constructive and wonderfully useful function . . .'

Slater may, perhaps, be granted the benefit of what one might call the ripple effect – that Slater Walker acted as some sort of bogeyman the mere voracity of which was enough to goad some firms into greater efficiency. But it is very far from self-evident that, after a decade of the activities of Slater Walker and its imitators, British industry is any more efficient than it was before; and the overall judgement of Slater Walker's industrial conglomerate phase must be that, once the financial gimmickry has been eliminated, on the whole the intervention of Slater Walker did not result in dramatic improve-

ment in real industrial profits. On the contrary, Slater and his colleagues quickly discovered that making money in industry took much
longer and was much harder than was to their taste; so they pulled
out again explaining that they were not in 'the ten years' hard labour'
business.

If Slater's reputation as an industrial genius was perhaps already
tarnished, his renown as investment wizard and talented dealer in
stocks and shares was more durable. 'Jim Slater sees shares roaring
ahead' sang the *Daily Mail* City Page headline on 27 January 1977 –
and the following day the index rose nine points. It had been the
original purpose of my inquiry only to see how far Slater's claim to
have 'contributed to the country's welfare' on the industrial front was
justified. But it proved impossible to limit it in this way, ignoring
share dealing activities. They were the foundation on which the
business was built and remained an essential part of the structure. It
became necessary to examine them in detail and to assess Slater's
other main claim that 'we're very good' at 'investing other people's
money'.

While Slater certainly did make money for other people, and
himself, in good times, he also lost it for them – and, it seems, himself
– in bad. His methods, however, do not stand up to detailed investigation, and there are a number of specific episodes in the story
that would have been unacceptable even by the standards of the time
if they had been generally known about; and just as Slater was in no
sense an industrial risk-taker, or 'entrepreneur', nor was he a genuine
speculator, in the sense of gambler, in stock market dealing. For the
essence of his technique was to try to control the market – buyers,
sellers and price – so that he could realize profits at will. Throughout
its life Slater Walker took on the appearance of many different things
– money manager, financial adviser, industrial renovator,
conglomerate, bank. But from Capitalist to Tokengate – and the Far
East – it was really about one thing: the manipulation of share prices.
Investment to Slater Walker did not mean the underlying worth of
industrial assets like factories and machinery but the only too
ephemeral values that companies could be given by stock market
promotion. It created a scale of values that had precious little
relation to reality.

The basic function of, and justification for, the Stock Exchange,
and indeed the City at large, is to channel the country's capital
resources into industry and trade, where the real wealth is created.
There is, however, a well-established suspicion in many parts of the
community that the stock market is really just a mechanism for
making money for a privileged group. The damage that the Slater
Walker brand did to capitalism was that this was precisely what it
used stock markets for: and during a decade when perhaps industry's

greatest need was for more capital investment, Slater Walker and its imitators were essentially reversing the flow to use industrial capital in share dealing and other financial activities of questionable social – or indeed material – value.

Postscript

Peter Walker does not agree with many of the views I have expressed.
He has asked me to include the following statement:

I have always kept my political and business life totally separate. The
description given by Mr Raw that the business life benefited my
political career and the two were inter-linked is totally false. I was the
youngest constituency chairman of the YCs prior to even embarking
upon a business career. I was the youngest Conservative Parliamentary candidate in the 1955 General Election prior to any of my business activities being known. I became National Chairman of the
Young Conservatives without any of the YCs who voted for me even
knowing of my business background. Various political observers and
press commentators at the time described my national chairmanship
in glowing terms including at that stage the prediction that I would
be a member of a future Tory Cabinet. I was elected as the Member
of Parliament for Worcester in a By-Election in 1961 with only a
factual reference to my business background and no play being made
of it within the campaign at all. I have always refused to transact
business for my insurance broking firm with any Member of Parliament or with any person or firm living in my constituency. Both at
Dartford and Worcester I had numerous offers of business which I
rejected on the grounds that I never wanted to be in a position of
having a business relationship with someone I was representing in
Parliament. As National Chairman of the YCs I expressed at Party
Conferences and elsewhere views that were described as being 'progressive' and 'To the Left of the Party'.

On entering Parliament I took an unpopular stand against the
Party leadership on the question of the Common Market primarily,
as the *New Statesman* profile points out, on the damage it could do
to future race relations worldwide. My first appointment was to Mr
Selwyn Lloyd who, like me, held the view as to the necessity of
Government intervention in economic affairs. I made my first

reputation in Parliament for the work I did on the 1965 Finance Bill, work which Shirley Williams described as being 'the best performance of what at that time was the longest battle on a Finance Bill for more than fifty years'. In the period prior to the 1970 Election, unlike the descriptions given by Mr Raw, I had no standing upon economic and financial arguments at the time. My position was that of Shadow Minister of Transport, Housing and Local Government where I made perfectly clear the need for increasing public expenditure and the need for a considerable range of intervention. In a pamphlet entitled 'Cities Fit for People' published prior to that Election I advocated a re-definition of the homeless to include many more people and a commitment to a campaign to eliminate homelessness. I outlined the need for a slum clearance programme and not to build slums for the future. I advocated a massive improvement grant campaign, extension of the voluntary housing movement, an improvement in the mortgage option scheme and the 100 per cent mortgages, the creation of housing advisory services and a reform of education so that education was available throughout a person's lifespan and not confined to childhood. I also set out the need to remove all of the derelict land in the country. This was the main type of contribution I made to the political atmosphere at that time.

On becoming a Minister I pursued policies which can be described as being very much against big business and the financial operators. I pursued far more restrictive planning policies for example towards the Green Belt and confirmed whole new areas of Green Belt against the wishes of the property companies. I stopped all out-of-town shopping centres much to the objection of big business and property companies. I listed a substantial number of London theatres thus preventing a whole range of property development taking place. I introduced for the first time rent rebates for all council house tenants and rent rebates for all tenants in the private sector in a Bill that was described by Dick Crossman as 'the most Socialist Housing Bill in history'. I made it clear that it was my intention to switch the budget of the Department so as to concentrate upon the worst environments of the country and my record as Secretary of State for the Environment showed I very much succeeded in doing this. I pursued very distinctive regional policy of which there is plenty of evidence in both the North-East and the North-West. I substantially increased public expenditure on urban renewal and concentrated upon those areas most in need. I retained, against the wishes of the property developers, the office development certificates and I retained, against the wishes of the Party, the Regional Economic Planning Councils.

In what is described as 'The Selsdon Park atmosphere' prior to the Election it is now known publicly that together with Edward Boyle and Reggie Maudling I was the only member of the Shadow Cabinet opposed to not continuing with some form of Prices and Incomes Policy. It was the general view when I was made Secretary of State for Trade and Industry that I was appointed to that position in order that it should be made clear that the 'lame-duck' policy had been reversed. In the period I was Secretary of State for Trade and Industry I actively used the Industry Act which had been passed by John Davies in assisting major firms in need of help. I succeeded in obtaining a bigger rise in industrial investment than for many years past and I embarked upon a major reform of Company Law and actively started pursuing the need for greater employee participation.

With this political background to depict me of all people as a great advocate of laissez-faire policies beneficial to financial operators is a total nonsense.

Since the 1974 Election I have continued to pursue the policies of social reform and the need for Government intervention and collaboration on the economy in spite of the unpopularity of those views with my Party.

Index

A number in brackets immediately after a page number indicates two or more separate references on that page.